# Cinemas
## OF THE
## BLACK COUNTRY
### NED WILLIAMS

**URALIA PRESS**
23 WESTLAND ROAD, WOLVERHAMPTON  WV3 9NZ

"Cinemas of the Black Country"
is dedicated to
Kiran Lee Frances Williams.
*Who arrived on 17th July 1980
shortly after her parents had been
to the cinema, and who put a
temporary stop to their thrice-
weekly film-going!*

The production of the book has
been helped by the Mercia Cinema
Society Publications Group, and
has been partly financed by
advance subscription.
Financial assistance has also been
received from :
West Midlands Arts
Dudley Arts Council.

Published by Uralia Press
23 Westland Road, Wolverhampton,
West Midlands. WV3 9NZ.
1982.

Hardback: ISBN 0 9500533 6 8
Paperback: ISBN 0 9500533 7 6

Designed by John Revill

Printed in the Black Country by
John Price & Sons
Bilston.

"I'm tellin' yo', Aynuk, we did our courtin' at the Quanes in double sates as wide as this"

"I wouldn't know, Ayli, I've never bin to them pictures".

"Yo' 'aven't lived, Aynuk, if they closed them down tomorrow, yo'd always be there".

Published in a limited
edition of 1,000 copies

Copy number _SSS_

Signed _J. Ned Williams_

On the cover and frontispiece (above): The Odeon, Wolverhampton, photographed on 8th September 1937, a few days before the cinema opened. It seemed that this magnificent Black Country cinema was doomed to close on 17th July 1982 just as this book reached the printers. At the last minute, on 9th July, the local magistrates refused to grant Rank Leisure a gaming licence and thus the Odeon will continue to greet filmgoers in this foyer for a little while longer. Alas, the foyer's decor has lost its period flavour and the pay box has been "modernised" and the crush hall beyond the doors on the right has boasted a bar in recent times.

*(Photos: John Maltby)*

# CONTENTS

This book describes the cinemas once to be found in the area now covered by the four Metropolitan Boroughs of Wolverhampton, Walsall (but excluding Aldridge and Brownhills), Dudley and Sandwell. The material is arranged as follows:

The peacocks at the Rink in Smethwick have looked down on half a century of local cinema history. Once they guarded a splendid super-cinema, now their domain has become a luxurious Bingo Club.

# MAP

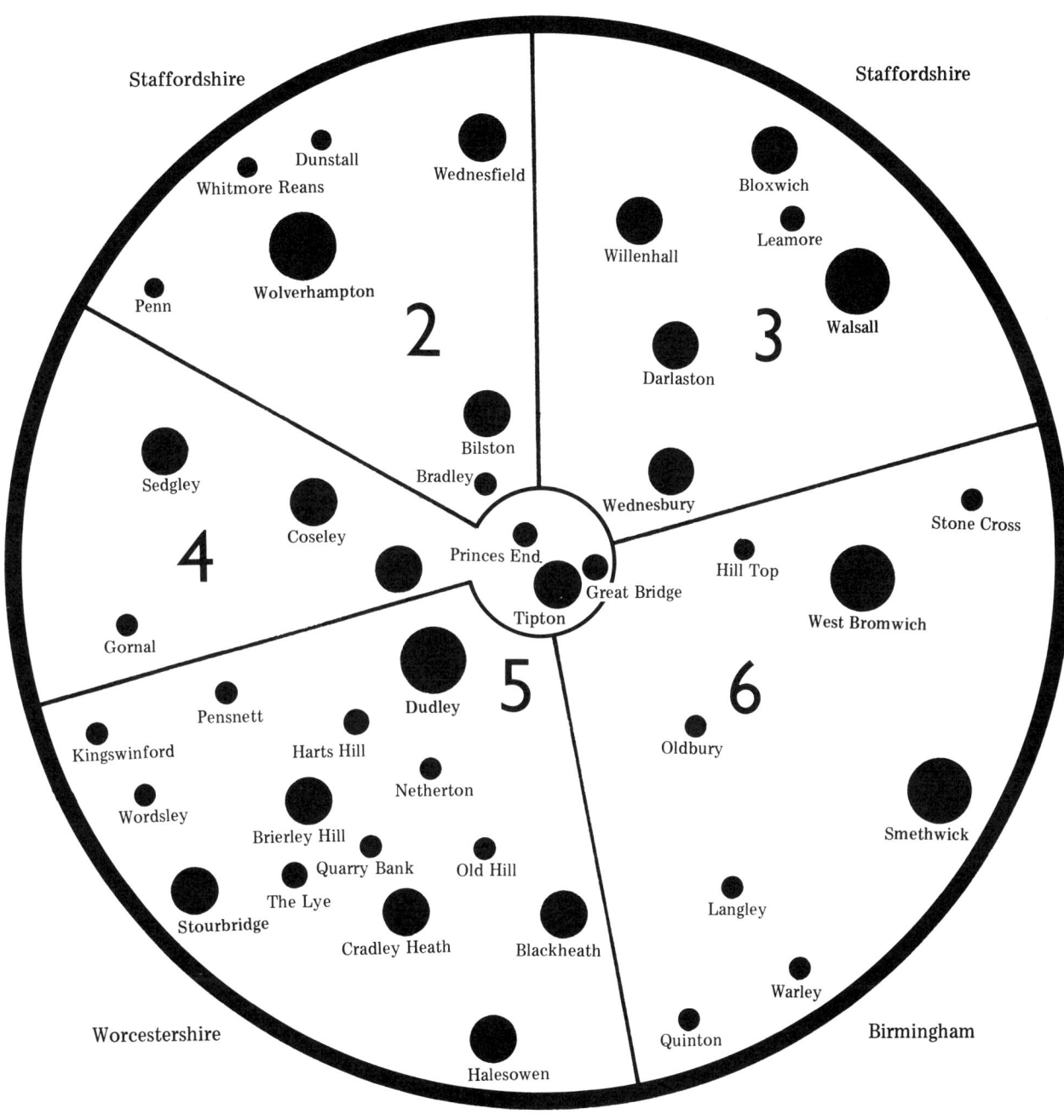

Staffordshire

Staffordshire

Dunstall
Whitmore Reans
Wednesfield
Bloxwich
Willenhall
Leamore
Penn
Wolverhampton
2
3
Walsall
Bilston
Bradley
Sedgley
Wednesbury
Coseley
Darlaston
4
Princes End
Stone Cross
Hill Top
Gornal
Great Bridge
West Bromwich
Tipton
Pensnett
Dudley
5
6
Oldbury
Kingswinford
Harts Hill
Netherton
Wordsley
Smethwick
Brierley Hill
Quarry Bank
Old Hill
The Lye
Langley
Stourbridge
Cradley Heath
Blackheath
Warley
Worcestershire
Quinton
Birmingham
Halesowen

---

Some Abbreviations Used:

| | |
|---|---|
| C.V.A. | Cinema Veterans Association. (Originally members had to be making or exhibiting films before 1903). |
| C.E.A. | Cinema Exhibitors Association. (Black Country members joined the Birmingham Branch). |
| A.P.P.H. | Associated Provincial Picture Houses Ltd. |
| P.C.T. | Provincial Cinematograph Theatres Ltd. |
| G.B. | Gaumont-British Picture Corporation. |
| A.B.C. | Associated British Cinemas. |
| B.T.H. | British Thomson-Houston. |
| B.T.P. | British Talking Pictures. |

A Warning to "furriners" on local pronounciation:

1. The sentence, "Are you taking us to the best seats in the Beacon?" would be pronounced thus: "Am yo' takin' we to the best sates in the Bacon?".

2. Wolverhampton is pronounced with the stress on the third syllable, never on the first syllable.

3. The word "bank", as in Quarry Bank, is pronounced "bonk".

4. Old Hill is pronounced Owd'ill.

5. Caldmore Green is pronounced Karma Green.

6. Birmingham is often called Brummagem, and should never be considered part of the Black Country.

This is a book about cinemas, not about films. It describes the business of showing films from the turn of the century to the present day, in anything that can legitimately be called a cinema, from fairground bio-scopes to triple-screens, via converted chapels and super-cinemas ! It is only concerned with such places that have existed in the Black Country.

The Black Country is that area of North Worcester-shire and South Staffordshire that became industrialized as a result of the proximity of a ten-yard seam of coal to the surface of the ground; from Warley to Wolverhamp-ton, from Walsall to Stourbridge. Coal, ironstone, lime-stone, canals, railways and the labour force itself forged this crystal-like network of villages into a smokey black conurbation. The cinema arrived to bring light into this darkness.

When Edward Hewitson opened the Windsor, Smeth-wick, he wrote :

"Here then is the answer to those who ask, 'Why all these places of amusement ?' They are centres of mental and physical relaxation, the reflex of hard industrial organisation. The more a people must work, the more it should play."

and of his new cinema he wrote :

"No one can cross its threshold without feeling a sense of exhilaration. It is a triumph of architecture graced by the art of the scenic decorator, a veritable place of luxury, comfort, and beauty. Here music, colour, soft lighting, all combine to provide an atmosphere of joyousness in which the mind can more easily cast aside those worries and problems of the office, the casting shop or the lathe."

All that — before the film has even begun its own seductive effect ! In this book you are asked to stand with your back to the screen and admire the auditorium itself, the exterior of the building, the men who designed and built it, the staff who ran it, the companies that invested in it, the patrons who supported it, the forces of destiny that opened it and closed it.

It might be asked how does a "furriner", who has only lived in the Black Country for twenty years, come to be writing such a history ? The short answer is that in April 1980 I drove past the Coliseum, Dudley Road, Wolverhampton to find the place being demolished. In the stalls a huge bonfire was consuming the paperwork accumulated in the cinema. It was a potent image that reminded me of many such occasions I had experienced since coming to this area in 1962; one arrives somewhere to find it "gone". I felt that it was now or never, so many buildings had already disappeared, probably so many people had passed on, so much had never been recorded. I resolved to put the matter right without further delay.

The long answer concerns my own long relationship with the cinema, as an eager patron. In London I lived half way between two cinemas: the Odeon, Gants Hill,

and the Coliseum, Manor Park. Ironically I later discovered they were designed by the same architect, George Cole, at opposite ends of his career. They were so different, one a magnificent super-cinema, the other a grubby flea-pit, that I learnt from an early age that no two cinemas were the same and that their variety provided as much enjoyment as the films themselves. At the Odeon I joined the Minors' Club on Saturday mornings. Who can call themselves educated who have not been brought up on children's matinees ? But at the Coliseum I encountered a more intriguing mystery concerning cinemas. The seediness of a run-down flea-pit attracted disapproval that suggested film going to such establishments might initiate one into the forbidden mysteries of the adult world. I longed to be old enough to understand what "I Was A Teenage Werewolf" was all about ! Television has changed all this.

During my teens I was fortunate to belong to the State Film Society: a cinema co-operatively owned by its staff and patrons, in Leytonstone. Eventually bingo was played on five nights of the week and our films were screened only on Wednesday evenings, but what wonder-ful evenings they were! I learnt that it was possible for people to love a cinema and that some individuals would make almost any sacrifice to enjoy the act of putting an image on that sacred screen.

When I came to the Black Country I found myself exploiting the variety of cinemas that still staggered into the sixties to do battle with declining audiences and advancing Bingo. It was still possible to catch a trolley-bus from my new home in Dudley to the Clifton, Wolverhampton, catch the blue and cream No. 74 bus in search of the Queens, West Bromwich, or mount a motorcycle to try and find the Royal, Cradley Heath, or Lyttleton, Halesowen. In the second half of the seventies I discovered the Black Country was a micro-cosm of the World. There is no end to the variety of the cinema-going experience. With Jane, I have frozen to death in a deckchair seat on a bare concrete floor in a cinema in Yeppoon on the Queensland coast, watched a spaghetti western in an open-air cinema in Albania and paid homage to Graumann's Chinese Theatre in Los Angeles, literally in the "footsteps of the stars". If cinemas have given me so much, I feel a sentimental compulsion to repay that debt with a record of the life and times of my adopted local cinemas.

The result has been that I have spent two years of extremely exciting work. It has been a process of assembling a fairly large and complex jig-saw from very tiny pieces. Cinema histories cannot be compiled from single sources and the quest for any sources at all has been as exciting as those matinee serials. While I have spent much time buried in newspapers and records in libraries, I have also engaged in so much social activity that I thought I would never have time to write every-thing down. I have met as many cinema proprietors, managers, usherettes, patrons, builders, projectionists, and "chuckers-out" as I could find. Everyone has been generous with their time, energy, and information, not forgetting cups of tea. I am still amazed about how much devotion people have felt towards their cinemas, whether they were patron or staff.

I have sometimes felt worried that people have imagined that I have come to denigrate or scorn their flea-pit, blood tub, or bug-hut, but readers will realise that the more obscure the cinema the more I have been fascinated by it. If I am guilty of displaying any negative feelings towards any local cinemas it is more likely to be a frustration with the anonymity of a super-cinema on a national circuit !

Some large cinemas that closed before I knew them still seem unknown quantities to me. On the other hand a glorious local flea-pit like the Rex, Whitmore Reans, now lives vividly in my imagination even though it had disappeared before I could possibly have known it.

I hope the reader will feel inspired to set out to visit the few surviving cinemas in the Black Country and will even visit Bingo Clubs, D.I.Y. warehouses, and shops that have once been cinemas, to enjoy the trail that has given me so much pleasure, and then talk to everyone you meet, as I have done, to revive the human memories, the legends, surrounding every local cinema. To talk about film-going will unleash a torrent of nostalgia and affection that is almost overwhelming. Be prepared to ride the range all over again in those great B Westerns, or sing and dance your way through an amazing extravaganza or try to untangle the plot of *"The Big Sleep"* for the hundredth time. Then turn your attention to the place in which all these dreams unfolded. Recall the welcoming manager in evening dress, the warmth, intimacy, and luxury of the auditorium, the craftsmanship with which the show was presented, and the dash for the last bus home.

May I end my introduction on a note of warning ? I have tried to make this account both accurate and comprehensive but there are still gaps to be filled and conflicting information to be more fully resolved. As the jig-saw has consisted of so many tiny pieces this has to be regarded as inevitable. I knew very little about this subject just over two years ago, if I spend a lifetime going any further the resulting account could be even more vast — and gaps could still exist ! If readers do have corrections to make, or information to add, naturally I will be delighted to hear from them.

*Spring 1982.*                                    *Ned Williams*

The cinema is the marriage of technology and magic. After all that restless material progress of the nineteenth century man deserved to sit back in some comfort and turn his inventions to the serious business of enjoying dreams. It is a cliche to describe the cinema as an art of illusion, but the statement becomes more interesting if it is applied to the entire business of "film-showing" and "film-going" rather than simply to the process of "film-making".

This book celebrates two illusions that were quite distinct from the movement of light and shadow on the screen. The first illusion concerns the environment in which the event takes place, it is revealed in their early name: the picture palaces. The showman's art was to provide an illusion of taste, comfort, luxury, and personal attention, that could all be yours for the price of an admission ticket. The second illusion was a trick played upon the showman himself: the illusion of profit! Individuals and companies set out to build palaces and super-cinemas at tremendous cost because they themselves were carried away by this illusion. A few were lucky, or astute enough, and turned the illusion to a reality, but others struggled for years to pay off mortgages long after the illusion had crumbled.

At the beginning of the century "animated pictures" were to be found at the fair. Even here the showman was carried away by his desire to present the novelty in the grandest possible way. Pat Collins' "Wonderland" needed an army of people to erect it and transport it. More candle-power was created by the bulbs on the facade than was ever reflected from the screen ! And for Black Country folk who preferred to see "animated pictures" in less dazzling surroundings, they could be found in Town Halls and Assembly Rooms, presented by gentlemen like Professor Wood or Waller Jeffs.

Conveniently for the historian the transition from that state of affairs to the business of providing cinematographic entertainment on a permanent site was accompanied by the passing of the 1909 Cinematograph Act. From 1st January 1910 onwards cinemas had to be licenced and observe various regulations, to receive such a licence. From then on the cinema has a charted history, however hard it may be to find the documentation today.

From 1910 to the First World War a variety of premises found themselves becoming cinemas. Shops, chapels, factories, and public halls were converted. Theatres installed projection equipment. The first purpose-built cinemas were constructed, and regional and national "circuits" emerged. All aspects of industry grew and developed at a great pace. Some modest halls presented heavy melodrama in short bursts while the chucker-out tried to preserve order, and the floor disappeared under a sea of pea-nut shells and orange peel. The audience, packed onto benches, howled for the death of the villain and if a baby howled the chucker-out

would cry, "Give that baby some breast". On the other hand, fine purpose-built cinemas presented relatively long and sophisticated "silent" films, with accompaniment from an orchestra, and tea and biscuits were served at the matinees.

The First World War checked the progress of the rapidly expanding cinema business. A few small cinemas operating in converted premises found it difficult to keep up with ever more stringent safety regulations and sometimes found themselves holding too few patrons to operate economically. They were often regarded as second class cinemas by their bigger rivals, who dismissed them as "Penny and a Pass" establishments. They "faded away by 1920 when the building industry returned to life. As materials gradually became available again, work was resumed on building new Picture Palaces and on extending old ones. There was sometimes opposition from those who felt that homes should be built before cinemas. There was also a considerable lack of confidence in the trade itself. Many felt the cinema had a poor future. When Tom Wood built Woods Palace in Bilston he encountered both views, and to take account of the latter it was built as a theatre as well as a cinema.

The cinemas of the early twenties began to establish an appropriate "cinema style". Woods Palace, Bilston, The Criterion, Dudley, and the Scala, Stourbridge are good examples. When P. Morton Shand came to write "Modern Theatres and Cinemas" at the end of the decade he denounced the vulgarity and eclecticism of such buildings and welcomed modernism with open arms. Yet many of them enjoyed a harmony with their High-Street-neighbours that supers failed to achieve. The transitional period at the end of the twenties possibly produced the most exciting variety of cinema-design, in my opinion. It was also the period of transition from "silence" to "sound". Musicians found themselves out-of-work while the public rushed to see and hear the first talkies in town. In some cinemas the orchestra pit was already overshadowed by the magnificent new theatre organs. Popular cinemas like the Regent, Dudley, and the Central, Stourbridge, opened as "silent" cinemas, but with fine organs, but soon installed sound equipment. An indication of the flurry of activity at this time is represented by events in Smethwick. Between September 1929 and December 1930 four substantial sound super-cinemas opened within the borough. All four, the Windsor, the Princes, the Rink, and the Beacon, although considered "modern" in their day, really illustrated the quality and variety of cinemas just before the dawn of modernism.

The following decade, the thirties, produced the "Super-Cinema", at first used to denote a degree of luxury and a seating capacity in excess of one thousand, but later strongly associated with the emerging architectural styles. Design became more functional. Possibly under the influence of art-deco, pleasing geometry became more important than eclectic ornamentation. Cinemas that truly celebrated the "modern" style were no less grand than their predecessors, and if anything even more firmly than ever created a tradition of what a cinema should look like. The Black Country's part in establishing this style is described later.

Many fine Black Country cinemas were built during the mid to late thirties; the Tower, West Bromwich, the Regal, Darlaston, the Cliftons and the Danilos. With the Odeon style emerging at the Warley Cinema, the Odeons at Wolverhampton and Dudley followed from the drawing boards of the Harry Weedon partnership in Birmingham. Some people felt they were something of a sham compared with the more genuine solid virtues of the Gaumonts designed by W. Trent, but for many the word "Odeon" is synonymous with super-cinema.

By the end of the thirties some of the older Black Country cinemas had really become flea-pits compared with the supers. (Many local people prefer the term "flea-pen", or "blood-tub", if the cinema was associated with melodrama). Flea-pits and super-cinemas alike were saved by the boom in film going that coincided with the Second World War. After the War one or two flea-pits even produced bold plans to have themselves rebuilt as super-cinemas. It seemed as if those Saturday night queues would go on forever. In reality very little post-war cinema building took place and from the early fifties onwards the industry has suffered a long decline. Some super-cinemas had a life of less than a quarter of a century: less than the duration of a person's career.

The long sad story of the cinema's decline has been considered many times. An excellent article on the subject, by Kevin Wheelan, has appeared in Mercia Bioscope No. 4. It is certainly not enough to simply blame the rise of television, even though many people in the cinema-business offer that as an analysis of what happened.

The Black Country, probably like any other area of Britain, provides many examples of the other changing circumstances that caused cinemas to abandon their cause. The small local cinemas, that had once so closely been a part of the community that immediately surrounded them, suffered when increased mobility and prosperity robbed them of the status they had once enjoyed. And, conversely, some of those large suburban fortress-like super-cinemas became victims of their own scale and grandeur. The longer one considers the story of cinema-closures the more incongruous it becomes, because of the alarming exceptions to every possible rule.

By the 1950's the exhibition of films was dominated by the two major circuits. As far as I can see the effects have been disastrous. Having acquired several cinemas in a single town the circuit often felt obliged to "rationalise", and often to do so for bizarre reasons. The Criterion, Dudley, the Kings, Stourbridge, and later the Gaumont, Wolverhampton, for example, all suffered in this way. The circuits also made life very difficult for the "independents" when it came to film supply. Even if an independent could eventually obtain a desired film he knew that, by then, much of its marketability had been exhausted. From the relatively large empire of Miles Jervis Cinemas, to small lonely enterprises like the Savoy, Netherton or the Lyttleton, Halesowen, the cry

was the same.

The cinema's decline ironically had strange effects. For a time cinemas were "going for a song" and amidst all the closures several cinemas were returned to life by entrepreneurs who still cherished that illusion of profit. Places like the Rialto, Wednesbury, the Coliseum, Wolverhampton, even The Temp in the Lye all re-opened at least once towards the end of the fifties. Later the Indian films arrived and from flea-pits like the Alhambra Bilston, to super-cinemas like the Princes, Smethwick, screens were filled with action for a further lease of life.

During the seventies the surviving super-cinemas often responded to the changed situation by twinning, or tripling. (At Quinton they have quadrupled!). For a time this was economically effective but increasing overheads have eventually caught up with such cinemas. At the time of going to press it is very difficult to be optimistic about the future of the remaining local cinemas. When I started writing eight cinemas were presenting English-language films in the Black Country, and a few were showing Indian films on selected evenings. Now, in Spring 1982, there are seven of the former and none of the latter. Of the "Magnificent Seven", two are threatened with closure at the moment.

Since the sixties we have witnessed the emergence of the "Bingo and Social Club". Many former cinemas have opted for this activity. Bingo has therefore actually saved, or "preserved" several cinemas for those interested in their design, as opposed to those interested in their function! While writing this book I have paid many enjoyable visits to Bingo Halls and found much inside to admire. At least two Black Country Bingo Halls are "magnificent": the Clifton, Stone Cross, and the Rink, Smethwick, but many others have interiors that faithfully preserve different cinema styles — the "modern" at the Danilo, Stourbridge and the "joyfully vulgar" of the Imperial, Walsall. Bingo Halls are usually bathed in bright light, strongly contrasting with the intimate warm darkness of a cinema, but all the better for appreciating the decor.

Having talked of decline, closure, and of Bingo, it is worth considering one final illusion that is impossible to shatter however unrealistic it is. This illusion concerns the belief in a "Golden Age". Each generation seems to have loved the cinemas and films of its own time, and therefore recalled such an age. I have spoken to many who loved the early silent era, who no doubt believe that cinema ended with the coming of sound. Many people have recalled the serials, *"The Clutching Hand"*, *"The Shielding Shadow"*, *"The Laughing Mask"*, and *"The Diamond from the Sky"*, and many have recalled the musicians of that era that helped bring these fantasies alive.

Naturally, most people have tried to convince me that the thirties and forties were really the Golden Age, not only in terms of the films produced at that time, but also in terms that relate to their exhibition. For example it was a time when the operator's craft had become a consummation of technology and art, plus a great deal of human skill. Shows were rehearsed and operators worked to rigid cue-sheets. Operators employed by Gaumont British had to earn their bonus by not breaking any film! For the patron, Hollywood, and the British Studios, produced the most outrageous escapism

— certainly worth queuing for hours to see.

Many of the staff who joined the trade in the 1930's stayed for the rest of their cinema's life. Try to imagine a career that began with the glamour and prestige of the business at that time and which ended a quarter of a century later in such sad circumstances ! Harry Crane, manager of Clifton Coseley, throughout its life, always wore evening dress every night even to the bitter end, and could always oblige the patrons with a tap-dance routine on the steps. Such a man was given a week's notice and had to find work elsewhere. There was no great financial reward for working in the cinema, but even when some of the glamour had faded there was always great comradeship and friendliness. On days off managers and usherettes alike would often go to the pictures, and share "intelligence" with friendly rivals down the road !

I was born too late to experience all this at first hand but even in my lifetime each decade has seemed wonderful in its own right, at the time. Even in the seventies I have never shared the often quoted view, "We don't go to the pictures anymore as there is never anything on worth seeing". This is the lie that has hastened the death of our local cinemas.

In the early days the "palaces" were often called "the Electric Palaces", due to their ability to flood their exterior in light, or generate their own power to put a picture on the screen. On reflection I wonder if the phenomenon that was really "electric" was the relationship between the events of the screen and the audience. The shared gasp, the huge hall-full of laughter, the mutual sitting on edges of seats, in a cinema, are things that television and video can never satisfactorily re-create. I am glad that even at the beginning of the eighties we have just about retained, for a little while longer, the opportunity of experiencing these things.

## SOURCES AND ACKNOWLEDGEMENTS

Research into local cinema history begins in the pages of the *Kinematograph Year Book* — an annual trade directory that provides a mine of information. I have extensively used a local private collection of KYB's and the collection in Birmingham Reference Library. *Kine Weekly*, the trade's magazine is also useful, and I have consulted copies at the British Film Institute and the National Newspaper Collection at Colindale.

Local newspapers are invaluable and most Black Country Libraries have good collections. *The Express and Star*, and the *County Express* allowed me to use their own archives. Local government records, like plans, licences, council minutes etc. are again invaluable but not always available. Some authorities have committed official vandalism with their own archives, particularly on the two recent occasions of local government reorganisation. Perhaps, on the other hand, we should be grateful for all that survives.

I have had much assistance from the following libraries: Wolverhampton, Walsall, Bilston, Wednesbury, West Bromwich, Tipton, Smethwick, Dudley, Halesowen, Brierley Hill, Stour-bridge, and, across the border, in Birmingham. Staff have often helped me find information that they themselves did not know they had ! Sandwell Planning Department conceals a good archive and I must thank the two ladies who unlocked some of its treasures for me. I hope individuals will accept a huge "thank you" directed at everybody. I particularly have to thank a host of individuals who have talked to me, written to me, and phoned me, to help assemble the story that follows. It could not have been compiled from archives alone. Chris and Rosemary Clegg of the *Mercia Cinema Society*, for not only supplying information, but also for typing much of the manuscript and being the first to write a cheque when the time came. Members of the *Cinema Theatre Association* have also helped, including the archivist, Richard Gray, and the following:

Hugh Sykes
Tony Moss
Terry Cresswell
Kevin Wheelan
Keith Skone
Alan Moore
Allen Eyles
Norman Robins
Eurwyn Jones

Others who have helped include:

Ewart Cook
Mrs. Harrison
Della Powell
Manfred Worton
G. E. Kay
Mr. & Mrs. L. Harvey
Doris Holden
Tom Watkins
Tim Williamson
Mr. & Mrs. Bernard Powell
Mrs. P. Charlesworth
W. H. Williams & Family
Mrs. C. Thornycroft
Vic Page
C. S. Joseph
Garton Hawkins
Ken & Doris Woodroffe
Derek Salberg
Mrs. H. Bennett
Bill Priest
Madge Attwood
Maureen & Jean Mee
Eddie Jones
Graham Simmonds
Bernard Williams
Wilf Hollyhead
Archie Williams
Mrs. A. Lee
Edith Johnson
Angela Bird
Reay Wood
Geoffrey Hewitson
Miles Jervis
Syd Griffiths

Malcolm Timmins
Arthur Griffin
Mrs. G. Bishop
George & Harry Siddall
Harry Taylor
Michael Dorsett
Ronald Farr
Fred Guy
Mary Siviter
Eric Turvey
Bernard Gash
John Garnett Jones
Bill Lockett
C. T. Jones
Mrs. A. Hyde
Mr. C. Pickering
Hilda Francis
Ken Waterhouse
C. M. Whitehouse
John Sharp
John McLeod
Monica Archer
Eileen Stables
Jack Haddock
Mrs. J. Stuart
W. B. Williamson
(of Theatre Administration)
A. P. Harper
Hilda Gould
Mr. Bartlett
Sandra Gwilliam
Fred Moore
Tom & Muriel Morgan
Mr. Grainger
Frank Harvey
Frank Fellows
Mr. Hingley
(of Wm. Jackson)
Harry Bayliss
Mrs. G. C. Wallbank
G. C. Billington
(of Hurley Robinson)
Tom Bray
Alf Wright
Mrs. Drinkwater
John Ward

Chris Willis
Alan Price
John Felton
Barry Moseley
G. A. Coombes
(of EMI)
Eira Benton
Dorothy Penn
Norman Tildesley
Howard Darby
Eva Willington
Chris Ingram
A. C. Vaughan
Arthur Collett
Ernest Highland
Gordon Mintern
Roy Mullender
Gerald Price
Margaret Woodhall
Joe Purshouse
Albert Brookes
Chris Gittings
Janet Miller
Bob Wareing
Les Castree
Zoe Joseph
W. T. Hunt
Les & Maud Gardner
Tarsem Singh Dhami
Colin Hunter
Peter Barnsley
John Saffell
Bill Winwood
D. W. Gilbert
Miss P. Entwistle
Ray Eggington
Fred Ward
Jane Williams

John Brimble, President of the Black Country Society and the following members of the B.C.S.:
Dave Whyley
Andy Rutter
Peter Glews
Keith Hodgkins

Mrs. Taylor and Mrs. Smit also helped type the manuscript, and the huge task of designing the book has been undertaken by John Revill. The manuscript was improved at a very late stage by the attention of Miss Chris Redler at Galataprint.

A great deal of photographic work was undertaken by Tony Wright, Kevin Wheelan, and Jan Endean of A. P. Eardley & Co. Tony Wright has also produced two excellent pencil sketches.

A final thank you to all the advance subscribers whose faith in the project made it financially possible.

Readers may feel that they would like to support the following specialist organisations:

The C.T.A.

For those interested in the history of cinema buildings a worthy organisation is the Cinema Theatre Association, founded in 1967 to promote serious study of all aspects of their design and operation. Regular visits and meetings, plus a bi-monthly newsletter.

The distinguished list of patrons is headed by Sir John Betjeman. Hon. Secretary: Marcus Eavis, 123B Central Road, Worcester Park, Surrey. KT4 8DU.

The Mercia Cinema Society

This organisation also promotes serious study of cinemas and would like to become involved in the preservation of cinema artefacts. The M.C.S. publishes a quarterly illustrated magazine; Mercia Bioscope. The Hon. Secretary is Mrs. R. Clegg, 64 Someton Drive, Erdington, Birmingham. B23 5ST.

This section of the book introduces you to the names of some of the people associated with the cinemas of the Black Country. If you become familiar with these names they will provide a cross-referencing system that relates different cinemas in different areas to one another. If one looked at cinemas solely in terms of architecture or their technical equipment these inter-relationships would not be apparent. It is the recognition of the "human element" that makes the history of local cinema meaningful. People "individualized" cinemas far more than the splendid exteriors of the buildings, and the people tie the cinema to its location. Ignore the people, and the history of the cinema of the Black Country is probably not very different from the history of the cinemas of any other area!

## 1. THE EXHIBITORS

People often ask, "Who was the first man to bring the cinema to the Black Country ?". Unfortunately even after a lifetime's difficult research I doubt whether one could produce a definitive answer. In the absence of a single answer it is worth looking at the work of several pioneers who could have claimed to have first shown films in the area and who went on to become exhibitors in the local cinemas, in the normal sense of the word.

### Pat Collins    1859 — 1943

It is fitting that we should begin by considering the life and and work of a fairground showman because the fairground was probably the place where the first cinematograph pictures in the Black Country were seen. Some books claim that one Harry Scard exhibited a flickering film at Bloxwich Wake Fair in 1895. This would make such an exhibition contemporary with the first shows given by the Lumiere Brothers in France, and would therefore be quite remarkable. However, one year later, 1896, the cinematograph was being demonstrated in London and the new medium had definitely "arrived". A public audience had sat down at London's Regent Street Polytechnic on 20th February to see some cinematography, and not far away, at Finsbury Technical College, Robert W. Paul was perfecting the equipment that later moved into the Alhambra, Leicester Square. In the remaining four years of the century the invention spread like wildfire and several fairground showmen immediately recognized its potential.

One such man was Pat Collins. He had been born into fairground life and grew up travelling the towns of Staffordshire, Cheshire and Lancashire, working on his father's roundabout. His biographer E. J. Homeshaw, wrote,

> "He was a cheerful lad and a born optimist. At 21 he had a hand-turned roundabout, a horse, a wife, and a few shillings in his pocket. His home was a horse drawn flat under which he slept at night."

His progress was from rags to riches. In the late 1870's the legend tells that he had to pawn his wedding suit immediately after his marriage, but by 1882 he had decided to settle in Walsall and began to prosper. He understood that the working population of urban areas like the Black Country sought escapism and excitement when they came to the fair. Pat Collins introduced new attractions and was quick to adopt any new technology that he could use on the fairground, for example the steam traction engine and generator. He bought a car as soon as such things were available, to keep an eye on all his interests. His success was partly due to skilful management of fairs and partly due to a reputation for fairness and strength. (He had valiantly fought off "opposition" in Walsall!). He later moved his headquarters to Bloxwich, just outside Walsall. At the Wakes Ground, Harry Scard is said to have shown his films and Pat Collins adopted the novelty as part of his show, advertising them as "animated pictures", and later, the "bioscope".

The booth, or tent, in which these shows were presented tended to become more and more elaborate and eventually they were bathed in electric light and enjoyed sound provided by a fairground organ. The zenith of the development of the bioscope was Pat Collins' "Wonderland". This was first presented at Olympia in 1907 and then went on tour with the fair. Its elaborate carved and gilded wooden frontage was said to have 5,000 electric lights and 14 arc lamps, powered by the generators on the huge traction engines. It must have been more impressive than many of the permanent cinemas that followed it ! The original Wonderland had a Gavioli organ. A second Wonderland was built, with a Marenghi organ and was even more like the permanent cinemas that followed in that the entrances were moved to the centre of the facade. The organ formed an ornate centrepiece, and has recently been returned to life after very extensive renovation.

After World War 1 It seems that Pat Collins realised the cinema had a future in proper permanent purpose-built theatres and he acquired the Alhambra, Dudley Port, the Olympia, Darlaston, and the Electric Palace in Bloxwich, not far from his home and the headquarters of his fair. At the same time he was making great headway in civic life. He had acquired great prestige and popularity as a major benefactor of local charities. In April 1918 he had been co-opted onto Walsall Council as representative of Birchills Ward, and in November of the same year he was adopted as the Liberal parliamentary candidate.

In the November 1922 election he was elected to parliament and was so busy that he was unable to attend the opening of his new cinema in Bloxwich, the Grosvenor, opened in the following month ! He was defeated in the October 1924 election and returned to the showground and the entertainment business with renewed vigour, none the worse for Tory insults and some disillusionment with life in the House of Commons.

He became a Walsall alderman in 1930, by which time he seems to have relinquished his interests in the Olympia and Alhambra, but he retained the Grosvenor into the sound era until the Odeon organisation acquired it. With his second wife at his side he went on, in 1938 to become Mayor of Walsall and celebrated his eightieth birthday while in office.

He died on 8th December 1943 and is buried in Bloxwich. His name is indelibly linked with the fairground, but his exploitation of the bioscope, the building of "Wonderland", and the grandeur of the Grosvenor cinema are all reminders of his contribution to the history of local cinemas.

## Waller Jeffs    1861 — 1941

The invention of the cinematograph was also seized by another breed of showmen, the presenters of travelling lectures, travel talks and magic lantern shows. These toured the drill halls and temperance institutes of the land while the fairs toured the wakes grounds. Their "educational value" gave them a respectability that no doubt the fairground lacked.

One man who was widely acclaimed as a travelling speaker and presenter of the lantern slide lecture was Waller Jeffs. At the turn of the century his shows at Birmingham's Curzon Hall were extremely popular. The Curzon Hall, at the top of Suffolk Street, was later the site of the West End Cinema, but it had been built to house dog-shows. Political meetings, boxing, variety, religious services, circuses, all came to the Curzon Hall. In May 1901 Waller Jeffs presented a complete programme of moving pictures, although it is possible that he had included short pieces of films in earlier shows. The programme of Edison films ran for two hundred performances and Black Country folk, as well as Brummies, flocked to see it.

Jeffs made his own films of local events and of local visits by celebrities like General Buller or Buffalo Bill and screened these. The fact that he was probably doing this before the turn of the century is suggested by the fact that he became a member, and later President, of the Cinema Veterans Association. He also arranged complete film shows in other towns, probably including the Agricultural Hall, Wolverhampton and the Public Hall in Dudley. His seasons of film shows continued at the Curzon Hall throughout the 1900's. In 1908, for example, he filmed a Wolverhampton-Birmingham cycle race and photographed the event from a car that dashed along in front of the cyclists.

His manager at the Curzon Hall was Irving Bosco and later, when Mr. Bosco became a cinema proprietor Waller Jeffs returned the compliment and managed one for him. This was at the Picture House, Harborne. About 1921 Waller Jeffs moved to the Picture House, Stratford-on-Avon, again in association with Irving Bosco, to whose family he was "Uncle Wally". Eventually the Stratford-on-Avon Picture House was bought by Sidney Clift and Waller Jeffs' new association with the emerging Clifton Circuit brought him back for at least one visit to the Black Country.

Then in his seventies, he came to the opening of the Regal, Wednesfield, on the 14th October 1935, and two of his films taken in 1908/9 were presented as the first part of the programme. He was always a man that was loved and respected, and his kind gentlemanly manner endeared him to everyone he met. He died, at the age of eighty, on 1st July 1941 and is buried at Brandwood End Cemetery, Kings Heath. I do not know if any of his films have survived.

## Irving Bosco    1870 — 1946

I have mentioned Irving Bosco in the previous section of this book. His name is occasionally to be found in the few printed references that are made to the life and work of Waller Jeffs, but I feel his part in bringing the cinema to the Black Country needs to be more widely recognised. He was a striking man with an equally striking assumed name. He was born as William Morris Bainton, on 13th October, 1870, at Keighley in Yorkshire. How he adopted the name Irving Bosco is an intriguing mystery, although it may have been a name found somewhere in his family's history, or a circus name.

1. Irving Bosco

*(Photo: Mrs. E. Willington)*

Towards the end of the last century he was to be found touring Ireland with Bosco's Circus. In his role as the Ring Master he introduced many of the leading acts of the day. He had also toured Britain with some kind of entertainment and had visited Dudley in the early 1890's. When the cinematograph was displayed in London in the middle of that decade he had turned his inventive skill to perfecting a machine of his own. He eventually patented part of the mechanism but later sold the idea to a London firm. It seems likely that he made his own films and showed them with the travelling circus.

The turn of the century saw him working with Waller Jeffs at the Curzon Hall, after which he seems to have toured with a cinematograph show for the Navy League. He was definitely in this area again by 1908 for the cycle race that has already been mentioned, and in 1909 he married Miss Ducie Saunderson. She also came from Yorkshire and was a mezzo-soprano, actress and dancer. She was appearing twice-nightly for sixteen weeks "non-stop" at the Curzon Hall. Waller Jeffs was the best man and that evening he brought the couple on stage at the Curzon Hall.

Mr. and Mrs. Bosco Bainton settled in Tipton and it seems likely that Irving Bosco showed films in Dudley sometime in 1909. Christmas film shows at Dudley's Public Hall were presented by Professor Wood but as soon as the Cinematograph Act became law it seems that Irving Bosco acquired the necessary licence and began his regular shows at the Public Hall as from 31st January, 1910.

He was also showing films at the Picture Palace, West Bromwich before the coming of the Cinematograph Act helped by his brother, James Bainton. In the years leading up to the War he broadened his operations considerably. In June 1911 he opened the Cape Hill Electric, a purpose-built cinema, and in April 1912 he began showing films at The Rink, Smethwick and The Empire, Dudley. The latter became the headquarters of "Bosco's Pictures Ltd.", which was formed in 1913. He moved to Smethwick as his interests began to include cinemas in the Birmingham area, the Picture House, Harbourne and the Picture House, Villa Cross. Shows at the Public Hall, Redditch were also presented by Bosco's Pictures.

During the First World War, or just after it, Irving Bosco relinquished his interest in the West Bromwich cinema, to Thomas Leach, and abandoned Dudley's Public Hall. Some pioneers, such as Professor Wood and his son decided to expand, but it seems that Mr. Bosco felt unsure of the industry's future. In October 1920 Kine Weekly reported that he was putting his cinemas up for sale. In a subsequent edition it reported that he certainly did not intend giving his cinemas away but a buyer materialised and Bosco's Pictures Ltd. was wound up at a special general meeting on 17th December 1920.

The man who bought the Empire, Dudley, the Rink and the Cape Hill Electric, the two Birmingham cinemas and the Public Hall, Redditch was E. C. Shapeero of the Record Cinema Circuit based in Nottingham. Although this deal marked the end of Irving Bosco's association with Black Country cinemas it is interesting to recall what happened next. From the same Mr. Shapeero, and a partner named Mr. Cook, Irving Bosco acquired the Picture House in Stratford-upon-Avon, and installed Waller Jeffs there as the manager. This cinema had opened in 1913 and had developed a few problems that its new owner was quite equal to solving.

To his staff at Stratford Mr. Bosco was always the "Great White Chief" and he regularly visited the cinema on Saturdays to see Waller Jeffs and see how business was going. Very quickly it became apparent that the unreliable electricity supply was the cinema's main problem. A power cut on Whit Monday 1921 while queues waited outside the hall convinced Irving Bosco that there was only one answer: they would generate their own power. A gas generator was installed and the

staff trained in its use. A lamp was erected at the top of a flag pole to proclaim their triumph and even during power failures in the mains supply they could annouce, "Bosco's Beacon shines nightly !". In 1924 he sold out, but he made sure that Waller Jeffs' position at the cinema was to be permanently safeguarded, as recorded in the previous section.

Like many of his fellow-members of the Cinema Veterans Association, Irving Bosco was definitely a great showman. He was a big impressive man with an engaging outgoing personality. He could combine a shrewd business sense with generosity, fairness and a sense of humour. These attributes, plus his continual inventiveness, made him an ideal pioneer of the new medium. He retired before the advent of the talkies, and when he died in 1946, many of the buildings in which he had shown films had disappeared or changed their use. His most lasting monument in the Black Country was the Cape Hill Electric, which survived into the mid fifties. His Picture House at Stratford has survived but is at present threatened by redevelopment of the site.

The Woods of Bilston :
Professor Joseph Wood    (1842 — 1927)
& Thomas Wood           (1868 — 1938)

If life should take you into the Bingo Hall in the centre of Bilston in the 1980's look above the proscenium arch and take note of a letter "W" cast in the plaster as a kind of heraldic mongram. One or two assistants talk of the building being haunted by the ghost of a professor and some of the elderly Bingo-players claim to remember that professor "reading their bumps". Unravelling these "mysteries" unfolds the story of the men who brought films to this part of the Black Country, one of which became one of Bilston's leading citizens.

Joseph Wood was one of four brothers born on a smallholding in Northumberland. He was born in 1842, had a "working childhood", and received no education. About the age of 10 he set off in search of a brighter future in Liverpool and found work in a flour mill. He then set about acquiring some education with all the drive and energy that some Victorians brought to the task of improving themselves. He studied anatomy and physiology and from an interest in medical matters he ventured into a number of subjects such as mesmerism, phrenology, palmistry and the interpretation of handwriting. He was largely self-taught but progressed far enough to be able eventually to make a living from demonstrating his skills and lecturing on them. These lectures, from the mid 1880's onwards, were accompanied by lantern slides.

The Professor's son, Thomas Reay Wood, born in 1868, became the projectionist, and in 1887 acquired an elaborated machine that could dissolve one image into the next and add movement, such as falling rain etc., to static views. A travelling show consisting of the Professor's demonstrations and his son's magic lantern slides was a success in the industrial towns of the North West.

In 1896 Tom Wood immediately recognized the potential of R. W. Paul's cinematograph, the Professor purchased a projector in the October of that year and they put on their first programme of animated pictures at Bury. By this time they had settled into a routine of

2. Thomas Reay Wood, his father, Professor Wood, his son Reay, his wife Zella Vondi and his daughter Angela, about 1925.

*(Photo: Reay and Angela Wood)*

living and working in Douglas, Isle of Man, each summer and touring the mainland industrial towns in the winter. Although strict Wesleyans there was no rest for them on Sundays, for on that day they presented sacred concerts!

While Tom purchased and projected films the Professor produced his own book, "Scientific Palmistry" published in Douglas in 1897. The future patrons however, seemed likely to find more enjoyment in animated pictures than in having bumps read. Tom was anxious to make his own films and eventually acquired his first camera, a Prestwich, in 1900. Like many of his fellow members of the Cinema Veterans Association, he was both exhibitor and film-maker. In 1902 he went down to London and made his own film of Edward VII's coronation, sending the results back to Douglas for screening at the Grand Theatre, the next night ! He also made a successful film of the King's post-coronation tour, including a visit to the Isle of Man.

While managing the Grand Theatre in Douglas in the early years of this century Thomas Wood met many of the show business personalities of his day. It was also probably where he met Miss Zella Vondi, an accomplished pianist. Her real name was Miss Nellie Hewitt, and she came from Handsworth. They married in 1906.

The winter tours with the travelling cinema continued and the Woods updated their technology as the years went by, adding a heavy electric generating set to their

equipment that had to be transported from hall to hall. Bilston Town Hall was on their circuit, as was the Public Hall in Dudley and probably other halls in the Black Country. They settled in Bilston in 1910 and rented a room in the Town Hall to be the first "Wood's Palace".

In the next four years they looked round for a suitable site for a permanent purpose-built cinema. About 1912 they found a site on the Wakes Ground at Willenhall but nothing came of this, although, after the Great War they leased the Coliseum, Willenhall, for a time. During the War itself Thomas Wood joined the St. John's Ambulance Association and performed duties with the Special Constabulary. He was also acting-manager at Leon Salberg's Alexandra Theatre in Birmingham for a while. As soon as peace returned he turned his attention, once again, to the expansion of his entertainment business.

In 1919 the Woods leased the tiny Electric Palace, opposite the Town Hall, in Church Street, and as materials became available again they set about building the magnificent Wood's Palace in Lichfield Street. In 1921 their shows in the Town Hall ceased and their purpose-built cinema opened. The full details are described in the section on Bilston's cinemas. They did not rest there; they acquired the lease of the Alhambra, in the High Street, and showed films there until 1927 when they opened their new purpose-built "Savoy" on

18

the opposite side of the road.

In the meantime they acquired the Theatre Royal in 1924, briefly showed films in Bloxwich, and, towards the end of the twenties, took over the Queens at Bradley. Thomas Wood was also a director of the Palace Cinema in Wednesbury and the Palace, Melton Mowbray. Added to all this activity he had become an important figure in the civic life of Bilston. He had been chairman of the Urban District Council in 1925/7 while also serving on Staffordshire County Council, and acting as a local magistrate. He was a Rotarian, and was on numerous committees, including the Childrens Holiday Camp Fund, the District Nursing Association, the Horticultural Society, and Swan Bank Methodist Church !

In January 1928 he held the first of Bilston's "Cinema Balls". The British film actress Marie Ault came to the Town Hall to judge the fancy dress competition and to join the four hundred and fifty revellers. They continued annually into the thirties and raised funds for the charities with which Thomas Wood was associated.

Professor Wood died in 1927 and Thomas Wood consolidated the business of "Woods Picture Halls" from then onwards rather than continue the expansion. His brother-in-law Leon Hewitt, acted as general manager in order to give "T. R." time for his many activities but even so he was often to be found at his office in the Palace.

As the thirties unfolded he installed sound in his cinemas and converted the Theatre Royal to a cinema as the talkies gained popularity. It later became a theatre again. He also took part in the organisation and planning that led to the rebuilding of the Palace in Wednesbury.

Since 1933 Bilston had become a Borough and Thomas Wood became its Mayor in November 1935 and spent a busy year in this office. Perhaps it is not surprising that at this time he decided to retire. Family businesses were being overtaken by the super-cinemas and the growth of the circuits. On 29th August 1936 the three Bilston cinemas: the Woods Palace, the Savoy and the Queens, were leased to C. S. Joseph's Astel Pictures for twenty-one years. Before leaving his office at the Palace, Alderman Wood gave an interview to Quaestor of the Express and Star. In this he reviewed his career from the days of travelling lantern-slide shows to the eve of the practical use of television.

"Films", he said, "have made home conditions better, improved behaviour, and made people dress better."
What would he say today ?

His civic life continued, for example he opened Bilston's Library in March 1937, in his sixty-ninth year. He died on 16th December 1938 and at his funeral were to be found mourners representing all aspects of the cinema, past, present and future, ranging from Charles Pindar, the Wednesbury member of the Cinema Veterans Association of Pre-1903 exhibitors, to John Davies who represented Oscar Deutsch, but who was later to rise to great heights in the Rank Organisation.

T. R. Wood's heirs continued to be the landlords of the picture houses while C. S. Joseph ran them on his twenty-one year lease. Thus in the mid fifties when C. S. Joseph chose not to renew the leases, they returned to the family. The Theatre Royal closed and the Forum was sold to Mr. and Mrs. Woodroffe, but Thomas Wood's son, Reay Wood, took over the Savoy, hoping that a buyer would be found. No buyer materialised and thus Reay Wood kept the family's association with cinemas going right into the sixties. For a time he added the Rialto, Wednesbury, to his task of running the Savoy, but the late fifties were difficult times to be running cinemas and their closure became inevitable. The Rialto enjoyed a further short lease of life in other hands, but the Savoy closed in 1963.

The Odeon, late Wood's Palace, which had been transferred directly from C. S. Joseph to Oscar Deutsch back in 1936 had seen its lease renewed by the Rank Organisation. It closed a year after the Savoy and became a Bingo Hall. Its connection with Woods Picture Halls was finally severed in 1971 when the Rank Organisation offered the Hutchinson Group a package deal of five halls which included the Dunstall Odeon and the Bilston Odeon. This brought the Wood family's association with Bilston to an end.

## The Poole Family

The pioneers of cinematography were showmen from a variety of backgrounds: the fairground, the lecture hall and the music hall. What they had in common was that they invariably travelled the length and breadth of the land while providing their entertainment. The building of permanent "cinemas" provided a break with this tradition and heralded the demise of that way of life. People like Irving Bosco, Benjamin Kennedy and the Woods then put down some roots in the Black Country. The same cannot be said of the Pooles, but as they contributed to the history of early film-showing in the Black Country they deserve to be included here.

This story begins in 1837 when a man named M. Gompertz formed a partnership with two brothers, George and Charles Poole. Legend has it that the former, a travelling presenter of "panoramas", met the two brothers while they were busking on the promenade at Margate. They teamed up so that they could provide a musical accompaniment to the show, which consisted of painted pictures being rolled across the stage. Some of the pictures were very elaborate and expensive, others used trick effects such as moving components, and they usually depicted great battle scenes, epic disasters and contemporary events.

Eventually the Poole Brothers took over the business entirely and were joined by a third brother, John Poole. John Poole's son, Charles W. Poole became the manager and they adopted the term "Myriorama" to describe their moving tableaux. The show was accompanied by an orchestra and included variety acts between each tableau. The show travelled from town to town and hired a public hall for a week. Special trains and fleets of horse-drawn pantechicons had to be organized to move the elaborate equipment and growing numbers of personnel. By 1900 seven such shows were on tour. About the same time films were introduced and included among the vaudeville turns while the next panorama was being mounted. Some of these films had mechanically coupled sound-on-phonograph, yet they still were only considered in third place, in terms of entertainment value, after the panorama and the variety acts.

Poole's Myriorama visited the Black Country on tour each year but their headquarters were established in Gloucester, so a stronger association with the area did not come about until they gradually started acquiring some of the halls they visited on a more permanent basis. Charles Poole and his son, John R. Poole, started running cinemas very soon after the passing of the 1909 Cinematograph Act.

They opened the Kings Hall in Stourbridge in November 1911, and the Queens Hall, Brierley Hill in May 1912, and eventually had cinemas in Edinburgh, Aberdeen, Oxford and Ipswich. "Pooles Perfect Pictures" never quite penetrated the Black Country as thoroughly as other early concerns, but their presence at Stourbridge survived the coming of sound and the advent of the super-cinema. The only male member of the fourth generation of the family, John K. S. Poole, born in 1911, was trained in all aspects of the cinema business and preserved his family's traditions. After celebrating the centenary of the business he set about rebuilding the Kings Hall as a modern super-cinema.

They were an old-fashioned family business and their employees often enjoyed a long association with them, for example Harry Wharton and Harry Morris in Stourbridge. Other people associated with cinemas in the Black Country, for example Cecil Couper in Brierley Hill and Jim Davis in far away Wednesfield, began their cinema-careers with Pooles. (Cecil Couper was related to the Poole family).

Their connection with local cinemas was severed in the mid-fifties when their Stourbridge cinema was sold to the Rank Organisation.

## Benjamin Kennedy    1867 – 1939

Ben Kennedy came to the cinema via the music hall, but he was not born into a theatrical tradition, nor was he born in the Midlands. He was born in London, the son of a furrier. It was intended that he would go into his father's business but legend has it that he ran away at the age of thirteen and joined a travelling waxworks show. He spent at least three years with the waxworks before drifting into the theatre where he played comedy parts. At one time he had a troupe known as the Kennedy Komics.

In 1890 he became manager of the Coliseum Theatre in Dalston, London, but it seems that his heart was set on a proprietorial role in the theatre. His association with the Midlands began with an interest in Birmingham's Gaiety Theatre. Both there, and at the King's Hall he started showing films with the variety acts. As he expanded his interests into the Black Country the films became more important but from 1910 to the mid 1920's both film and variety were often presented at the same theatre. At one time he had an interest in thirteen theatres, but some of these were short-lived. He showed films at halls in Tipton, Wednesbury, Dudley, West Bromwich and Smethwick.

His name is particularly associated with Dudley. In October 1920 he acquired the Opera House, and the adjacent Scala ten years later. The Scala was demolished and rebuilt as a super-cinema, opening in May 1936. About six months later the Opera House was burnt down. Ben Kennedy then set out building his ultimate

3. Benjamin Kennedy

*(Photo from Plaza opening brochure)*

achievement. From the ashes of the Opera House a huge brand new theatre was built to stand alongside the Plaza. He was now in his seventies but in December 1938 he struggled to attend the opening of the Hippodrome in an invalid chair. It was a brave and proud gesture to build such an immense theatre when super-cinemas seemed to rule the entertainment world.

Not long afterwards, on 10th April, 1939, Ben Kennedy died at his home in Wollaston, near Stourbridge. His sons continued to run the halls in Dudley and one in West Bromwich, but the Plaza was eventually sold to Miles Jervis and the Hippodrome closed on 15th March, 1958, not long after its twenty-first birthday. The Hippodrome was sold and re-opened for a short time as a theatre but was not a success. Today it is a Bingo Hall and Discotheque, and the two fortress-like brick buildings still stand at the foot of Dudley's Castle Hill as a monument to Ben Kennedy.

## Edward Hewitson    1874 – 1936

It presents a very neat straightforward picture for the historian if one person can be given the credit for bringing the cinema to a particular town; for example Professor Wood, and his son, in Bilston. Smethwick seems to have been equally fortunate. In this case Edward Hewitson introduced films to the town.

Edward Hewitson came to Smethwick in 1897 to be manager of the Theatre Royal, Rolfe Street, on its opening. He was, therefore, a man of the theatre, as much as the cinema, and it was in the Theatre Royal that he first showed films, introducing them after the stage show about 1905. Like other early exhibitors he also made his own films and occasionally hired the Town Hall in which he put on shows. Following the passing of the Cinematograph Act he does not seem to have rushed into the business of showing films on a full-time basis. Films still mingled with the theatrical offerings at The Theatre Royal and at Ben Kennedy's rival theatre, The Empire.

Irving Bosco opened the first purpose-built cinema in Smethwick, at Cape Hill, in 1911, just at a time, presumably, when Edward Hewitson was making up his mind that exhibiting films had a future. Edward Hewitson left the Theatre Royal on 2nd December, 1911 after a Benefit evening held in his honour. A few months later he opened "Pictureland" at the Town Hall while his own cinema was being built. The new cinema, The Prince's Hall, was built nearby, on the site of an old post-office. This opened on 19th December, 1912 and the shows at the Town Hall ceased.

During the same period Thomas Jackson, in Wolverhampton, was expanding like wildfire, but Edward Hewitson proceeded more slowly. He added the Majestic, Bearwood, early in 1916. Perhaps its completion had been held up by the outbreak of war. By the end of the First World War he had also acquired The Coliseum, Bearwood, and the Ring Palace, West Smethwick. I do not know whether he had any wish to purchase Irving Bosco's two Smethwick cinemas, the Rink and the Cape Electric, after the war. In the event the only further addition to his "chain" was the Empire, acquired in 1922 and turned into a cinema.

Running five local cinemas he was now an exhibitor of some importance and he became a prominent member of the local Cinema Exhibitors Association and joined such battles as the campaign for Sunday opening. He became the C.E.A.'s National President in 1927 and also entered the world of politics. His interest in his cinemas was still strong and towards the end of the twenties a great deal of activity took place, anticipating the coming of sound and the super-cinema.

First of all the Coliseum was replaced by an entirely new cinema, built just across the road. This new hall was The Windsor, opened in September 1930 with the wonders of sound, and a Compton theatre organ. Three

4. Edward Hewitson
*(Photo from Windsor opening brochure)*

months later a new Prince's opened in Smethwick itself as a fine replacement for the old Prince's Hall. The Windsor, however, was the company's 'flagship' and the head office was established there. The Rink had also re-opened in 1930 and thus Smethwick enjoyed three new large cinemas, each containing a Compton organ !

The Empire was updated with sound equipment but the Ring Palace was abandoned after a short period of survival as a "silent" cinema surrounded by sound ones !

Edward Hewitson's civic life was still to reach its summit. He became Smethwick's Mayor in 1935. Unfortunately, a few days after the end of his year of office, he died on 19th October, 1936. Thus he did not live to see the last part of his cinema empire join the Windsor and the Prince's as a modern super-cinema. The final touch was the rebuilding of the Majestic, which was completed just before the beginning of the Second World War.

Surrounded by the growing circuits, the four halls, now run by Edward Hewitson's son, Alan, provided an oasis of independence and remained as such until their closures, thus linking the family's name indelibly with cinema entertainment in that borough.

Thomas Jackson

The men who built the first cinemas and recognized that films could bring profit to permanent establishments were not always men from the traditions of the theatre, or travelling showmanship. Sometimes local entrepreneurs were simply businessmen who seem to have alighted on the new toy just at the right moment and who adopted it as their main concern. One such man was Wolverhampton's early film magnate: Thomas Jackson.

While the Cinematograph Bill was going through Parliament it seems that Mr. Jackson was still baking cakes at his bakery in Whitmore Reans, an industrial quarter of Wolverhampton. He lived nearby at 78 Gatis Street. Perhaps inspired by the success of the Quigley's at the Olympia, he decided to convert his bakehouse into a cinema. This became The Strand, opened in 1912. Following its success he opened the Alhambra in Bilston and the Electric in Bloxwich. He formed a company called Wolverhampton, Walsall and District Cinemas, with a capital of £15,000. His meteoric rise was accompanied by the building of larger premises, considered quite a novelty because of their size; The Coliseum, Wolverhampton and the Cinema de Luxe, Walsall.

In a bewildering maze of activity the Midlands County Cinema Circuit Ltd., was also formed early in 1914. This company had its headquarters in Market Harborough, Leicestershire, and owned both of Mr. Jackson's Walsall cinemas, the De Luxe and The Palace, the Coliseum, Wolverhampton, and the Picture House, Kidderminster. The Palace, West Bromwich and the Little Picture House, Victoria Street, Wolverhampton, were also brought under his control. The latter became his headquarters, and, at some stage he moved from his home in Whitmore Reans to a grand house in Merridale Road: "The Firs". Apparently Thomas Jackson managed to supervise all his cinema interests personally, with the help of his daughters, and a speedy chauffeur-driven car!

In May 1922 Kine Weekly announced that he intended selling his chain of six cinemas and "The Firs". The six cinemas at that time were the Picture House and Coliseum, Wolverhampton, the Palace and the Cinema de Luxe, Walsall, and the cinemas in West Bromwich and Kidderminster. The Strand was to be re-built as The West End, the Alhambra, Bilston, was by then being run by Thomas Wood and the Bloxwich cinema had passed to Pat Collins. It seems that Mr. Jackson wished to move to Leicestershire and concentrate on his interests there.

No sale was forthcoming and it seems that he was forced to form a new company to run the circuit. He went into partnership with a Mr. C. D. Allen and formed Jackson Allen (Cinemas Consolidated) Ltd. Unfortunately the partnership did not thrive and on 16th March, 1923 Pathe Freres presented a petition for the liquidation of the new company. It was heard at Wolverhampton County Court on 6th April and the company was compulsorily wound-up. Further court proceedings occupied the remainder of 1923 and Thomas Jackson's bankruptcy was finally recorded in the 1926 Kine Year Book. The six cinemas mentioned above were then operated by the Midland Counties Circuit - run by L. A. Thompson, the official receiver.

The rise and fall of this Black Country cinema proprietor is interesting in several respects. Firstly it illustrates the attraction that the new medium had for anyone of an entrepreneurial disposition, and the fact that the prospect of great wealth was possibly an illusion. Maybe the day to day administration of such a scattered and quickly established empire created problems, although men like Irving Bosco and Benjamin Kennedy had managed it. Later men built circuits of cinemas each separately financed by individual companies, but the cinema business was always a world where distant profits were often preceeded by daunting initial capital investment.

Another aspect of Thomas Jackson's career is the speed with which such a man can "disappear" into history. Just over half a century after his difficulties, his life and work seem as remote as King Arthur and the Round Table ! I have spoken to a few of his ex-employees and to a few of the patrons of his cinemas from those far off days before the First World War. Yet as a person I know very little more about him than I first imagined on initially encountering his name in those cryptic entries in the Kine Year Books. A few people alive today remember eating his cakes, popularly known as "kill-me-quicks" ! He transformed himself from a baker to a showman. He adopted the tricks of men like Irving Bosco and Thomas Wood. For example, in July 1914 he filmed Wolverhampton's annual flower show and screened the results at the Strand, the Picture House and Coliseum. Yet today few people know his name or can provide memories of the man himself.

If he left Wolverhampton about 1924, I wonder what became of him ? Perhaps he did manage to pursue his interests in Leicester. I have heard other more romantic stories including one in which he emigrated to Canada and ran cinemas in Saskatchewan !

## The Bray Family and Wally Davies

When I first came to the Black Country in the early sixties I remarked to someone on the number of little cinemas that had closed in the area around Dudley. The stranger said that all the cinemas belonged to either the "Brays or the Coupers" in the south west of the Black Country. It was not quite true, but the names had obviously become part of the folklore regarding local cinemas and only now, nearly two decades later, have I begun to sort out who these people were and which cinemas were which !

At the turn of the century the Brays were an established business family in Dudley. They had no previous show business connections but cinematography obviously attracted a young Sidney Bray. Mr. Bray's sister married another local man, Walter Davies. Mr. Davies' grandfather had been a noted Netherton brewer and early this century his father kept the Criterion Public House in the Market Place, Dudley. Music hall entertainment was to be found at the Criterion and eventually films. At some stage it ceased to be a public house altogether and the entire site was converted into a cinema, only about thirty feet wide, but nevertheless a cinema. By this time Sidney Bray had already established himself as a cinema proprietor, by putting on shows at the Drill Halls in Halesowen and Langley and at the Palace cinema in Brownhills.

Wally Davies, born in Springmere, Dudley in 1891 and educated at Holly Hall School, had started work at "The Earl's" (Round Oak Steel Works) in 1907 as a clerk and draughtsman. He first joined his brother-in-law Sidney Bray, in the cinema business on 30th January, 1911. After work he made his way to the Drill Hall, Halesowen, and described what happened next in his diary :

"At 6.30 p.m. I opened and started to take the money for the pictures. It was a terrible scramble, they knocked my pay office over and the money on the floor. At the two houses I took £7.10.0 in about fifty-five minutes. (I was very ill, I, foolish-like, had a glass of bad ale)".

From August 1913 onwards he was running Sidney Bray's Langley Cinema in the Drill Hall in that town.

As from the beginning of January 1915 Sidney Bray became the licensee of the Criterion on his homeground in Dudley, but it seems that the cinema was still only a very part-time interest of brother-in-law Wally. Wally Davies was extremely inventive and persuaded Sidney Bray to be his partner in a number of schemes. First of all he became the first Dudley aviator when he took off from a field near the Priory on 27th May, 1911 ! He built his machines in the large workshop space available at Sidney Bray's home at 90 Aston Road, Dudley. In September 1913 he had emerged from this workshop with a glider which was tested at Lapal, near Halesowen.

While Mr. Bray was establishing his place in the cinema world, therefore, Wally Davies was involved in more technical matters and the First World War took him away from the area while employed by the Bournemouth Aviation Company in their design team. After the War Sidney Bray turned his attention to rebuilding the Criterion while Wally Davies turned his attention to hydroplanes. Once again these were built at 90 Aston Road and the two men tested them on the River Severn. Sidney Bray's son, Bernard, born 1910, used to come along for the ride, and inherited his uncle's love of speed.

The Criterion opened in November 1923 but, as far as I know Wally Davies, had nothing to do with this particular venture. His involvement in cinemas was rekindled the following year when he became Sidney Bray's partner at the Palace, Brownhills, and this somehow became his cinema while the Brays were more preoccupied with their interest in the Black Country itself. Sidney's younger brother, Clifford Bray, had taken over the management of the Criterion which left Sidney more time to concentrate on their interests in Halesowen.

Following his success at the Drill Hall, Sidney Bray had acquired the Picture House, Halesowen, from the Rose Brothers. In February 1924 it was gutted by fire, doing £3,000 worth of damage. It took over three years to rebuild the cinema, by which time the local cinema proprietor was facing the advance of the combines and the impending arrival of sound. These threats were felt particularly strongly in Dudley and the Criterion was sold to A.P.P.H. which was about to be merged into P.C.T. at the end of 1927. Clifford Bray left Dudley to develop his interest in the Central at Stourbridge and Sydney Bray continued to concentrate his activities in Halesowen.

After re-opening the Picture House, Sydney Bray also acquired the Cosy Corner in Peckingham Street, thus establishing his monopoly in Halesowen. In the early thirties he also showed films at the Victoria Palace in Lye for about four years. Clifford Bray's work in Stourbridge was more spectacular. The building of the Central was undertaken by a public company, as the Criterion had been. F. J. Ballard, an important local businessman, was on the board of both, and both cinemas were built by the Dudley firm, A. J. Crump of Aston Road. It was built on a scale and grandeur that could rival the work of the combines. (For example, it was certainly as good as P.C.T.'s new hall in Dudley; The Regent!). It opened in May 1929, shortly before the talkies arrived.

As the manager of the Central, Clifford Bray earned the popularity of the well-liked genial local cinema manager never quite acquired by his brother. He organized money-raising charity shows for local hospitals and was often in the foyer to greet his patrons, although by the mid thirties he no longer enjoyed good health. He died on 23rd April, 1937 at the early age of 52, having been confined to bed for the last few weeks of his life. In the same year Oscar Deutsch acquired the Central and in 1938 it became the Odeon.

During the mid thirties Sidney Bray still fought for the cause of the independent private cinema proprietor! In Brownhills, he and Wally Davies bought their rival, the Regent. The demolition of the Palace helped pay for extending and improving the Regent. In Halesowen the Cosy Corner seemed to be running into difficulties and its licence was only renewed temporarily in 1935 because it was understood that Sidney Bray was intending to build a brand new cinema in Halesowen. In the 1930's this was easier said than done by a lone individual but somehow the Lyttleton, as the new cinema was called, managed to reach completion and defiantly opened in April 1938. It was an attractive cinema, a small super-cinema in fact, built in the prevailing "modern" style, and a fitting conclusion to Sidney Bray's career. His son, Bernard Bray, was old enough to manage the cinema, and at the end of 1940 he inherited

5. The Brays and Wally Davies at the Lyttleton's opening: 11th April 1938.
Standing, left to right: Wally Davies, K. Choate (job architect), Bernard and Bessie Bray, C. E. Wilford (architect), John Felton (the builder) and W. Harrison (electrical engineer).
Seated, left to right: Mrs. Bray, Alderman Downing (Mayor of Halesowen), Mrs. Downing and Sidney Bray.
*(Photo: O. Ford-Jones, from the Collection of John Felton)*

both Halesowen cinemas on his father's death. He also became Wally Davies' partner in the Regent, Brownhills.

Wally Davies had never ceased experimenting with hydroplanes and hydro-gliders. For example, in 1938 he had built a fairly large craft at Aston Road, which was sold to the Maharajah of Bhopal. During the Second World War both Bernard Bray and Wally Davies worked hard with an A. T. C. squadron in Halesowen building a ground-model training aircraft which was copied all over the world. Bernard Bray's interest in speed and mechanical matters usually took the form of motoring and rally-driving. A fast car parked outside one of the Halesowen cinemas was a sign that he was "in residence".

The Halesowen cinemas prospered thronght the War years. Bernard Bray making a particular success of the new Lyttleton. Like most other cinemas they suddenly encountered new circumstances in the mid fifties. Bernard Bray died at the early age of forty-nine, thus escaping the final decline of his cinemas. The Picture House closed soon afterwards, but the Lyttleton struggled on, owned and run by his daughters, and his widow. It made a spectacular survival through those difficult times and into the seventies. After the new owners turned it into a Bingo Hall, films still made a "come back" for a short period. It still survives as a Bingo Hall and a monument to the Brays as cinema proprietors.

Wally Davies also survived into the seventies. He died at 90 Aston Road, Dudley, in the house that had once belonged to Sidney Bray, in 1972. In his lifetime he had witnessed, and participated in, almost the entire span of the Brays' involvement in local cinemas.

## Cecil Couper and Mr. Bishop

Cecil F. Couper's name appears in the old Kinematograph Year Books in a number of entries concerning the small cinemas in the south western corner of the Black Country. One cinema, the Savoy at Netherton, was a joint venture with another local exhibitor: Mr. Bishop. It seems sensible to bring their careers together in this section although their business association was fairly brief.

Cecil Couper was actually a native of Southampton and was born in 1885. He was a nephew of one of the Poole's and presumably via this connection eventually found work with the travelling "Myrioramas". He became one of the lecturers who addressed the audience while the panoramas were presented. As they were interspersed with variety acts he became well acquainted with the artistes from the world of "variety". He married "Inez" of "Inez and Pim", a famous acrobatic team.

In 1912 the Coupers came to Brierley Hill to manage the Queens Hall — the Poole's new cinema in the Town Hall, which replaced Mr. Colin's variety shows, known as "The Tivoli". Mr. Couper's cheerful showman's geniality won him many friends and a year later he took over the lease of the Queens Hall in his own right, and continued to enjoy their support. It also seems that about 1914 Mr. Couper took over the Palace Theatre on the other side of Brierley Hill's High Street.

Further immediate expansion was interrupted by the First World War. During the War Cecil Couper served in the Army and as a result of his service suffered ill health for the rest of his life. However, once peace was restored he vigorously set about expanding "Coupers Enterprises".

First of all they leased the Cinema Hall, High Street, Tipton, and then in 1923 they acquired the Olympia at Wordsley near their base in Brierley Hill. The Coupers' home was at "The Firs" in Albion Street, Brierley Hill, and therefore, this outpost in Tipton must have seemed quite remote from the rest of their operations. The Queens Hall, the Palace, and the Olympia were within easy reach and were very much under his personal supervision. Cecil Couper ran matinees for the children and special Christmas shows in the grand showman's tradition.

He rebuilt the Palace sometime in the mid twenties and, thereafter, it devoted more time to presenting film than live theatre. His daughter, Irene, accompanied the films and Mrs. Couper played a large part in the management of the halls. In September 1928 Irene Couper married Harold Roberts and Mr. Couper's new son-in-law became involved in the cinema world ! The wedding at St. Michael's Church, was hailed as the first such occasion in Brierley Hill to be recorded on film. The film was subsequently screened on their three local screens so that patrons could share the family's happy event. Charles Poole himself was present and a representative of the Cinema Veterans Association, of which Cecil Couper was a member. Irene's younger sister, Celia, was a bridesmaid. Later her wedding was filmed by Pathe and screened at the Coronet and Savoy !

With the coming of sound Cecil Couper abandoned his outpost in Tipton and later at Wordsley. He began a programme of building small cinemas ideally suited to

6. The Coupers and Mr. Bishop Jnr.
Left to right: Charles Bishop, Cecil Couper, "Ma" Couper, and Kathy Clark (Cashier at the Coronet).

*(Photo: Mrs. Bishop)*

the village communities of that part of the Black Country.

Early in 1933 he opened the Coronet in Quarry Bank. The four shareholders in this enterprise were Mr. and Mrs. Couper and Mr. and Mrs. Roberts — their daughter and son-in-law. Mr. Roberts maintained his connection with the Coronet for its entire life. Then Cecil Couper began his business association with Howard Bishop of Netherton. Mr. Bishop had been presenting films at the Netherton Institute since before the War. He had also presented films at Dudley's Temperance Hall and at Cradley Heath's Institute, usually presenting films under the banner of "Pictureland". In the early thirties business was bad and Howard Bishop sought Cecil Couper's help in installing sound to bring the talkies to Netherton and regain a reasonable audience. With sound installed the hall became the Imperial.

Business picked up at the Imperial but the future of the lease was uncertain. Howard Bishop died, but his son, Charles Bishop, carried on his father's cinema activities, while working for the Great Western Railway by day. To overcome the uncertainty of the Imperial's future Mr. and Mrs. C. Bishop joined forces with Mr. and Mrs. Couper to build a new cinema almost "next-door". This cinema was the Savoy, and was opened in 1936.

Mr. Couper's final achievement was the building of the delightful little cinema in Pensnett; the Forum. Ill health prevented him from attending the opening of the Forum in January 1937 and he died not long afterwards at a nursing home in London.

The funeral was at Holy Trinity Church, Amblecote. The family were joined by mourners representing many branches of the cinema world, including the Cinema Veterans Association, Charles Bishop, his Netherton associate, D. H. Pass representing the Odeon circuit, and Mortimer Dent of the Danilo circuit (both circuits were now present in Brierley Hill), and the general manager of Poole's Theatres Ltd., along with Harry Morris from the Kings Hall, Stourbridge.

His early death, at the age of 52, robbed the Brierley Hill area of its enterprising showman who had built "village cinemas" where no super-cinema would have dared to venture. These three new purpose-built cinemas carried on but the Queens Hall and the Palace closed. (The former may have closed earlier). The Olympia had been sold to Mr. F. C. Leatham.

The Savoy continued to be run by Mr. and Mrs. Bishop, although Mrs. Couper booked the films for a time, then Irene Roberts did it. Harold Roberts ran the Coronet, and the Forum was managed by Kitty Stewart and her husband Alfred. The Stewarts were variety artistes who had worked for Poole's way back in the past. Mrs. Couper died in 1947, before the little cinemas began to suffer any decline in their popularity. The Forum was then sold to Mr. F. C. Leatham. It was the first of Cecil Couper's little cinemas to close, in 1959, but by then it was in other hands. Mr. Roberts struggled on at the Coronet until early in 1960 and Mrs. Bishop kept the Savoy open until the end of 1960. The Coronet has been demolished, the Savoy is a carpet store, but the Forum still brings entertainment every night to Pensnett, in the form of Bingo.

## Miles Jervis : Father, Son, and Son

The Black Country's newest cinema does not belong to one of the major circuits, but to Miles Jervis Cinemas of West Bromwich; a name long associated with the cinemas of this area. The senior male Jervis of each generation has been given the name Miles and this, at first, might cause some confusion. I have adopted the American style of numbering them !

Miles Jervis I began his association with the cinematograph in the days of the fairground and travelling show. Although he loved the fairground, he realised the potential of permanent cinemas. His brother Edward (Ted) Jervis had been showing films in the Market Hall at Chase Town, first for five days a week and then, when the market ceased to be held, on a full six day week. It was known as the Palace de Luxe. During 1920 Miles Jervis I purchased the Palace from his brother and began to build up a small circuit of cinemas. In 1922 he opened the Chase Cinema at Sankey's Corner. He acquired cinemas in Hednesford from a Mr. Bayliss, and one in Walsall Wood. Edward Jervis built the Regent in Brownhills, which was later sold to Wally Davies and Bernard Bray, before coming to Miles Jervis III at the end of its life !

Miles Jervis I did not concentrate all his attention in the area of the Cannock Chase Coal Field. He made one interesting excursion into the Black Country, by acquiring the Alhambra at Dudley Port. He took it over from Pat Collins in about 1926, and, at the end of the silent era sold it again. But this was not the last connection between the Jervis family and Dudley Port's cinema.

Miles Jervis II was born in 1909 and started work in his father's cinema business in 1926. He acquired his first cinema in 1937; the Valentine, at Kidsgrove in North Staffordshire. He "joined up" during the Second World War but returned to Kidsgrove when demobbed in 1945. His wife had looked after it during the War.

His debut as a Black Country cinema proprietor came very quickly after the War was over. At the Grand Hotel, Birmingham, on 26th July, 1946 he purchased the Queens and St. George's, West Bromwich, and the Savoy, Oldbury, by putting in the top bid of £25,575 at an auction of the estate of the late Tom Leach. These three cinemas had been leased to the F. J. Emery circuit, a Lancashire-based firm, and the leases still had twelve years to run.

As owner of the freehold Miles Jervis II first took a closer look at the cinemas and found them to be fairly run-down. He therefore went to see the lessee, Sir Frederick Emery, and while discussing the state of the cinemas he discovered that Sir Frederick was willing to relinquish the leases. Sir Frederick's son, who had acted as general manager of his circuit, had been killed during the War while serving with the R. A. F. The father had no enthusiasm for continuing the operation of these particular cinemas.

Thus Miles Jervis II's career as a local independent exhibitor began in these three ancient cinemas, all of which had been rather eclipsed by the emergence of the super-cinemas of the 1930's. However, the next decade gave Miles Jervis II the opportunity of acquiring more modern halls. At the beginning of 1952 he acquired the Alhambra, Dudley Port, from S. T. Cinemas. Mr. Suffolk, of S. T. Cinemas, had acquired the original Alhambra from Miles Jervis I but the cinema that now changed hands was the brand new replacement that had opened on the site in 1935.

Two years later, in 1954, Miles Jervis obtained the Plaza, Dudley, from the trustees of the estate of Benjamin Kennedy. Collecting cinemas, and therefore acquiring a larger number of seats, was one way of improving one's place in the pecking order of cinemas for an independent exhibitor. However, the major circuits still had first use of the films, and a film could be well exposed to the public by the time an independent exhibitor was able to show it. Strangely enough, at the time of acquiring the Plaza, the independents were seizing an opportunity to fight back. The major companies were reluctant to make any major re-investment in the cinemas, and one circuit had fallen

7. Miles Jervis II

*(A photo from his own collection)*

25

out with a film company. The result was that the introduction of cinemascope gave people like Miles Jervis II a chance to screen new pictures unseen at Rank Cinemas. Miles Jervis II made a deal with Twentieth Century Fox for the exhibition of their films and felt that the problems and expense involved in showing cinemascope films would be worthwhile. When *"The Robe"* opened at the Plaza in summer 1954 he was proved right. The Odeon, directly opposite, looked on as huge queues formed outside the Plaza and the film was retained for a second week.

In 1954 Miles Jervis II became deputy chairman of the local branch of the Cinema Exhibitors Association. He seemed youthful compared with many of the other members, but no-one could deny his commitment to the cinema business. He regarded this commitment as the secret of his success. He looked at other exhibitors, such as Arthur Griffin, from whom he later acquired the Imperial, and decided that, for them, running cinemas was only a sideline. Even Pat Collins had only run his cinemas as a sideline, his heart was in the fairground. The families that had 100% devoted themselves to their cinemas, the Brays, the Coupers, the Woods, the Hewitsons were now disappearing, or had already left the cinema business. Miles Jervis II was unique in that he preserved this commitment through the most difficult years ahead and passed on the enthusiasm to Miles Jervis III.

Miles Jervis I had died in 1948 and the cinemas at Chase Terrace and Chase Town were then administered by his widow. Although these suffered the misfortunes and decline of the 1950's, Miles Jervis II's Black Country empire continued to expand. In 1957 he acquired the Kings, West Bromwich, from the trustees of the estate of Benjamin Kennedy, and, a few years later, the Imperial from Arthur Griffin. West Bromwich therefore, became the centre of his local operations.

He obtained Dual Pictures and Haven Pictures from C. S. Joseph and took on leases of the Palace, Wednesbury, and Haven, Stourport. (At the former he ventured into Bingo when the 1960's developed a taste for such things). At one time or another he also controlled cinemas in Cheshire, and one in Bedworth. In the Black Country, the Savoy, Oldbury and St. George's, West Bromwich had closed by the end of the fifties. The Queens and Kings in West Bromwich prospered, possibly because films could be shown a week after they were seen in Birmingham and thus seemed reasonably new.

Following some ill health in the mid sixties the control of the cinemas gradually passed from Miles Jervis II to his son. Miles Jervis III realised what was happening during the sixties; the "family audience" was disappearing quickly and the tastes of the 18-25 year old age group would determine the future success of cinema programming.

Miles Jervis III inherited his father's dedication to the cinema, and in the early seventies when Compulsory Purchase Orders and the wholesale redevelopment of West Bromwich threatened to close the Kings he took the brave, and unusual, step of fighting for a new cinema to be included in that redevelopment.

When the Kings closed the Imperial abandoned Bingo to enjoy showing films again while the new Kings was built. The Kings opened in June 1975; a brand new purpose-built triple screen cinema, opening at a time when many other important local cinemas had become history.

Miles Jervis III now runs the business, but Miles Jervis II is still very much present in a consultative capacity, and can justly feel proud of his family's record of loyal devotion to showing films, and particularly of their continued success in doing so in the Black Country.

## Sidney Clift — (1885 — 1951) & The Clifton Circuit

Three names of Black Country cinemas stand out among the super-cinemas built in the nineteen thirties: the Cliftons, the Danilos, and the Odeons. Each were developed by Birmingham men, and, of course, the Odeons became a national circuit. The story of Oscar Deutsch and his Odeons has become well known, but the story of the other two circuits is less known and belongs very much to Birmingham and the Black Country.

Sidney Clift was a Birmingham solicitor whose association with the cinema business went back as far as 1914. His father-in-law, William Astley, had opened the Empire at Stirchley and I assume this is where his interest began. He later became a prominent member of the Cinema Exhibitors Association in Birmingham and at the beginning of the Sound era worked hard in their battle with the authorities for Sunday-Opening in the city. The battle was won at the end of 1932, and a few years later he became chairman of the C. E. A. in Birmingham. When he became its national president in 1944 he was the first Brummie to occupy that post.

The circuit that bore his name, began to emerge in the early thirties, as construction of super-cinemas gained momentum. He became associated with the construction of the Grove at Smethwick, opened in 1932, and then The Rock, in Birmingham. As the possible projects multiplied Sidney Clift joined forces with Leon Salberg a theatre proprietor often associated with Birmingham's Alexandra Theatre and the production of pantomimes. They were the two directors of The Regal Cinema (Wednesfield) Ltd., which, despite its name, was really the first Clifton ! It opened in 1935.

As the subsequent cinemas were opened, each was nominally owned by a separate company and this has led some people to feel that the word "circuit" is incorrect. However, the management of the cinemas was handled by a single company, they shared a common house-style, and usually the same name: Clifton. The management company was formed in 1934 as Cinema Accessories Ltd., and was responsible for staffing and equipping each cinema as well as for booking the films and purchasing all the ancillary sales.

As time went on Sidney Clift and Leon Salberg were joined by other directors, and some cinemas, such as the Rosum, Walsall, were built as a result of Sidney Clift's partnership with a local entrepreneur. In this case the directors were Sidney Clift, Edgar Summers and the architect, Ernest Roberts, and the cinema opened in 1936. The architects, Ernest Roberts and Roland Satchwell, had particularly strong ties with the Clifton Circuit and helped establish its house-style. The circuit rapidly developed in many parts of the West Midlands, and even further afield, but the Black Country cinemas

8. Sidney Clift at the Regal, Wednesfield.
Left to right: Area Manager (name unknown), Ken Jones
(General Manager), Mr. Smith (Manager of the Clifton,
Wolverhampton), Sidney Clift, Mr. Davis (Manager of the
Regal) and Marjorie Westbury.

*(Photo: Mrs. Charlesworth Collection)*

which are this book's concern developed as follows.

In 1937 the Cliftons at The Lye and Sedgley opened.
The former was the only Clifton to materialize in the
south western corner of the Black Country but others
were planned, for example at Amblecote. These sites
were in the villages rather than the large towns of the
area and in the following year, 1938, Cliftons opened in
areas of the Black Country that were, in a sense,
"surburban", firstly at Stone Cross, and then at Fallings
Park. Other sites were chosen and plans drawn but the
cinemas did not materialize. The last brand new Clifton
to open in the Black Country was at Coseley, in July
1939, not long before the declaration of War, and the
end of the age of building super-cinemas. Again it was
a village site but the cinema boldly faced the
Birmingham-Wolverhampton "New" Road as if future
patrons would drive to the cinema from miles around in
the new age of private motoring.

Other local cinemas were brought under the control
of Cinema Accessories Ltd. The New Theatre Royal in
Wolverhampton became a town-centre "Clifton", the
Empire and the Classic in Walsall joined the clan but

retained their existing names. In 1939 the little
Alexandra in Lower Gornal became part of the group.

During the Second World War the Clifton cinemas
made a striking contribution towards the War Effort, led
by Sidney Clift, who had two daughters in the services.
Concerts and special shows raised large sums of money
for war-time charities. A collection to raise the money to
build a Spitfire collected £5,000 in no time and the new
plane was duly named "Clifton Cinemas"! Sidney Clift's
other great interest in life was poultry and this led him
into war-time work that earned him a knighthood,
awarded in 1947 "for services to charity and
agriculture". He was not a pretentious man and I doubt
whether he insisted on being called Sir Sidney Clift anymore than he had insisted on being "Captain Clift"
before that. (He had acquired the rank of Captain while
serving in the First World War, in the Royal Artillery and
the R. F. C.). Ken Jones, the General Manager of the
circuit always regarded him as a good friend, ready wit,
and sympathetic listener and said that Sir Sidney was
always known as "The Guvnor".

During the forties "The Guvnor" operated over thirty

27

cinemas and continued his work for the C. E. A. and the Trade Benevolent Fund. He never saw the industry decline, as he died on 18th October, 1951. He collapsed at Birmingham's Snow Hill station, on his return from a business trip, and died before the arrival of the ambulance. After his death the circuit continued to be managed by Ken Jones for at least another decade, after which the closures began.

Theatre Administration Ltd., took over the work of Cinema Accessories Ltd., and continues to exist to this day although it no longer brings films to any cinema in the Black Country.

## Mortimer Dent and the Danilo Circuit

Captain Clift often appeared at the opening of his Cliftons, and at special events. In the same way Oscar Deutsch was an identifiable figure associated with the Odeons. When it comes to the Danilo circuit, the man behind it seems a much more shadowy figure at this distance of time. Mortimer Dent, sometimes known as "Micky" Dent, seems to have created the name in an attempt to recall the name of Dan Leno, and the name "Danilo" appeared on three Black Country cinemas. The cinemas themselves were as grand as the Cliftons and Odeons but the circuit was a much smaller affair and its history seems more obscure.

It seems that Mortimer Dent had been in the cinema business since just after the First World War. In the early twenties he joined Joseph Cohen to form C. D. Cinemas Ltd., the initials taken from each surname. They built up a circuit by purchasing old theatres and converted skating rinks, mainly in Birmingham but including a few in the Black Country such as the Olympia, Darlaston. The smartest hall in the Black Country was the Plaza, West Bromwich. By the time they opened the Plaza, in September 1927, the circuit was running fourteen halls.

At the end of the silent era Joseph Cohen and Mortimer Dent decided to go their separate ways. As a result of a good offer from A.B.C. they "sold up", all their cinemas apart from two city-centre halls which later became "News Theatres". Joseph Cohen went on to build his own super-cinemas in Birmingham while Micky Dent appeared to look further afield. In the next decade he built about eight "Danilo" cinemas, three of which were in the Black Country.

The first was the Danilo, Brierley Hill, which opened at the end of 1936. The Danilo, Quinton, opened in August 1939, became Mortimer Dent's headquarters as it was relatively close to his Edgbaston home, and the Danilo, Stourbridge had the distinction of being the last of the circuit to open, in May 1940. By that time, the other Danilo cinemas were operating at Redditch, Cannock, Stoke, Longbridge, and Hinckley.

They were large elegant buildings observing the traditions of the super-cinema: staff in distinctive uniforms, a house-style established in the furniture and fittings, a place in the community on the scale of an Odeon or Clifton. Is it possible that the man responsible for building eight such palaces remains so obscure ? He visited his cinemas, sometimes bringing two huge dogs with him, and often personally appointed his staff, but has left no imprint on history to compare with Oscar Deutsch or Sidney Clift.

At the end of the War the Danilo circuit was acquired by S. M. Super Cinemas Ltd., the expanding empire of Mr. Southan Morris. In 1961 they passed to the Essoldo group and the survivor, at Quinton, is now part of the Classic circuit. Having sold his circuit to Mr. Southan Morris, Micky Dent retired. He died in Eastbourne far away from Birmingham and the Black Country.

## Oscar Deutsch (1893 — 1941) and the Odeon Circuit

Much has been written about Oscar Deutsch, and the story of the Odeons is the one aspect of cinema history that seems to have reached a relatively wide audience. He was born in Birmingham, in 1893, the son of a prosperous scrap metal merchant who had enjoyed some association with the places of entertainment of the Black Country. Oscar Deutsch himself was possibly associated with places like the Scala, Wolverhampton, and the Regent, Tipton, in the early unsettled history of these places, as a result of his interest in Midland Amusements Ltd.

During the twenties Oscar Deutsch realised that an exhibitor's major problem was obtaining the right "product" and knew that power as an exhibitor could only be acquired if one controlled or owned enough cinemas. Some of the principal exhibitors, for example Gaumont, were also involved in film production and thus exhibited their own products. Oscar Deutsch hoped that he would be able to deal directly with the producers and obtain favourable terms by having a big enough "circuit", and by not being seen as a rival producer. This he eventually achieved in a deal with United Artists.

The Black Country can be proud that his first purpose-built cinema was opened in the area. This was the Picture House, Brierley Hill, opened in October 1928. It was not his first cinema, nor his first Odeon, but as it was the first brand new cinema built for Oscar Deutsch it surely deserves a place in history.

With the arrival of the talkies Oscar Deutsch set out on his ambitious plan to build a cinema in the High Street of every reasonably sized town in the British Isles. At first no strong house-style emerged and the first Odeon, opened at Perry Barr in 1931, was in an exotic style more associated with the twenties. Oscar Deutsch commissioned a variety of architects, many of them famous names in cinema-design.

Once again the Black Country played a significant part in his progress. At Warley, on the very border of the Black Country and Birmingham, Oscar Deutsch's new cinema was designed by Cecil Howitt and the Birmingham firm of Satchwell and Roberts who were responsible for so many local cinemas. Harry Weedon was asked to act as a consultant on the interior decor. Within a short time Harry Weedon had become the Consultant Architect to Odeon Theatres Ltd., and his office produced the house-style that has become so well known.

In passing it is interesting to note that the other directors of the Warley Cinema, as it was called when it opened in 1934, included Captain Clift and W. H. Onions, both of whom played a part in developing cinemas in the Black Country ! Further Odeons were built in the Black Country at Dudley and Wolverhampton, both in 1937, and both superb examples of Harry Weedon's style. It is also interesting to note that the Blackheath Odeon, opened a couple of months before the Warley, was the product of a Black Country architect and, therefore, not in the established style. Odeons to other people's designs also came into being by acquisition, for example the Dunstall, Wolverhampton, the Central, Stourbridge and Woods Palace, Bilston.

The classic Odeons of the rapidly growing circuit that poured off the drawing-board in Harry Weedon's office were built in a particular way. After all, the economy had barely recovered from the 1929 — 1931 slump, and the introduction of the talkies made the capital investment needed to build a cinema even more daunting than it had been in the twenties. Each super-cinema was the property of a separate company.

A local builder, grateful for such a major contract, would offer to work in return for payment partly in debentures, or even a seat on the board. Once a tenth of the work had been completed Eagle Star provided a mortgage and construction carried on. Oscar Deutsch only had a nominal liability and interest in each company but at the same time developed a strong interest in the companies that supplied fittings and equipment to each cinema, and the management company.

The house-style replaced the eclectic styles of the early cinemas and was much more related to the function of the building. As the style developed the proscenium arch, for example, disappeared and the walls swept directly to the large screen in a way that dramatically focused attention on the film. Sight lines and acoustics were improved, fussy decorative light fittings disappeared and were replaced with hidden lights, exterior facades began to reflect the influence of art deco and the Modern Movement. Neon lighting added the final touch to these buildings and the name Odeon has become strongly associated with the lettering used ever since the thirties.

The Warley Odeon looked particularly impressive at night, standing at the new gateway to the Black Country — the commencement of the "New Road" which had opened in 1927 to herald a motoring age. By 1937, when the two major Odeons of the Black Country were opened, Odeons were opening at the rate of two or three per week and the event was often treated with the excitement nowadays associated with the hysteria that greets pop stars. Two years later the pace had slowed down and the shadow of War was to bring further expansion to a halt.

In December 1941, a decade after the opening of the first Odeon at Perry Barr, Oscar Deutsch died at the age of forty-eight. By this time he had opened one hundred and forty cinemas and had acquired about as many existing ones. He had successfully challenged the existing national circuits such as Gaumont British and A.B.C. His initials were now preserved in the name of these superb super-cinemas and, for many, "Odeon" had become a common noun to be used for any such cinema.

His financial interests passed to his widow and in 1942 they passed to J. Arthur Rank, who became the new chairman of the board. J. Arthur Rank had been on the board since 1939 and also had a controlling interest in Gaumont British. John Maxwell of A.B.C. had also died in 1941 and Mr. Rank had tried to buy the family's holding in that company, but failed to do so.

J. Arthur Rank became as famous a name as Oscar Deutsch in post-war Britain. By 1947 the Rank Organisation embraced over eighty allied companies. The three hundred and five Odeon cinemas plus the two hundred and forty G.B. cinemas, when combined, outnumbered the four hundred and fifty-eight operated by A.B.C.

The organisation of the two circuits was amalgamated in 1948 into the Circuits Management Association. In that year the C. M. A. controlled five hundred and sixty-four cinemas. Oscar Deutsch's dream of a cinema in every major High Street was outstripped by the reality of the Rank Organisation often owning two cinemas in each town centre ! In Wolverhampton the number was four, plus two more nearby. Not only that, but the Rank Organisation was directly engaged in film-production, something never considered by Oscar Deutsch.

Naturally my own views on monopolies in a capitalist economy colour my attitudes towards the suitability of such organisations to provide entertainment in the changing social scene that followed the War. By the mid-fifties the closures had begun. Cinemas like the Criterion, Dudley, and the Cape Hill Electric closed after a quarrel between the Rank Organisation and the Government on the question of entertainment tax. It began the process that has continued ever since, in a series of waves, and often it has seemed to happen without any relevance to the ability of a local cinema to supply a local need or respond to a local situation. In the meantime the circuits' stranglehold on distribution had done much to affect the survival of everyone else.

## Other Exhibitors

### Cyril Joseph

Cyril Stanley Joseph was born in 1898 and was educated at the King Edward Grammar School in Birmingham (also attended by Oscar Deutsch and Sidney Clift). By the mid-twenties he was a sales representative for Ideal Films and by the end of that decade he had entered the world of exhibitors in Shrewsbury, having acquired a lease on the Central. During the thirties he built up a small circuit of nine cinemas, eight of which were in the Black Country. While others were building super-cinemas he built up his circuit by acquiring older existing cinemas and re-vitalised them in time to enjoy the boom of the late thirties and early forties.

Separate companies existed to operate two or three cinemas, but each were administered by the same three directors. The three men who pooled their talents were Mr. Joseph himself, as leader and "showman", Mr. Harry Gompertz, who was an accountant, and Mr. Alfred Parton Smith, a solicitor. They made their Black Country debut by acquiring the Picture Palace at Great Bridge in 1933 in the name of Storer Pictures.

The major development came at the end of August in 1936 when, in the name of Astel Pictures, they acquired a lease from Thomas Wood on Woods Palace, The Theatre Royal, The Savoy, and the Queens, Bradley. The lease on Woods Palace was sold, in turn, to Oscar Deutsch. This helped finance improvements to the cinemas and further expansion. For example, the Queens was refurbished and became the Forum.

A year later it was possible to lease the Palace at Wednesbury in the name of Dual Pictures. The company re-building the cinema at the time had run out of funds and C. S. Joseph stepped in to complete the cinema and re-open on 27th September 1937. Very soon afterwards similar events led to the acquisition of the Rialto, also in Wednesbury, in the name of Clifford Pictures. Early alterations in 1927 and 1931 had still not brought the Rialto up to date. Cyril Joseph acquired the lease from Mr. I. Kraines, reconstructed the place in six weeks, and re-opened on 17th August 1938.

Cyril Joseph's interests in the Black Country were completed in 1939 with the formation of Pine Pictures to acquire the Olympia and Coliseum in Wolverhampton. Compared to the new super-cinemas many of the halls on the circuit were "flea pits" doing poor business in poor districts of the Black Country, but Cyril Joseph put them back on their feet with a degree of showmanship coupled to refurbishing and better programming. He used stunts and promotions to advertise his shows. For example, the first fifty ladies coming to see a "weepie" like *The White Rose* were given paper roses, an old £5 car was set alight to advertise *The Great Fire*. In this way he competed with the elaborate promotions mounted by the managers of the supers, and it brought success to his cinemas. He also followed the example of other successful early cinema proprietors and kept a watchful eye on his enterprises by visiting them regularly.

The eight Black Country halls, plus the Haven, at Stourport, prospered as an independent circuit through the War and the period immediately following it. In the mid-fifties the twenty-one year lease on the halls in Bilston expired and was not renewed. In Wolverhampton

Pine Pictures was sold to V. J. H. Wareing, along with the Palace, Great Bridge. The lease on the Palace at Wednesbury was acquired by Miles Jervis. The Rialto was acquired by Reay Wood. As an exhibitor he had the remarkable good fortune of acquiring the cinemas at what turned out to be an opportune time and parted with them before their final decline. His showmanship had earned him a long retirement on Dudley Golf Course perched on a windswept ridge high above the Black Country !

### F. C. Leatham    1902 – 1962

While commenting on the career of Thomas Jackson of Wolverhampton, I drew attention to the fact that some people connected with local cinemas simply seem to "disappear". Their names stare at us from the contemporary entries in the old Kine Year Books but research can fail to bring them back to life in the imagination of the historian. F. C. Leatham is another such intriguing character. Read through those dusty trade directories and his name appears all over the place, undoubtedly earning him a place in this account of Black Country cinemas, but when some kind of bio-graphical jig-saw is assembled I still feel the man is remarkably elusive. I still feel this after two years research and several conversations with his relatives and a few people who knew him !

Frederick Charles Leatham was born in Cardiff on 19th May 1902, he was one of four children, two sons and two daughters. His father, Frederick William Leatham, was a leather belt maker in the days when most industrial machinery was driven by such belts. The family came to the Black Country during the First World War. As a child he had constructed make-believe theatres from old cardboard boxes to entertain his family but otherwise had no family tradition of "showbusiness" that might have directed him towards the world of running cinemas.

His principle interest was music and after qualifying as a music teacher he gave piano lessons in Dudley. His encounter with the cinema world appears to have come via Mrs. Jones of the Picture House at Princes End, Tipton, later known as The Bruce. At this little cinema he found employment playing the piano accompaniment to silent films. Later he relieved Mrs. Spicer at Dudley's Criterion and played in the orchestra at that grand establishment.

In October 1927 he became the manager at the Rialto, newly "re-opened" by Mr. and Mrs. Jones, in Wednesbury. He stayed there for about three years, until purchasing his first cinema, "The Cinema", High Street, Tipton. Presumably he acquired it as a silent cinema from Cecil Couper, and one of his first tasks was the installation of sound. He then sold it to his father and never again showed much interest in the place, even when the twists and turns of fate brought him back to another Tipton cinema.

At this stage he may have briefly acquired a cinema in Longton, but his next appearance in the Black Country came in the mid-thirties when he again acquired The Olympia, Wordsley, from Cecil Couper. He ran this hall until the beginning of the War when he became associated briefly with the Scala in Stourbridge.

Sometime during the War he acquired the Victoria at Horseley Heath, Tipton. To me this seems something of a "come-down" after the Scala in Stourbridge, but it must be remembered that in the early forties the Scala was very much the "poor relation" of Stourbridge's cinemas, surrounded by three "supers". It was also a very low point in Mr. Leatham's fortunes. Apparently he had hoped to move into the world of live theatre, and had intended re-opening the Theatre Royal in Rolfe Street, Smethwick. For a time he lived in a flat "converted" from the dressing rooms in the theatre that had once been managed by Edward Hewitson but the project collapsed, and Mr. Leatham returned to Tipton.

At the Victoria Mr. Leatham was not only proprietor, but also chief operator. Although this had the possible advantage of being a "reserved occupation" and Mr. Leatham was back in business, it hardly seems a good position from which to continue the pursuit of the glory of live-theatre or the illusive fortunes to be made in the cinema business.

At the Victoria Mr. Leatham was not only proprietor, but also chief operator. Although this had the possible advantage of being a "reserved occupation" and Mr. Leatham was back in business, it hardly seems a good position from which to continue the pursuit of the glory of live-theatre or the elusive fortunes to be made in the cinema business.

At the same time his father, and brother Leonard, were running the Cinema, in High Street, Tipton, not very far away, but Fred Leatham seems to have little to do with that enterprise. When his father died the latter passed to Mrs. Leatham and ultimately the four children, the Cinema was managed by brother Leonard, but still Fred Leatham had little to do with it.

Immediately after the War some improvements were made to the Victoria and a manager installed to run the place while Mr. Leatham went on to further projects. He acquired the Forum in Pensnett, again following in the footsteps of Cecil Couper, and the West End in Whitmore Reans, then operating as The Park. At the latter, refurbishing and new sound equipment gave the place a new start when Fred Leatham re-opened it as the Rex in August 1947.

It seems possible that the cost of the work on the Rex was Fred Leatham's downfall. The post-war decline in cinema fortunes was perhaps just too far away to be predictable. Apparently Fred Leatham himself felt that television would only be a "passing phase". Ironically, at last he was truly a cinema magnate — with three little cinemas under his control, in Tipton, Pensnett and Wolverhampton. He lived in Wolverhampton in a house called "Edenfield", now demolished, but not far from the author's home.

Possibly he felt his career was still ascending. In August 1952 he disposed of the Forum to two old associates, F. Ward and R. Eggington, and took over the Plaza in Dover. The latter held over a thousand patrons and perhaps he felt at last he had acquired a "super-cinema". As usual he set about making improvements and installed cinemascope about the same time as closing the Rex and putting it up for auction.

Things went wrong. The Rex could not be sold having failed to reach a reserve price at the auction on 20th January 1953. Presumably Fred Leatham had to leave

Dover and try and restore some value to his two remaining Black Country cinemas. In 1956 he bravely installed cinemascope at both the Rex and the Victoria but the decline could not be halted. A last minute attempt to remain in the cinema business involved a "swop" with the Victoria and a cinema in Market Drayton but this did not work out successfully. The Victoria then became difficult to dispose of as the Council refused to grant the necessary "change-of-use" that would have made it a potential industrial property. When his appeal was heard by the Ministry of Housing and Local Government he claimed that he had lost a "terrific amount of money" in the cinema business, including £4,000 on the sale of the unfortunate Rex.

His appeal, in 1958, was lost, but ironically today the site has been put to industrial use.

The quiet pianist whose career as a cinema proprietor had crossed the histories of so many diverse Black Country cinemas for a time became a rent-collector for Wolverhampton Council, but later returned to business in a Bilston hardware store. As with the cinemas, he had already sold that one and acquired another by the time he died in November 1962. Apparently he had never enjoyed good health.

Unlike some of the men described in this part of the book, he died without obituaries recording his part in the operation of local cinemas. Even within the trade I doubt he was a well known figure, but his restless career in so many Black Country cinemas deserves to be remembered as a tribute to the small independent exhibitor, tenaciously pursuing financial survival in an industry where even the major exhibitors found it difficult to adapt to the social changes that overtook their trade.

---

### Charles Dent

To clear up any confusion between Charles Dent and his heirs and Mortimer Dent of the Danilo circuit, it is worth detailing the careers of the former who became associated with two Black Country cinemas. Charles Dent had first become an exhibitor at the Grand, Tamworth. By 1919 he also owned the Palace, Erdington and entered the Black Country by acquiring the Palace in Freeth Street, Oldbury.

A decade later, on the arrival of sound, Mr. Dent opened a brand new, much larger, Palace at the same address, and his son, John Marshall Dent, became its manager. John Marshall Dent not only inherited the cinemas, but also expanded his interests in the Black Country by taking over the Regent at Langley Green. His son, Malcolm Dent, worked in both cinemas. J. M. Dent also had plans drawn up by Hurley Robinson for a cinema in Warley but this was never built.

During the War J. M. Dent had the rare distinction of being able to build a cinema. This was the Lido at Lichfield, which had to be rebuilt after a fire, started, according to local legend, by an American serviceman's cigar! No such excitement interrupted the lives of the Palace or the Regent and they both survived until the end of the troublesome fifties without incident. About that time J. M. Dent opened La Reserve Restaurant and provided cabaret entertainment there. Perhaps its success led him to convert the Regent to a variety club. The

Palace defected to Bingo.

J. M. Dent died in 1970 and the cinemas had to be sold to pay death duties. The Regent went on to have a remarkable old age and even became a cinema again for a while.

## Thomas Leach

Not far from Mr. Dent's "Palace" at Oldbury stood the Picture House, Birmingham Street. This had begun its life as a converted market hall in the spring of 1911, when it was known as The Picturedrome. By the end of the year Thomas Leach had acquired it and turned it into something much more like a cinema and reopened it as "The Picture House".

Thomas Leach therefore became an exhibitor about the same time as Thomas Jackson in Wolverhampton. Although he survived much longer he is now an equally shadowy figure, despite building up a small empire in Oldbury and West Bromwich.

Just after the First World War he acquired the St. George's Hall in the centre of West Bromwich and at some stage ran both the Queen's and the Hill Top Cinema. It also seems that he had at least two cinemas in the Birmingham area.

In the mid twenties the Picture House in Oldbury was substantially rebuilt becoming a very lofty building into which a far bigger audience could be crammed. When the talkies were introduced in this building in early 1930 the acoustics were found to be awful, and I have the feeling that the thirties saw a decline in the fortunes of the cinemas of Tom Leach. About 1937 the Picture House, the St. Georges and the Queens were leased to F. J. Emery, owner of a Lancashire-based circuit.

By 1946, when Miles Jervis acquired these cinemas Thomas Leach had passed away and his estate was being auctioned. Despite energetic management by Miles Jervis these cinemas were relatively early casualties, only the Queens surviving into the sixties. Thomas Leach and his cinemas have vanished into the dark pages of history!

## Thomas Cooper, Walter Williams & Benjamin Priest

In the south western corner of the Black Country three towns became associated with individual independent exhibitors.

Blackheath became the province of Thomas Cooper, a strict Methodist, who like J. Arthur Rank, was said to have never watched a film! Cradley Heath's cinemas are usually associated with the name of Walter Williams, and in Old Hill we encounter Benjamin Priest. The latter also ran cinemas in Kidderminster and Kinver.

Each of these gentlemen, at some time, ran more than one cinema, but never became exhibitors on the scale of the people described in the previous chapters. Their work is described in more detail in Section Five of this book.

## Mr. & Mrs. Woodroffe

Although it seems inconceivable, in the light of cinema's decline over the past twenty-five years, that anyone should have entered the business during the 1950's and built up a small "circuit" of local cinemas in that era,

that is just what happened in the Black Country.

Mr. Ken Woodroffe and Mrs. Doris Woodroffe acquired the Alhambra Bilston in the early fifties just before national audience figures were about to plunge. With some drastic modernising and refurbishing the cinema was a success.

In 1955 they acquired the Bruce, in Princes End, Tipton, and refurbished it. When C. S. Joseph declined to renew the lease on the Forum at Bradley in 1957, they purchased the building from Woods Picture Halls and again kept that cinema alive while commercial television came to the Midlands and a set became an essential part of every home. All three cinemas were small, and enjoyed a very local patronage. The Bruce and the Alhambra were pre-First World War buildings and the Forum belonged to the first wave of cinema building after that War. Somehow they continued to thrive as if the super-cinema, never particularly close by, had never come into existence. Like Cecil Couper's three little cinemas of the thirties, I think they correctly fitted the particular "cinema-needs" of the communities they served: they were village cinemas.

The Bruce, closed first, followed by the cessation of regular shows in the Alhambra, and the Forum became a Bingo Hall, all in the early years of the sixties. The Woodroffe's little "circuit" of three cinemas seems like the last brave stand of the small independent exhibitor, although less dramatic than the survival of Miles Jervis or the indestructability of the Royal at Cradley Heath.

## The Final Generation

While Mr. and Mrs. Woodroffe valiantly ran one of the last independent Black Country cinema enterprises towards the end of the fifties, a new generation of film goers was emerging to challenge the prevailing orthodoxy of the major circuits. Their enthusiasm for the cinema was going to keep several cinemas alive for the next two decades. By the mid fifties the Asian minority in the Black Country was large enough to demand its own films and film-shows. The Indian cinema industry was in the process of becoming one of the world's largest film industries, and was developing a relationship with its patrons that reflected the relationship between Hollywood and the English-speaking world a decade earlier.

The first products from the Bombay studios to come to the Black Country were screened by J. S. Sidhu's Eastern Film Society on Sunday mornings in Darlaston. A sympathetic manager, Leslie Taff, and an independent cinema provided the ideal location. Later the Eastern Film Society moved to the Alhambra, Bilston. At first they hired the cinema from Mr. and Mrs. Woodroffe but later bought the cinema and began showing Indian films more regularly, again with some help from Leslie Taff.

Meanwhile Ajit Singh Bains had presented a few Indian films at the Olympia, Wolverhampton, while Vincent Wareing tried to run the place in the twilight of its existence. It was impossible to buy the Olympia after Mr. Wareing's departure in mid 1960 and Ajit Singh eventually persuaded the owner to lease him her other cinema, the moribund Coliseum, Wolverhampton. The poor old Coliseum had suffered badly since Mr. Wareing's last bold attempt to revive it, and Ajit Singh had to put in a great deal of work to make it a cinema for the last time. He reopened it in 1963 and ran it for over a decade.

On the far side of the Black Country the Beacon, Smethwick, had been showing Indian films since the late fifties and continued to do so until December 1980. A number of proprietors had run the place, and towards the end, shows were reduced to Sundays only, but it had shown Indian films for as long as some local cinemas had shown English-language ones! Also in Smethwick, Nirmal Singh Sanghera made a success of running the Princes from 1970 until February 1980. It must not be assumed that the Indian patron supports the Indian cinema indiscriminately simply because the films are in his own language. The Indian exhibitor had to gauge the popularity of certain films and obtain them early enough in their release to earn success.

One exhibitor's name appears in the history of a number of Black Country cinemas: Tarsem Singh Dhami. As a child he had watched travelling cinemas erect their shows, couple their heavy equipment to their generators, and put on film shows. He developed a passion for films and the art and business of showing them. When he came to the Black Country in 1953 he systematically visited the great variety of cinemas still operating at that time, from the Odeons to the struggling independents like the Rex and Carlton in Wolverhampton. His career as an exhibitor began in 1962 at the Clifton, Stone Cross. At first occasional Sunday shows were presented, but from 1964 to 1968 he presented regular programmes until Ladbrokes acquired the premises.

By organising shows at the Dale, and with the co-operation of J. S. Sidhu at the Alhambra, Bilston, Tarsem Singh Dhami was able to book Indian films on their first release in this country and bring them to these three Black Country screens.

Later, in partnership with others, he leased the Queens, West Bromwich from Miles Jervis. For just over the last three months of its life the Queens showed only Indian films, while the owners and lessee waited for the C.P.O. to take effect. On Sunday 27th July 1969 the demolition men started work while the audience was watching an Indian film inside the cinema!

In 1972 Mr. Dhami formed the Silver Cinema Company and purchased the Odeon, Wednesbury. It ran for two years, showing films in English and Hindi, until purchased by Ladbrokes in 1974. His enthusiasm for the cinema was unabated and in April 1978 he acquired the Grove, Smethwick. However, as the decade came to a close, the Indian audience disappeared as Video swept the land. The last film was shown at the Grove in November 1981 and the Black Country's last generation of exhibitors gave up the battle. Even the erstwhile Eastern Film Society which was still showing Indian films at the Wolverhampton Civic Hall on Sunday afternoons at the beginning of the eighties gave up in August 1981.

A few other Black Country cinemas had shown Indian films at one time or another. In Walsall the Imperial and the ABC had put on occasional shows, and Surinder Kumar opened the short-lived Rex. In Langley Mr. Gupta acquired the Regent and leased it to several others making a fine "last stand" in the mid seventies, showing English-language films as the Astra, and finally Indian films as the Milan.

The most interesting result of Indian cinema coming to the Black Country might have been the building of a brand new purpose-built cinema, the "Raj", at Pleck, but the project never materialised, partly due to planning objections.

At the time of writing Indian films have disappeared from local screens faster than the general decline in the fortunes of the cinema business. Their great contribution to the final years of a cinema's life was to fill those seats once again and pack the screen with more action, song, dance and drama than Hollywood ever dared to pour into one production.

## 2. THE ARCHITECTS AND THE BUILDERS

It has often been pointed out that cinema architecture has reflected the cinema's fairground origins. The bright elaborate facade merely concealed a plain, functional auditorium. The quest for a dramatic interesting facade led the cinema to present itself to its patrons in a variety of styles, until settling for the relatively functional simplicity adopted by most super-cinemas of the mid to late thirties. It is the variety produced during that development, lasting approximately only a quarter of a century, that makes the buildings so fascinating. However simple the needs of a film-viewing auditorium, the patron might be entertained in surroundings suggesting anything from chapel to a mosque, something Tudor, something Egyptian, or Spanish, be seduced by the apparently simple lines of Art Deco, or be bewildered by an eclecticism that could defy description.

The Black Country by no means provided anything like the full range of possibilities of cinema architecture and interior design, but did include enough variety to show the cinema's development. Converted chapels such as The Central at Bloxwich or the Ideal, Wednesfield, converted market halls like the Grand, Kingswinford, converted theatres like the Clifton, Wolverhampton or original Kings, West Bromwich, converted factories and skating rinks, all survived alongside purpose-built cinemas until the decline of the industry.

The architects who produced the first purpose-built cinema were not specialists, nor were quite certain upon which tradition they should draw, apart from a theatrical tradition.

In 1910, a Wolverhampton architect, Marcus Brown, was designing extensions and alterations to public houses. Often this involved the provisions of an assembly room with space for music-hall style variety acts, or occasionally the cinematograph. This work led to designing conversions of premises to cinemas, for example, the Globe, Wolverhampton, and the first Palace, Oldbury. Eventually this experience led to designing purpose-built cinemas, but, in Marcus Brown's case, not in the Black Country.

In Birmingham by 1910, Archibald Hurley Robinson (1884 — 1953) was not only designing cinemas but was already a director of the Aston Cross Electric Theatre Company Ltd., thus forecasting the future trend of architects becoming involved in the ownership of cinemas. After the First World War he produced such fine Black Country cinemas as Woods Palace, a building that seemed to link the original theatrical tradition with the developing sense of what a cinema should be. He later designed the Savoy for Woods Picture Halls, and via John Tyler's admiration for Thomas Wood's cinemas, he came to design the Dale, Willenhall, and the Dunstall, each showing the changes in style that accompanied the transition from the twenties to the thirties. His designs for the Plaza and Hippodrome in Dudley show how he had absorbed the functionalism of the later decade.

It would be wrong to imagine that the most impressive Black Country cinemas were always the work of nationally known architects from Birmingham, or London. In Dudley, the firm of Webb and Gray designed three very elegant local halls; the Criterion, Dudley, the Central, Stourbridge, and the Majestic, Cradley Heath. From Walsall the firm of Hickton and Farmer designed the beautiful Grosvenor at Bloxwich (1922), having been connected with the business since the earliest days. (In 1910 they were the architects to Electric Picture Palaces, Midlands, Ltd., responsible for the Palace, Walsall, and probably one of the earliest attempts to create a Black Country circuit.).

Oscar Deutsch's first purpose-built cinema, the Picture House, Brierley Hill, was designed by local Stourbridge architect, Stanley Griffiths. In the first flurry of building the Odeons, Mr. Deutsch employed a variety of architects to cope with the volume of work and therefore the little known Stanley Griffiths found himself designing the Blackheath Odeon just as Harry Weedon was about to decisively establish the circuit's style. The building thus never quite seemed truly an Odeon — but rather a Black Country "special" variation of the national style! And it is interesting to recall that the same man designed those perfect Black Country mini-cinemas for Cecil Couper, the Savoy, Netherton, and Forum, Pensnett. His devotion to the "stadium" style of auditorium came to its zenith at the Kings, Stourbridge.

The Odeon style, often regarded as the climax of 1930's cinema design, was best examplified by the work of Harry Weedon and the Odeons at Dudley and Wolverhampton are excellent examples. Although not a Black Country architect, and not responsible for many cinemas in the area, no account of cinema architecture would be complete without some mention of Harry Weedon's career.

Harry Weedon (1888 — 1970) qualified as an architect just before the First World War and designed cinemas at Birchfield and Perry Barr. He served in the Royal Flying Corps from 1914 to 1917 and then again set up an architectural practice in Birmingham. He became associated with Oscar Deutsch in 1934 when called in as a consultant on the interior decor of the Warley Cinema, later the Odeon. Within a year he had become the Consultant Architect to Odeon Theatres Ltd., and in the next five years was involved in the design of over one hundred and fifty cinemas throughout the British Isles. During the Second World War he was involved in the dispersal of industry and this renewed association with industrial building took him into a post-war career of work connected with the expansion of the motor industry.

Thus Harry Weedon was involved with cinema-design only for a short part of his total career, but he, or possibly his chief assistant, Cecil Clavering, was largely responsible for stream-lining the super-cinema and making architectural virtue out of the rather basic functional requirements of a building in which to show films. Apart from the Odeons at Wolverhampton and Dudley, their approach is also well illustrated by the Tower, West Bromwich.

Super-cinemas built by the other circuits were often the work of their Consultant Architects rather than local men. For example, the A.B.C.'s new cinemas of the thirties were often the work of W. R. Glen, the Savoys in Walsall and Wolverhampton being good examples. Gaumont British often favoured the work of W. E. Trent, for example, the Regent, Dudley, the Gaumont, Wolverhampton, and the Gaumont, Wednesbury, but W. T. Benslyn produced the beautiful new Rink in Smethwick.

The most prolific designers of local super-cinemas were Ernest Roberts and Roland Satchwell. They are particularly associated with the cinemas of the Clifton circuit, and they both became directors of that circuit. They had worked in partnership, and individually, on a great number of cinemas, and I do not know if it is possible to distinguish their work. The Cliftons at Sedgley, Lye, Coseley and Wednesfield are all credited to Roland Satchwell. The Clifton at Fallings Park on the other hand is credited to them both, and the Rosum, Walsall, to Ernest Roberts. The Penn, Wolverhampton was Roland Satchwell's work, the Danilo, Stourbridge, was Ernest Robert's yet both were large, very rectangular structures with huge frontages of plain brickwork relieved by five high vertical windows. Perhaps Ernest Roberts preferred plain brickwork, after all it was a feature of his earlier work on the Alhambra, Tipton, and possibly Roland Satchwell favoured faience as found at Sedgley and The Lye and his own cinema at Aldridge, the Avion. But there seem to be too many exceptions on which to try and establish the rules and perhaps history is right to bracket them together as "Satchwell and Roberts".

Wherever the architect might come from, the builder of a cinema was usually a local firm, and a firm that had built one cinema would often be asked to build another. Sometimes builders became owners of cinemas, possibly in default of payment. For example, William Jackson of Oldbury, who built cinemas for Edward Hewitson of Smethwick, and for the Danilo circuit, found himself running the Regent, Langley, and the Cosy Corner, Halesowen, for certain periods of time, although apparently having no real interest in being an exhibitor.

When a small independent exhibitor like Sidney Bray set out to build Dudley's Criterion, it made sense to invite the builder, A. J. Crump, to join the board. Having established a connection with the Brays, it is not surprising to find the same builder working on the Central, Stourbridge, for Clifford Bray. In other instances local builders put up sufficient cinemas to become somewhat expert at the task, for example, J. and F. Wootton of Bloxwich, H. J. Amies of Wolverhampton, B. Whitehouse and Sons of Birmingham, Housing Ltd., J. Hickin, T. Elvins, and J. M. Tate of Cradley. Wherever possible their work is credited in the account of each cinema.

Building cinemas provided work for other local people besides the main contractor. Local steelwork was often used, local bricks were used, and in the thirties, many a super-cinema included leaded glasswork by the local firm of T. W. Camm. Local craftsmen, carpenters, painters, electricians, plumbers, all saw cinema-construction from their own point of view and should write their own book on the subject one day. To give just one example, the ornamental plasterwork, often the work of the Birmingham firm, Bryan's Adamanta Ltd., was a craft that found a particular place in the cinemas of the 1930's. Today the mysteries of the craft are becoming forgotten. Try and work out a formula for fixing the price for plastering a cinema on the basis of the number of its seats! That is how it was done. No doubt the suppliers of light fittings, the hangers of curtains and the installers of organs could come up with equally "mind-boggling" problems.

Perhaps a final word on the designing and building of cinemas should be devoted to the speed with which the work was often accomplished. The super-cinemas were often built at a "super-speed" and I am sure it was not only the Dunstall Cinema that opened with wet paint on the emergency exit doors. What a pity that some of these palaces had such a short-lived existence.

Theatre Furnishings

## 3. THE MANAGERS — AND THE STAFF

By the time the architect and builders had done their work every cinema could expect to have a manager and staff ready to admit the first patrons. In some cases the proprietor acted in a managerial capacity, but even in cases where the proprietor owned only one small cinema the place was often left in the hands of a manager.

In the early days managers seem to have come and gone very quickly. Some were incompetent, some lacked showmanship, some were dishonest, but as the cinema business matured, the manager became more professional. Today the managers of the past have become legends and a stereotype has been established. The typical manager of folk memory is well-groomed, distinguished, and worthy of great respect if only for the variety of his talents. In evening dress, bow tie, brightly polished shoes and well oiled hair, he was expected to be in the foyer to greet every patron with personal care and with a concern for their well-being and entertainment. To the staff he had to be like a benign ship's captain: a sociable disciplinarian. To his employer he had to be enterprising, efficient and honest. To his family, he was probably unknown: he was always at work.

Many managers seem to have matched the ideal, but to enlarge any further is to say what is true of cinemas in any part of the country. It just seems worth identifying a few of the local managers who became well known in the Black Country and preparing the reader to meet them later in the text as each cinema is surveyed in turn.

Occasionally a manager ran a particular cinema throughout its life. For example, Harry Crane at the Clifton, Coseley, or Frank Bills at the second Alhambra, Dudley Port. More often they graduated to a cinema and then stayed a considerable time. For example, Jim Davies of the Regal, Wednesfield (1938 — 1962). He had worked his way up through the trade, with Pooles, of Gloucester, from chocolate boy to projectionist. At the Clifton, Lye, he had been groomed for a managerial post and then devoted his life to Wednesfield's cinema, and then left to find a new life when the closure abruptly came.

If a man gave a dedicated life's service to the cinema business he risked the misfortune of being in a business whose boom was followed by a lengthy decline. Sometimes this could be seen clearly in a man's career at one cinema, such as the Clifton, Coseley, but often it was a trail that was pursued through several cinemas. Imagine how Charles H. Kettle felt in December 1935 when he was the new manager appointed at the opening of the Tower, West Bromwich. He was in charge of a splendid super-cinema complete with organ, and the care of up to two thousand patrons at each performance. Suddenly his cinema is swallowed by A.B.C. with its own ranks of managers.

In September 1937, less than two years after opening the Tower, Charlie Kettle opened the Palace, Wednesbury, for Cyril Joseph's Dual Pictures. Perhaps the Palace did not seem as grand as the Tower, but it was certainly no flea-pit. Over twenty years later, Charlie Kettle was still working for Cyril Joseph. Since the War he had managed the Olympia, Wolverhampton. He made a virtue out of the difficulty of obtaining films and showed the continental films so loved by film societies.

9. Staff at the Strand, Whitmore Reans
Believed to be about the time of the First World War,
when Mr. Van Lachterop (seated left) was Manager.

*(Photo: Wolverhampton Libraries)*

10. Staff at the Penn Cinema, Wolverhampton, in the 1950's.

Gentlemen seated, left to right: Eric Turvey, Cyril Moore, and Gordon Mintern (the Manager).

Ladies seated, left to right: Mrs. Mintern (Cashier), Mrs. Pope (Sales) and Mrs. Goodway (in charge of cleaning staff).

*(Photo: Eric Turvey Collection)*

Through the difficult fifties he was respected and liked as a manager who cared about films and preserved the traditional qualities of a cinema manager. Then Pine Pictures' lease on the Olympia expired and Mr. Kettle found retirement forced upon him.

Sometimes a manager had proprietorial aspirations. For example, Cecil Couper, who came to the Black Country as a manager for Pooles and became an entrepreneur. Similarly, Fred Leatham had worked as part-time pianist at the Princes End Picture House then gone to the Rialto, Wednesbury, as manager, but seemed to be driven by a compulsion to own cinemas.

Organists sometimes became managers; the two most outstanding examples, William Sykes and Leslie Taff, being described later, but operators tended to stay in their boxes, except in small cinemas, where the job of management often included some work in the projection room, sometimes stoking the boiler and a hundred and one "odd jobs".

In the cinemas of the larger circuits, managers often had to move from cinema to cinema, not only within the Black Country, but sometimes nationally. Even so, three Wolverhampton managers, Cliff Lloyd-Davies, Tom Lloyd and Mr. Felton, managed to establish a local

permanence by only making very local moves. Earlier Harry Shawcross had worked at a number of Wolverhampton cinemas until ending his career at the Penn. In the Dudley, Brierley Hill and Stourbridge area several Odeon managers established long Black Country careers. Some managers moved "upwards" within the circuits. For example, Ken Jones managed the Cape Hill Electric and the Grove before ascending to the position of General Manager of the Clifton Circuit, in which position he visited their Black Country halls. More recently Euan Lloyd, from Wombourne, one time assistant manager of the ABC, Walsall, has risen to become a film-producer, and once appeared on the stage of a Black Country cinema to introduce his work!

The popular picture of the manager is definitely "male", but many cinemas were effectively run from the paybox, and no doubt a thesis will be written one day on the role of women in running cinemas. For example, Eleanor Webster, who ran the Coliseum, Wolverhampton, for twenty-five years, and Minnie Wallis, of the Classic, Walsall, who did the job for thirty years.

Many a manager must have had a tale to tell if his career went back to the pre-cinema days. Jack Riskit briefly managed the Palace, Wednesbury, but his vaudeville background made it sensible for Cyril Joseph to transfer him to the Theatre Royal at Bilston which abandoned films and returned to live theatre. Charles Pindar, who also managed the cinemas of Wednesbury, was a member of the Cinema Veterans Association, and therefore must have had tales to tell of films before 1903. Sometimes a local man without theatrical or early cinema background could seem right for the job. One such man was Harry Wharton from Stourbridge. While working fourteen years as a seedsman for Messrs. Webbs at Wordsley, he had vigorously pursued his interests in amateur music and dramatics. When Pooles opened their skating rink in Stourbridge in 1911, he was put in charge of it and almost immediately it became a cinema presenting both films and variety. Harry Wharton was such an energetic man and so full of ideas that he was forever organising concerts and carnivals and raising money for local charities. During the twenties he transferred to the Scala for a time, changing places with Harry Morris, an equally popular figure who also had a long association with Pooles where he had once been a scenery painter. Just as Tom Wood introduced "cinemaballs" to Bilston, Harry Wharton once did the same for Stourbridge. Perhaps we shall never see their like again.

Without much chance of earning fame or a named place in history, the rest of the staff of a cinema were really as important as the manager and many notched up a long record of service. Sometimes a cinema could come and go within an individual's working life. Two Wolverhampton cinemas witnessed first and last films projected by the same operator: Cyril Moore at the Penn, and Harry Bayliss at the Dunstall, the latter specially invited back to perform the task. Many an operator showed bravery and quick thought in dealing with burning film and one operator died in a local cinema fire; Frank Danks of the Alexandra. Many worked in cramped conditions and all worked unbelievably antisocial hours.

Presenting a film show was a craft, and like all crafts it had to be learned via a long apprenticeship which began with re-winding films, carrying films to the station, speeding newsreels between cinemas on a bike in all weathers, or keeping the operating room clean, yet it was a job many a fourteen year old school leaver felt would be worthwhile. If you joined the business during one of its rapid periods of growth, 1910 − 1914, or 1932 − 1939, and had your wits about you, there were opportunities for advancement. Harry Bayliss began work at Woods Palace the same day as he left school. He learnt the trade from the "chief", Reg Lloyd, an ex-Pat Collins employee, and entertained John Tyler of Willenhall who often visited Woods Palace before setting up his own cinema, the Dale. When John Tyler built the Dunstall, Harry went to become its chief just before his twenty-first birthday !

The age of the super-cinema demanded a great deal of the operator and often shows were rehearsed to work out cues, volumes, timings, etc. in great detail. If anything went wrong a watchful manager immediately rang the box. Large cinemas sometimes had large operating staff and the "chief" was a very exalted figure. Often he exercised a tyrannical insistence on the absolute spotlessness of his projection suite. As managers and chief operators both seemed such powerful figures, it can be

38

imagined that occasionally some personalities did not get on well with each other.

During the Second World War Herbert Morrison recognised the work of a "Chief" as a Reserved Occupation but other operators could be conscripted. In their place came a generation of lady-operators and many a "chief" had to make an adjustment to the fact. Lady-operators had certainly existed long before this, at least in the Black Country, but they were in a minority and many had found work in the operating room in the similar circumstances during the First World War.

11. Assistant Operator Eric Turvey, a spotless operating box and a new Philips projector, at the Penn Cinema.
*(Photo: Eric Turvey Collection)*

Like other trades, it was sometimes passed on from father to son, or from brother to brother, and one family could collect considerable experience of the Black Country's cinemas. For example, James Powell worked at the Public Hall, Dudley, for Irving Bosco and went with him to the Empire. When Gaumont British eventually took over the Empire he worked for them and transferred to the Regent when they showed the first talkie in Dudley. Ultimately he transferred to Poole's at the Kings Hall in Stourbridge. Meanwhile his son, Bernard Powell, had trained as an electrical engineer with Gaumont British, at the West End in Birmingham.

When Gaumont British found themselves short of operators, Bernard Powell was asked to become a relief operator and he travelled far and wide in the

12. A historic moment in the projection room at the ABC, Stourbridge. Alongside an ancient Ross GC 3 projector are posed Vic Court, retiring chief operator, and Jan Bruton, the new senior operator. Vic Court's retirement in March 1982, with the film, *"Last Feelings"* ended a fifty year career that included work at the Temp, and Clifton, in The Lye, the old and new Kings, in Stourbridge , and 28 years at the ABC. Jan Bruton began a cinema career as an usherette in the Odeon, Stourbridge, but was trained as an operator by her cousin at the Danilo, Brierley Hill.

*(Photo : County Express)*

Black Country, on his motorbike, working at the Cape Hill Electric and the Rink in Smethwick, or the Empire and Criterion in Dudley. At the Empire, where his father had worked for many years, he met the girl who was to become Mrs. Powell. The cinema staff worked unsociable hours but were often happy together as a group. The G.B. staff thought nothing of holding their own dances at midnight on Saturday night, collecting their G.B. colleagues from other cinemas, and dancing into the small hours. Sunday-closing was important and the staff often used to assemble for Sunday-morning bicycle rides or day trips to the sea.

Bernard Powell followed his father at the Kings Hall in Stourbridge and in 1939 saw the new cinema being constructed around the old one. He liked working for Pooles but by the end of the War had accepted a job at the Clifton in The Lye. At this cinema he was occasionally summoned by Mr. Entwistle to come and solve a problem at the Temp. He then left the cinema business for a while but returned to be a relief operator for the Odeon circuit, working at such places as the Warley Odeon. Between them, James Powell and Bernard Powell had witnessed almost the entire history of the cinema and worked for a variety of employers in every type of cinema, and their experience was by no means unique.

Few patrons ever met their operators to thank them for the show. The patron's relationship with the cinema tended to focus on the other staff; cashiers, attendants, ice-cream girls and doormen.

The way these figures presented themselves changed over the years as can be seen in a comparison between the pictures of the staff at the Strand before the First World War and staff at the Penn after the Second World War. The super-cinemas set the pace in smart uniforms and military-style training for the staff.

Muriel Morgan was an usherette at Quarry Bank's Coronet but had set her heart on working in Brierley Hill's Danilo. Mr. Roberts of the Coronet encouraged her and she obtained the job at the Danilo. She was in a team of eight usherettes and acquired a made-to-measure uniform. At the Danilo cinemas the girls dressed in smart emerald green frocks, trimmed with orange and gold lace,

and their coats had brightly polished brass buttons. As well as showing patrons to their seats she sold the chocolates, and loved every moment of her eight years work. There was a pride in being at the point of contact between the glamorous world of show business and the public. For many girls it followed a daytime job elsewhere, and the rush from the days work to the cinema could not be so hurried that one's appearance suffered, as a good usherette also took pride in her hair and make-up.

The service they gave is now part of the nostalgia that several generations feel for their cinema-going past. Such labour-intensive extravagance has gone forever, but is occasionally evoked by the dashing attendants at Wolverhampton's Odeon in their blue suits, and often parodied elsewhere by ladies in smocks who ought to be out playing Bingo instead of snarling as they tear one's ticket!

The doorman and male attendants were the descendants of that great Black Country tradition: — the "Chucker-out". Some of the earliest Chucker-outs seemed to be chosen for their eccentricity, deformity or physical handicaps if the legends are to be believed. The business of maintaining good order, as well as being a suitable front-of-house "presence", was sometimes combined in the skill and personalities of some latter-day doormen. In Wednesfield everybody remembers Albert Brookes.

Janet Miller worked for four years as an usherette at the Regal, Wednesfield, and recalls :

"We had a commissionaire of great strength; Albert Brookes. No-one messed around with Albert. If there was any noise he merely stood in the aisle near the wrongdoers for peace to reign. Albert had a method with nuisances: they were never allowed in again. Many begged to be allowed in, but there was no hope. Sometimes one would get in when Albert was missing from the foyer, and huddle in their seat only to be ejected forcibly when discovered."

Even the cleaners played a vital part in the history of every cinema and ultimately it would be impossible to name every person who had worked in every Black

13. Tommy Stanford, doorman of the Clifton, Coseley, poses outside the cinema in June 1953, in full uniform.

*(Photo: Sandra Gwilliam Collection)*

Country cinema. However, as each cinema is described in more detail I have tried to recognise and name the staff where appropriate. Those mentioned are merely examples of the many many others that there is neither time nor space to name.

## 4. THE MUSICIANS — (INCLUDING OF COURSE, THE ORGANISTS).

No "silent" film was ever shown in silence. Literate patrons read the subtitles aloud, in Black Country dialect of course, for the benefit of those who could not read or could not afford spectacles, and often the action encouraged a certain amount of cheering and hissing. Meanwhile, the management provided some form of musical accompaniment. The piano was the minimum that would suffice. A trio, piano, drums and violin, for example, were preferred. The bigger cinemas might provide a seven piece orchestra which had rehearsed the official score.

An army of part-time musicians devoted their time to providing this music, and for many, the bitterest blow in their lives was the coming of the talkies. Many were so good that the patrons came to the cinemas to hear them play rather than to see the films and today, over half a century later, the mention of their names evokes powerful nostalgia.

Alfred Van Dam at the Queens, Wolverhampton, had a huge following. As leader of the orchestra, and as a violinist, he has become a local legend. In Stourbridge two orchestras and their leaders vigorously competed: Norris Stanley at the Kings Hall and Charles Bye at the Scala. Both went on to establish reputation in the musical world when times changed. The third jewel in Stourbridge's crown was Mr. Barrs Partridge, a brilliant pianist, violinist and organist. He came from Cradley Heath and had played at the Royal. He graduated to Birmingham's West End but in 1929 came to the Central, Stourbridge.

When sound arrived at the Central he stayed on as organist, but in 1938 he joined the B.B.C. He was finally leader of the second violins for the City of Birmingham Symphony Orchestra. His work included composition, including a comic opera, and maybe his career is still waiting to be re-discovered and re-evaluated.

In Halesowen, Bert Holden's career was typical of the rise and fall in the fortunes of a local musician. He first played the piano for Mr. Bray at the Drill Hall. Matters improved and he was joined by Mrs. Wood on the violin. In 1927, when Sidney Bray opened the newly rebuilt Picture House, Bert Holden went there to be part of an orchestra until the talkies arrived. He survived by playing the solo piano at the Cosy Corner that struggled on as a silent cinema into the mid thirties. Finally he became a projectionist. That pattern was duplicated by many others.

In Dudley, Syd Griffiths brought some of the plaster down from the Criterion's ceiling with his drumming while "*Ben Hur*" was on the screen. He believed that Mr. Anton at the Castle Cinema was a brilliant conductor, illustrating his theory that minor cinemas often enjoyed major talents. Perhaps that is why patrons went to the Olympia, Wordsley, just to hear violinist Lena Wood, the same lady that had joined Bert Holden in Halesowen!

The list of musicians could be endless. I have tried to include their names in the story of each individual cinema wherever possible, but cinema organists possibly deserve a section all to themselves.

## The Organists

The first cinema organ in the Black Country was also the first Wurlitzer to be installed in Great Britain. It was opened by Jack Courtnay at the Picture House, Walsall, in 1925. Fifty years later it was removed and made its way to Devon via Sedgley. The two-manual, six unit instrument still exists today in a church at Beer.

From the mid twenties onwards many new cinemas did not feel complete unless they had an organ and a full orchestra. The fashion, for their installation, lasted about a decade, but their popularity lasted much longer, and today I would regard it as something of a cult. An illuminated console rising mysteriously from the stage into the spotlight was undoubtedly something very magical, and if the chambers were correctly arranged in the building, and if the acoustics were right, the full-bodied sound of a large cinema organ was an overwhelming experience. But this was true in all parts of Britain and to concern ourselves with Black Country matters we must look only at the organs and the organists of this area.

The men associated with the organs at the Regal, Darlaston, and the Majestic, Cradley Heath, will be described in a moment. First let us survey the other instruments once to be found locally.

When the Gaumont in Wolverhampton opened in September 1932, the Compton organ was opened by Frederick Bayco. Again, it was the first instrument of this kind to be opened in the Black Country and was much more than a three-manual and pedal organ.

After bringing himself and the organ up on the electric lift, the organist could produce virtually any sound effect he wanted from the machine buried below. He could also control the volume by controlling the louvres to the chamber, hidden from the auditorium by a gauze "wall". In building this organ Compton had used over a thousand pipes ranging in length from three quarters of an inch to sixteen feet. If all the copper wire was unwound from the organ it would have stretched from Wolverhampton Low Level to Paddington, and over five thousand silver contacts in the instrument had been soldered by hand. Frederick Bayco was succeeded on this magnificent instrument by Leslie Taff, moving from the Rink, Smethwick. To some extent the tradition of an organ on this site went back to the days of the Agricultural Hall where a straight organ had existed since 1916. The Compton stayed at the Gaumont until 1966. When the Gaumont closed in November 1973, Graeme Hawkins played a special organ farewell to the cinema on a Rodgers theatre organ specially installed for the final week.

Meanwhile, in Dudley, a great Wurlitzer had been filling the Regent with sound for several years. Although work on it was not quite finished, this instrument was opened by young John Howlett when the cinema opened in September 1928. When new, this Wurlitzer cost £4,000 but probably played its part in establishing the popularity of this cinema. By the early seventies it was dilapidated and forgotten and many of its six ranks of pipes had been stolen. The Rank Organisation considered that the cost of restoration was too high and were glad to sell it to Roy Mosley. He removed it in 1975, and began its painstaking restoration and

14. Twenty-two year old cinema organist: John Howlett, at the time of opening the Regent, Dudley.

*(Photo: Peter Glews Collection)*

installation at Peterborough Technical College. With a great sense of history, John Howlett was to have reopened the organ in its new home on 8th March 1981. In the event, it was reopened by John Mann, but John Howlett, prevented by ill-health from attending, sent a recorded message to everyone there.

John Howlett had only stayed at the Regent for a few weeks. He was followed by none other than Reginald Dixon who went on to fame in Blackpool. When Reginald Dixon left Dudley in May 1929, he was replaced by Sidney Wallbank, who had already been "orchestral organist" at the cinema since its opening. Sidney Wallbank had been Musical Director on a P. & O. Liner on the run from Tilbury to Sydney. At the latter city he had gained some experience on a Wurlitzer at the Prince Edward Theatre. P.C.T. sent him to Dudley. He stayed until 1932, when he went to London, finishing his career at the Gaumont, Holloway, when it was bombed in 1940. He died in May 1980, just after the research for this book began, but before I could make his acquaintance. The last resident organist at this cinema was Stanley Harrison, seen in the picture of organists at The Rink.

In Stourbridge, John Howlett returned to open another Black Country organ at the Central. (In the meantime he had been to Belfast and Preston). This time he found himself opening a Compton organ, on 16th May 1929. It was a three-manual, ten-unit instrument, and again cost about £4,000. It was later played by Mr. Barrs Partridge but when the Odeon circuit took over the theatre its importance declined. It was broken down and removed in 1958 and I believe parts of it are to be found in Netherton Parish Church.

The organ of the Tower, West Bromwich, will be mentioned again in relation to Leslie Taff. He opened

15. Sidney Wallbank at the console of the Wurlitzer at the Regent, Dudley.

*(Photo: Mrs. G. C. Wallbank Collection)*

it when the cinema opened in December 1935. It was a three-manual, ten-unit Compton, with a Mellowtone electronic attachment. With the illuminated surround to the console it was the archetype of the cinema organs that patrons love to remember. The organ in Darlaston and Cradley Heath will also be dealt with subsequently. It remains for us here to consider the organs of Smethwick.

Edward Hewitson's replacement Princes Cinema was being built just at the time that organs seemed so important and although the talkies had arrived a Compton organ was installed. It was a two-manual, five-unit instrument, and was opened by Wilfred Southworth. In 1936 it was moved from the Princes to the Empire and rebuilt with six units. It was re-opened by George Hunt. After the Empire closed as a cinema it was removed piece by piece by the boys of Holly Lodge Grammar School with the intention of rebuilding it at the school. I do not know what happened to it subsequently.

When Edward Hewitson replaced the Coliseum with the Windsor, he again installed a Compton organ. It was a three-manual, eight-unit instrument and was opened by Reginald Maynard on 29th September 1930. In his comments on the organ in the opening brochure, Mr. Maynard revealed that the organ consumed fifty thousand cubic feet of air per hour. It was removed in 1960 to Oxley Parish Church, newly built in Wolverhampton. Only seven units were installed but

once again a local organ has found a permanent home in the Black Country.

Just over two months earlier Gaumont British's new Rink opened in the Cape Hill area of Smethwick. G.B. particularly favoured Compton organs and equipped their palatial new cinema with a three-manual, nine-unit instrument. Leslie James rose into the spotlight to open the organ when the cinema opened on 7th July 1930, and apparently stayed all week to play in this two thousand seater cinema. It probably survived in regular use longer than the Smethwick's other two Comptons, but was removed in 1961, and survives at Quinton Parish Church.

A few small cinemas were not to be outdone by the new super-cinemas, their organs, and the wonders of sound. For example, the West End, tucked away in Whitmore Reans, Wolverhampton, revived their "orchestra" on Friday nights for old time's sake after sound had made them redundant. Later the proprietors, O. G. Pictures Ltd., introduced their own "home-made" organ complete with illuminated console. It was basic-ally a Hammond model A, and it had to stand permanently beneath the centre of the screen but the organist, Arthur Collett, played nightly to an enthusiastic audience. He received some coaching from William Davis who was then playing the organ at Wolverhampton's Gaumont. Like many other cinema musicians, he eventually realised there was a better future in other aspects of the business and went to the ABC to become a projectionist.

16. Midland cinema-organists at the Rink, Smethwick, about 1951.

Left to right: S. Harrison (Regent, Dudley), W. Gregory (Tower, West Bromwich), G. Blackmore (Gaumont, Birmingham), R. Bentley (West End, Birmingham), Harold Nash (Savoy, Northampton), John Madin (Granadas, London), Leslie Taff (Regal, Darlaston), Syd Gustard (New Victoria, London), Hubert Coster (Empire, Coventry), Henry Croudson (Gaumont, Haymarket), Clifford Bayliss (Savoy, Coventry), Harold Hunt (Gaumont, Coventry), William Sykes (Majestic), and Jack Evans (The Rink).

*(Photo: Harry King, from Collection of Mrs. Drinkwater)*

## William Sykes    1890 — 20/8/75

As the reader will have gathered, the theatre organs in the super-cinemas were often played by a whole succession of organists. It is interesting to consider, therefore, two men that devoted their careers to the Black Country. In the case of the Majestic, Cradley Heath, which remained independent of the circuits throughout its life, one man devoted twenty-five years of service to the cinema and its community. That man was William Sykes.

William Sykes was born in Mirfield, Yorkshire, and trained under Edward Bairstow, the organist at York Minster. He joined the Army in 1916, and in France he formed the 5th Brigade Remount Depot Concert Party and gave concerts around Calais.

He first provided music in a cinema at The Crescent, Dewsbury Road, Leeds, when that opened in August 1921. He stayed there until he came to the Black Country in 1933. He was attracted to the new Christie organ being installed at the Majestic because it was the first Christie organ in Britain with an all-electric action and was the largest of its kind to be built up until then. It was a three-manual instrument with ten extended and distinctive units and a fifteen hundred seater super-cinema seemed a good opportunity.

The organ and the cinema were opened on 27th March 1933 when Mr. Sykes began the proceedings by playing the National Anthem to a capacity audience. His family settled in Stourbridge but he devoted his life and work to Cradley Heath. By the end of 1933 he was appointed Manager of the cinema as well as organist. As well as his administrative duties, he still performed every night for half an hour on the organ before the shows, and took special pride in organ interludes during the programmes. He made his own slides to be projected on the screen while he played below, and wrote his own compositions. The Majestic's reputation for good music spread and trade papers described Cradley Heath as "a centre of musical activity".

During the Second World War all this musical activity greatly increased. For two War-time Christmases he organised recitals at the Majestic that raised money to buy over seven hundred five shilling postal orders that were sent to ex-patrons that were then serving overseas in the Forces. They were accompanied by a letter: "Be of good courage, you are not forgotten, and the time may not be far distant when victory will be ours and you can return home to a better world and to the ones you love. William Sykes".

He was appointed Musical Director for Rowley Regis during the "Holidays at Home" scheme and organised Sunday concerts at the Majestic for the Mayor's Forces Fund. Someone suggested that the Hallelujah Chorus should be heard from the stage of the Majestic and the Cradley Heath Choral Society was formed. *"Judas Maccabaeus"* was performed on 14th November 1943 and then they began work on *"The Messiah"*.

Isobel Baillie and Kathleen Ferrier came along to augment the local principals. The C.H.C.S. provided two hundred voices in the chorus and Mr. Pecks conducted the forty piece Reddal Hill Orchestra. Joined by Mr. Sykes on the Christie it must have fill the Majestic with a mighty sound on 6th February 1944. Kathleen Ferrier was so popular, she returned to the Majestic on 29th October in *"Elijah"*. Mr. Sykes later confessed that he had sometimes been tempted to leave the Black Country but he had created too many strong bonds.

He stayed at the Majestic through the post-war era when the circuits made it difficult for an independent cinema to acquire reasonable films, and organs became unfashionable. In 1955 he invited members of the Cinema Organ Society to come to the Majestic to hear the Christie. He dazzled the audience with his skill in extemporisation and treated them to one of his own compositions: *"Moorland Mists"*. He was still very proud of his cinema, and only the year before it had celebrated its coming-of-age, by introducing reduced prices for pensioners at matinees.

He retired in 1958 and was thus spared the agony of running the Majestic for the last few years of its existence as a cinema. Immediately after its closure it became a Bingo Hall and the Christie languished. Fortunately, during the seventies, it was restored by Mel Edwards, and the organ returned to life just before William Sykes' death on 20th August 1975

at the age of eighty-five. He had lived near Bristol while writing and composing in his retirement, but was brought back to the Black Country for burial at Stourbridge Cemetery.

The Christie has been played regularly at the Bingo Club, and is the only Black Country organ to have survived in its original home. When it celebrates its fiftieth birthday this will have seemed quite an achievement.

---

## Leslie Taff    1910 — 25/4/73

Born in Tividale on the outskirts of Tipton, Leslie Taff began his long career in the cinema at a picture house of that town. He obtained an associate degree of the London College of Music when he was twelve years old, and started to play piano accompaniment to silent films at the Victoria Cinema, Railway Street, when he was fourteen. He worked every evening at the Victoria for over four hours and worked in a mineral water factory by day!

A year or two later he graduated to the post of orchestral pianist at the Palace, Oldbury, and from there he moved to the Empire, Dudley. Provincial Cinematograph Theatres owned three cinemas in Dudley and Leslie Taff played in all three, passing from the Empire, to the Criterion, and finally to the Regent.

While he played in the Regent's orchestra he watched the Wurlitzer organ being installed. John Howlett opened the new organ but Leslie Taff was allowed to practice on it, with the encouragement of P.C.T.'s Musical Director. This led to his appointment as an organist and he left the Black Country to play at the Regent, Swindon.

At the end of the twenties, an up-and-coming organist had to be prepared to move around and from Swindon he returned to this area to play at the Rink, Smethwick, and the Gaumont Palace, Coventry. In 1932 he appeared at the Gaumont, Wolverhampton, not long after it had opened.

P.C.T. had become Gaumont British by this time and Leslie Taff left the company at the end of 1935 to open the Tower, West Bromwich. This cinema's Compton organ was opened on 9th December 1935 and Leslie Taff not only opened it — but also returned to close it thirty years later. His first number at the Tower, where

18. Leslie Taff, at the console of the Tower's Compton organ, both photographed at Marston Green in December 1970.

*(Photo: John D. Sharp)*

he was billed as "Our Singing Organist", was *"Tea for Two"*, and this became his signature tune.

He left the Tower after it was taken over by ABC and on 19th September 1938 he opened the Regal, Darlaston. The Regal's organ was a Compton Theatrone electronic instrument and became famous when Leslie Taff began B.B.C. broadcasts from the Regal. The first was on Boxing Day 1938.

At the Regal he had entered the world of cinema management and over the years this gave him less time to appear at the organ console. The organ itself grew unreliable and by the time the Regal had turned to Bingo it had been replaced with a modern electric organ.

His last recital was on the Tower's organ. In December 1970, this organ, which he had opened and closed at the cinema, was installed and reopened at Marston Green Hospital. Despite ill health it was a memorable recital, within four days of the anniversary of his debut at the Tower. When he died, three years later, the world lost not only a notable organist, but also a man who had given almost fifty years service to the entertainment industry. He played the organ, played the piano to accompany Alfred Van Dam, organised concerts, managed a cinema and helped organise the earliest specialist film shows for the ethnic minorities of the Black Country — a career truly spanning the history of the cinema.

## 5. THE PATRONS

While conducting the research for this book a great many people have contacted me not because they worked in cinemas, but because they were part of the audience. It might be thought that a dark building, in which one often did one's courting, would not have attracted much attention from the patron, but this does not seem to have been the case. Many patrons have recalled their cinemas and the staff who worked in them, in great detail, and sometimes the staff have returned the compliment.

Not much can be said that would not be true of the audience in any part of Britain. The cinema set out to acquire enough respectability to attract customers who could afford to pay to come in. Bringing tea and biscuits to the patrons in their seats, and later providing elegant cafes was as important as reassuring everybody of the good taste of the films themselves. The survey that follows will show how each cinema strived to do this.

Many Black Country cinemas, however, exploited a very local patronage and had no need to feel ashamed of providing entertainment for a working class audience, that preferred action, melodrama and excitement, to romance and borrowed theatricals. Many small cinemas were called "The Blood Tub" as a mark of their success in providing a suitably violent and melodramatic diet.

If you arrived late at the Electric, in Church Street, Bilston, you risked walking through the beam of light from the projector, and if your silhouette appeared on the screen there would be cries of, "Shif your yed out the rode!"

In such cinemas the films always seemed to be breaking and the audience could hardly be expected to endure such matters in polite silence. Of course noisy rowdy audiences enjoying themselves seemed very immoral to some, and the chucker-out was appointed to deal with the situation. When the Regent replaced the Tivoli in Owen Street, Tipton, the proprietors went to great trouble to publicly state that the rowdiness of the audience in the former theatre would not be tolerated in the new one!

When the cinema matured and sound arrived, a quiet and respectful audience was more deserved and for twenty years, from 1930 to 1950, a hushed audience was carried away be some of the greatest films of all time, enjoyed by all social classes, and by all age groups. The period that followed was a difficult one, not only because audiences declined, but the social fabric of post-War Britain was changing and has continued to change. *"Rock Around the Clock"* slashed its way through the cinema seats of the Black Country as it did elsewhere. My loyalty to my own generation prevents further comment but many a cinema proprietor seems to have seen it as the beginning of the end. By the end of the sixties the remaining cinema-goers were predominantly in the sixteen to twenty-five age group, plus a few pensioners at the matinees.

In recent years the Black Country has lost all its truly local cinemas, apart from the Royal, Cradley Heath, and has been left with a handful of town-centre cinemas with multiple screens. The only way you can tell you are sitting in the Black Country is by the laughter that greets the mispronounciation of local names in the advertisements by ignorant southerners!

Two great legends concerning the patrons have become part of the folk-lore of the cinema: bugs and children. Many a local cinema was nick-named the "Bug Hut" or "Flea-Pen". (The word "flea" is pronounced "flay".) Managers and proprietors always adopted the same policy regarding this matter. If a patron complained about the bugs it was politely pointed out that the patron had brought them in.

The usual practice was to spray the auditorium with a perfumed disinfectant between the shows, and from the White City in Willenhall to the Scala in Dudley, to the Cosy Corner in Halesowen, patrons have recalled the perfumed scent of that spray more vividly than a D. W. Griffith's classic.

Children traditionally were provided with their own matinees: the "Penny Rush", later the "Tuppenny Rush". The price of admission often paid for oranges, sweets, comics and special prizes and the audience was seldom docile. Usually they were admitted by the side entrance to the cinema, used by patrons reaching the cheapest seats. The noise and the litter problem were both enormous but it was a recruiting ground for future patrons and few local cinemas failed to provide such shows. The first super-cinemas, particularly the Cliftons, carried on this tradition throughout their lives, but the Odeons and ABC Savoys were a little more cautious.

The Odeon, Blackheath, claimed to be the first Odeon to start a children's club but I do not know whether this is true. The town-centre super-cinema moved the show forward to Saturday morning, and to a post-war generation it was always known as "The Saturday Morning Flicks". They spread through the larger cinemas during the forties. For example, A.B.C.'s "Minors' Club" did not start at the Tower, West Bromwich, until 1947. The first member still keeps his membership card and can sing the club's song on demand!

As late as 1960 three thousand children went to the Saturday matinees in Wolverhampton alone. At the ABC Tim Whittaker claimed he had a thousand members. Rank's cinemas were doing so well they were about to divide the patrons. John Alexander was going to look after the under 13's at the Gaumont while the teenagers were directed to Reg Felton's care at the Odeon. Two years later the pattern was reversed and the Gaumont played such shockers as *Rock Around the Clock* to teenagers that were about to become Beatle Maniacs. Only six years earlier the same film shown to an "adult" audience had resulted in calling the police!

The last children's matinee in the Black Country was presented while this book was being researched. At the Odeon, Wolverhampton, Colin Hunter issued the last ticket (for 15p) to an eager patron on 12th July 1980, after thirty-six years of such shows. They had ceased at the ABC, Stourbridge, one week earlier.

How will future Black Country folk ever acquire the habit of cinema-going?

## 1. Introduction

"Out of Darkness, cometh Light" might have been a slogan adopted by early cinematographers, but, in fact, it is the motto of the Borough of Wolverhampton. Today the enlarged Metropolitan Borough covers the entire north western corner of the Black Country, including Bilston and Wednesfield and even parts of Coseley. Like all the towns occupying the "corners" of the Black Country, Wolverhampton has traditionally regarded itself as slightly separate from its neighbours. Its coat-of-arms displays symbols of its pre-industrial past: its ancient educational and ecclesiastical institutions, the wool trade and early locksmithing. However, when Queen Victoria emerged from mourning to visit the town in 1866 she drove from the station to the town centre through arches of coal. This was surely a realistic nineteenth century recognition of the fact that the town's wealth was built on coal and the resulting growth in manufacturing industry, and that the town was therefore, to all intents and purposes, a part of the Black Country.

Growth and prosperity produced many fine buildings in Wolverhampton, and the continuing recklessness with which they have successively been replaced. Georgian, Victorian, and Edwardian elements of the townscape have survived to mingle with post-war modern architecture; Cinemas have come and gone in the same way. Two super-cinemas perfectly reflecting the quality of the "modern" style of the thirties have remained, but splendid buildings like the Queens and the Gaumont have gone, however much a permanent part of the town they once seemed to be. With the kind of "surprise" that is Wolverhampton's speciality, the cinema enthusiast could, until very recently, behold the Clifton in Bilston Street, an excellent example of a late nineteenth century theatre's survival as a cinema, and Bingo Hall. Even in 1982 Bingo players at the Scala in Worcester Street can enjoy cinema architecture of 1913. The Olympia and Pavilion buildings still survive.

Reflecting the size and importance of Wolverhampton, the town had a large number of cinemas. In this survey the cinemas of the town centre will be dealt with first, in chronological order. Four cinemas in the suburbs of Wolverhampton will then be described, before proceeding to Bilston and Wednesfield. Several 'town-centre' cinemas at one time attracted a very local audience, and my definition of 'town centre' might include areas that, in the past, people would have regarded as being on the way out of town. (For example the Coliseum, Blakenhall, and the Globe, Horseley Fields.) I have therefore tried to describe the cinema's place in the social geography of the town wherever it seems relevant.

19. The Pavilion, Wolverhampton. 1981.

*(Photo: Ned Williams)*

## 2. Films in Wolverhampton before 1910 (The Drill Hall, The Pavilion, etc.)

Like most towns, Wolverhampton certainly saw films before the passing of the Cinematograph Act of 1909. Besides the fairground there were one or two other places that films appeared during the first decade of this century.

Films were occasionally shown at the old Drill Hall in Stafford Street. I have no details of these shows but one Wulfrunian remembers being a small boy at one of these shows about 1905, and remembers being more fascinated by the beam of light and the temporary fireproof projection box erected in the middle of the hall than with the films themselves. It also seems fairly likely that travelling cinematograph shows came to the Agricultural Hall as described in the chapter on that establishment, and possibly to other public halls.

The earliest "theatrical" shows seem to have taken place at the Pavilion. This was a variety theatre which was basically a fairly long low building stretching from Tower Street to Castle Street. A small raked gallery was provided at the Tower Street end, where the building can still be seen to this day. Films were being shown by 1909 between the variety acts and people were being admitted for "a penny and a pass".

Whatever the relative importance of live variety and films, the Pavilion seems to have obtained a Cinematograph Licence after the passing of the Act and used to appear in the Kine Year Book when that first appeared. It is recorded as belonging to Messrs. Bennett & Stone and is said to have held 1500 patrons but that is very difficult to imagine even if they were all crammed onto bench seats.

The Pavilion seems to have closed during the middle of the First World War, and the building has seen a variety of uses since. In 1959 a gas-lit chandelier which used to hang from the ceiling forty years earlier was unearthed while the building was undergoing alterations. The frontage still has a theatrical look about it, but like the Electric/Imperial in Queen's Square, which also closed in the First World War, there are few people around today who can remember the place in any detail.

### 3. The Electric Theatre — later The Imperial
*38 Queen's Square*

In order to prepare premises that would fulfil the requirements of the 1909 Cinematograph Act, would-be cinema proprietors had to start work in that same year. Enterprise Developments Ltd. asked a London architect, Herbert H. Gissing, to draw up plans of a cinema they proposed opening in Queen's Square. The plans were approved on 8th December 1909 and involved making several alterations to the existing building. A raked floor had to be installed, a pay box at the entrance, and a small operating room immediately behind it, reached by climbing four steps.

20. The Electric Theatre, much enlarged from a Bennett Clarke photograph of Queen's Square.

*(Photo: Wolverhampton Libraries)*

It was designed to accommodate three hundred people on benches and tip up seats reached from one side gangway. Nowadays it seems strange to imagine so many people squeezed into premises the size of a shop but at the time it was fairly typical of the places used for showing films in many high streets throughout the country. Such was the novelty of the picture house that the local magistrate issuing the licence for music and dancing in respect of the Electric Theatre could not understand what was happening. The licence was required as the silent films were to be accompanied "by a small piano, played by a lady artiste". The applicant, Mr. R. A. Willcock, assured the magistrate, Alderman Jones, that there would be no other music and certainly no dancing. Alderman Jones gave up, and turned his attention to the inflammability of films and their possible offensiveness. The owners offered to allow the Chief Constable to review the films privately every Monday morning if necessary!

Such was the rush to enter the cinema business that the Electric Theatre first opened to the public on 24th January 1910. The narrow cramped auditorium seems hardly to have provided enough space for a pianist to accompany the films, but apparently there was room behind the screen for a sink. The sink was used for washing cups, as patrons at some matinees could have cups of tea brought to their seats. Along with this image of a tea-drinking audience some Wulfrunians have recalled that the Electric showed many British films. When it opened the most expensive seats, which could be reserved, were a shilling: a high price in those days.

Business carried on at the Electric until about 1915 without any change. While being managed by a Mr. J. B. Stephenson, it seems that a new company was formed to improve the place. Messrs. Imperial Playhouse Ltd. submitted new plans, by Frank Clark, for approval in November 1915. A new half-timbered facade was planned that would have given the cinema a more imposing frontage and would have made it seem less like a converted shop. It was also planned to move the screen so that it occupied the centre of the rear wall of the hall. This meant that the screen would have to stick out slightly across the existing rear exit to Cheapside. The plans were not given approval.

However, the Imperial Playhouse, as it wished to be called, carried on under its new name from 1916 until it closed sometime in 1918. Mr. Stephenson found a new job for a short while at the Coliseum and the little cinema became a shop. Today it is Green & Hollins, the outfitters.

### 4. The Olympia
*Thornley Street*

The early shows at the Drill Hall in Stafford Street were probably presented by a Mr. & Mrs. Quigley, and to them goes the honour of the opening of Wolverhampton's second cinema. While the 1909 Cinematograph Bill was becoming law they seem to have been looking for suitable premises. The Thornley Street Odd-Works, not far from the Drill Hall, seemed ripe for conversion. The falling ground meant that an auditorium constructed parallel to Broad Street would have a natural rake. Plans, drawn by the architect Joseph Lavender, were submitted for approval in January 1910, and work began on alter-

21. The Olympia, Wolverhampton. 1960. Display cabinets and Mr. Wareing's poster, "You Can't See Films Like These On The Telly", still in place.

*(Photo: Wulfrun College Collection)*

ing the premises into a cinema.

Mr. James Joseph Quigley was a Derbyshire man who played for the County Cricket Team, but he now devoted himself to his future in Wolverhampton. He had recently married Frances Appleby, whose sister claimed to have shown films privately to Edward VII and Alexandra in Scotland. Frances had the interest in films and a flair for presenting them, he kept the books and ran the business side of the venture. Together they became the town's first cinema magnates.

The Olympia opened for business on 14th March 1910. It held eight hundred people, and in the theatrical tradition, the best seats were at the front, near the screen. The cheaper seats, benches with a back-rail, were at the rear of the hall. At first there was only one projector and programmes featured a gap between reels. Mr. Frank Whild was the musical director and sometimes sould effects were provided for the silent films. Early in its life the Olympia did present an early "talkie"; a man singing a song with sound provided by mechanically synchronised disc.

Ten years after opening their cinema, the Quigleys acquired the freehold of the property, and sixty years later it is still owned by their daughter. Kine Weekly reported this fact in April 1920 and told its readers,

"The hall itself is of neat appearance and arrangement; they get a wonderfully clear picture, and it would be difficult to improve on the showing".

Kine Weekly was also impressed by the warm welcome the regular patrons extended to Frank Whild, who had been away on War Service, and had worked briefly at the Scala.

The Olympia managed to keep its regular customers and survive the growing competition from other cinemas in town by specialising in serials, strong melodramas and action films. It also received the very personal attention of its proprietors, who prided themselves on such matters as the brightness of their picture.

A new operating box and loudspeaker room behind the screen had to be added in 1930 when Western Electric Sound was installed. For many years the chief operator was Harry Poncherry. He was an electrical and mechanical genius. He came from a high-wire

circus family but his inventive skill was just what was needed to help run a small cinema.

The Quigleys maintained their operating interest in The Olympia until early 1939. Mr. Quigley was now fifty-seven years old and decided to lease the cinema to C. S. Joseph. The latter's company, Pine Pictures, took over the Coliseum and the Olympia and he announced plans to refurbish and revitalise them. Although Pine Pictures had inherited two of Wolverhampton's oldest cinemas, the popularity of film-going during the War meant that they were not such a bad proposition.

After the War the Olympia survived partly due to the enterprise of its manager, Charlie Kettle. It began to specialise in continental films and sometimes advertised as the "Olympia Continentale". Mr. Kettle took the unusual step, for a cinema manager, of joining the committee of the town's Film Society soon after it was re-formed in 1948, I wonder if the expertise and help he offered the Society was repaid by members visiting his theatre to see some of the classics of the foreign cinema?

Towards the end of the 50's, C. S. Joseph began to pull out of the cinema business and Pine Pictures Ltd. was acquired by a Mr. Vincent Wareing. The arrival of Mr. Wareing led to the departure of Charlie Kettle, precipitated into retirement after a varied career in the management of Black Country cinemas. Ageing premises and declining audiences provided Mr. Wareing with problems, to which could be added the problems of fulfilling quota regulations. The Olympia gave up the struggle in July 1960. In this respect it was outlived by its original proprietor as Mr. Quigley lived until his eightieth year. In February 1962 he was buried in his adopted town. The last show, on 9th July 1960 had featured *"A Lift to the Scaffold"* supported by Fellini's *"Cabiria".*

To this day the premises in Thornley Street bear flaking paintwork testifying to the existence of the Olympia Cinema, although subsequent lessees have put the premises to a variety of uses. It even seems that one potential lessee had wanted to reopen the Olympia as a cinema, but could not obtain the lease. If he had done so it is tempting to wonder if the town's first cinema would have survived to a greater age.

## 5. The Picture House
*69 Victoria Street*

While cinemas established themselves in Wolverhampton in 1910, other town-centre sites had to be found for conversion for the new mode of entertainment. A Wolverhampton architect, A. Eaton Painter was asked to produce plans for conversion of some premises at the back of the Villiers Club in Victoria Street. The plans, approved by the Council on 14th November 1911, were commissioned by Messrs. Evans, Brown and Myatt of the Villiers Club. This club was to be found next door to Hudsons, a leather goods shop that is still in business today.

Work must have proceeded very quickly as little over a month later the Midland Evening News carried an advertisement for the opening of the Picture House at 6.00 p.m. on 21st December 1911, under the management of Clifford Wormersley.

It was usually known as the *"Little"* Picture House and many people remember the narrow entrance in Victoria Street and the corridor that led down to the cash desk and entrance to the hall. As in the Electric, Queens Square, there was a feeling of narrowness to the hall itself, and of a long slope down to the screen. It held about three hundred and fifty people and it could become quite hot when packed!

Within a couple of years of opening it had come within the growing empire of Thomas Jackson. Several people have told me that he used to stand by the cash desk to welcome patrons and that his daughter played the piano accompaniment to the films, but I imagine that this figure was one of the succession of managers.

After the War, Thomas Jackson seems to have planned to enlarge and improve the Picture House. He had plans prepared by Messrs. Hickton and Farmer, of Walsall and Birmingham, for a new overhead ventilation system, and extension to the auditorium, and for a new system of back projection to be installed behind the screen. The old projection room at the Victoria Street end of the hall was to become a fan chamber. As he was also planning to replace the Strand with a new cinema, Mr. Jackson entered a partnership with a Mr. Allen to form Cinemas Consolidated Ltd.

Under the control of this new partnership work began on the Picture House, but in October 1922 the Licensing Justices refused to renew the music licence because proper sanitary accommodation was not available. For a time films were shown in silence while work on the alterations went on!

It was officially reopened on 17th May 1923 and audiences were invited to enjoy the new "ray-less" pictures, and back projection was promoted as less likely to cause eye strain.

While audiences enjoyed the rather yellowish pictures that appeared on the cinema's translucent screen the proprietors began to experience further financial problems. Jackson-Allen (Cinemas Consolidated) Ltd. was compulsorily wound up during 1923. The property had been conveyed to the Bank and to two trustees for the purpose of raising capital. The Bank now sold the property to recover its debt and ultimately the Picture House passed to the Midland Counties Circuit Ltd., along with the Coliseum, Dudley Road.

The Midland Counties Circuit sold the freehold to Beatties, the adjoining department store, in June 1926, but the Picutre House continued to operate as a cinema until plans for the expansion of Beatties' premises and rationalisation of the building line in Victoria Street led to its demise. While Beatties owned the freehold films were presented by the company showing films at the West End. It closed, just as sound films were reaching town, on 28th September 1929, and the last film was *"His House in Order"* starring Tallulah Bankhead. Demolition began a few days later on 2nd October.

However, a few reminders of the Little Picture House were incorporated into Beatties extensions. If you climb the stairs by the electrical department and look out the window it is possible to imagine where the Picture House stood, and for many years an elaborate piece of plaster work and ornate ceiling support on one of the walls of the electrical department also reminded customers of the cinema. This is no longer visible to the public.

## 6. The Coliseum

The little cinema on the Dudley Road that was being demolished in April 1980 was the inspiration for starting this book. The demolition contractor's bonfire made me realise that the story of our local cinemas had to be sorted out before it was all too late. There was something significant in the fact that the building was in a sorry state and nobody seemed sad to see it go. Surely, if only the story could be unravelled, it would reveal that even a little flea-pit would have once had its day, and been as proud a picture house as any mighty Odeon. Its glory could have reflected the vitality of the area in which it had been built, now a twilight zone on the outer fringe of town, shorn of any surburban purpose, swallowed by ring roads and the changing pattern of the town's life.

In the decade before the First World War, Blakenhall was an important suburb of Wolverhampton. Many of the town's famous firms had their factories there and the network of late Victorian and Edwardian streets housed a large working class population. Nowadays only the Ring Road seems to separate Blakenhall from the town centre but in those days it was a tram-journey away and it seemed perfectly reasonable to build a cinema on the Dudley Road, the main artery of the area, to serve a local need.

The man who brought the cinema to Blakenhall was Wolverhampton's cinema entrepreneur, Thomas Jackson, possibly inspired by his success in Whitmore Reans, a similar "suburb" on the west side of town. He planned a cinema on the site of a stone-mason's yard, and the local architect, William Oliver, drew up plans which were submitted for approval in May 1912. The single storey auditorium was set back from the Dudley Road and only a narrow entrance reached the street alongside some shops. It was a simple building with a Belfast roof.

The grand opening took place on 14th November 1912, in time for Christmas. There were to be new programmes three times a week and admission to the twice nightly shows ranged from 2d to 6d. A Children's matinee was held on Saturday afternoons.

In July 1913 William Oliver produced more plans

22; The Coliseum. 1973.

*(Photo: Terry Cresswell, C.T.A.)*

for Thomas Jackson in which he sought to extend the cinema up to the Dudley Road with a much more imposing frontage, pitched roof and a small balcony. This extension turned the shell of the cinema into the building that lasted until 1980. Later in 1913 it was improved still further by adding a canopy-style shelter across the front of the cinema and down the side of the cinema in Bell Place. This time the architect was Marcus Brown.

One Blakenhall resident recalls that the first manager was a Mr. Walker but that he was replaced by a Mr. Williams. As a child about to leave school just before the First World War he remembers assisting the operator, Mr. Jesse Lewis, occasionally running errands to the Strand in Whitmore Reans. The doorman, Bill Hall, was a well known local character as he weighed twenty stone or more! The cinema's place in the life of Blakenhall is emphasized by the screening of film taken of a comic football match played on the Sunbeam Football Pitch, and the fact that the cinema's staff used to participate in the annual Blakenhall Carnival. One manager, in those early days, was Charles Norton, and his fifteen year old son Percy began work at the "Col", later working at a number of local cinemas until retiring from the Penn fifty-six years later.

Thomas Jackson regularly visited the Coliseum, in his chauffeur-driven car. One night he raced to the cinema thinking that it was on fire but the blaze was at the Star Motor Works nearby in Frederick Street. After the War, Thomas Jackson formed a partnership called Cinemas Consolidated Ltd., and the Coliseum, like his other cinemas, floundered as the partnership ran into difficulties in 1923. The Coliseum, along with the Little Picture House in Victoria Street, were taken over by the Midland Counties Circuit. The latter company ran the place for the rest of its silent-cinema life, and was controlled by Mr. Thompson, who had been appointed official receiver after Mr. Jackson's bankruptcy.

In the twenties music was provided by an orchestra under the direction of Claude Fenn-Leyland, who came from the Palace, Walsall, and a two-manual orchestral organ was in use. However, with the coming of sound the cinema went through another change of ownership. The Quigleys, of the Olympia, Thornley Street, acquired the cinema from the Midland Counties Circuit as a twenty-first birthday present for their daughter Madge, in mid 1930.

Madge Quigley spent as much money as the cinema had cost on renovating the place. It was re-seated and the canopy outside was renewed. New bronze doors were installed that lasted until April 1980. The local architect Marcus Brown, planned a "new horn recess" behind the screen for the new loudspeakers, and a bright new Coliseum reopened with *"Gold-Diggers of Broadway"* on the 24th November 1930. Sound was by Western Electric.

The Coliseum held just over eight hundred patrons and for a time was personally supervised by Miss Quigley assisted by usherettes in the balcony and male chuckers-out downstairs. Miss Quigley married in 1934 and therefore had less time to devote to her cinema as the thirties

51

went on. Her marriage, and her father's retirement, led to the disposal of both the Olympia and the Coliseum to a new lessee.

C. S. Joseph's Pine Pictures took over both cinemas in 1939. He felt that they were both doing poor business and that the areas they served had declined in prosperity during the thirties. Mr. Joseph set about building up business again. He improved the programmes, set up "promotions" and publicity. For example, the first fifty ladies coming to see *"The White Rose"* were given hankies to cry into! Unconsciously the cinema had "moved" and was now one of four on the fringe of the centre of Wolverhampton, along with the Olympia, the Globe and the Scala. Blakenhall was no longer significantly separated from the centre of town.

The Coliseum continued one other interesting tradition that had begun with Madge Quigley's management. It continued to be run by women. The Manageress from 1940 to 1955 was Mrs. Eleanor Webster. She was assisted by Mrs. Gladys Hill, the cashier, and five usherettes. In the projection box the operators were Irene Batty and Maisie Carter. The chief, George Darby, was the only man on the premises!

By the mid-fifties time seemed to have caught up with the Coliseum again, and its audiences were declining. It closed on 17th January 1959 with *"Naked Alibi"* and a *"Zorro"* serial. However, Pine Pictures Ltd. was sold to Mr. Vincent Wareing, and reopened on 6th June of the same year with *"Carry On Nurse"*. The Canopy of the building boldly exclaimed, "Back from the Telly"! It closed, for the second time that year, on the 19th December with *"Horrors of the Black Museum"*.

Having suffered two closures in 1959 it seems surprising that the building stood for another twenty years! History repeated itself as Blakenhall revived in the sixties and new tower blocks rose into the sky by the Dudley Road. Several people developed schemes for using the Coliseum. In the early sixties it seemed that it might become an indoor golf school, but the state of the building always deterred would-be developers.

In the end the new Indian community in Blakenhall came to the rescue and the cinema once again served its local community as it had done in its early days. Ajit Singh and his two brothers acquired the lease in 1963 and reopened with Indian films, after virtually rebuilding the cinema within the existing shell.

A decade later they found themselves threatened by the advance of the new Ring Road. The cinema clung on to a precarious existence through several years of uncertainty. The blight caused by the impending Ring Road meant that little money could realistically be spent on the place. Towards the end of the seventies it looked very sorry for itself and it entered the eighties waiting for the demolition men. As I said at the beginning of this chapter; when they arrived in April, I began the research for this book. The fortunes of the Coliseum rose and fell many times. For many more years many Wulfrunians will not even be aware that it has gone! Despite that bonfire, every day that I have been working on this book people have assured me that the "Col" is still there. No wonder such cinemas become legends.

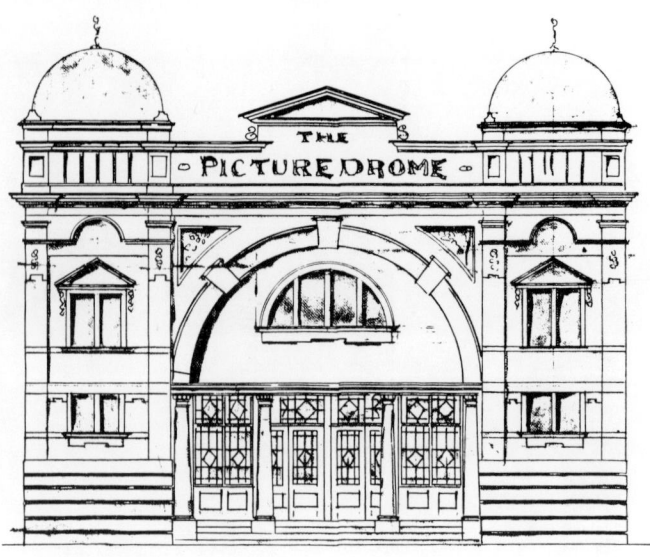

### 7. The Picturedrome, later The Scala
*Worcester Street*

While Thomas Jackson's "Picture House" and "Coliseum" were settling down to reasonable business in the two or three years that preceeded the First World War, other local businessmen planned bigger cinemas. Wolverhampton Picturedromes Ltd., led by F. Evans and G. Lewis, proposed to build a twelve hundred seater in Worcester Street. The plans, drawn by A. Eaton Painter, were submitted for approval in July 1913. Its rather grand frontage, featuring domes, arches and pillars, was the first such facade to bring the "cinema style" to Wolverhampton, and it had much in common with several cinemas being built in Birmingham at the same time. Behind the facade the auditorium had to be squeezed into a slightly triangular site but it was still thought possible to house 942 people downstairs plus 248 in the balcony.

Work must have proceeded apace during the second half of 1913, perhaps prompted by a desire to have the cinema open by Christmas. I have failed to find any advertised opening date but it was certainly opened in December of that year, having received its licence on the 8th of the month. It was open for the Christmas week which began on Monday 22nd December. The programme included *"Dancing Lessons on Film"* which would seem an ideal film to show if the seats had not yet been installed! The vagueness surrounding its opening is carried on into the years of the War. Whatever happened, it does not seem to have had a smooth start to life.

After the War it was bought very cheaply by Edgar Hounsell of Midland Amusements Company whose interests were mainly in West Bromwich. Oscar Deutsch is also believed to have been associated at sometime with this Company. It was re-named The Scala and Vic Hornblow was installed as manager. Some rebuilding, good management by Mr. Hornblow, and better programmes led to better box office success. A new orchestra, led by a Mr. Beard, was engaged.

Despite its success Edgar Hounsell soon seemed keen to dispose of the Scala. In 1920, in the middle of its most successful month of trading it had ever known, the cinema was sold to a firm calling themselves Midlands Entertainments Ltd. Vic Hornblow's services were retained but he only stayed till early 1921.

23. The Scala, the last day, 1st December 1956.

*(Photo: John Van Leerzum)*

By the mid twenties it was acquired by a national circuit; Associated Provincial Picture Houses, who also owned the Queens and the Agricultural Hall, in the town. On 11th July 1925 A.P.P.H. closed the Scala for complete refurbishing, an operation they had just completed on the Agricultural Hall. It was reopened on 28th September 1925 with *"Winning Through"* and *"The Mirage"*. The advertisement declared, "Forty souvenirs to be given away nightly!"

Mr. C. Lloyd Davies, a name long associated with local cinemas, was the manager and Louis Ronnie was in charge of the orchestra.

Apart from losing a few seats the Scala remained fairly unchanged over the years. When sound arrived British Acoustic equipment was installed. Its place in a national circuit provided stability and an uneventful life in terms of changes of ownership. It effectively served a population living in the Graisley area as well as serving the fringe of the town centre. The former area provided the "regulars" and when post-war movement led to a fall in that population the cinema's audience declined. Thus it was outlived for a few years by its flea-pit rivals!

The Scala closed on 1st December 1956 with Cornel Wilde's *"Beyond Mombasa"*. More significantly, it had revived James Whale's *"Bride of Frankenstein"* for the first two days of its final week of operation. The building was then put up for sale and began another chequered career similar to its early career as a cinema! It has settled down, and survived, as a Bingo Hall, probably serving the population of the new rebuilt Graisley just across the Ring Road. Some of its original

frontage survives but the grandeur is missing. The Bingo hall's floor is at balcony level but the decorative plaster work of the ceiling and the top of the proscenium arch still remind visitors of its one-time life as a cinema.

## 8. The Queen's
*Queen's Square*

Every town seems to have had a favourite cinema that the populus took to its heart. Places like the West End and the Coliseum may have had their local following but usually a centrally sited cinema stood the best chance of being the premier picture house. Such a cinema had to aspire to respectability to win the middle classes to its cause. The Queens, in the centre of Wolverhampton, was just such a place. People who would not have dreamed of entering any other picture palace felt it was acceptable to visit The Queens. A "posh" atmosphere was obtained by incorporating such features as a tea room into the complex, but the elegance and "social safety" had to be spiced with a little of the vulgar excitement that film-going was really all about! In the twenties, which was the golden age of such cinemas, Hollywood's films themselves provided this same formula, a subtle blend of vulgarity, sophistication, and moral propriety!

The Queens, significantly, was part of a growing national circuit. It was built for Associated Provincial Picture Houses who specialised in providing this kind of cinema. Local xenophobia, just before the War, seemed to create a distrust of A.P.P.H. and they were constantly denying that they had any German connection. Up until 1914 many local cinemas had been

53

pioneered by local men. Even A.P.P.H. were not as "foreign" as they seemed as will be made clear in the chapter on Walsall.

The plans were produced by Robert Atkinson and George Alexander, London architects, during 1913, with a few modifications being made to the foyer and tea room in early 1914. Work on the building proceeded in 1914 and the contractor was Messrs. H. Willcock and Co.

On 30th September 1914 Wolverhampton's eighth cinema opened. (Including the Strand out in Whitmore Reans in the other seven). The opening speech was made by Mr. A. E. Newbould of A.P.P.H. and he stressed his local connection and again denied any German sympathies. Indeed he had been born in Wolverhampton and had attended the local Art School. The Mayor, Alderman Bantock actually declared the cinema open, and the films that followed included *"Jelfs"* and *"Her Uncle"*. Norman Williams, from Covent Garden Opera House, sang *"Shipmates of Mine"* and *"Land of Hope and Glory"* to underline A.P.P.H.'s patriotism.

Accommodation was provided for just over one thousand people, slightly less than the Scala, but probably in greater luxury. Its frontage, dominated by three arched windows at balcony level, and its elegant foyer provided suitable grandeur for its imposing position at the top of Queen's Square. The cinema obviously took its name from this square. Other A.P.P.H. theatres were usually simply called "The Picture House", but this name was already used locally by the rival in Victoria Street. A commissionaire, page boys and ushers, in splended blue uniforms, greeted the patrons plus one solitary usherette, Edith Causer, who also helped out occasionally as a waitress in the cafe. She obtained the job through her sister Kate, who was an assistant in the operating room under the "chief", Mr. Collett.

Managers came and went fairly quickly in the first few years but later individuals stayed for longer periods and became closely indentified with the cinema. In the early twenties it was the leader of the orchestra who was the personality most strongly associated with the cinema

24. The Queens
*(Photo: Wolverhampton Libraries)*

in most people's minds. This gentleman was Alfred Van Dam. Many people went to hear him play in his own right, as well as admire his accompaniment to the films.

Miss Causer had graduated from usherette to 3rd operator by the early twenties and used to open the projection room portholes when Van Dam was playing and used to sing along with the marvellous music. One day the manager sent a note up to the box saying, "Tell Miss Causer the orchestra is supplying all the music that is needed!"

It must have been a sad day when the talkies came to the Queens despite the excitement of the new medium. Unexpectedly, the Queens was not the first Wolverhampton cinema to be wired for sound, A.P.P.H. granted that honour to the Agricultural Hall. However, on 23rd September 1932 *"Weary River"* introduced the phenomenon to the Queens. Three members of the orchestra were retained on the staff.

The cinema had been managed for a year by Cliff Lloyd-Davies from the Scala, but he was destined for the new Gaumont that September, so was replaced by Tom Lloyd. The latter stayed twenty-seven years until the cinema closed. His long stay, and Cliff Lloyd-Davies' long stay at The Gaumont later joined by Mr. Felton at the Odeon, earned them the local nick-name, "The Three Musketeers". Successfully they managed the local cinemas and promoted the films shown, for quarter of a century.

The Queens was provided with Western Electric sound and through the thirties and forties continued to hold its own against newcomers like the Odeon and Savoy. The Earl of Dudley, and occasionally his guest, The Prince of Wales, came to the Queens without any special fuss being made, and several generations of courting couples regularly went to the cinema or the cafe. Future husbands and wives actually met at the Queens, proposals were made there, and even honeymoons often started there! Although its "golden age" may have been the twenties, each subsequent decade provided people with memories of the place right up to its closure at the end of the fifties.

By the mid fifties the owners, the Circuits Management Association of the Rank Organisation, were undergoing the first of their endless series of rationalisations. Thus Dudley's Criterion disappeared as early as 1956. In July 1957 Rank revealed plans for converting The Queens into a ballroom, but these were apparently shelved in September when snags arose over licensing.

In May 1958, it was announced that the cinema would be auctioned. A month later, in the London auction room of Goddard and Smith, it was withdrawn when bidding reached £74,000, probably about £6,000 short of the reserve. For a while it seemed a private sale might still take place, but by the end of the year it was clear no sale would take place and that Rank themselves would re-develop the site.

The end came on 7th February 1959. The final programme was *"The Square Peg"*, starring Norman Wisdom, plus *"The Lavender Mob"* starring Alec Guinness. The restaurant remained open while "alterations" commenced. It was to become a dance hall after all. The £30,000 conversion was planned by Dennis

Patterson and K. W. Brookes of the Harry Weedon Partnership, and was carried out by A. W. Gibbons and Son of Coventry.

Ironically the conversion made the place seem more "theatrical" inside than it had looked for years in the view of the Express and Star reporter. He viewed the place as the scaffolding was being removed in May 1959. Deep reds and blues, and gilt panelling created this atmosphere. The strongly horseshoe-shaped balcony where courting couples had once sat in the double-seats, was retained and linked to the dance-floor at the former screen end of the hall. The Canadian maple dance floor was installed at the level of former rear stalls. As the stalls were steeply raked this left considerable space under the floor at the screen end, but brought the dancers nearer to the original ceiling which was retained. The lavish plaster work was "lost" by being painted all over in midnight blue. Someone remarked that it would make an ideal intimate cinema!

The Queens Ballroom opened on 15th May 1959 but lasted just under a decade. For some it had strong nostalgia as a dance hall, but generally there was a flood of nostalgic letters in the local press about the place as a cinema when, almost another decade later, the building was demolished. Demolition began in 1977 but staggered on into 1978. Even on a valuable town centre site it seemed that a cinema could just "fade away" rather than promptly disappear. The site was redeveloped in 1980 by Lloyds Bank.

## 9. The Globe, later the Carlton
*Horseley Fields*

Although I am including The Globe in my survey of Wolverhampton's cinemas of the central area, there is a distinct feeling as one walks down Horseley Fields today that it was in an area quite remote from the life of the centre. Like the Coliseum in Blakenhall, there is feeling that this cinema never shared the bustle of town-centre life, and that the cinema belonged to its own inner suburb that has also now disappeared.

The eastern approach to the town is visually the most depressing way to encounter Wolverhampton. Perhaps it was different when this cinema's neon lights were the "brightest in town", as one fan of the Carlton informed me.

The Globe was promoted by Captain W. J. A. Cresswell and his father-in-law, Mr. Hawthorn. The building on the site in Horseley Fields was formerly Hollingsworth's Pork Sausage and Pie Factory. (They still have a factory nearby today). The local architect, Marcus Brown, drew up plans for converting the building to a cinema and these were approved on 9th June 1926. A new roof was provided, a small foyer put in, with a projection room above it, plus an entrance in Mary Ann Street to provide access to the bench seats at the screen end of the auditorium, but basically the outline of the building did not change very much. There was only a tiny orchestra pit and narrow stage with the screen mounted on the rear wall.

To make the entrance a little more imposing an overhanging canopy was planned while the local contractor, H. J. Amies, was working on the conversion. It had a hanging iron framework, was glazed and bore the name

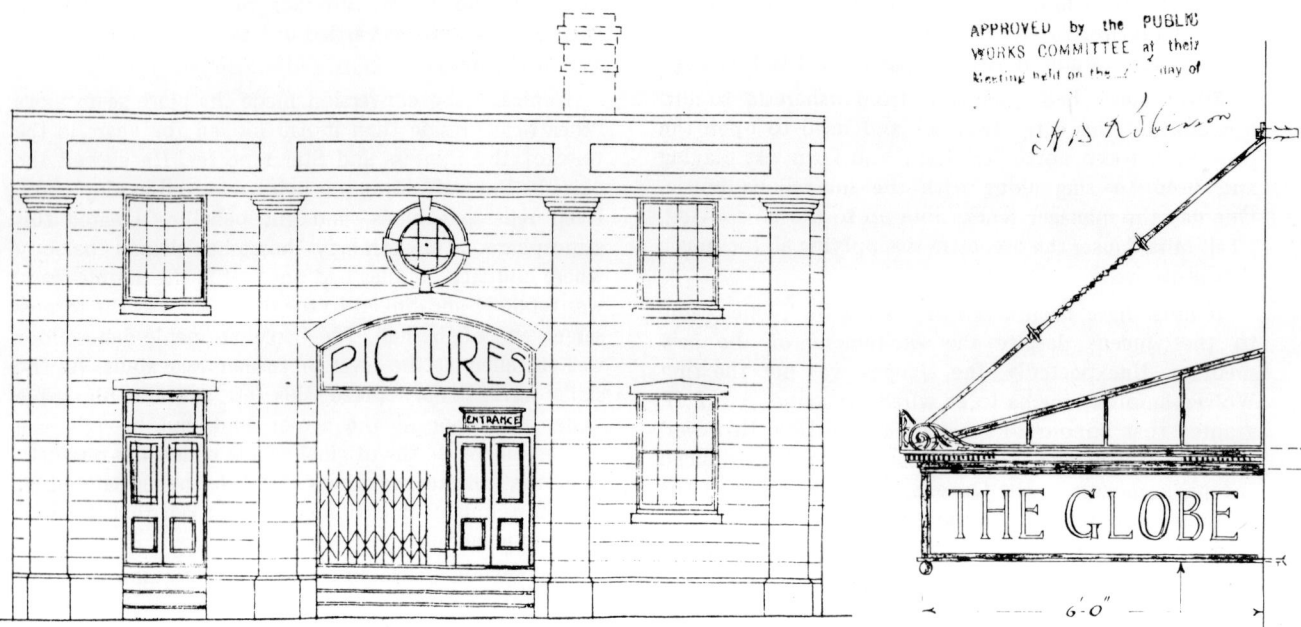

PICTURES

ENTRANCE

THE GLOBE

6'-0"

of the cinema. Again, it was the design work of Marcus Brown. When all was ready and the cinema prepared to open one local paper apparently ran a story headlined, "From Pigs to Pictures", which did not please Captain Cresswell very much.

On 24th January 1927 the Globe was opened by Mayor of Wolverhampton, Alderman F. A. Willcock, at the matinee performance. The first film was *"The Midnight Sun"*, a film of pre-war Russia. Captain Cresswell welcomed the Mayor and the latter praised good wholesome entertainment. He dismissed crime thrillers with the words, "We don't want the rising generation shown how to become burglars". Chief Constable Webster was also present and, addressing himself to the natives of Horsely Fields with a broad smile declared, "You now have a church, a pub, and a cinema, what more do you want?" (The Globe was sited opposite Mount Zion Church and that has also disappeared).

The Globe advertised "Amusing, instructive and wholesome pictures, with orchestral music, in comfort — at popular prices", and from 1927 onwards that is just what it did, although the orchestra disappeared about four years later and B.T.H. sound equipment was installed. It was a small cinema, holding about six hundred people, and for the first decade of its existence it had an uneventful life.

About the middle of 1937 it seems that Captain Cresswell decided to dispose of his cinema. This plunged the place into a series of changes of ownership over the next six years. By the end of 1937 it was owned by Mr. Hawtin of Cannock, and he had an extension put on the Mary Ann Street side of the building, principally as a garage, and built a car park at the rear of the building stretching from Mary Ann Street to Gough Street. At the beginning of the Second World War a Mr. Funnell was involved, and the cinema was associated with the West End in Whitmore Reans for a time. Mr. Walter Palmer, managed both cinemas for a short time and engaged Ron Farr as a re-wind boy following a rapid turnover of lads in this position. Forty years later Mr. Farr can still remember crawling under the stage in

the darkness to manually wind the curtains at the right moment.

The cinema was thriving during the War, with long queues outside, just like the super-cinemas, but that did not seem to stop the confusing changes that seem to have taken place in the Globe's ownership, plus short periods of closure. On 10th November 1941 it reopened after closing briefly for refurbishing, this time under the banner of the Marks Circuit, a Manchester firm also represented locally at the Regent, Tipton.

Two years later it closed again. On 13th June 1943 it presented its last show as The Globe. On Sunday 14th November of that year it reopened as The Carlton. The first film was *"International Squadron"*, starring Ronald Reagan. The cinema was now in the hands of H. F. N. Burton, of Walsall, and, at last, had found an owner who was going to stay to the bitter end.

When the War was over Norman Burton improved the cinema and put up its new name in neon light. The little six hundred seater marched on into the post-war era. Although it advertised regularly I have spoken to many Wulfrunian cinema-goers of that period who seem unaware of the Carlton's existence, perhaps indicating how remote Horseley Fields seemed, or the unfair way it was dismissed as a flea-pit. By early 1960 Norman Burton was in ill health and the cinema was put up for sale.

The Carlton closed on 2nd April 1960, the last film being *"Tommy the Toreador"*. The building was sold to Bergs of Wolverhampton, owners of The Household

Stores, and Mr. J. Berg found himself trying to give away six hundred tip-up seats.

I am not sure how long it survived as a warehouse. However, it was eventually demolished, and a new building, occupied by a credit company, now stands on the site in a Horsely Fields that has become increasingly derelict and uninhabited.

## 10. The New Theatre Royal, later the Clifton
*Bilston Street*

When a cinema earns the nickname, "The Blood Tub" we do not expect to find it standing on a prime site in the town centre but the Clifton was just such a contrary place. The building enjoyed an extraordinary history. It was built on the site of a slaughter-house and opened in 1865 as The Prince of Wales Theatre, providing music hall entertainment. It was also known at various times as The Star, the Hippodrome and The New Theatre Royal, to distinguish it from the former Theatre Royal that stood at the end of Garrick Street. It was equally well known as The Blood Tub, in honour of the stirring melodramas presented, and "Kimberley's" after one of the proprietor's; Mrs. Kimberley. Local legends claim that Vesta Tilley and Marie Lloyd played there but they are more likely to have played at The Empire. On the other hand, Harry Lauder's only visit to Wolverhampton was at this theatre.

In 1913 the building caught fire, not for the first time, and the rebuilding that followed created the frontage that survived until recently. The plans were drawn up by Marcus Brown in 1914 and the work was completed the same year. It reopened with Mrs.

Kimberley's *"Australian Nell"* and the proceeds went to a war-fund. The ornate plaster work across the front of the building seemed more appropriate to a theatre than a cinema and the interior certainly always retained its theatrical atmosphere.

On 23rd August 1928 Leon Salberg, proprietor of Birmingham's Alexandra Theatre, purchased it for £25,000 and decided to concentrate on higher class drama, revues and pantomime. Repertory Theatre was presented just as the "talkies" were beginning to take the world by storm. The New Theatre Royal decided to join the craze and Leon Salberg converted his theatre into a cinema. The last play was presented on 25th May 1931 and the conversions took less than a month. The plans had been drawn up by Satchwell and Roberts and had to contend with problems such as improving sight lines in the circle. This was solved by modifying the upper circle, or balcony, reducing its previous figure of 274. A screen was dropped at the front of the stage and an operating box was constructed right up in the roof of the building. The resulting angle of projection was ridiculously steep. Even with the screen angled it was impossible to prevent some distortion or loss of focus. With such impossible projection conditions it seems fitting that the only chief operator who could be found who would not suffer vertigo was a man with one eye: Tom Edkins. Special appertures were cut in the machines but it was never very satisfactory. A Western Electric sound system was put in. As the stage took up a fairly large proportion of its size, the building only held just over a thousand patrons.

The cinema opened on 15th June 1931 with *"The Widow From Chicago"*, not long before the Empire

25. The Clifton in June 1974.

*(Photo: Chris Clegg)*

began a short period of showing films. Thus the decade of the Super-cinema began with two of the town's theatres courting the new improved medium. Whether it was intended to show films at the Theatre Royal for long I am not quite sure.

Leon Salberg also owned the "old" Theatre Royal just round the corner in Garrick Street. In mid 1930 Cinema Proprietors Ltd., the partnership of Leon Salberg and Sidney Clift, proposed re-developing the site as a huge 3,000 seater to be called "The Garrick". Again this was to be designed by Messrs. Satchwell and Roberts.

However, before this plan had progressed very far A.B.C. seem to have entered the picture. A new set of plans for a cinema was finally submitted to the local authority the following year, by Leon Salberg, but these were drawn by William Glen — A.B.C.'s resident architect. Next we hear that A.B.C. themselves are to build their own "Savoy" on the site, but some "special relationship" presumably existed between A.B.C. and Messrs. Salberg and Clift because the Theatre Royal was then leased to A.B.C. while the Savoy was being built.

When this lease expired, and the Savoy was open, the cinema returned to the Clifton circuit. Presumably it retained the name "Theatre Royal" to avoid confusion with the Clifton at Fallings Park. For the first decade of its life it had been managed by Harry Warburton, but about 1940/1941 Howard Smith became the manager, and licensee of the Clifton Bar at the Tower Street end of the theatre. He remained there until its closure as a cinema.

In the summer of 1948 the "New Theatre Royal" name plates were removed from the front of the building while it was repainted. As from 19th September it was to be known as the Clifton, but as the building was known by so many of its names this made little difference to anybody. A more important problem was to find suitable films to show there now that the two major circuits had tighter control over the availability of film, and a more monopolistic control of town centre cinemas.

The Clifton began its long association with revivals, foreign films and films rejected by A.B.C. and Rank. Thus films such as *All Quiet on the Western Front* reappeared in Wolverhampton and the work of Bunuel, Bergman and Fellini popped up among cheap horror films and dubbed Italian epics. In September 1949 Howard Smith actually approached the town's film society and begged its members to support the Midlands premiere of *"Paisa"* at the Clifton. Sadly the middle classes who supported such films in the rarified atmosphere of the Film Society rarely seemed to venture into the Olympia or the Clifton to see the same material. When I arrived in the area in 1962 I was amazed to be able to see films that I had previously gone to the Academy in London to see, but often had to sit through a Harrison Marks supporting film to enjoy a Bergman classic!

The Clifton seemed such a tatty contrast to the ABC opposite, but its theatrical atmosphere was far more exciting than the plainess of the ABC. It was obvious its days were numbered. The Clifton circuit disposed of both the Clifton and the Rosum, Walsall, to Star Associated Holdings in February 1966.

The final show for the old proprietors was on 12th February with a magnificent double bill, *"Curse of the Fly"* and one of my favourites, *"Duel of the Space Monsters"*, but it seems probable that Star Holdings ran the place as a cinema for a further week. The last show was therefore probably on 19th February, but as it was not advertised I have been unable to find out what was shown.

It was transformed into a Bingo Hall even more quickly than it had been transformed from a theatre to a cinema. The screen and orchestra pit disappeared and an attempt was made to streamline the interior of the auditorium and give it a feeling of brightness and luxury. It opened for Bingo on 3rd March 1966, and survived for a decade in which it was taken over by E.M.I. Bingo; A.B.C.'s second association with the site.

By 1978 the building was being declared unsafe and was acquired by the County Council was part of the process of acquiring land associated with extensions to the final phase of the town's ring road. For the last two or three years of its life it presented a very sad and dejected face to cinema-goers emerging from the ABC. One even wished it had survived longer as a Bingo Hall.

Demolition began early in 1981 but even that proceeded slowly until W. Jones and Son replaced the original contractor in April. Work then speeded up in a dramatic way. The eastern wall of the building was ripped away exposing a magnificent side-elevation transect of the building from projection box, through both circles, down to the stage. A huge gas-engined generator was unearthed beneath the stalls, and on 5th April 1981 the frontage came down; leaded windows, art-nouveau tiles on the staircases, bronze doors, and decorative plaster work all disappeared without any ceremony.

---

## 11. The Agricultural Hall and the Gaumont
*Snow Hill*

Following a chronological pattern it is logical to proceed to a description of the Gaumont, Wolverhampton's first "modern" cinema, but the story and chronology are complicated by the fact that the Gaumont was built on the site of the Agricultural Hall and that story takes us back to the early days just before the First World War.

The Agricultural Hall was built in 1863 at Snow Hill, the junction of the roads from Bilston and Dudley — the corner itself determining the distinctive curved frontage of the Hall, and later of the Gaumont. A weekly corn market was held there and above the building's entrance was a decorative device featuring a stook of corn, a plough and agricultural produce. Various additions were made to the building as time went on and it could be used for public meetings, conferences, exhibitions etc.

Early travelling cinematograph shows were put on at the hall. For example, Poole's travelling shows came there. The hall was used by the Birmingham showman Waller Jeffs in 1908 as the finishing line in a marathon race from The Curzon Hall in Birmingham. Irving Bosco organized the race in connection with the Wolverhampton Cycling and Athletic Club. It was filmed from a car supplied by Charles Clark and Sons. The film of the event was certainly shown at the Curzon Hall but it is not clear if it was also screened at the Agricultural Hall.

26. The Agricultural Hall, Snow Hill, in the mid-twenties.
*(Photo: Wolverhampton Libraries)*

27. The crush hall at the Agricultural Hall.
*(Photo: Wolverhampton Libraries)*

28. The auditorium at the Agricultural Hall.

*(Photo: Wolverhampton Libraries)*

From 1910 onwards, as the town's early cinemas were emerging, the Hall seems to have concentrated on concerts and public meetings. The touring film-exhibitors usually occupied the hall during the winter. For example in September 1912 a new season of "Perfect Pictures and Vaudeville" is advertised to start on the thirtieth of that month. The presenters call themselves "Pictureland" but it may have been Poole's. At Christmas 1912 this gave way to a film presentation of *"From the Manger to the Cross"*. A very pious attitude was adopted towards this, and it must have been more like attending a religious meeting than going to the pictures. It seems to mark the hall's determination to become a cinema. During 1913 it closed for proper modification to a cinema. Plans were drawn up by Norfolk and Prior of Catford and a new raked floor capable of holding 1248 patrons was provided. The magnificent foyer and crush hall with fountain provided many patrons with lasting memory of the cinema. It opened, in its new form, sometime during the latter half of 1913, coming half way between the openings of the Picture House and the Picturedrome in terms of a chronological view of the town centre's cinemas.

The proprietor was the Wolverhampton Playhouse Company but this local name disguised a firm that had its headquarters at the Rink Cinema, Finsbury Park, in North London. The company later became North Metropolitan Theatres, but by 1919, the Agricultural Hall had been acquired by Associated Provincial Picture Houses, who owned the Queen's, and later the Scala.

Several managers came and went, but from 1924 to 1927 Fred Studd ran the Hall. While he was there in September 1924, a film caught fire in the projector. The operator, Mr. Fielding, managed to contain the situation but the last two reels of the film were destroyed. A common enough cinema story of that period, but two factors were interesting. First, this "red-hot" piece of film was suitably, *"Sodom and Gomorrah"*, and secondly, the resourceful Mr. Studd managed to acquire two replacement reels within ninety minutes and the doors were opened to allow the audience to see the end of the film!

During his stay at the Agricultural Hall Cinema, as it was called, Fred Studd saw the place refurbished. It closed for a few months for this to be carried out, and reopened on 13th July 1925 with *"The Snob"*, starring John Gilbert. Although not originally a purpose-built cinema it had become a cinema in quite a grand way. Its huge auditorium could hold eighteen hundred people and its entrance hall had an elegance to rival the Queens. There was also a three manual straight organ to accompany the films in silent days. It is not surprising therefore that the Agricultural Hall was the first cinema in the town to present sound films. These arrived in 1929.

Despite all this nothing could really disguise the fact that the place was a rather old Victorian building, and, perhaps naturally to its owners, it seemed to be sitting on an ideal site for a new 1930's style super-cinema. Thus its days were numbered. The last film was shown there on 19th September 1931 and the building was demolished to make way for the new Gaumont.

## The Gaumont

The demolition men began their work on the Agricultural Hall on 21st April 1931, the Monday after the last show. A.P.P.H.'s successor's, Gaumont British, owned three sites in Wolverhampton, the Queens, the Scala and the old Agricultural Hall and, as stated in the last section, the site at Snow Hill provided an ideal location for a new super-cinema. The architect, W. E. Trent, who designed a number of Gaumonts, drew up the plans which were given local approval in July 1931, and work was carried out as quickly as possible. G.B. maintained their presence on three sites meanwhile by using the Hippodrome.

The builders were McLaughlin and Harvey Limited, and their foreman was named James Risk! However, construction went smoothly and soon the towering structural steelwork dominated the corner of Snow Hill. The balcony girder alone weighed thirty-five tons, yet it only took ten weeks to erect the steelwork. The hall was horseshoe shaped and was built to accommodate nearly two thousand people, six hundred and fifty of which were in the balcony. The age of the "super-cinema" had truly arrived in Wolverhampton.

The large sweeping exterior wall was of brick, relieved by narrow horizontal bands and a canopy ran the entire length of the wall facing the town centre. A canopy, nearly the width of the pavement, covered the entrance where two columns headed skywards to the illuminated sign, "Gaumont Palace", at roof level. Three pairs of swing doors led into the walnut-panelled entrance hall and further doors led to a crush corridor that circled the rear of the stalls.

In the auditorium the walls were lined with fabric in pastel shades of green, fawn and gold, which was thought to enhance the acoustics of the theatre. The dado was deep blue and the tip up seats were upholstered in a rose moquette. The ceiling had a small central dome and throughout the theatre elaborate and novel lighting was deployed. Most of the ornamentation was concentrated around the proscenium and the stage was fully equipped for theatrical use.

Up in the projection room two of the latest Gaumont machines were installed and Western Electric sound apparatus was brought along from temporary use at the Hippodrome. The final touch was the provision of a Compton organ, a 3c/7 model, housed in a special chamber under the stage. The console rose on an electric lift.

The huge half page advertisement in the Express and Star announced that the opening would take place on Monday 5th September 1932, fifty weeks after the Agricultural Hall had closed. It was opened by the Mayor, Alderman J. Haddock and the film shown was "A Night Like This" supported by "Northern Lights" and "Mickey's Troubles". On the opening day Frederick Bayco played the Compton organ.

Wolverhampton thus acquired a super-cinema of which it could be proud fairly early in the decade associated with such buildings. Like the Queens, it had a certain respectability and style about it. It also provided

29. The Gaumont — the day after closure —
11th November 1973.

*(Photo: Terry Cresswell, C.T.A.)*

a cafe which, in this case, closed before the cinema did. However, it never seemed to command the same devotion as the Queens. Mr. Shawcross came to manage it having served earlier at the Queens and was already well-known in the town. He left to manage the Dunstall and Cliff Lloyd-Davies began his long reign.

By the end of the thirties the Gaumont had stood by and watched two more large super-cinemas join it in the town centre but the popularity of film-going during the Second World War kept them all busy and produced special events in the cinema's life. For example, on 18th September 1944, the film *"This Happy Breed"* was screened after which the local auctioneers, Bussey and Swallow, ran a sale of donated goods, including a captured Nazi flag, to raise money for the local "Comforts Fund".

In 1945 the Gaumont was selected for the world premier of George Formby's *"I Didn't Do It"* and from then onwards various premiers were put on as special late night shows to raise money for various charities. In the 1950's the cinema decided to make greater use of its stage facilities and tried to obtain the necessary licence. Each year this was opposed by the Grand Theatre and some years the license was granted, some years it was not.

In the auditorium itself a little drama was provided in 1965 when a policeman's killer was arrested in the rear stalls. On stage occasional concerts were presented. One evening in the mid sixties I tried in vain to fight my way through Snow Hill to reach the Film Society but the traffic was at a standstill and policemen and screaming girls blocked my way. The Beatles were appearing at the Gaumont, in the wake of Bill Haley and Henry Hall! The Gaumont also tried late night film shows, firstly in the early sixties, with films such as a revival of the Boris Karloff *"Frankenstein"* and the Bela Lugosi *"Dracula"* and then in the late sixties, with foreign films such as Bunuel's *"Viridiana'*. Saturday morning matinees for teenagers were tried featuring material like *"Rock Around The Clock"* which by then was considered rather tame!

In the seventies it seemed unlikely that the Rank Organisation would wish to keep both the Gaumont and the Odeon running in the town centre while audiences were allegedly dwindling. Many people felt the Gaumont was the more attractive of the two cinemas and that its stage facilities were a valuable part of the town's entertainment provision. The Gaumont went through a bad period when its programmes were dominated by sex films and oddities. One wet afternoon I sat in the huge cinema with three old pensioners, two wearing dirty raincoats, snoozing through Fellini's *"Satyricon"*.

When the Odeon was chosen for tripling it was clear that the Gaumont would eventually be abandoned. It carried on bravely under the careful management of Colin Hunter, who would later go to the Odeon. The last live show featured Cliff Richard on 11th October 1973.

Colin Hunter made sure the Gaumont went out in fine style. A Rodgers theatre organ was installed for the final week, provided by the Wolverhampton Organ Centre, and on the last night, six hundred patrons heard it played by Graeme Hawkins. The show consisted of Mario Lanza's *"The Great Caruso"* plus Gene Kelly's *"Singing In The Rain"*. On the 10th November 1973

at 10.40 p.m. precisely the local paper's film critic, Ray Seaton, switched off the power after everyone had joined in singing Auld Lang Syne, and the Gaumont was dead.

The demolition men were supposed to be ready to pounce on the building to clear the potential real estate as quickly as possible but the Gaumont did not completely vanish until the following spring. To everybody's amazement the redevelopment of the site took a long time to materialise. This book was already being written by the time Allied Carpet's new store graced the corner of Snow Hill.

## 12. The Empire/Hippodrome
*Queen's Square*

This building was primarily a theatre but it was used for a year as a full-time cinema and therefore has to be included in this survey. Its theatrical history goes back to the middle of the nineteenth century when entertainment in the Music Hall style was provided on the site in the Cheapside Tavern. On 22nd May 1897 the "Gaiety Syndicate" of Birmingham made an application for the rebuilding of the tavern as a proper theatre. It closed in its original form, on 17th July 1897.

The new "Empire Palace of Varieties" cost £30,000 to build and turned out to be a magnificent place. The architects were Messrs. Owen and Ward of Birmingham and they provided the theatre with a bizarre frontage, even by Victorian standards. It should be compared with the same architects' work on Her Majesty's Theatre, Walsall. The Empire was crowned with a golden dome, rising above a row of small cupolas across the top of the facade, and the facade itself featured Moorish windows! Somehow it had a capacity for nearly two thousand people, at least half of the patrons being crammed into a huge gallery.

The Empire opened on 5th December 1898 and many music hall stars appeared there. It was also used for meetings and people like Ben Tillett — the dock workers' leader with a voice like silver, and General Booth of the Salvation Army also stood on its stage. Like many variety theatres, films were occasionally shown and during the summer of 1910 the Empire had presented film matinees every afternoon using the name "Cinematinees". It closed briefly very early in 1921, re-opening on 21st February of that year as the Hippodrome.

Ten years later it started its short career as a cinema. Variety entertainment ceased on 19th September 1931 and the theatre closed for a week while the equipment from the Agricultural Hall was installed. Keeping the Western Electric Sound System in use was apparently one of the main reasons for transferring the cinema shows to the Hippodrome while Gaumont British built the new Gaumont. Film shows commenced beneath the golden dome on 28th September with *"Derelict"* and *"No Lady"* starring Lupino Lane.

Harry Shawcross managed the Hippodrome while the Gaumont was being built and then, with the equipment, went back to Snow Hill. The last film show was on 27th August 1932, *"The Impatient Maiden"* and the theatre then closed for another week for conversion back to its original use. It reopened as a variety theatre on the same night as the Gaumont opened its doors; 5th September 1932.

Once again great names appeared live on the Hippodrome's stage. Somehow its pantomimes were always second to the ones at the Grand, but in later years it gained prestige with some of the bands who gave concerts there, including a visit by Louis Armstrong. On Sunday morning, 19th February 1956, the building was destroyed by fire, although the bar survived! For a while, the site was an eyesore but eventually it was redeveloped and today a furnishing store occupies its position.

# ODEON
Regd.

## THE HALLMARK
## OF
## LUXURY ENTERTAINMENT

30. The Odeon under construction, 8th April 1937, revealed the standard method of 1930's super-cinema construction. The finished result can be admired on the front cover.

*(Photo: Wolverhampton Libraries)*

## 13. The Odeon
*Skinner Street*

Cinema building reached its zenith in Wolverhampton with the construction of two super-cinemas in the mid-thirties, the A.B.C.'s "Savoy" and Oscar Deutsch's "Odeon". For those who love the super-cinema, the Odeon is undoubtedly a very fine example and a classic example of what could be expected from Harry Weedon's architectural practice. The individual architect in charge of the project was P. J. Price, but, as with the Odeon, Dudley, it is Harry Weedon's name that will always be associated with the building and its style.

The front elevation of the building is dominated by a tower and the biscuit coloured faience alternated with thin green tiles. At a pedestrian level black faience and the canopy provide a horizontal base from which the verticals soar skywards. Every part of the building was functional. For example, the tower contained the air intake for the air conditioning system, as well as "flying the flag" in the form of the neon light, in the characteristic lettering we associate with the name "Odeon". The huge auditorium could hold just under two thousand patrons (1272 in the stalls and 668 in the circle) and featured a fairly simple decorative style. A series of rectangular panels across the walls and ceiling direct ones eyes towards the screen. Standard BTH equipment was fitted. The general contractors were Housing Ltd.

The cinema was opened on 11th September 1937 and despite the fact that so many of his cinemas were opening at that time, Oscar Deutsch himself attended the ceremony. This was performed by the Mayor of

Wolverhampton, Councillor Sir Charles Mander and was followed by a musical interlude provided by the band and pipers of the First Battalion, King's Own Scottish Borderers. The film was *"Dark Journey"* starring Conrad Veidt and Vivien Leigh.

The first manager at the Odeon was Edward Pike from the Odeon, Perry Barr. A couple of years later he was replaced by Percy Stanwick but its best known manager was Reg Felton.

The first chief operator was Frank Harvey and he remained there until 1950. He was followed by John Warrilow who gave twenty-five years service as an operator and had in fact been in the industry locally since 1929 when he had started as a page boy at the Queens. Often people gave long periods of service at the super-cinemas whose existence was more stable than that of older, smaller theatres. Back in 1967 Colin Hunter came to Wolverhampton to look after the Gaumont and Odeon, and still manages the Odeon at the time of writing. His quiet dedication to the cinema has been much appreciated.

Childrens matinees began at the Odeon on 19th August 1944, after the Odeon, Dunstall, and the Gaumont, and survived until 12th July 1980, the last such show in the Black Country. Like the Gaumont, the Odeon occasionally ran late-night premieres and special promotions. In the sixties a few late-night shows were put on for the Wolverhampton Film Society, using the balcony seats only, presenting films like Godard's *"Weekend"*. Like other cinemas it celebrated significant birthdays, and on its fortieth birthday in 1977 ran a week of one night double bills of film-classics. We went to the Odeon four times in one week!

The major event in the cinema's history was its tripling in the early seventies. Modernisation and re-furbishing was planned way back in 1968 but the early seventies brought in the fashion of dividing cinemas into smaller units. On 4th August 1973 the stalls were closed and the £40,000 conversion work began. The three screens came to life on 7th October 1973, with *"Live and Let Die"* on Screen 1, now seen from 622 seats in the former circle, *"Fist of Fury"* in Screen 2, which only holds ninety-six seats, and *"Sleuth"* in the 111 seater, Screen 3. Screens 2 and 3 are tucked beneath the former balcony and share a new projection box. Rather unusually the seats in the front stalls have been left in place but I do not know if they have ever been used to seat patrons watching Screen 1.

The Odeon has repeatedly sought a licence to serve drinks. Their first application was turned down in 1974 but in February 1981 they were successful and a bar has been built in the ground floor crush hall.

Inside, the Odeon's conversion is more pleasant than many; outside the Odeon is still a pleasure to behold. At the time of writing one prays that it will continue to exist despite video entertainment and despite Rank's continued withdrawal from the cinema world.

Postscript

At the time of going to press the future of Wolverhampton's Odeon as a cinema is threatened by the plan to convert the premises to a Bingo and Social Club. Outline planning permission for the scheme had been obtained some time ago and therefore, to some extent, approval has been fairly automatic. Individually, and on behalf of the Wolverhampton Film Society, the author tried to present the idea to all concerned that some film-showing capacity should be retained. It seems, however, that the last film at the Odeon may well have been shown by the time this book appears.

## 14. The Savoy, later the ABC
*Corner of Garrick Street and Bilston Street*

As mentioned in the chapter on The Theatre Royal, A.B.C. had some interest in providing a cinema in this area from the early thirties onwards, probably purchasing the site from Leon Salberg, who provided A.B.C. with a screen in Wolverhampton at the New Theatre Royal, while the new cinema was being built.

The site had been vacant for some time when ABC submitted William Glen's plans to the local council for approval in January 1936, and it took nearly two years for the cinema to be completed, beaten by several months by its rival new super-cinema, the Odeon!

The contrast between the early "modernism" of the Gaumont, only a few yards away, and the later "modernism" of the ABC built only five years after, was quite interesting. Glen's design was very austere and simple. possibly even forbidding in its lack of decoration and its massive expanses of brickwork. The pleasing geometry of this simplicity can only really be appreciated now that surrounding buildings have been demolished and roads widened. The rather cracked facing on the lower part of the building has been repainted in 1981 and now, as the traveller walks along Garrick Street, the massive brick built structure has all the majesty of an ocean liner seen alongside its berth!

Apparently, while it was being built it was intended that it would be known as The Regal, but by the end of 1937 the name "Savoy" was adopted. The Savoy, there-fore, opened on 20th December 1937 with a programme consisting of *"Let's Make A Night Of It"*, starring Charles Rogers and June Clyde, plus *"Last Train from Madrid"* starring Lew Ayres and Dorothy Lamour. The opening was performed by the mayor, Councillor R. E. Probert. Although he did not say so at the time, the Mayor was no stranger to cinemas, as he had once been Managing Director of the Dunstall Cinema Company. Mr. A. S. Moss of A.B.C. presided at the function, and at the Reception held afterwards at the Victoria Hotel. Everyone seemed very impressed with the latest cinema, admiring the autumnal shades of the internal decor and the size of the cantilevered circle, capable of holding 622 patrons. (Another 1155 could be seated in the stalls). The acoustics did fine justice to the sound provided by the Western Electric system.

The Savoy was the last town centre cinema to open in Wolverhampton, although two other large cinemas were to open in the suburbs. With its completion one could say that the town was now well served by cinemas and that the major circuits, Odeon, Gaumont British, and A.B.C. were all now represented and ready to "do battle". The other striking thing about the Savoy was its contrast to the Clifton directly opposite on the other side of Bilston Street. Rarely can two such contrasting establishments have faced one another.

As a modern super-cinema the Savoy has had a less

31. The ABC, now seen in all its glory! 1981. The site of the Gaumont, now occupied by Allied Carpets can be seen on the right.

*(Photo: Ned Williams)*

hectic life than many a smaller or older theatre, and the managers of the Savoy never seem to have become as well known locally as their counterparts in the Rank cinemas. Children's matinees on Saturday mornings did not begin until 1948, over a decade after the cinema's opening.

In the 1950's as managers began to experience the challenge from television, the cinema went in for the usual promotional activities. For example Manager L. Spurgh challenged a member of the public to come forward and sit alone in the theatre through a midnight showing of *"The Phantom of the Rue Morgue"*. Mrs. Pat Evans volunteered and photographs of her reaction to the film appeared in the local weekly paper. A more interesting event occurred in January 1951 when Manager Ken Hall screened a 16 mm copy of *"Annie Get Your Gun"* to a bedridden 81 year old Wolverhampton woman who, in 1888, had met Annie Oakley and Buffalo Bill in person.

In December 1960 the name "Savoy" was dropped and "ABC" adopted in line with company policy throughout the country. In the same month seven years later the cinema was celebrating its thirtieth birthday, and the special cake was cut by the mayor, Councillor E. Fullwood. Manager Ron Trevor ran a competition in which one had to guess how many miles of film had been projected at the cinema in thirty years. The answer was 104,500 miles.

In July 1968 ABC celebrated the success of its local protegé, Euan Lloyd, by asking him to personally introduce *"Shalako"*, a film he had produced, before it was screened. Perhaps a more significant sign of the

times came in December when "The Clock", A.B.C.'s fifth pub, opened on the corner of the theatre, on the site once occupied by the cafe. Its name referred to the clock in Golden Square where A.B.C. had its headquarters, a reference that was rather lost on the local public.

The major event in the cinema's history unfolded in the mid-seventies. EMI, now owners of the ABC circuit, had tripled and twinned a number of theatres before turning their attention to Wolverhampton. The ABC was surveyed early in 1973 but by the summer of the same year it seemed that the proposals would be shelved. Meanwhile Rank unfolded similar plans for the Odeon. EMI then changed their minds and decided to triple the ABC after all.

The cinema closed on 27th April 1974 and work began on providing two small cinemas under the existing circle and a centralised projection box to serve them. The stalls had been closed since the February but the cinema naturally wished to close completely for only the shortest possible length of time. ABC 1, the former circle now holding 590 patrons, used the existing projection box and screen. ABC 2 was provided with seats for 127 patrons, and ABC 3 seats 97. The entrance foyer was also slightly modified. The new complex opened on Monday 13th May 1974.

I must admit a personal dislike of ABC 2 and 3, but if tripling has kept the ABC open I suppose we must be grateful that it has survived into the eighties. As I said at the beginning of this chapter, it is only now that its architectural splendour can be appreciated.

## Outer — Wolverhampton

Four cinemas were built sufficiently far from the centre of Wolverhampton to earn the right to be dealt with separately. Three were the products of 1930's cinema building when suburban sites were often a popular choice, but the other had a long history going back to those pioneering days before the First World War and, in my opinion, enjoyed one of the most exotic histories of any Wolverhampton cinema.

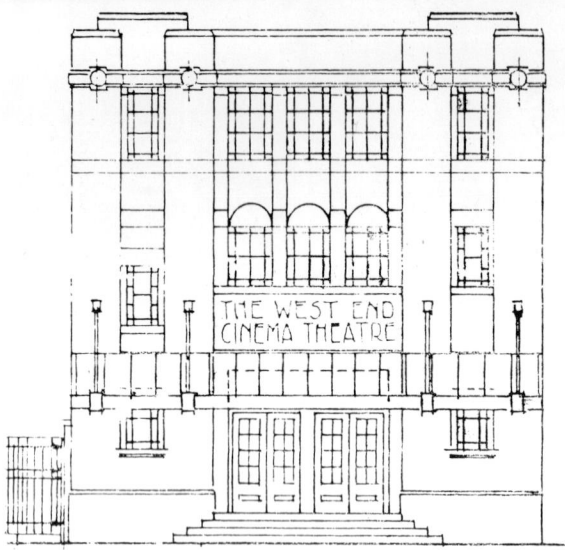

### 15. The Strand/West End/Park/Rex
*Coleman Street, Whitmore Reans*

The entire history of Whitmore Reans as an industrial suburb of Wolverhampton is a fascinating subject although an outsider to the area would be privileged to have even heard of the place. Today, new signs have been erected to welcome people to "Whitmore Reans", but the place must have changed beyond all recognition in the last two decades and the last generation that properly recognised it as a place in its own right has passed away or moved away! The latter are the people who still carry with them the legends of Whitmore Reans' own cinema. Redevelopment has totally obscured even the site of the cinema, but the legend lives on.

Long ago, at the end of the Edwardian era, there lived a baker and confectioner in Whitmore Reans named Thomas Jackson. On the site of his bakehouse he decided to build a picture house. Some plans were drawn by William Oliver in the early summer of 1912 and conversion of the bakehouse proceeded very quickly because the Strand was opened on Monday 22nd July of that year. The first show was at three o'clock but normally shows were to be presented twice nightly, at seven and nine o'clock. For the payment of 2d, 3d or 6d the Strand promised "Finest, Steadiest and Most Up-To-Date Pictures Will Be Shown!". By the autumn of 1912 Marcus Brown had provided plans for further extensions and better use of the site was made, making the place more like a cinema. (Following a similar pattern of development as Jackson's venture in Blakenhall; the Coliseum).

The little 350 seater was now well established in Whitmore Reans. The entrance, or front of the theatre was in Coleman Street, opposite the junction of Gatis Street and Evans Street, but only a stones throw from

the hub of the local community at "Leicester Square".

The cinema prospered and Thomas Jackson prospered, as detailed elsewhere. By the early twenties it was obviously worth rebuilding the place on a larger, grander scale. During the latter half of 1922, plans were being drawn up to build the new cinema. Unfortunately, however, this coincided with the period of Thomas Jackson's financial problems, already detailed in relation to the Little Picture House and the Coliseum. The new cinema was to be built by Edward Garfield to the plans of Leonard Voisey, whose design was formally approved on 10th October 1922. A company was formed called the West End Cinema Company, by these two gentlemen, plus four others and they acquired the Strand. The licence was transferred from a Mrs. Baker to Edward Garfield and for a little while longer the Strand continued to show films. The renewal of this licence was refused on 24th September 1923 because no work had yet started on either improving the Strand or building its successor. It seems that work on building the "West End" began soon afterwards. Edward Garfield had an interest in other cinemas at that time, for example, Ye Arden cinema in Solihull.

Leonard Voisey's plans provided Whitmore Reans with a building grand enough to be recognised as a proper cinema. A flight of steps up to a double set of swing doors, a canopy and a tall facade greeted patrons, and the furnisher, Mr. W. Turner provided seven hundred

32. The Rex, just before demolition, about 1960. ("Rex" has been painted over "Park" on a board covering stone lettering: West End Cinema Theatre!)

*(Photo: Wolverhampton Teachers Centre)*

and fifty seats in the new auditorium, which included a balcony. One ex-operator complained to me that the only way out of the re-wind room was back through the projection room and, that in the event of fire, you would have had to escape through the fire itself. Meanwhile, patrons inside the building were beguiled by broad staircases, a cosy lounge with orange walls and blue and gold Chesterfields.

The West End formally opened on Saturday afternoon 29th August 1925. Mr. Berresford, the manager, greeted the Mayor, Councillor J. Clark, on behalf of the directors, Messrs. Garfield and Voisey and the others under the chairmanship of a Mr. Parker. The event was an ominous warning that the cinema could expect a chequered career because the audience was very small. Everyone had gone to watch the Wolves in their first match of the new season! The cinema made a better start on the following Monday, 31st August, when it opened properly for business with *"The Flaming Forties"*.

Edward Garfield's company ran the West End for the next decade. During that time, sound was installed and "talkies" commenced on 13th April 1930, probably at first using a BTH system. Later, Western Electric sound heads were fitted. The popularity of live music at the West End is illustrated by the fact that three years later the orchestra was "re-instated" on Friday evening for a time.

From the early 1930's onwards, the West End Cinema Company leased the cinema to various people. One well remembered lessee was Captain Bert Riego who commanded the Saturday afternoon matinees with his striking presence. As usual, children came away with sweets and comics. About 1936 the enterprise was acquired by F. S. Sandover whom we will meet later in this book in connection with the Regent, Langley Green.

The cinema enjoyed the privilege of being the monthly meeting place of the Wolverhampton Film Society, and on one Wednesday night each month, classics like *"The Cabinet of Dr. Caligari"* and *"Battleship Potemkin"* flickered across its screen.

Towards the end of the thirties it becomes increasingly hard to unravel the history of the West End through a number of apparent changes of ownership. For a time it was owned by E. K. Hawtin, the Cannock-based businessman who ventured into the Black Country to run such places as the Globe, Horseley Fields and the Alhambra in Bilston. Early during the War a Mr. Funnell appears and Walter Palmer jointly managed both the West End and the Globe. Then Mr. Funnell seems to have become associated with Messrs. E. A. Oakey and H. Godsall. The latter pair as O. G. Pictures Ltd. assumed control of the West End during the middle of the War.

O. G. Pictures Ltd. brought an organ to the West End, a Hammond Model A, with a home-made surround of glass panels that could be illuminated by lamps of various colours. It was set up just below the centre of the screen as there was no stage and the screen itself was virtually on the rear wall of the hall. Stan Bannister crossed the town from the Coliseum to become the new manager and with him he brought Arthur Collett to play the organ. If the picture was a good one, the combination of Mr. Bannister's talent at promoting custom and Arthur Collett's performance on the organ, could bring people from all over the town to Whitmore Rean's little cinema.

The organist also helped out in the projection room and was shocked by the age of the equipment. The old Ross projectors with hand-fed arcs could hardly be neglected for a moment and although Western Electric sound heads had been installed the old sound-on-disc equipment was still in position. Possibly the problem of reinvesting in the cinema's improvement caused the various changes of ownership. On Sunday 16th January 1944 the West End became the Park cinema, taking its name from its proximity to West Park. On the Saturday it had been the West End, the next day it had a new name, but for most local people the old name stuck. The new proprietors were the Marks Circuit, the Manchester firm that six months earlier had relinquished the Globe.

There were now one hundred less seats (650) than provided way back in 1925 but the general feeling was that the cinema continued to remain remarkably unchanged. It was sometimes more difficult to book a good film than to fill the cinema and with this kind of problem a small suburban flea-pit struggled into the post-war era. As the Park, the cinema closed in July 1947.

The phoenix rose from the ashes very quickly. Fred Leatham reopened the cinema on 10th August 1947 as the Rex with the announcement in the local paper, "The management welcomes back old and new patrons to Whitmore Reans' "Little Super Cinema". Some refurbishing of the cinema had taken place and an RCA sound system was now installed. It opened in fine style with *"Kismet"*, starring Marlene Deitrich and Ronald Coleman. At the time, the government was trying to introduce a tax on American films and the Americans were threatening to refuse to send films to Britain, but such matters seemed a long way from life in Whitmore Reans.

Life did not run smoothly at the Rex for very long. By January 1953 the cinema was up for sale once more. It was to be auctioned at the Grand Hotel, Birmingham on 20th January by Messrs. Harris and Gillow. The reserve was £10,000 and the top bid fell just four hundred pounds short of this figure. This seemed to give the agents confidence that the cinema would soon be sold. However, nothing seemed to come of it and Mr. Leatham struggled on until early in 1956. The cinema then closed for six months while Mr. Leatham had trouble disposing of the Victoria in Tipton.

Remarkably, the Rex reopened once more. Cinema-scope was added and on 30th June 1956, the cinema returned to life with *"The Student Prince"*. The final respite was short and the Rex closed for ever in December 1956. The building remained unused for a time and then became a warehouse. Since then the whole of Whitmore Reans has undergone considerable changes and Coleman Street no longer reaches Leicester Square. The position of the Rex is obscured by the new Avion Shopping Precinct. Its history across four changes of name, two buildings, countless proprietors, lessees and managers, its first association with Thomas Jackson, its final association with Fred Leatham and everything from organ to Cinemascope, make it one of the most fascinating cinemas of the Black Country. What Odeon has a story to compare with it?

---

### 16. The Dunstall Picture House/Odeon
*Stafford Road*

It is fitting to proceed from the Whitmore Reans cinema to its nearest neighbour, not far away as the crow flies, at Dunstall. They both served industrial suburbs on the north western side of the town, in the "good ol' days" when the girls who worked at Courtaulds were courted by the young men who worked on the railway at Stafford Road Works, and both areas had clear identities of their own.

Leaving Wolverhampton by the Stafford Road the traveller at one time passed the G.W.R.'s factory, much extended across Dunstall Hill in the early thirties, then crossed the valley of the Smestow where the canal and railway viaduct now dominate the scene, and then climbed out of the valley after passing the Electric Construction Company's works on the right. Opposite the junction with the road to Bushbury four local businessmen decided to build a cinema.

The project began as the brainchild of Jack Roper and John Tyler. Jack Roper was a fishmonger who developed an interest in the cinema, particularly its technical aspects. At one time he ran a mobile cinema putting on shows at hospitals. He often visited the projection room at Wood's Palace in Bilston, saying to Harry Bayliss, who was working there, "One day I will have a cinema of my own". John Tyler was a business-man from Willenhall. He was proprietor of the Dale, which had opened in 1932 and in many respects the Dunstall was modelled on the Dale, which, in turn, was inspired by Wood's Palace! Dr. Hamp and R. E. Probert, a local butcher, completed the team. The latter becoming chairman of the board. At the time the cinema opened he was a local councillor. When he became mayor of the town he performed the opening of two other cinemas!

The cinema, which was going to cost about £20,000, was designed by Mr. Hurley Robinson whose work at the Dale and Wood's Palace was already appreciated by the directors. The plans were approved early in 1934 and construction began in the spring in the hope that the contractors, J. & F. Wootton, could have the work completed by the autumn.

Construction proceeded quickly. Harry Bayliss, the young operator at Wood's Palace, remembers watching the huge circle girder being swung into place while the Stafford Road was closed to traffic. Jack Roper's dream of having his own cinema was becoming a reality. A few months later Harry Bayliss was offered the job of chief operator at the new cinema, thus becoming Wolverhampton's youngest "chief". It was a large building, holding 1400 patrons, and at the time, its facade was described as "bold and dignified" but unfortunately over the years its snowcreted frontage suffered the ravages of the weather. Four main entrance doors were approached by a few steps under a steel canopy. The spacious auditorium featured a slightly rising floor for the front stalls and a huge screen was placed 30 feet in front of the nearest seat. The stage, 19 feet deep provided some facilities for live presentations.

When Harry Bayliss arrived a month before the cinema was due to open he recalls that no one knew which curtain was to be hung to the left and which to the right. No-one ever knew whether they were hung correctly! There was a rush to complete the building. Bryan's Adamanta worked hard to finish the fibrous plaster work and internal paint work. Even so, it is believed that paintwork was wet on some of the exit doors as the first show began! Harry Bayliss found himself in a huge operating suite of no less than seven

33. The auditorium of the Dunstall.
*(Photo: John Maltby)*

34. The Dunstall, after being taken over by Oscar Deutsch.
*(Photo: John Maltby)*

rooms extending the whole width of the building above the balcony foyer. The contrast with the conditions he had worked in at the Palace was staggering. The Western Electric Wide Range system was quite awsome, and together with the Kalee Eleven projectors, gave Mr. Bayliss the feeling that he had stepped into a mighty Rolls Royce. Another show piece was the rectifier supplying current for the High Intensity arcs. This was supplied by the E.C.C. — the firm situated directly opposite the cinema on the other side of the road.

The opening was arranged for Monday afternoon, 19th November 1934. The cinema was to be declared open by the mayor, Councillor Morris Christopher, but the event was to be made more exciting by a personal appearance of Winifred Shotter. She was the British star of the opening film *"Lilies Of The Field"*.

Unfortunately the 19th November turned out to be a foggy day in London and Winifred Shotter's train was late in arriving at Wolverhampton. She was met by the Mayor and whisked away to the Victoria Hotel for a meal. Tension mounted at the cinema where every seat was taken and the operator nervously waited to start the show. Three-quarters of an hour late, manager Roland Matthews was able to welcome the star to the Dunstall Picture House and she said a few words to the audience before the show, concluding with "I haven't seen it myself so I cannot tell you anything about it". Whether she stayed to see it on this occasion is not recorded. The first screening of *"Lilies Of The Field"* raised £45 for local charities.

As they were running late, the second house had to follow the first as soon as the audience could leave, and the second audience reach their seats. Dr. Hamp's wife thoughtfully took some sandwiches to the men in the operating box. After such a hectic start the Dunstall settled down quickly, but its independent life was short.

In the opening brochure the company declared, "The Dunstall is a non-combine, privately owned super-cinema ....... not bound by mass control, routine and the general regulations which are inseparable from the officialdom of the large organisation ....". Bold declarations of independence were not enough! Two years later the cinema was absorbed by the Odeon circuit, becoming the Dunstall Odeon, and in 1942 the name simply became Odeon. Harry Bayliss remembers John Maltby coming to the cinema to take the official photographs for the Odeon records. John Maltby set up his plate camera, opened the shutter, and then walked round the operating room with a lamp in his hand to illuminate the shadowy areas. He explained that it would not register on the negative unless he stood still for several seconds!

One aspect of life in a large circuit was the sharing of newsreels. The newsreel was shared with the Odeon in the town centre and the lad who was the youngest operator at that cinema had to collect the newsreel from the railway station on Sunday afternoon and then shuttle it back and forth between Skinner Street and Dunstall on an Odeon bicycle. Meanwhile, Harry Bayliss kept his operating room spotless and one assistant told me, "The floor had to be polished so brightly that you could see the usherettes knickers reflected in it!".

Several managers came and went, including Harry Shawcross, associated with several local cinemas, who went from Dunstall to the Penn. Its last manager was none other than Cliff Lloyd who had come to Wolverhampton to manage the Scala in 1925 and had managed the Queens and Gaumont before coming to Dunstall. The head cleaner, Doris Price joined the cinema in 1936 and stayed there throughout its life. The "chief", Harry Bayliss left in 1950, but that was not the last he saw of his beloved cinema.

As the Rank Organisation continued to find reasons for abandoning its cinemas throughout the fifties, the future did not look too bright for Dunstall's Odeon. After closing the Queens and the Scala in the town centre Rank announced that they were really only interested in town centre cinemas and therefore the Odeon Dunstall would be the next to go! The closure was announced for 5th November 1960.

With a great sense of history, Harry Bayliss was invited back to show the last programme, even though he now worked outside the industry. He has the rare distinction of having projected the first and last film in a cinema, events separated by a mere twenty-six years. The last programme consisted of *"The Savage Innocents"* and *"Dead Lucky"*.

After this sad day the cinema was more "dead" than "lucky" as it remained empty and unused for over a year. It was not wide enough to become a twelve lane bowling alley and Rank already had one cinema in town converted to a dance hall. Eventually bingo saved the day and the hall reopened for Top Rank Bingo on 16th February 1962.

As a bingo hall it passed to the Hutchinson Group (Surewin Bingo) in 1971 and survived for another decade. The exterior became shabby but the bright lights and atmosphere inside provided a valued social amenity to the residents of Dunstall and Bushbury. Meanwhile the Stafford Road was being widened, and on both sides of the cinema great changes were being made to the landscape. Bingo was last played in the old cinema on 23rd September 1981 and on the following night a brand new Surewin Bingo Club opened in a purpose-built hall a few hundred yards away in Bushbury Lane.

On 19th November 1981, forty-seven years after the cinema's opening, the demolition contractor, J. J. Gallagher of Birmingham moved in. By the end of the year only some rubble remained.

## 17. The Penn Cinema
*Warstones Road*

When Harry Shawcross left the Dunstall in 1938 to go to the Penn cinema, he found himself in a much less industrialised part of the town. Here was the truly "suburban" cinema, surrounded by pleasant inter-war housing estates of tree-lined avenues and semis. In the thirties the Clifton and Danilo circuits had contemplated such sites, the Clifton at Fallings Park being the only one to materialise, so it was left to an independent to promote this suburban super-cinema and to see it become a success.

The Penn Cinema Company was formed by a Birmingham accountant, B. T. Davis, in association with the architect, Roland Satchwell and a number of local men, G. T. (Tommy) Whitehouse, who supplied the locally made Baggeridge Bricks to build the place, and

Mr. French, the electrical engineer. Mr. H. Yoward occupied the chair. B. T. Davis did not have much to do with the cinemas of the Black Country but in Birmingham his interest in cinemas was well known. He figured largely in the local branch of the Cinema Exhibitors Association and became the CEA President in 1947/8. In many respects the Penn was "his" cinema, but Mr. Whitehouse apparently liked to bring his friends on tours of the projection room to admire what he regarded as "his" cinema!

As the building took shape in 1937 it began to look like a typical Roland Satchwell cinema of the period. It was fairly plain and its solid rectangular form was undisguised. Five large vertical windows to the balcony foyer provided relief to its huge brick frontage. It was built to provide accommodation for 1122 patrons.

The Penn cinema was opened on 27th December 1937 by Geoffrey Mander M.P. The first film was *"A Day At The Races"* featuring the Marx Brothers. After the show the directors entertained one hundred and twenty guests at the Bradmore Hotel.

Up in the projection room behind the Ross projectors was the new chief operator, Mr. Cyril Moore. He had started his cinema career at the Coliseum and had worked at least three other Wolverhampton cinemas before coming to the Penn. Like Harry Bayliss at the Dunstall, he had the distinction of showing the first and last films screened at his cinema. He gave over thirty-five years of devoted service to the Penn, inspiring affection and the respect of his colleagues. At the age of

sixty-three, the closure of the cinema forced his retirement. He was presented with a replica "Oscar" to mark the event. A replica "Oscar" was appropriate because the Penn used a picture of an Oscar on its monthly programmes. Some of his friends felt that the closure of the cinema had broken Cyril's heart and when he died just under a year later a screen-shaped wreath appeared at the funeral to pay tribute to his dedication to the cinema.

Returning to the chronological history of the Penn, we must go back to its early life. The first manager, Mr. Rogers, was replaced, as we have already noted, in 1938, by Harry Shawcross. The patrons of the Penn now enjoyed the attention of a man who was the epitome of a cinema manager. He ran the cinema with attention to discipline regarding his staff and with a personal welcome for his customers. He ran the Penn until the early fifties.

When war broke out, Mr. Shawcross had to remove the sign from the front of the cinema and the building was "fortified" with piles of sand bags placed across its frontage. The home guard, the police, and the ARP all used the premises and the shows carried on. Childrens matinees were popular at the Penn and were only suspended during the war for a short period of three weeks. Sunday concerts were also put on and proved quite popular.

B. T. Davis seemed keen to maintain his cinema and after the war there seemed to be more reinvestment in the Penn than in many independent cinemas. As well

35. The Penn Cinema, 3rd March 1973, just before closure.
*(Photo: Terry Cresswell, C.T.A.)*

as refurbishing the auditorium, the Penn also saw several major changes in the projection room. The theatre's acoustics were good and the Western Electric Sound System worked well but in July 1948 the projectors themselves were replaced with Simplex machines with Peerless Magnon arcs. Three years later the Penn became the first cinema in the country to install Philips F.P.7 projectors with a Philips sound system. The Penn's huge screen also had to be modified, with some difficulty, to accommodate Cinemascope.

A certain pride could therefore be felt in working at the Penn. The only problem that remained unsolved since its opening was the question of heating the place! This problem was finally solved by Gordon Mintern, the cinema's manager from the early 50's onwards. He managed to make the Penn a warm place. It says something for the loyalty of the Penn's patrons that they endured the coldness of their cinema through the War years and its aftermath! Gordon Mintern would also have liked to install an organ at the Penn but he was not allowed to do so.

While other cinemas began to flounder as the 1950's unfolded, the Penn continued to do good business. It was certainly easier to park at the Penn than in the town centre and often people caught up with a film there having missed it at its earlier town centre screening. Local patrons patiently waited for the big epics like "The Ten Commandments" and "Ben Hur", or popular musicals, to reach their nearest screen. Coffee and drinks could be obtained during the interval and the personal atmosphere continued to give the cinema a pleasant ambience.

Gordon Mintern left during the mid sixties and Frank Crane became the manager. He maintained the traditions of the Penn for the remainder of its life, a period when its possible closure was often the subject of rumour and most of Wolverhampton's other remaining cinemas succumbed. As early as 1966 B. T. Davis was busy publicly denying that the Penn would close so that the site could be redeveloped.

Another figure to join the Penn for the last seven years of its life, was Percy Norton. We have first encountered him at the Coliseum where he started work before the First World War. At one time he had managed the Little Picture House in Victoria Street and the Palace, West Bromwich, but he had left the cinema business in 1931. He returned in the mid sixties to become second operator at the Penn. He was slightly older than the chief, Cyril Moore, and retired a short while before the cinema's closure. One ex-assistant operator from the Penn still calls his budgies Cyril and Percy in memory of the grand old men from the operating room!

One sign of the times came at the end of the sixties. Childrens matinees had been running since the cinema opened but they ceased with the final show on 26th April 1969. Average audiences were still two to three hundred children, but Frank Crane explained to the local press that it was no longer possible to obtain suitable films.

As the cinema bravely lived on into the seventies rumours about its closure became more frequent and more intense. Film supply problems meant the Penn could not sometimes show material that suited it needs.

I remember being one of an audience of four watching a sub-titled print of "Onibaba" one sad evening.

In March 1972, local residents held a "Save the Penn" public meeting and tried to push forward the idea that the cinema could provide community facilities and need not be the victim of redevelopment. Interest in the cinema led to increased attendances in 1972 but meanwhile a London property company, Old Burlington Street Estates, relentlessly pursued its plans for purchase and redevelopment. The original plan for a 10,000 square foot supermarket, shops and car park was modified and resubmitted for the council's approval later in 1972. The new plan proposed included a few amenities such as squash courts. Councillor Frank Clapham of the planning committee declared "I think any hope of it continuing as a cinema is out".

B. T. Davis was growing old, the future of the cinema industry seemed uncertain, the early continual reinvestment in the cinema had slowed down and economies had been made. To be offered a quarter of a million pounds for a cinema in such a situation was to make an offer that no independent proprietor could refuse. The council saw no possibility of intervening and thus planning applications were granted, the cinema was bought and its closure announced.

Cyril Moore laced up the projectors for the last time on 24th March 1973, with Dick Emery's film "Ooh, You Are Awful", Frank Crane and his staff of fifteen were to be made redundant, after throwing a farewell party at the cinema after the last show. There were sad farewells, marking not only Cyril Moore's retirement, but also a goodbye to people such as Violet Goodway who had been head-cleaner at the Penn for thirty-four years.

Many of the cinema's fittings were sold. The projectors are alleged to have gone to India. Gordon Mintern returned and preserved the curtains and clock. They can now be seen at the Regal, Henley-on-Thames. The demolition men quickly knocked down the building and a new MacMarket went up on the site. (Now an International Stores).

There must be many ghosts that haunt the site and many memories of the cinema surviving in the area! For a suburban cinema it had some great times. For example in 1960 a midnight matinee had been presented to raise money for Boys Clubs. Richard Attenborough came along to introduce, in person, his film "I'm Alright Jack". It was an unfortunate choice of film as its political content led to a mighty row between B. T. Davis, the Birmingham accountant and businessman and Wolverhampton's Mayor, an engine driver who disliked the film's attitude towards the working class! But of such bizarre moments is the story of a local cinema made. The Penn proves that cinemas were not just bricks, mortar and electrical equipment; they were also the result of the personalities of the people who ran them and visited them.

## 18. The Clifton, Fallings Park

This cinema had the distinction of being the last to open in Wolverhampton and enjoyed a short life of only twenty-three years. It occupied a good site on the Cannock Road, which was one of several sites considered by the Clifton circuit for cinema building in the mid thirties. Plans drawn by Messrs. Satchwell and Roberts had been approved as early as March 1934, but the cinema actually built was the result of new plans drawn in 1936!

Plans drawn by Messrs. Satchwell and Roberts had been as early as March 1934, but the cinema actually built was the result of new plans drawn in 1936!

Approaching the cinema from the town centre it presented itself with a rather castle-like frontage as two octagonal towers seemed to grace each side of the flight of steps up to the three sets of swing doors. The large expanses of brickwork were plain but the three high vertical windows above the canopied entrance gave it a certain grace. Their leaded panes let light into the balcony foyer but there were no windows at the projection room floor level, nor in the sides of the cinema. Like several other cinemas by Satchwell and Roberts it expressed a great feeling of solidity.

As the building neared completion, Alex Tuck moved over from the Regal, Wednesfield to prepare for the opening. It was declared open on 24th October 1938.

The visitors were welcomed by Captain Clift, and the Mayor, Councillor Probert, performed the opening ceremony. This one time director of the Dunstall Cinema had previously opened the ABC during his year of office. The first film shown was *"Happy Landing"*.

Like the other Clifton cinemas it was provided with BTH equipment and one operator recalled that a mushroom shaped light fitting at one time obscured the operator's sight lines. The building accommodated 1186 patrons and looked to the large estates on each side of the Cannock Road to provide the custom. It provided some competition for the Dunstall cinema and even for the Regal, Captain Clift's own cinema in Wednesfield, but such was the industry's optimism at that time. Mr. Kenyon took over from Mr. Tuck just before the War and enjoyed a fairly long association with this cinema.

Graham Simmonds, who eventually became the Clifton's chief, began work there as a trainee in 1953. At the time it was still a busy place and queues could still be seen around the building. He recalls how spick and

36. The Staff of the Clifton, Fallings Park.

*(Photo: G. Simmonds Collection)*

## THE STAFF OF THE CLIFTON

**Back Row. Left to Right:** Mrs. J. Sayce, Cleaner; Mr. G. Simmonds, Ch. Projectionist; Mrs. L. Gough, Cleaner; Mr. T. Glover, Projectionist; Mr. T. Harley, Projectionist.

**Second Row:** Mrs. V. Howell, Chief Sales; Mrs. M. Gale, Cleaner; Mrs. E. Douglass, 2nd Projectionist; Mrs. M. Osborne, Cashier; Mrs. C. Austin, Cleaner.

**Front Row—Usherettes:** Mrs. D. Leadbeater; Mrs. E. Audsley; Miss H. Cottrill; Mrs. N. Wearing; Miss E. McCarthy; Mrs. D. Aston.

**Centre:** Mr. A. Goodwin, Theatre Foreman.

span the projection room had to be. For £1.50 a week he spent the first eighteen months polishing the floor. The pride and sense of purpose enjoyed by the cinema was soon to be eroded.

The Clifton did last long enough to enjoy a twenty-first birthday party in 1959. A special programme brochure was produced and *"Carry On Teacher"* was presented for the week commencing 25th October. For one *"Carry On"* film Charles Hawtry made a personal appearance at Fallings Park but I do not think it was on this occasion. The manager, Maxwell Gordon, later of the Clifton, Sedgley, expressed the hope that ".... you will continue to find many happy hours at this cinema during the years to come". However, its fortunes were rapidly declining.

As the decade closed, staff were reduced, bingo was briefly tried at afternoon sessions and the prospect of putting on wrestling was considered but rejected. At one time rumours circulated that an American firm was considering buying the premises from Midland Lease-holdings Ltd., who owned the place after Captain Clift's demise. The family clientele that had once come to the cinema had disappeared and the takings were often ridiculous.

The end came fairly abruptly. Some demolition contractors appeared — also spreading rumours about the closure of the Regal, Wednesfield, and not long afterwards the final show was announced. The last film was shown on 4th November 1961; *"Can Can"* starring Frank Sinatra and Shirley MacLaine, and after the National Anthem, Auld Lang Syne was played from the projection room. Demolition followed and the site has now been redeveloped as a Fine Fare supermarket.

The smell of fish and chips can no longer rise from the back row one night a week as the girls from the Ever Ready eat their tea and take in a film. The natives of Fallings Park have had to look further afield for entertainment in the swinging sixties and ever after.

## 19. Wolverhampton's Unbuilt Cinemas

In every Black Country town there must have been various proposals made regarding cinemas that never came to be built. It might be interesting to consider what might have happened in Wolverhampton and leave readers to imagine the similar examples that occurred throughout the conurbation. Perhaps thirty or forty cinemas were planned in the region that never materialised.

During the pre-First World War period the local architect Marcus Brown drew plans for at least two unbuilt cinemas. For George Lovatt he designed a cinema in 1912 that was to be built in Church Street, not far from the Picturedrome. When nothing came of it, Mr. Lovatt possibly fulfilled his dreams of cinema-proprietorship by running the Gem in Dudley for a short time. Marcus Brown also designed a small cinema that someone proposed building in Heath Town. A very attractive little cinema was planned by Frank Clark for a Mr. W. H. Maynard. This would have been built in Owen Road, Penn Fields, but unfortunately, nothing came of it.

Twenty years later at the height of the "craze" for building super-cinemas at least two were planned in Wolverhampton, but not built. A large fifteen hundred seater should have occupied Graisley Hill on the Penn Road and the Plaza, Tettenhall, should have been built at Newbridge. Both cinemas were planned by Roland Satchwell in 1935 for the Clifton Circuit. Both ran into delays in gaining planning approval although the Tettenhall cinema was approved on appeal. By early 1938 the land at Newbridge seems to have been sold to the Danilo Circuit and Mr. Hurley Robinson had drawn up some more plans. Again, nothing came of it. This gives some indication of the possible number of proposals that local circuits may have had for super-cinemas.

Even in recent times, proposals to build cinemas have

37. The Clifton, Fallings Park.
*(Photo: G. Simmonds Collection)*

caused interesting speculation. In 1966 the Classic Cinema Group talked about opening a brand new

Even in recent times, proposals to build cinemas have caused interesting speculation. In 1966 the Classic Cinema Group talked about opening a brand new purpose-built five hundred seater cinema as part of the Hammerson Group's new Wulfrun Centre. About the same time there was talk of a West Midlands Regional Film Theatre coming to Wolverhampton. When this did not materialise the Wolverhampton Film Society ventured in several schemes to build a local arts centre that would have included cinema facilities, none of which materialised.

The most incredible "cinema-that-never-was" story concerns a proposal to build a "drive-in-cinema". A Leicester based firm proposed opening Britain's first "drive-in" at Wolverhampton Racecourse. By October 1977 the scheme, including a forty foot screen and space for three hundred cars, had gained planning approval despite impending traffic problems and opposition from local residents. The idea made no further progress.

## Wednesfield

Heading eastwards from Wolverhampton along the old road to Lichfield one comes to the one-time village of Wednesfield. This community, with its fine Saxon name, at one time saw itself as quite remote and distinct from Wolverhampton. Circumstances conspired to foster this independence. For example, the twists and turns of the canal, and the Wolverhampton — Walsall railway line managed to cut off Wednesfield from the surrounding world and many amenities reached the town quite late in life. In recent times its Urban District Council bravely tried to fight the overspill advance of Big Brother Wolverhampton towards the fields of Ashmore Park. It can come as no surprise to find that such a place

supported two cinemas of great individuality and that these cinemas are much loved and remembered by those who lived in Wednesfield in the "good old days".

## 20. The Regal
*High Street*

Rather than deal with Wednesfield's cinemas chronologically let us consider the Regal first because it seems to be passionately remembered with the greater affection, and its story can be told in more detail. For many people it was the finest building in Wednesfield and in the mid-thirties was a symbol of the community's march into the modern world. The site, on the corner of the High Street was possibly the site of one of Wednesfield's early manor houses and was selected by Captain Clift and Leon Salberg for one of their early "Clifton" cinemas. Why the name Regal was adopted rather than "Clifton", I am not quite sure, although the "circuit" was still in its infancy and maybe each project was still named individually. Certainly each cinema was built by a separate company, in this case the Regal Cinema (Wednesfield) Ltd., but Captain Clift and Leon Salberg had the major financial interest in it.

The Wolverhampton building contractor, H. J. Amies & Sons erected the cinema, the first of several for Captain Clift and the plans were prepared by Roland Satchwell. Stage facilities were provided as well as luxurious accommodation for 1028 patrons. Like the later Cliftons it was equipped with BTH apparatus. As children came out of the Sunday School at the Parish Church, almost opposite the Regal, each week they counted the new brickwork to record the progress made by this huge new edifice.

In the Autumn of 1935 Alex Tuck came over to the new Regal to become the new manager. He had been at the Dunstall Cinema since April 1935, but had previous-

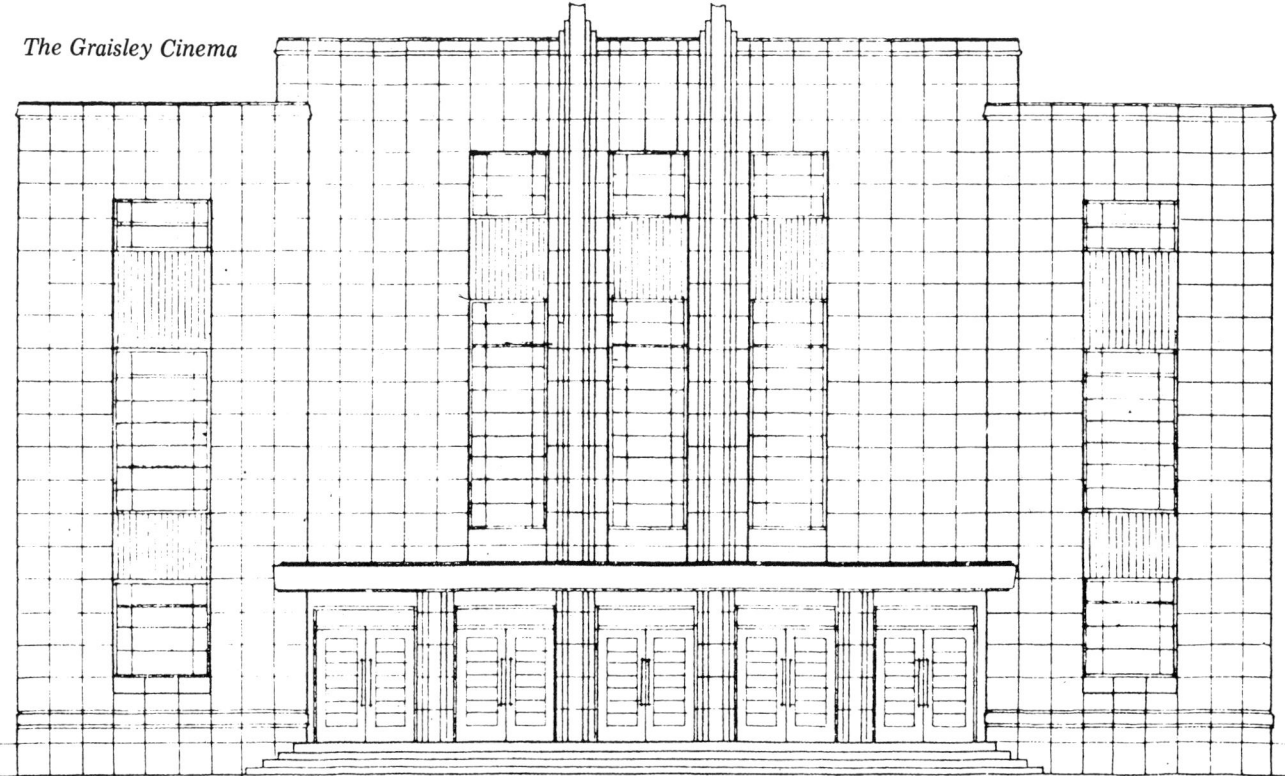

*The Graisley Cinema*

ly enjoyed a career in the industry that went back a quarter of a century. He had started work as a chocolate boy in a cinema in Selby owned by his father and had experience of most aspects of cinema work on the way up to management. He prepared the Regal for its official opening on 14th October 1935.

Unlike other cinemas that opted to open during the afternoon, the Regal chose to commence work at 7.30 p.m. that Monday night. It was an interesting evening. The feature film, Jack Hulbert and Fay Wray in *"Bulldog Jack"* plus supporting film, cartoon and Universal News were preceeded by events reflecting Captain Clift's sense of history. First of all, R. H. Morgan, the Stourbridge M.P. formally opened the cinema. He had recently been campaigning in Parliament for a reduction in Entertainment Tax, a cause dear to the heart of Captain Clift and the Cinema Exhibitors Association, of which he was an active member. Then none other than Waller Jeffs was asked to introduce a screening of two of his early films, one made in 1908 of *"Veterans of the Indian Mutiny"* and the other made in 1909 of the *"Stratford-On-Avon Shakespeare Festival"*. Mr. Jeffs was in his seventies and it was then thirty-five years since he brought his film shows to the Midlands, but he had recently become associated with Captain Clift and Leon Salberg by being manager of their newly acquired cinema in Stratford. It is appropriate that six years before his death he was invited back to the West Midlands to show this Wednesfield audience his early pioneering work.

The Regal was an immediate success in Wednesfield, faring much better than the other Clifton cinemas that opened in village-like communities already served by smaller, older independent cinemas, e.g. Sedgley and Coseley. Perhaps it was well served by its managers. Alex Tuck left after three years to open the Clifton at Fallings Park and then to become a circuit supervisor. His replacement, Mr. H. J. E. Davis, was the man who became indelibly associated with the Regal for the rest of its life. Like Alex Tuck he had entered the industry as a chocolate boy, working for Poole's Theatres Ltd. at Stourbridge and in Edinburgh. He worked on the last "Myriorama" there and on the first "talkie". He joined the Clifton Circuit in February 1937 as the Chief Operator at the new cinema in Lye and began to prepare for a managerial post.

His style of management was characterised by diligence, organisation and efficiency rather than charisma, but he was a practical man who could both appear in smart evening dress to see the patrons arrive, and who could understand the "electrics" and operating side of his cinema's life. During the war he organised many concerts for the benefit of several charities and during one Christmas season the Regal's stage facilities were enjoyed by a full blooded pantomime, *"Babes In The Wood"* featuring Della Neil as Robin Hood!

Mr. Davis was also at the Regal when the *"Great Nixon"* came to town. He was billed as "the world's master mind reader, astrologist and original blindfold wonder" and appeared at various Clifton cinemas. A

38. The Regal, Wednesfield.

*(Photo: Mrs. Charlesworth Collection)*

local publican, James Howe of the Angel, was asked to hide an article somewhere in Wednesfield. The Great Nixon, blindfolded, then walked through the town, followed by a growing procession, until he "found" it. In the evenings he performed his mind reading act on stage, between the films.

After the war, the Regal continued to be busy. Many local people have emphasised to me that its luxury, in particular its carpetted floors and warmth, were far more inviting than many a local home. Its doormen gave you the feeling you were entering an expensive hotel and yet it was truly "your" local cinema. Mr. Davis in immaculate evening dress and greased jet black hair always stood at the foot of the stairs to the balcony. Often, Harry Taylor, the chief operator, leaned on the radiator. Outside, the commissionaire, Albert Brookes, looked after the patrons. Albert Brookes became another well-remembered personality associated with the Regal. If he evicted some nuisance from the cinema, that nuisance would never succeed in entering the Regal again. Mrs. Benton and her fellow cleaners kept the place spotless, Albert maintained good behaviour!

Local community feeling ran high in the 1950's with the publication of a small broadsheet, "The Wednesfield News". As from April 1954 Mr. Davis made sure the Regal's programmes and special events such as children's painting competitions, were given publicity in this paper. In 1956 he organised a special 21st Anniversary Programme, presenting *"The Student Prince"* on Monday 15th October. (The 14th October, being a Sunday, only featured a one-day-only screening of *"The Red Badge of Courage"*).

The Regal seemed to be surviving. Its neighbouring Clifton cinema at Fallings Park had closed suddenly and the demolition men had been heard muttering "It's the Regal next!". However, Mr. Davis felt his cinema was "safe". Since Captain Clift's death, it had been in the hands of "Clifton Cinemas Management Ltd.". Unknown to Mr. Davis, Newbold Securities, the Solihull firm that had purchased and demolished the Clifton, Fallings Park, were also intending to do the same in Wednesfield.

The end came very quickly and at short notice. The "Wednesfield News" interviewed a shaken Mr. Davis in the office he had occupied for twenty-seven years, and on 17th March 1962, *"The Naked Edge"*, starring Gary Cooper had the honour of being the last film to be shown. It was followed by a party for the staff and then the Regal was dead. Albert Brookes looked after the place for a few weeks while various items were salvaged for use in other Clifton cinemas. For example, it seems that some of the seats went to the Alexandra, Lower Gornal.

The demolition men moved in, despite protests from the Wednesfield community. Ironically the new supermarket building that was erected on the site, now Fine Fare, was of roughly the same proportions as the once elegant and beautiful cinema.

## 21. The Ideal
### Rookery Street

Wednesfield's two cinemas were as alike as chalk and cheese! The Regal is the historian's dream: everyone remembers it, plenty of documentation concerning it survives and its birth and death can be clearly and precisely located. The Ideal is just the opposite; it is a historian's nightmare, putting a few facts together seems like constructing a dinosaur from a few random bones.

Ironically the building still stands, defiantly greeting travellers from Wolverhampton as they come into Wednesfield after crossing the Wyrley and Essington Canal. It is on the main road that abruptly swings into the High Street where the Regal once stood. Today it is Norton's Carpet Store and only a few remnants of the decor remind the visitor of its past.

In the nineteenth century the building was a chapel, built in 1852, and used by the Methodists until 1886. The building may have had a variety of uses in the following years but by the early twentieth century seems to have become some kind of public hall.

It has been impossible to pinpoint the exact date when the hall became a cinema. The earliest mention of it as the "Electric Theatre" appears in the Midland Evening News of 15th November 1912 when it is described as being "in business" and pursuing a policy of "Civility and the latest pictures". Advertisements in the same paper appear in January 1913 and the entertainment column states, "The new Picture House in Wednesfield has certainly "caught on" with the local people."

For most of its life this little cinema enjoyed the services of a local man named Joe Purshouse, known as "Joper". He started work at the cinema at the age of eight in 1917 and his father had worked there before that. At the time the cinema was owned by a Mr. Marchant and later a Mr. Aldridge but Joe's father effectively ran the place. Joe worked at Sidbotham's by day and at the cinema by night. He started by re-winding the films and doing jobs like fetching the comics and oranges for distribution at the children's matinees. The operator, George Ainsworth, taught Joe that side of the business.

As a silent cinema the audience entered the auditorium from the canal-end of the building and the screen was at the end nearest Rookery Street. Its proximity to the canal meant that it must have been one of the few cinemas where the patrons' entertainment was sometimes marred by the noise of canal boats chugging past!

About 1931 the cinema was acquired by John France, a building contractor, from Trench in Shropshire. It seems that this was when it became the "Ideal", and possibly John France had ambitious plans for rebuilding a larger and more luxurious cinema on the site. In the event The Ideal carried on showing silent films while Wednesfield's new "super-cinema", the Regal, was built a few hundred yards away. This was not a death blow to the little cinema as many people went to the Ideal at the beginning of the week for a cheap night out and then to the Regal at the end of the week. Even at the end of the week the Ideal took the "overspill" turned away by the Regal!

The Ideal was rebuilt towards the end of the thirties and turned into a sound cinema. The screen was now installed at the "canal end" and a porch and projection room built at the new "front" of the cinema. Two Kershaw Kalee 8 projectors provided the picture and Gyrotone equipment provided the sound. A raked floor and tip up seats added to the transformation, but it still only held about three hundred and fifty patrons.

It seems likely that John France died before the alterations were completed and the cinema was left in the hands of the trustees of his estate. His daughter, Maisie Withington was in charge but in reality Joe Purshouse still ran the place. During the War he often ran it virtually single-handed, sometimes staying up all night waiting for sound engineers to come over from Coleshill to look at the Gyrotone equipment when it went wrong.

At some stage the executors of the estate of John France sold the cinema to a Mr. Sankey, and in turn he sold it to William Severn, a waste paper merchant from Solihull. It remains a mystery why such a small local cinema continually found itself owned by proprietors from far afield. In William Severn's case it seemed that it

39. The Ideal, Wednesfield, surviving in 1982 as a carpet store.

*(Photo: Ned Williams)*

was the nearest cinema he could find that he could afford. He was fanatically interested in the cinema as a hobby and seemed obsessed with the idea of running a real cinema. He had bought some projection equipment at a house sale at Blythe Hall, Solihull after the death of a Mr. Bird, a one-time High Sheriff of Warwickshire. With this equipment and an organ, he built his own private cinema at his home. Somehow, this was not enough to satisfy him and his desire for a real cinema lead him to purchase the Ideal.

Joe Purshouse, and Mr. Britain, from the nearby fish shop, helped manage the place, and Mr. Severn, or his son, popped over whenever they could to keep a proprietorial eye on it. If technical troubles arose help was often forthcoming from the operating room at the Regal. In this way the Ideal survived into that difficult decade; the fifties. For a while it competed with the Regal by having details of its programmes printed in the

Joe Purshouse, and Mr. Britain, from the nearby fish shop, helped manage the place, and Mr. Severn, or his son, popped over whenever they could to keep a proprietorial eye on it. If technical troubles arose help was often forthcoming from the operating room at the Regal. In this way the Ideal survived into that difficult decade; the fifties. For a while it competed with the Regal by having details of its programmes printed in the little "Wednesfield News" but the announcements ceased in the summer of 1954. Hard times had come to the Ideal and as far as I can work out the last film was probably shown in the autumn of 1957. Mr. Severn, now in his sixties, suffered a long period of ill health but still believed his cinema could return to life.

In 1959 he bravely refurbished and partially re-equipped the place but during the summer of that year vandals broke in and wrought £500 worth of damage, slashed the new screen, stole the curtains and smashed heating and lighting fittings. The reopening that Mr. Severn had planned for that September never took place.

Just before the Regal closed in March 1962, the Ideal entered a brief new lease of life as a dance hall! Tommy Burton's Rock and Roll Group came over from Bilston to open the place and dancers jived on the raked floor. Tommy Burton went on to acquire fame at the key-board but the poor old Ideal could not survive as a place of entertainment. At least it has enjoyed a sedate retire-ment as a carpet store.

As sketchy as this outline of the cinema's life has turned out to be, one fact about the Ideal is known to every proud inhabitant of Wednesfield. This fact, now legend, concerns the nickname by which the Ideal was always known: "The Smack".

## 22. The Tivoli
*Hall Street*

The third site of cinematic entertainment in Wednesfield is even more obscure. Apparently a building in Hall Street was used for showing films before the First World War and several people have referred to it as "The Tivoli" but the only written evidence I have discovered of its existence is a small entry in "The Bioscope" for 2nd June 1910. It is described as having opened during the previous week and, under Bert Dawes'

management, was bringing films and variety to the people of Wednesfield. Here it is called the Palace Electric Theatre, but I have never heard it called by that name in the village. Whether it continued to show films when the "new" electric theatre opened in Rookery Street, I do not know.

## The Cinemas of Bilston

Today, Bilston is part of the Borough of Wolverhampton. In October 1980 Bilston's blast furnace, Lizzie, was ceremoniously demolished, and a symbol of the town's past as an important iron and steel-making community vanished from the Black Country landscape. Two centuries earlier, Iron-mad Wilkinson had brought iron-making to the area and built furnaces by the canal near Bradley. Bilston had developed and prospered in a way that reflected the identity of the Black Country — man's exploitation of coal, iron and labour. Its products became world famous: cast iron baths, domestic cookers, etc.

The market towns that had been important before the Industrial Revolution often acquired Borough status long before the new industrial communities like Bilston, but travelling showmen recognised the size of their population and identified a potential audience waiting for entertainment. To Bilston came Professor Wood and his son and their story unfolds in the following account of Bilston's cinemas, along with other Bilstonians who brought light and shadows to the town's screens for about half a century. Bilston no longer has its giant steelworks and Bilston no longer has an operating cinema.

## 23. The Town Hall and The Drill Hall

The principle room in Bilston Town Hall was used by Professor Wood for his winter tours of industrial Britain from the turn of the century onwards. He presented demonstrations of mesmerism and phrenology and advised the audience on their health, while his son, Thomas Reay Wood, projected elaborate magic lantern slides and short films. Entertainment gradually supplanted the lectures and by 1909 Professor Wood advertised his show as a "Musical and Pictorial Combination" and promised that the films "will delight and please you ..... a thousand laughs in ninety minutes." Elaborate heavy generating equipment had to be set up to project the films and it is implied that sound was sometimes provided with early phonographic synchronisation. To put on such a show on a travelling basis must have been quite hectic and perhaps the "coming to rest" in Bilston, with the passing of the Cinematograph Act, was quite a blessing. From 1910 onwards Joseph Wood and Son leased the room for film shows on a regular basis.

For the next decade, the room at the Town Hall was advertised as "Wood's Palace" and a sign to that effect appeared on the exterior of the building. The shows continued until 1921 and ceased with the opening of the new "Wood's Palace" just across the road in Lichfield Street.

After the passing of the Cinematograph Act a licence was issued to the Drill Hall in Mount Pleasant, almost next door to the Theatre Royal. I assume occasional film

79

shows were presented there up until the First World War but I have been unable to locate any details concerning them. The Drill Hall is now the Rising Star Club and still brings live entertainment to the centre of Bilston.

## 24. The Electric Palace/The Grand
*Church Street*

The little cinema in Church Street, now the furniture shop of J. Forrester & Sons Ltd., was Bilston's most short lived cinema. It was opened about 1913, by a Mr. Hallet, to provide an income for his three single daughters after his death. The Bilston Electric Theatre Ltd. was registered in May 1913 with a capital of £2000. Although it only held about three hundred and fifty people, it had a small balcony with an operating box underneath and was typical of the small "electric theatres" opened in such premises just before the First World War.

In the autumn of 1919 it was taken over by Joseph Wood & Son who ran it until the spring of 1921, although it was only across the road from their own shows in the Town Hall. At the same time their new Palace was being completed just round the corner of Lichfield Street, but they relinquished their shows in the Electric Palace about six months before their new cinema opened while taking a lease on the Alhambra a

few hundred yards down the High Street! The little cinema was acquired by J. Forrester and adapted for use as a furniture sale room. At first the appearance of the building altered very little but now there are very few traces of the furniture shop once having been a cinema. Some cinemas closed just after the War when their licences were no longer renewed as they failed to meet safety regulations and this may have been another factor in its demise.

## 25. The Alhambra

It is interesting that Bilston's other pre-World War One cinema, the Alhambra, is still standing today although its "temporary closure" seems ever more likely to remain permanent. It probably opened before the Electric Palace but the precise date of its opening is lost in the general obscurity surrounding the rapid expansion of the cinema interests of Wolverhampton's Thomas Jackson. It may well have opened on Thursday 7th November 1912 with the show, *"On the Brink of the Abyss"*. This is the earliest show for which I have found an advertisement.

The auditorium, on a single raked floor, held about six hundred patrons but looking at its brickwork today it may have undergone several alterations. The entrance onto Bilston's High Street was separate from the

40. Church Street: On the right; The Electric Theatre, and on the left; Bilston Town Hall, temporary home of Wood's Palace.

*(Photo: Wolverhampton Libraries)*

41. The Alhambra, photographed on its re-opening after refurbishing in the mid-fifties.

*(Photo: Mr. and Mrs. Woodroffe)*

auditorium and formed the central part of a parade of shops, lacking the grandeur of a facade appropriate to a cinema.

Thomas Jackson's financial difficulties followed the First World War, but when Joseph Wood and Sons acquired the lease of the Alhambra and began showing their programmes from September 1921 onwards, the freehold was already in somebody else's hands. Although not really very far from the Town Hall, the Electric, or the new Wood's Palace, that end of Bilston High Street must have served a different community because the Woods continued to operate the Alhambra until their lease expired in the Spring of 1927, by which time they were building their new replacement for it on the opposite side of the street.

After 1927 the Alhambra began a long series of changes of ownership designed to send the cinema historian crazy! Among those who showed films there were H. J. Whittaker, T. A. Webb, and E. K. Hawtin of Cannock. Mr. Hawtin acquired various Black Country cinemas during the thirties. At a time when the super-cinema was making its presence felt he seemed to be building up a small empire of relatively unimposing halls. However he took his role of cinema magnate seriously and for example, in July 1937 he, his wife and

his daughters took the staff of the Alhambra and the Forum, Cannock, on a Sunday outing to Aberystwyth at his own expense! Ironically, there had been talk of replacing the Alhambra with a modern super-cinema in the mid thirties but it had come to nothing.

The changes in ownership, or lessee, continued during the forties, by the end of which it seems that the freehold was in the hands of H. J. Barlow of Wednesbury. Early in 1950 Sidney Saunders took on a lease to run the Alhambra. He had resigned as manager of the Essoldo in Penge to come to Bilston. Perhaps the Alhambra failed to realise his dreams! About two years later it seems that he relinquished the lease and Mr. Barlow sold the cinema to Mr. and Mrs. Woodroffe.

The Alhambra now took on a new lease of life. It was refurbished by Modernisation Ltd. With its smart interior and the excellent Western Electric sound the Woodroffes felt that they could put on the best shows in Bilston. Even modernised inside, the Alhambra was an old building and featured problems like damp. A stream ran under the floor near the screen and when its beautiful clear waters rose they needed pumping out now and again. However, Mrs. Woodroffe was ably helped in running the Alhambra by several dedicated staff who had survived the various changes of proprietor.

42. The Alhambra. The interior after refurbishing by Modernisation Ltd. To keep the place smart the cleaners, Mrs. Winsper, Mrs. Wilde and Mrs. Fellows scrubbed the floor regularly with very hot water.

*(Photo: Mr. and Mrs. Woodroffe)*

During the fifties, the Alhambra had still been a busy little cinema but by the beginning of the sixties life had become much more difficult and new business was sought. First of all bingo was tried on three evenings a week, but by 1964 the Odeon could provide much grander facilities for bingo. Asian films were screened on Sunday afternoons for the Indian community. The Woodroffes probably gave up showing English language films towards the end of 1963, out-living the Savoy by a short time but succumbing before the Odeon.

It was sold to a group of Indian businessmen and when the licence became due for renewal in 1964 it was in the name of Leslie Taff of the Regal, Darlaston. He had been associated with screening Indian films at the Regal, but apparently did not in fact renew the Alhambra's licence. Instead, the cinema was used for private shows and to gain admission, one had to be a member of the Eastern Film Society. In August 1968 the Express and Star reported that complaints had been made about the discomfort, dirt and dampness at the Alhambra. However, J. S. Sidhu, for the lessees protested that it was clean and had just been redecorated despite the fact that it was only open three nights a week.

Open on a part-time basis for private shows of Indian films, the Alhambra limped into the seventies to become Bilston's last surviving cinema. Since then it has been "temporarily closed" awaiting refurbishing. Although I have heard rumours that it could reopen I find it difficult to believe it will ever happen. The building still exists while this enigmatic question mark hangs over its fate, and in April 1982 a planning application was submitted to the council to turn the building into a clothes shop.

## 26. Wood's Palace/The Palace/The Odeon
*Lichfield Street*

As stated previously, while the Woods were taking on the Alhambra, in 1921, they were also busily putting the finishing touches to their brand new "Palace" in Lichfield Street. They had always called their shows in the Town Hall, "Wood's Palace", but the new building was going to be truly worthy of the name. It was the top show place in Bilston.

I imagine that it would have been built earlier but for the intervention of the First World War. The War created shortages of labour and material and restrictions on the kind of building work that could be undertaken. There were also doubts being expressed about the continuation of the new medium's popularity, and therefore the new hall was equipped as a fine theatre as well as a cinema, although its magnificent stage facilities were relatively little used.

Mr. Hurley Robinson was engaged as the architect and it was built by J. Hickin and Sons at a cost of £30,000. The interior design was by Val Prince. To Lichfield Street it presented a beautiful Renaissance-style facade, and the front elevation was treated in white faience. A cafe and billiard hall shared the facade but these have since ceased operations. Even so the entire frontage still has a unity that makes it an impressive part of the street scene.

The interior designer was carried away, filling the great arch-roofed auditorium with luxurious colour and atmosphere. Val Prince himself wrote,

"The colour schemes are strong, but I feel harmonious — orange, black, violet and blue, toned with a pearly irridescence. The wall panels are erratic, but, I hope, not aggressive ...... on either side of the proscenium are painted panels emblematic of song and dance, strong in colour, but designed to stand amongst the brilliance surround of orange. The seating, in rich purple, and painted draw-curtains in the same tone, pulls the whole together."

Fourteen hundred tip up seats were provided in the stalls and balcony, both fully raked and the screen was set back behind the proscenium. An orchestra pit was provided to accommodate up to twenty musicians and dressing rooms were provided off stage for theatrical use. With everything provided on such a splendid scale it is interesting to note that the original operating room was small and almost inadequate. The hall's own generators were supplied by the E.C.C. of Wolverhampton, and a Kalee Indomitable projector and a Powers No. 6 provided the shows for many years.

Messrs. Wood were described as "plucky promoters", and Kine Weekly stated that it opened, "at a time when others are holding back". The opening took place on 17th November 1921 and the ceremony was performed by Councillor Haddock, who was presented with a souvenir key by the contractor. On stage were the oldest shareholder in the venture, Professor Wood in his mid-seventies, and the youngest, his grand-daughter Angela, who was one year old exactly! The Professor said that many people had said that they were making it too fine for Bilston, but he thought that Bilston people deserved as fine a palace as anybody in the world. The first public show followed later that evening with *"The Old Nest".*

The orchestra, under the director of Mr. Salisbury soon acquired a reputation for good music at Woods Palace and it must have been an impressive cinema to visit during the silent era. A larger screen was installed in July 1930, larger than anything in neighbouring Wolverhampton at the time and then the "talkies" arrived. BTH sound equipment was installed at Woods Palace, and to improve the acoustics of the hall celotex panels were hung on the walls over Val Prince's murals. By the time the cinema celebrated its twelfth birthday in 1933 it had been refurbished throughout. The Mayors of Wolverhampton and Bilston came along to a birthday party and screening of *'The Good Companions".*

Professor Wood had long since retired to North Wales and had died in 1927 before the advent of sound. His son Thomas Wood always maintained a presence at the Palace despite his busy civic life and the fact that day to day running of his cinema interests had to be delegated to managers. In 1936 "T.R." decided to retire, and on 29th August 1936 the cinema, along with his other halls, were leased to Cyril Joseph. As from September it simply became "The Palace" and very quickly the lease was transferred to Oscar Deutsch and the cinema became part of the Odeon circuit. Traditions die hard, and even as the Bilston Odeon, it continued to be known as "Wood's". The building itself underwent little change and continued to thrive as a result of capable management by Billy Tyrer who had long association with Black Country cinemas

# Wood's Palace
## Bilston.
### Tel. 25.

43. & 44. Woods Palace at the end of the twenties. The decoration on this page comes from the handbills produced to announce the coming of sound. The talkies were introduced to Bilston on 14th October 1929 with *"On Trial"* starring Pauline Frederick. A British Filmophone system was installed, later replaced with B.T.H. equipment. Note acoustic panels covering the side-wall murals!    *(Photo: Collection of Angela Bird)*

including service in Oldbury and Halesowen.

Billy Tyrer organised successful war time Sunday concerts in his Odeon that made good use of its stage facilities and throughout the forties it was still Bilston's number one cinema as its place on the circuit guaranteed good films relatively early in their release.

When the twenty-one year lease expired the Rank Organisation exercised their option to renew it and in the October that year, 1957, they installed £2000 worth of automatic projection equipment. The small operating room in which Reg Lloyd, the chief operator in the thirties, had struggled to do his best was at last enlarged to a reasonable size.

Only seven years later the closure of the Odeon as a cinema was announced. The last film was shown on 22nd February 1964 and it was "Heavens Above", starring Peter Sellers. Conversion for use as a Bingo Hall was put in hand immediately and the Top Rank Bingo Club opened on 5th March. The opening was performed by Pat Astley, and hundreds had to be turned away!

The freehold still belonged to Woods Picture Halls, but in 1971, the Rank Organisation made a deal involving five properties (which included the Dunstall Odeon) and not only was their lease terminated, but the freehold itself was sold to the Hutchinson group, operating as Surewin Bingo. For a decade it has survived, the exterior has been repainted, but the auditorium when I last visited it, still had an atmosphere laden with the cinema's history. The "W" monogram in the ornamental plaster work, gold on a blue background, still dominates the proscenium arch and the staff talked about dusty old volumes on phrenology and medicine which had recently been found in a haunted office. A few days later after I had laughed about the idea of Professor Wood's ghost still patrolling the cinema, I came across an article in the Express and Star for 17th January 1964 announcing the closure. The article added that the cinema had "a long standing reputation for being haunted".

Although it still stands as a monument to the Woods, father and son, I would like to think that others who gave loyal service to the cinema could also be remembered. Some kind of record could be claimed by Sally Price who started work at the Palace as an usherette when it opened in 1921 and gave almost fifty years unbroken service, including work as projectionist and later cashier, until her retirement in March 1971. Within her working life many other entire cinemas had come and gone!

Postscript

At the time of going to press Woods Palace has closed for extensive refurbishing by United Leisure. It will reopen as the Cascade Bingo and Social Club.

## 27. The Theatre Royal
*Mount Pleasant*

The Theatre Royal opened in 1902 and only became a "proper" cinema in 1932, so the reader may wonder why an account of its history appears apparently out of chronological order. The reason is that the history of entertainment in Bilston revolves around the development of the Wood empire. It so happens that the

Theatre Royal was acquired by Wood's Picture Halls for the sum of £3000 in 1924. In other words, they bought the theatre half way between opening their two purpose-built cinemas; the Palace and the Savoy.

Let us go back to the theatre's beginning. It was built on the site of an earlier theatre, at the time when Music Hall was enjoying its heyday. The proprietor, Mr. H. Battersby, called his new hall the Theatre Royal as, in 1902, Edward VII's coronation had made such names rather popular. Nearly seven hundred people could be accommodated in the stalls and balcony, the latter shaped like a huge horse-shoe in the style more associated with theatres than cinemas.

After the passing of the Cinematograph Act, E. C. Jazon acquired a kine licence and films were introduced between the variety acts. About 1912 it was called, for a short time, "The Royal Hippodrome and Picture House" but variety and drama still filled the bills. Strong melodrama was popular in Bilston, but touring Shakespearian productions also appeared.

It was closed for a time in 1924 when Thomas Wood acquired it, but reopened on Boxing Day of that year with a review called "Cheer Up". At the time, variety acts occasionally supported the films at the Palace, but, as described in the chapter on Thomas Wood, he was no stranger to the live theatre and already had many contacts in that business. He was also a patron of the local Bilston Operatic Society and as from 1927, they also began to use the Royal for their annual shows. Thomas Wood installed Mr. A. Holland, the man who had produced "Cheer Up", as his first manager. Under his management the Royal continued its theatrical career with great success until the advent of the "talkies" stole the patrons of live entertainment.

The Royal closed for a time in 1932 but was slightly rebuilt and refurbished with a view to reopening as a cinema. A BTH sound system was installed and Ross projectors were mounted behind the screen. Back projection was considered quite a novelty, although "ray-less" pictures had been seen earlier in Wolverhampton and Dudley. Its short life as a cinema began with a presentation of James Whale's "Frankenstein", starring Boris Karloff, probably chosen to continue the tradition of melodrama rather than to celebrate the Dudley-born film-maker's success.

Four years later in August 1936, the Theatre Royal was leased to Cyril Joseph's "Astel Pictures" and it soon reverted to theatre. About 1941, Mr. Joseph transferred Jack Riskit from the Palace, Wednesbury, to the position of manager at the Royal.

Jack Riskit, born Jack Evans, was a remarkable man. He had once been a Music Hall entertainer performing a high wire gymnastic act. Now in his sixties, he was a popular manager at the Royal, both with the public, whom he usually greeted in the foyer, and the performers who came to Bilston. The latter included such stars as Max Bygraves, Tommy Trinder, and Hylda Baker. Jack Riskit retired in 1953 and died in Bilston two years later.

Towards the end of his career he had seen the theatre encounter hard times. By the fifties, even "Jane" of the Daily Mirror, and nude shows such as "Fig Leaves and Fun" and "Bearskins and Blushes" could not pack the

45. Mount Pleasant: on the extreme left; the Drill Hall, in the centre; the Theatre Royal.

*(Photo: Wolverhampton Libraries)*

auditorium. Occasionally repertory companies visited the theatre, and pantomimes, circuses, and the Operatic Society's shows provided some successes, but Astel Pictures must have been quite relieved when the lease expired in 1957. They were certainly not interested in renewing it and Thomas Wood's son, Reay Wood, announced to the press that the theatre would not re-open after its usual summer closure.

The Royal was put up for sale by auction but failed to reach its reserve price. Eventually the local authority bought it and towards the end of 1961 the building was demolished. The site is now a car park. After the demolition, Councillor Beards told the Public Works Committee that nobody had regretted its passing. Surely someone must have felt nostalgia when recalling its theatrical history, and a few perhaps remembered those rear projected pictures.

## 28. The Savoy
*High Street*

As we have seen already, Messrs. Wood expanded their film showing empire to the other end of the High Street with their acquisition of a lease on the Alhambra. This lease expired in the spring of 1927, but by then Thomas Wood had already made plans to continue his company's

presence in that part of Bilston.

In the November of 1926 Mr. Hurley Robinson had drawn up plans for a new Alhambra to be built on a site on the opposite side of the road to the old one. He produced a far less imposing plan than he had drawn up for the Palace. In fact, he followed the Alhambra's tradition of hiding the auditorium well behind an entrance foyer that formed a central part of a parade of shops. Impressive columns guarded a small vestibule between numbers 45 and 49 High Street and this gave access to the two pairs of swing doors that led to a long main entrance hall. The auditorium held only seven hundred and fifty patrons. There was no circle but the four rows of seats furthest from the screen were higher than the rest of the hall and were reached via a separate entrance. The front rows were raked upwards towards the screen to improve viewing. It had similarities therefore with the Regent, Dudley, planned at about the same time, suggesting a fashion for the "stadium" style.

Mr. Hurley Robinson improved on Woods Palace in one respect: a more generous operating room was planned situated above the pay box and that long entrance hall. The latest Kalee machines were installed in it. The orchestra pit held five performers and a deep stage was provided. All this was built by J. Hickin & Sons of Willenhall, the contractors who had built the

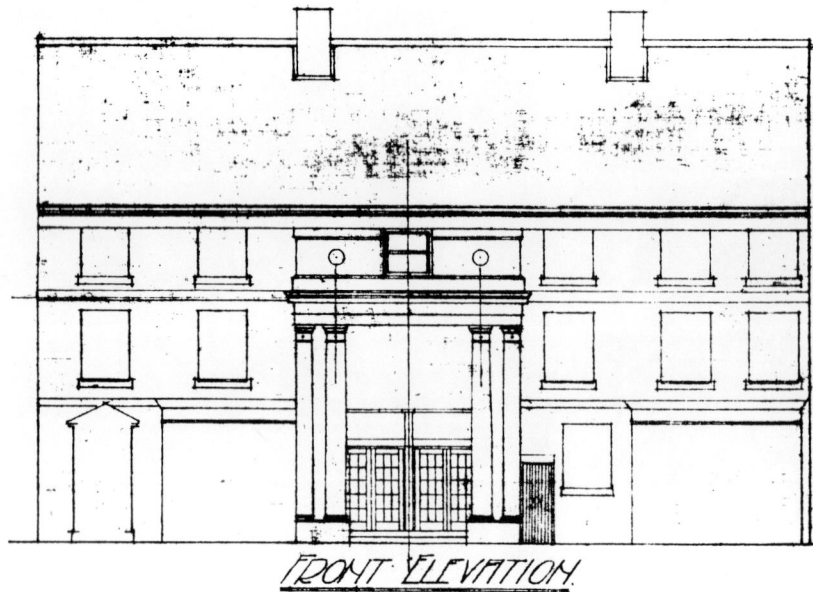

FRONT ELEVATION

The front elevation of the Savoy, from Hurley Robinson's plans. Only the extreme right hand corner of this building now exists and can be recognized from this drawing.

Palace. The only problem that remained was what to call the new cinema as the old Alhambra was going to continue using that name. Thomas Wood organised a competition in which future patrons had to select their favourite name and by this process the cinema became the Savoy.

The Savoy opened on 10th October 1927 and the ceremony was performed by the seven year old Angela Wood, who had been carried on to the stage of Wood's Palace by her grandfather on her first birthday. Thomas Wood spoke of his regret that the Professor had not lived to see the completion of the Savoy. Councillor W. M. Hughes, chairman of the Urban District Council lent a civic presence to the proceedings. The first film shown was *"Remember"*, a story based on a song by Irving Berlin.

The silent film era was coming to a close and the Savoy, along with the other Wood's Picture Halls, was converted to sound, using the B T H system. It also shared their fate in 1936 when they were all leased to Cyril Joseph for the next twenty-one years. Mr. Joseph's company, Astel Pictures, ran the Savoy, the Theatre Royal and Bradley's cinema, until that lease expired. In the case of the Savoy, this was for the larger part of its life.

Thus, in August 1957, the Savoy returned to the fold and Reay Wood, Thomas Wood's son, found himself running it in the hope that a buyer would materialise. The proprietors of the Alhambra had taken the opportunity to acquire the Forum, Bradley, but no-one seemed keen to acquire the Savoy. Presumably as an economy, the Savoy ceased advertising in the local press in 1959 and in the July of that year, the Express and Star reported that the building was for sale. Reay Wood was helped by his manager, Reg Lloyd, who had worked there since leaving the operating box at Woods Palace where he had been a well-liked "chief". The cinema outlived him and towards the end of its life it was run by Mr. Fullwood, the chief operator. It seems that the Savoy limped on until June 1962.

Once sold, the building was demolished to make way

for a Tesco supermarket, but even today, a remnant of Mr. Hurley Robinson's building can be seen clinging to the edge of the supermarket. As a cinema it lacked the dignity and prestige of Wood's Palace, and the longevity and idiosyncrasy of the Alhambra. However, it did have a nickname, "the Savvy" and this suggests that it meant something personal to its patrons and deserves to be remembered.

### 29. The Queen's Picture House, later known as The Forum
*Salop Street, Bradley*

One last cinema must be included in our survey of Bilston, but as it was really in the village of Bradley it had more in common with the cinemas in the areas I have chosen to call the "Central Villages" of the Black Country. In other words, it served a distinct and separate community from its counterparts nearer the centre of Bilston. However, while its patrons may have been local people, for most of its existence its ownership linked its history with that of Bilston's cinemas.

The original proprietor was a man called Ernest Hall and the building was erected by Messrs. Crewe of Dudley, at the same time as Wood's Palace was being built. The Queen's opened before the Palace but was probably far enough away to avoid any feeling of competition. The South Staffordshire Times exclaimed,

"The Town which has no cinema is out of date. Bradley is now abreast of the times and on Monday night a commodious cinema is to be opened within its borders".

The first show began at 6.30 p.m. on 17th October 1921, featuring Madge Titheradge and C. M. Hallard in *"His Story"*. The supporting programme included Charlie Chaplin's *"Shoulder Arms"*, Pathe News and the first episode of a serial, *"The Invisible Hand"*. Prices were 5d, 9d and 1/-, which I suggest were rather high, even if all six hundred seats were upholstered, and the lofty auditorium enjoyed the wonder of electric lighting and good ventilation! For 1/-, patrons could sit

86

in the small "balconette" and the cheapest seats, although upholstered were only benches. Later, when the seating was improved, the cinema's capacity was reduced to about three hundred and fifty. A small orchestra accompanied films at the Queen's, not quite on the scale of Wood's Palace, but grand enough for Bradley!

Towards the end of the twenties the cinema was acquired by Wood's Picture Halls and thus, when sound arrived, BTH equipment was installed, as in their other cinemas. From 1936 onwards it was leased to Cyril Joseph's Astel Pictures and in his hands, a new foyer was added to the original building and it became the Forum.

When Cyril Joseph's lease expired in 1957 the Forum was acquired by Mr. and Mrs. Woodroffe of the Alhambra. They redecorated the inside of the cinema and put in a new screen and reopened with a Tommy Steele film. Ironically, the Forum seems to have ceased advertising in the local press at about this time, but perhaps this was a realistic reflection of how such cinemas were used. Nobody travelled from far afield to an obscure second-run cinema, but if the community in the immediate vicinity supported your venture you could be a success. The Woodroffe's enjoyed this kind of very local success both in Bradley and in Princes End at a time when other cinemas felt their audience had deserted them for commercial television. A second run film could fill the Forum provided it had plenty of action.

When the audience figures did begin to decline in the sixties, bingo was introduced for half the week. The Forum ceased showing films altogether some time during the summer of 1964, although Mrs. Woodroffe continued to renew the cinematograph licence and the equipment was not removed immediately. In August 1964 about fifty young people, led by Bilston Grammar School pupil, Linda Bayliss, converged on the cinema in a demonstration to demand its reopening. Mrs. Woodroffe responded by explaining that bingo was played five nights a week and a dance was held on one night. Monday night was free and could possibly be used for a youth club, showing films when available.

I do not think anything came of this and the Forum has been whole-heartedly devoted to bingo ever since. Mr. and Mrs. Woodroffe retired in the early seventies and the club is now operated by Jarglen Ltd.

46. The Forum, Bradley, 1981. The original entrance has been bricked up, but its position is still clearly visible. The new entrance, still in use, is thought to have been added after 1937.

*(Photo: Ned Williams)*

WOOD'S PICTURES.
WEEK COMMENCING MONDAY, OCTOBER 17th, 1921.

PALACE, BILSTON.
Mon., Tues., Wed.,
THE EDGE OF YOUTH.
Five part Drama.
TWO LITTLE URCHINS, Episode 4.

Thurs., Fri., Sat.,
THE BROKEN ROAD.
An Anglo-Indian Drama.
SHERLOCK HOLMES, Episode 5.

ALHAMBRA, BILSTON.
Mon., Tues., Wed.,
WITH ALL HER HEART.
A Powerful Drama in Six Parts.
ELMO THE FEARLESS, Episode 11.

Thurs., Fri., Sat.,
FACE AT THE WINDOW.
A Six-part Melodrama.
BRIDE 13, Episode 6.

QUEEN'S PICTURE HOUSE, BRADLEY.
PROGRAMME FOR THE OPENING, MONDAY, OCTOBER 17th, at 6.30 p.m.
MADGE TITHERADGE and C. M. HALLARD in –
HIS STORY.
CHARLIE CHAPLIN in SHOULDER ARMS.
FIRST EPISODE of the Great Serial: THE INVISIBLE HAND.        PATHE GAZETTE

Thursday, October 20th: MALLA TALBOT in
THE PRICE OF INNOCENCE.
Supported by SYD CHAPLIN (Charlie's Brother) in the SUBMARINE PIRATE.
PATHE GAZETTE and PICTORIAL.
Note Times of Commencing.– Monday and Saturday, 6.30 and 8.30; Tuesday, Wednesday, Thursday and Friday, continuous from 7 to 10.  Prices:– 5d., 9d., and 1 -.

47. The Cinema de Luxe, its facade buried beneath the current promotion!

*(Photo: National Film Archive)*

## Introduction

Walsall occupies a position in the north-eastern corner of the Black Country, corresponding to Wolverhampton in the north-west. Like Wolverhampton, it has a background and history that slightly separates it from the Black Country, but industrial development and the patterns of urban growth have united it with the area where the presence of the Ten Yard Seam was more obvious. In this section of the survey the cinemas of Walsall itself will be considered first, followed by surveys of Bloxwich, Willenhall, Darlaston and Wednesbury. I realise that Wednesbury, unlike the other places, is now in the Metropolitan Borough of Sandwell but I have felt no obligation to be a slave to the Boundary Commissioners!

With Pat Collins' connections with Walsall and Bloxwich it would be very surprising if his fairground bioscope shows did not play a part in bringing the earliest film shows to this corner of the Black Country. Film shows were also to be found in public halls. For example, for six days in January 1903 a show was put on in Walsall Town Hall. The drama-feature was *"The Sand Man"*, but it was supported by colour film of the Delhi Durbar. Unfortunately the contemporary advertisements do not reveal who was presenting the show. Professor Wood certainly came to Willenhall and Bloxwich and so may have come to Walsall, but usually mentioned himself in the advertising! A press report indicates that the show was popular, but possibly not particularly unusual. We will probably never know who showed the first film in Walsall.

Thus while the Cinematograph Bill was becoming law in 1909, films were already familiar to the people of Walsall. Messrs. Melville and Stuart put on shows, with piano accompaniment by Selwyn Hay, at the Town Hall, from Christmas 1909 through to the New Year. Films had already been presented at the Imperial and, although not a purpose-built cinema, the Imperial has the strongest claim to being Walsall's first cinema by probably being the first to operate with a kine licence.

From then on Walsall's cinemas developed on similar lines to other Black Country towns, with the Palace and De Luxe opening near the town centre before the First World War. They were joined by the Grand's defection from theatre to films, and by comrades in the "suburbs" at Caldmore Green and Bloxwich. The Picture House, which had sister cinemas in Wolverhampton, Willenhall and Wednesbury was delayed by the War and problems arising out of a site so close to the waters of Walsall's mighty river, the Tame. For a cinema built above a river it, and its successors, were strangely cursed by fire!

Although A.B.C. acquired four halls in the town and set about replacing Her Majesty's Theatre with the Savoy, an excellent example of the large 1930's super-cinema, the "modern" style never quite arrived in Walsall as in other towns of comparable size. Oscar Deutsch did not build an Odeon there and the Clifton

circuit built nothing closer than the Rosum at Leamore. Nevertheless, by the end of the thirties, six cinemas flourished within the fairly compact centre of the town, plus others within easy reach.

Writing about her cinema going in Walsall, Eileen Stables recalls:

"I can still vividly remember the happy hours I spent with a friend during the Second World War at the cinemas of Walsall. Practically every night saw us at the "flicks" and neither our school work nor morals ever seemed to suffer.

As the Palace has long since closed, it can now be said that I had a relative there who was an usherette who let us in, via the fire doors, free of charge, in the absence of the manageress. Being a cinema that changed its programmes three times a week, i.e. Monday, Thursday and Sunday, and showing rather ancient films, that was our entrance to three trips of Hollywood fantasy, and how we thrived on it. Her two complimentary tickets to the Classic or the Savoy provided us with two more shows.

In those days it was a continuous performance and many was the time we went in at 2.00 p.m. and watched the wartime classics through three times (the relation bringing us a sandwich at 5.00 p.m.). Our signal for the "free admission" was to stand outside Taylors Record Shop in the Old Square and watch the little window, high above the foyer (if one could call it that at the Palace, for let's face it — it was pretty low on the list — just one above the Classic). When my cousin's head appeared at the window, we would shoot round to the fire doors and into another world.

The Classic "De Luxe" let us use the free pass, but we were never very happy there, the fact that we had been told it was infested with mice may have had something to do with it. As the pass took us upstairs, we had a brave feeling that maybe the rodents wouldn't have the audacity to invade that hierarchy. I distinctly remember seeing the great Bing Crosby in *"Bells of St. Mary's"* at the Classic.

How strange it seems now that one could walk into a cinema in those days half way through a film, immediately get engrossed, watch round to the exact word you caught as you sat down and then get up and say "Come on, this is where we came in".

Nowadays I never cease to wonder how two young girls used to walk through a blacked-out town, full of GI's, Dutch soldiers and other allied troops, up the Birchills Hill, and never have a care in the world, no muggings in those days. If Antonio and his hot potato machine happened to be outside the Grand (before the fire) we would, if funds permitted, buy a hot potato each to eat on the way home. They were like nectar. Only one night we were scared, that was after seeing *"Maria Marten and the Murder in the Red Barn"*. We ran past the iron foundry in Birchills Street that night!

As we got older and the war finished, we graduated to boy friends. Then it was the New Picture House on the Bridge or the very elite Savoy. Of course the boy-friend worth cultivating was the one that took you "upstairs in the one and nines". That carpet on the staircase was sheer luxury. And how strange it now seems that every cinema in town could leave the "stills" in glass cases all day and night and they remained intact. To be given a spare still was like receiving a medal, to be filed away with the weekly Picturegoer."

No doubt the cinema-goers of Willenhall, Darlaston and Wednesbury could equally vividly recall that "golden-age". Now, in 1982, only the ABC (former Savoy) remains in business in an area inhabited by over a quarter of a million people.

Walsall

### 1. The Imperial
*Darwall Street*

To the Imperial goes the honour of first showing films in Walsall on a regular basis, following the passing of the Cinematograph Act. On 1st January 1910 films were being presented there nightly by the American Bioscope Company.

The building had started life as an Agricultural Hall, built in the 1860's. It was later rebuilt, and was reopened in 1887 as St. Georges Hall. In turn, in 1889, it became the Imperial Theatre. The successive changes had reduced the building in size but, at the turn of the century it still held about one thousand five hundred people. I am not quite sure at what stage it acquired its present frontage but there is something about its appearance that seems to owe more to the theatrical traditions and the public-hall tradition, than to any cinema-style.

It became the property of the Walsall Theatre Company, but from 1910 onwards seemed whole-heartedly devoted to an existence as a cinema, unaffected by the opening of the Palace and the De Luxe. During the twenties it headed its advertisements, "The Royal Academy of "Real" Life"! Such was its dedication to silent movies it seemed reluctant to have to abandon them. Although W.T.C. quickly installed sound at the Palace they left the Imperial to make a virtue out of silence: "Silence Pictures Supreme", claimed the Imperial's advertisements. Sound, by Western Electric, eventually arrived on 20th October 1930 with *"All Quiet On The Western Front"*.

In April 1936 A.B.C. took over the four halls in Walsall owned by W.T.C. Their little triangular motif appeared on either side of the entrance, but the exterior of the building seems to have undergone very little change over the years. Even today, as an EMI Bingo

48. The Imperial, 1946.
*(Photo: Collection of Kevin Wheelan)*

Club, the name "Imperial" still exists, on part of the facade.

During the Second World War a small office on the left of the foyer was used as a signing-on point for the local fire-watchers. Before going on duty the fire-watchers were allowed to see the evening's programme free of charge and were also allowed to spend part of the night sleeping upstairs at the back of the cinema in the room used by the usherettes. On many occasions the fire-watchers on stand-by heard a buzzing noise in the auditorium and would come down to find the manager, Sammy Hipkiss, cleaning his cinema with the vacuum cleaner! Apparently he just loved doing it.

The Imperial may have been Walsall's first cinema but its prestige seems to have diminished over the years. It went sound fourteen months after the arrival of the first "talkie" in town. By the mid-fifties the installation of cinemascope took place a year after A.B.C. had bought the wide screen to the Savoy. "Bedevilled" filled the Imperial's new wide screen on 29th August 1955. At this time the Imperial held just over eleven hundred patrons — about half the number accommodated at the Savoy. A.B.C. then closed The Palace, which held a similar number of patrons but for some reason the Imperial survived.

Although small and old-fashioned the Imperial seemed a popular cinema right into the sixties. My one and only visit to the cinema was early in 1967 when I joined a packed house to see Vincent Price pretending to be Richard III in "Tower of London". One felt glad that a cinema still existed to bring such obscure gems to the Black Country after Wolverhampton's Clifton had closed.

During 1965 the Indo-Pakistani Muslim Welfare Association hired the Imperial for Sunday morning shows. This created a little crisis because Sunday opening was permitted in Walsall on the understanding that children were not admitted to a cinema before five o'clock. (Presumably after attending Sunday School). Great concern was expressed when it was realised that Muslim children were possibly seeing films in the Imperial on Sunday mornings. The Council seemed reluctant to alter their rule without consulting local clergy. A change was opposed by Councillor O'Hare on the grounds that it would be, "Another intrusion into the sanctity of the Sabbath." The Imperial had closed by the time the rule was relaxed.

When the cinema's demise was announced someone obviously decided that its farewell to Walsall should be presented in a style appropriate to its seniority. For the four weeks preceeding closure the Imperial ran a "Big Film Month", reviving many of the favourites that had been popular there, such as "The Ten Commandments". This culminated with its final film show on 4th May 1968 featuring "Assignment K" and the superb, "Cat Ballou".

The manager, Mr. R. Maher, stayed on to see the eighty year old building enjoy a "face lift", but once again it was the interior of the building that must have received the attention. He then prepared the Imperial for its opening as a Bingo Hall on 23rd May 1968. Today the interior still has a strong cinema atmosphere and is painted in strong lurid colours!

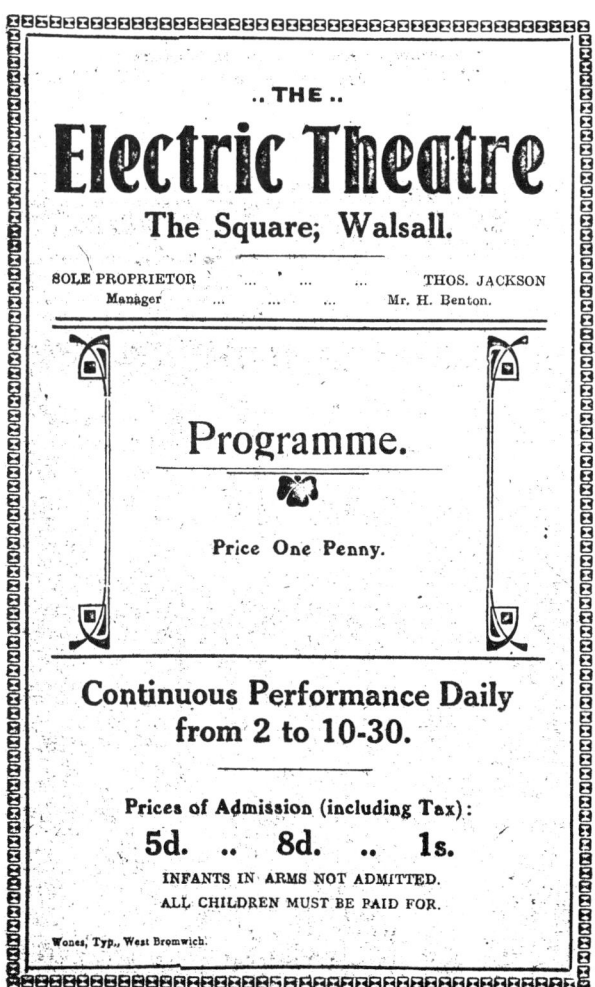

.. THE ..
# Electric Theatre
## The Square; Walsall.

SOLE PROPRIETOR     THOS. JACKSON
Manager     Mr. H. Benton.

## Programme.

Price One Penny.

## Continuous Performance Daily from 2 to 10-30.

Prices of Admission (including Tax):

### 5d. .. 8d. .. 1s.

INFANTS IN ARMS NOT ADMITTED.
ALL CHILDREN MUST BE PAID FOR.

Wones, Typ., West Bromwich.

## 2. The Palace
*The Square*

As soon as the Cinematograph Bill became law an attempt was made to create a chain of Black Country cinemas. Electric Picture Palaces (Midlands) Ltd., with a proposed share capital of £50,000 set out to build six theatres, in Walsall, West Bromwich, Smethwick, Darlaston, Wolverhampton and Handsworth. Only two of these materialized, and Walsall's was the first. The directors were from London but the company's office was in Birmingham. The company's architects were Hickton and Farmer, of Walsall.

No time was wasted on building The Palace, Walsall. The builder was S. Wootton of Bloxwich and most of the sub-contractors were local firms. It was erected in three months but, nevertheless, lived up to its name. It was built to accommodate just over a thousand patrons and was solidly constructed from brick. (No wooden frame and corrugated iron for the Palace!). The Walsall Observer described it in some detail:

"......The outer elevations present an attractive scheme executed in modelled fibrous plasterwork, the open Loggia front having Corinthian columns carrying an open ballustrade surrounding the dome, from the centre of which arises a figure of Electra......

On entering the main doors, on the left is the manager's office, and next comes a lounge, luxuriously furnished with upholstered bays in green, and the floor is covered with a rich Rose du Barry carpet .....

49 The Palace, 1946.
*(Photo: Collection of Kevin Wheelan)*

From the lounge, in which refreshments are provided, the theatre proper is approached. This is a magnificent building with tip up seats, and is carpetted. The seats are upholstered in two shades of green and the walls and ceiling are panelled and finished in red paper, while the beautiful electric torches are shaded with pink silk hankerchiefs ....."

The paper made only one complaint: "The building is a most imposing one, and/it is to be regretted that it could not be found a place in a more prominent thoroughfare of the town."

The Square was not far from The Bridge and therefore the Palace was in a reasonably central position, but was often regarded as being "tucked away". Today the site is obscured by the development of a new shopping precinct.

The Palace opened on 12th April 1910; Walsall's first "purpose-built" cinema. The ceremony was performed by Lady Holden in the presence of an influential gathering which included the Mayor. Mr. Harry Farmer, of Hickton and Farmer, was presented with a silver rose bowl and everyone congratulated everybody else. In the words of The Bioscope: "An exhibition of pictures followed, some remarkably fine films being shown."

One of the early features of the programmes at The Palace was "sequence pictures". These were not "serials", but involved the same characters in a series of self-contained stories. They were projected by a Mr. Robinson on two Pathe projectors from his fireproof operating room. The resident manager was Alex Grant but the company also employed Mr. H. Stanley Marks, from Pathe Freres, as General Manager. This gentleman probably found his job more demanding when the company's second "Palace", in West Bromwich, was opened a month later.

Sometime in 1912 these two "Palaces" were taken over by United Electric Theatres, the grand circuit of six cinemas never becoming a reality for the original company. The new proprietors redecorated the cinema and offered free afternoon tea to patrons in the stalls. They described themselves as "The only fashionable Picture Theatre in Walsall", and, "The Rendezvous of th the elite". Continuous performances ran from 3 p.m. to 10.30 p.m. but the full orchestra only accompanied the evening screenings.

It seems that not everything went well for the Palace. It was probably acquired by Thomas Jackson, the Wolverhampton baker and confectioner whose empire had spread to the Walsall area, to include the De Luxe and the Palace, Bloxwich. It may have closed for a time while Thomas Jackson tried to renovate the place. Such a task may have been specially difficult during the War and it seems that it was not reopened until 17th December 1917. The occasion was marked by a showing of D. W. Griffiths' *"Intolerance"*. After the War, the

Palace adopted the slogan, "The House With A Big Following".

In March 1920 this slogan was replaced in the advertisements with "The House that is Becoming Different", and after Easter this became "The House That Is Now Different". The changing slogan does not do justice to the work Thomas Jackson undertook. The theatre was turned round! The screen had originally been at the entrance end of the auditorium. It was now transferred to the other end to which a twenty-five foot extension had been added. A new balcony was built over the main entrance, reached by broad staircases, and the projection box was moved. Much of the work was accomplished while shows continued, much to the pride of the manager, Mr. Reynolds Benjamin.

The new Palace reopened on 3rd April 1920 and "Spiral of Death" filled the new washable silk screen with light from the Powers No. 2 projectors. The orchestra was now directed by Claude Fenn-Leyland, late of the London Opera House. The financial strain may have been the beginning of Thomas Jackson's downfall but the cinema was packed that Easter Monday.

Along with the De Luxe in Stafford Street, the Palace was acquired by L. A. Thomson's "Midland Counties Circuit" when Thomas Jackson's empire was dissolved in 1922/3. There it remained until it was taken over by Walsall Theatres Company in the summer of 1930. W.T.C. briefly closed the Palace in order to install the BTH sound system, and reopened on 4th August 1930, with "The Gold Diggers of Broadway". The Palace must have become accustomed to changing hands every six or seven years because on 1st April 1936 it was taken over by A.B.C. The cinema now held one thousand, one hundred and sixty-four patrons.

Like the A.B.C.'s Imperial, the Palace eventually found itself overshadowed by the company's brand new Savoy. It only screened the best releases when they were on their second time round. However, its proximity to the Picture House and the Empire meant that during the Second World War when all three cinemas enjoyed long queues, the Palace gratefully accepted the patrons who were unsuccessful in getting in at the other two places!

When audiences faltered it was natural that A.B.C. should prune at least one of its three cinemas surviving in Walsall. The Imperial was an older building but the Palace was the first to be abandoned. The last show was on 24th September 1955 and featured Norman Wisdom's second film, "One Good Turn". The last advertisement carried a "thank you" to the patrons for their loyal support, and possibly the question of re-developing the site was more relevant to its closure than a real loss of patrons. Five days later the site was sold to the Walsall Observer, becoming the Commercial Printing Department. The new owner's canteen occupied the site of the balcony. As mentioned earlier, the site has been again redeveloped and all traces of the Palace have gone.

### 3. Cinema De Luxe/The Classic
*Stafford Street*

For a couple of years the cinema-going public of Walsall had only the Imperial and the Palace to provide them with a choice of entertainment. However, on Monday 23rd December 1912 they were joined by the Cinema De Luxe at the opposite end of Walsall's central area.

This appears to have been built by Thomas Jackson in his first flush of success after opening the Strand, in Wolverhampton, five months earlier. It was opened by Walsall's mayor, Councillor John Venables, and held about one thousand patrons. Little seems to be recorded of its early history although it seems that Thomas Jackson was keen to enlarge the place, but his plans were held up by the First World War. The work was done in 1920, increasing its capacity to about one thousand five hundred.

After Thomas Jackson's collapse in 1923, the cinema was administered by the Midland Counties Circuit, as was the Palace. When they were put up for sale, it can be assumed that the Walsall Theatres Company did not want the De Luxe. It was bought by a neighbouring garage proprietor and motor-car dealer, Mr. T. Birch.

Sound was installed in November 1931 using the Western Electric Mirrophonic system. The De Luxe, the last cinema in Walsall to introduce the "talkies", showed its first sound film, *The Easiest Way* on 30th November 1931. The new proprietor probably gradually improved the seating as its capacity fell to about eight hundred and fifty and later to about a hundred less than that. Miss Minnie Wallace, who had been a secretary in the garage, was later given the job of managing the place, knowing that she would be one of the few women given the opportunity to occupy such a position.

When the De Luxe was sold to the Clifton Circuit Miss Wallace retained her position of manageress and worked for that company until the mid-sixties. The

cinema ceased to be the De Luxe on Sunday 25th February 1940, Sunday opening being allowed during the Second World War, despite strong denunciations of such practices in Walsall. The cinema was then redecorated and refurbished by the Clifton Circuit and some technical changes were made although the cinema's equipment continued to be rather antiquated. The cinema reopened as the Classic on 4th March 1940 with "OHMS" starring John Mills. The new name implied that the cinema intended making a virtue out of showing old films! It was going to be policy to show the "classics"; films that had already proved popular in Walsall. The advertising also described the three hour double feature programmes at other cinemas as "wearisome" and announced that the Classic would specialise in two hour shows consisting of a feature supported by only a short and Universal News. Patrons were to be charged sixpence downstairs or a shilling in the balcony.

Miss Wallis became secretary of the local War Aid Committee, organising variety shows, concerts and dances for war-time charities. After 1945 she carried on such work for local charities. Tommy Trinder, George Formby, Norman Wisdom and bandleaders, Billy Cotton and Joe Loss, all found themselves answering Miss Wallis's charity call. In 1951 Miss Wallis was presented to Princess Margaret as a "cinema manager and charity worker".

The Classic was literally overshadowed by the Savoy and naturally seemed something of a "flea-pit" by comparison, but it had its own pride and a determination not to give up too easily in the fifties. It celebrated the Coronation by being lavishly decorated externally and by reducing seat prices to one shilling downstairs, two shillings upstairs. Mr. Moseley who went to the cinema as third operator and had risen to second operator, assured me that the sound and picture were always the best that could be obtained on the rather old equipment provided. He and his chief, Bill Prescott, had to be on their toes to get the best from their Kalee 8 projectors with BTH arcs, although helped by good maintenance by the Clifton Circuit engineers.

The age of the building and its slightly awkward site added to its problems and the Classic finally gave up the struggle to survive on Sunday 22nd June 1958. The last show was a one day only presentation of "Johnny You're Wanted" and "Phantom from 10,000 Leagues".

In recent years the building has been occupied by the Mazda Price Supermarket and was not obviously an ex-cinema until one stood well away from the frontage to be able to see the roofline. Until November 1981 the operating box could be seen clearly projecting through the forward slope of this roof, but was removed after fire had destroyed part of the building. At the time of writing, the site is about to be redeveloped.

## 4. The Rink, The Arcade and The Grand

Three other establishments presented films in Walsall before the First World War. For convenience they will be dealt with together in this section.

The Rink, as its name suggests, was a converted skating rink in Darwall Street, not far from the Imperial.

It opened on Saturday 10th May with "Broken Wings" and "Undine". The following week brought a forty minute silent version of "Romeo & Juliet". It claimed to hold two thousand patrons at two and three pence a time. (In 1913 seats at The Palace were one shilling, sixpence and threepence!).

The Walsall Observer reported: "The Skating Rink has been admirably adapted to the requirements of a Picture House". However it does not seem to have been a great success, or its licence fell foul of safety regulations, because films at "The Rink" seem to have ceased fairly quickly, probably within a year of opening. It was managed by one Alfred Jacobs, but beyond that I have discovered very little!

A kine licence was also issued for a time before the First World War to W. T. Comer of the Arcade. Mr. Comer was an optician, and one of the original tenants of Walsall's Arcade. During 1913 or 1914 he may have organised film shows in the Assembly Rooms at the Arcade but I have not found them advertised, nor recorded elsewhere.

Walsall Theatre Company has already been mentioned in relation to the Imperial and the Palace. At the time when these two places were pioneering film entertainment in Walsall, the two theatres owned by W.T.C., the Grand and Her Majesty's, were still presenting drama and variety. By 1912 Her Majesty's had thought it worth obtaining a kine licence and successfully showed twice-nightly film programmes during the summer.

Mr. Westwood of W.T.C. declared that he had decided the cinema was here to stay, and that Walsall could support another cinema. The Grand, in Park Street, had been built as a theatre in 1890 but closed in 1912 to be converted to a cinema.

Four hundred and fifty new tip up seats were installed in the stalls. The seats in the circle were regarded as too good to change and the gallery was left as it was, to provide cheap seats, apart from a section used to house the operating box. New heating was installed to overcome its reputation as a cold theatre and a new screen was mounted behind the proscenium arch.

The Grand opened as a cinema on 4th November 1912 with "The Mysteries of Paris", but did not formerly change its name to "Grand Picture House" until the following May. Ironically by this time some variety acts had crept back into the three hour programmes! It had an orchestra led by a Mr. Blakemore, and could accommodate about one thousand five hundred patrons. It occasionally returned to theatrical use in subsequent years and was presenting plays when sound films arrived at Walsall's cinemas. It was briefly closed in mid 1931 and reopened on 15th June, with "Just Imagine" as the Grand Talkie Theatre.

When it was acquired by A.B.C. in April 1936 it served a useful purpose in maintaining their presence at that end of the town while they demolished Her Majesty's Theatre and replaced it with the Savoy. The Grand closed on Saturday 1st October 1938 and the Savoy opened two days later. The final show featured "Sea Devils", starring Victor McLagen.

The Grand languished for a short time and was then reopened as a live theatre, by Pat Collins Junior. Unfortunately it was destroyed by a fire in 1939.

Park Street and Theatre, Walsall.

50. The Grand, on the left, and distant centre, Her Majesty's Theatre.

*(From a postcard in the Collection of J. S. Webb)*

### 5. The Picture House — Gaumont — Odeon
*Bridge Street*

Just before the First World War, Associated Provincial Picture Houses began work on a prestige cinema for Walsall. This was to be The Picture House in Bridge Street, virtually built over the River Tame itself. The site had formerly been part of the George Hotel, an old coaching inn, right in the centre of town. The foundations were laid and then the problems began.

First of all construction had to be suspended during the War, due to shortage of labour and materials, then building restrictions. By the time work could resume the foundations were flooded and expensive piles had to be sunk to try and put things right. A.P.P.H. had managed to open their cinemas in Wolverhampton, Willenhall and Wednesbury and were doubtless keen to open in Walsall as quickly as possible. Eventually the contractors were working at nights and on Sundays to try and finish the cinema. Even then the frontage was not quite finished in time.

The front elevation of the cinema was particularly handsome. It was faced in cream glazed faience and was dominated by marble pillars above the main entrance doors. The lofty windows of the cafe at balcony level, and the ballastrades, added to the effect of grandeur. The foyer was panelled in oak, there were lifts to the balcony level and the best seats were of a cosy arm-chair type. Everything suggested luxury and good taste to reassure the middle classes that A.P.P.H. had made cinema-going respectable. The architect was Percy Browne, and Glover.

The Picture House opened on 29th July 1920 in the presence of Walsall's Mayor. Mr. Darbyshire, of A.P.P.H., made a speech explaining why Walsall deserved such a fine cinema. He said,

".....Many of her sons have devoted their brains to the development of the picture industry. Dr. Jupp, who was the first to conceive of the idea of the super-cinema was a native of the town, while many senior men in A.P.P.H. were born locally. Walsall men had shown America how to build Picture Houses .....and when the history of cinematography came to be written Walsall would occupy a high and honourable place....."

It is interesting to see the term "super-cinema" in use so early. The Picture House held one thousand five hundred patrons and was therefore a "super" in the numerical sense, but I think A.P.P.H. were referring to the luxury, refinement, good quality music, fine cafe and general "atmosphere" of their cinema when using the term.

The first film shown was called *"Woman"* and the orchestra provided musical accompaniment that included themes by Strauss, Wagner and Gounod. The orchestra's director was a Signor Cinganelli. The proceedings culminated in the presentation of a gift of £100 to the mayor by A.P.P.H. for the War Memorial Fund. (Walsall Theatre Co., immediately gave a similar amount!).

The Picture House confidently settled into its role in Walsall's life. It overlooked the principal town centre

tram terminus and no doubt filled everyone with awe. The only distraction was a huge advertisement for the Imperial, and its programmes, standing alongside the Picture House's facade. When the cinema had been built the old City and Midland Bank buildings next door had been truncated and its new gable end was entirely devoted to the Imperial's advertisement!

Flooded foundations and war-time delays had no doubt been forgotten by 1923. On the evening of 1st September of that year the audience in the Picture House saw William S. Hart's film *"Travellin' On"*. After the performance the manager, Mr. Pain, inspected the premises, locked up and went home. He was summoned early Sunday morning to find his sumptuous theatre was reduced to a wreck by fire. During the night a P.C. Lewis had smelt burning but could not locate the fire. He had aroused the landlord of the George, and the two men suddenly saw a tongue of flames shoot out of a ventilator cover on the cinema's roof. The Fire Brigade worked for an hour and a half bringing the fire under

control, rescuing two kittens and damping down the wreckage.

A.P.P.H. had now been absorbed by its associate P.C.T. and the company resolutely took up the task of rebuilding the Picture House. Once again it was built on a grand and luxurious scale. The new interior seemed brighter, and a rich Renaissance-style ceiling was added. Oak panelling was retained and the foyer still featured its old-time fireplace. The proscenium was flanked by two new electric pedestal lights, capable of flooding the entire stage in light and the screen could now be drawn up into a fly tower if the stage was required. At the same time, the seating capacity was increased to one thousand seven hundred. P.C.T. claimed it was second in size only to their Regent in Brighton. The Picture House opened, for the second time, on 26th December 1924, with *"Down to the Sea in Ships"* and once again it had been a great rush to have everything finished. Everyone worked all hours right up to the last minute.

After such an exciting career, Walsall's Picture House

deserved the honour of being the first Black Country cinema to have a Wurlitzer installed, indeed, it was the first Wurlitzer in any British cinema. The two manual, six unit instrument was opened by Jack Courtney in 1925. The Picture House was also the first Walsall cinema to present the "talkies". *"The Singing Fool"* was shown on 26th August 1929 and the film drew massive queues to the cinema all week. The Picture House used the Western Electric system. P.C.T. eventually became part of Gaumont British and the cinema had the latest G.B. Kalee 21 projectors.

The name, "The Picture House", was retained until July 1948 and then it quietly became the Gaumont. Perhaps the name seemed more "modern". Despite the relative newness of the Savoy, the Gaumont still had its own special quality. Projectionist John McLeod, who joined the cinema just after its change of name, and who worked there for a decade recalled:

"....Of course, the Gaumont had one major advantage over other cinemas in Walsall: it possessed a restaurant, as well as a private room that could be hired for special occasions (The Oak Room). What a thrill it was to take that special girlfriend for a meal in the lush surroundings, before plying her with the most expensive box of chocolates, in the best seats. The seats at the front of the circle were like theatre-boxes with seats just for two."

Meanwhile the projectionists apparently flirted with the chambermaids from the George Hotel. The latter's quarters were clearly visible from the operating room and each party no doubt felt sympathy for others, each assigned to remote parts of buildings! During John McLeod's time in the operating room he saw the Wurlitzer taken out of the theatre. Its departure, in 1955, seemed to mark the beginning of the period of decline. He had often been able to sit at the organ's console on Sunday mornings and imagine the well known organists who had occupied the same seat; Arnold Loxam, Hubert Selby and Wilf Gregory. Like the organ at the Regal, Darlaston, Walsall's Wurlitzer had starred in radio broadcasts. Today the organ is in the Congregational Church at Beer, Devon.

The Gaumont changed its name once again; on 22nd October 1965 it became the Odeon. Whether its fortunes would have declined, or whether it would have survived to this day, we shall never know because once again fire destroyed the building. Unfortunately the Odeon had not long been completely modernised. It had closed in May 1967 for the interior to be re-modelled at a cost of £70,000. New seats, carpets, new silver curtain, and a new larger screen were installed. The old timber fireplace in the foyer that survived the fire of 1923 was abandoned, the restaurant was rebuilt and even the marble pillars were replaced with Hoganas tiling. Two hundred and forty seats had been lost in the modernisation but it was still a reasonably sizeable theatre.

It "reopened" on 26th June 1967 with a special gala performance of *"Casino Royale"* and the manager, Philip Cross, probably felt confident that the much-renewed cinema would last for decades. The following week *"Privilege"* was screened and many young folk in Walsall went to see themselves or their friends appearing as "extras" in the parts of the film shot in Birmingham.

Less than four years later all the modernised interior was destroyed when fire broke out on the night of Tuesday 2nd March 1971. *"Hello Dolly"* was being presented that week, but the fire broke out while the cinema was empty. Eighty firemen from several Brigades tackled the dramatic fire, at the height of which, the roof caved in and collapsed. When Philip Cross was summoned to the scene he felt he was watching a nightmare. He went into the cinema's office to retrieve money and records while the auditorium still blazed. As before, the front of the cinema was relatively little affected.

It was one of the worst fires ever known in the centre of Walsall and it was a miracle that it did not spread to the Walsall Observer offices or the George Hotel. At first there seemed to be no evidence that it was anything but an accident but later a man was convicted for arson. From Bridge Street it seemed as if the Odeon was still in existence, although the frontage was partly boarded-up. Behind the facade the remains of the auditorium were demolished and thus it remained for a year or two until the site was sold and redeveloped. The Savoy, now the ABC, was thus left as Walsall's sole surviving cinema, and the Bridge Picture House, as it was often known, has passed into history.

---

## 6. The Empire
*Freer Street*

After the opening of The Picture House in 1920 there was no further cinema building in the centre of Walsall for over a decade. The same could not be said of the other major Black Country towns, and it is interesting to wonder why this was so. The only genuine "super-cinema", of the style expected of the 1930's, to be built in the centre of Walsall was the Savoy, opened in 1938. The only town-centre cinema to open between 1920 and 1938 was the Empire.

The Empire was built on the site of Walsall's Temperance Hall in Freer Street. This building had been erected in 1866. In December 1931 a poorly attended farewell gathering was held in the hall, presided over by Alderman Joseph Leckie to mark the sale of the hall. He recalled the more active days of the Temperance Movement and the decline of the hall. The decline had followed the collapse of the roof about 1921. The Movement had never financially recovered after facing the cost of repairs. It was bought by a Mr. T. Jackson who set about turning the ruin into a new cinema at a cost of £13,500. Mr. T. Jackson was a resident of Bournemouth and, of course, it has been tempting to wonder if he was none other than Thomas Jackson, the Wolverhampton cinema proprietor who had ventured into Walsall at the De Luxe and the Palace. I have found no evidence to suggest that it was the same man.

The new cinema was designed by J. H. Hickton and the work was carried out by J. & F. Wootton, of Bloxwich. The frontage of the original building was used, but was totally transformed by a white cement facing over the brickwork, effectively contrasting with marble terrazzo steps and plinths. The pairs of handsome recessed swing doors replaced the old entrances. A raked floor had to be installed in the stalls, plus nine hundred upholstered seats. Three hundred such seats were positioned in the balcony. The walls and ceilings were

52. The Empire, 1964, on the eve of closure.

*(Photo: The Walsall Observer)*

decorated in eau de nil, ivory and gold, while each side wall contained six panels, each of which was filled with a landscape mural.

Mr. Jackson hoped to open the Empire on 24th August 1933, but in fact it opened the following Monday: 28th August 1933. Naturally it was built as a sound cinema, using the Western Electric system, and the opening programme featured the musical comedy, *"Letting In The Sunshine"*, directed by Lupino Lane. It was supported by *"Slightly Married"*, described as a "ticklish comedy of married life" and Universal News. Although no organ was installed in the Empire the proprietors did the next best thing: they showed a short sound film of Jesse Crawford playing a Wurlitzer!

Mr. Jackson did not remain the proprietor of the Empire for very long. In February 1936 a film renter named Henry Smith introduced Mr. Jackson to Captain Clift as a would-be purchaser of the Empire. The negotiations ceased but were resumed in 1937, when Captain Clift finally agreed to purchase the Empire for £20,000. The Empire then became part of the Clifton circuit. When the Rosum at Leamore was opened in 1936, and the De Luxe was acquired in 1939, the Clifton circuit had quite a presence in Walsall although the name "Clifton" never appeared there. The Empire

and the Classic (one time De Luxe) shared newsreels during the War as a result of being part of the same circuit, but in many ways they seemed to pursue their independent ways.

During the fifties patrons may have guessed that the Empire and the Rosum shared the same proprietor because both cinemas installed cinemascope simultaneously. The Empire brought *"The Robe"* to central Walsall on 4th October 1954, one day after the Rosum. Such was its success that it had to be brought back for a further run a few weeks later. The Empire was the first *town-centre* cinema in Walsall to present cinemascope.

When Clifton cinemas started closing in the early sixties rumours began to circulate about the future of the Empire. Even managers were kept completely "in the dark" until the last moment. When *"Cleopatra"* was screened at the Empire on 24th October 1964 Clifton Cinemas would still not confirm or deny that the cinema was closing! In the event, that show was the last, and the cinema only remained empty and unused for a very short time. In February 1965 it was demolished.

The area around Freer Street and Leicester Square has been fairly dramatically redeveloped and all trace of the Empire has disappeared.

53. Her Majesty's Theatre running as an A.B.C. cinema, before replacement by the Savoy.

*(Photo: D. W. Gilbert)*

## 7. The Savoy — ABC
*Town End Bank*

The history of Walsall's super-cinema begins with the history of its predecessor; Her Majesty's Theatre. The latter was opened by Sir William Pearman Smith in March 1900 for Walsall Theatre Company. Its bizarre architectural eclecticism dominated Town End Bank, at the top of Park Street. Two thousand people could be accommodated in this colossal structure, which had taken Messrs. Whittaker & Co., of Dudley, nearly four years to build. It was designed by Messrs. Owen & Ward of Birmingham and had a suitably ornate interior and proscenium arch. The first show was *"The Belle Of New York"* and there followed many quality plays and pantomimes.

Leading actors of the day, such as John Forbes-Robinson and Laurence Irving came to Walsall to appear at Her Majesty's Theatre and when drama gave way to the popularity of Variety, Charlie Chaplin is said to have appeared there in *"Casey's Court"*. Like other theatres, Her Majesty's obtained a kine licence and occasionally showed films between variety acts. Their popularity led the proprietors to devote The Grand to showing films. Her Majesty's survived as a theatre until about 1933 but then spent most of its time showing films. Along with the other W.T.C. properties, it was acquired by A.B.C. in April 1936. I assume their intention from the start was to demolish the building

and replace it with a modern purpose-built super-cinema.

William Glen, A.B.C.'s principal architect, produced an elegant cinema that would dominate Town End Bank with its simple sweeping straightforwardness just as dramatically as the exotic theatre had done. Once again it was to be a large building, holding 1358 patrons in the stalls, and 811 in the circle. It was built by Messrs. Fox & Co. of Norton-on-Tees. There was some participation by the local architects Messrs. Hickton and Madeley.

The five pairs of swing doors across the semi-circular entrance to the cinema led the patron to a large foyer with a terrazzo floor. The walls and ceilings were pink with blue and gold relief. These colours were continued in the auditorium. Around the screen and proscenium arch there was a decorative scheme in dark blue and gold and the screen itself was draped in gold silk that rose in billowing festoons.

The new cinema, the Savoy, opened on 3rd October 1938 and the ceremony was performed by Walsall's Mayor, Dr. E. P. Drabble. He had opened the Avion at Aldridge a week or two earlier but gave this task a distinctive quality by welcoming Sir William Pearman Smith to the stage and recalling Sir William's similar function when the theatre had opened thirty-eight years before. The opening programme featured *"A Yank at Oxford"* starring Robert Taylor and Vivien Leigh. The

54. The Savoy, 1946.

*(Photo: Collection of Kevin Wheelan)*

Newsreel showed Mr. Chamberlain at Munich and the audience heard the Prime Minister's voice, via the wonders of the Western Electric Mirrophonic Sound, announce, on his return, that there would be peace in their time. The opening party then went off to a reception at the George Hotel.

The Savoy was the last cinema to open in Walsall, forgetting the Rex for a moment, and thus, the A.B.C. circuit owned the first cinema in Walsall, the first purpose-built cinema in Walsall and the last purpose-built cinema in Walsall. Like many super-cinemas built by the major circuits towards the end of the thirties the Savoy has had a fairly uneventful history and suffered no major changes until the seventies.

The A.B.C.'s Minors Club started at the Savoy on 20th April 1948. On one of the annual celebrations of the club's anniversary, its eleventh, the cinema presented a premier of the N.C.F.F.'s production, *"The Cat Gang"*. Shows continued until 1980. The name "Savoy" was dropped in favour of ABC at the end of 1960, but such details do not add up to an exciting history!

The major event in the cinema's life came in 1973. During the summer it closed for three months for tripling. Screen 1 was the first to reopen as this made use of the balcony, now reduced in capacity to five hundred, and the existing projection box and screen. It opened on 30th September 1973 with *"Love Thy Neighbour"*. Screen 2, a 278 seater, and Screen 3, a 143 seater opened on Friday 16th November with *"Man At The Top"* and *"Scorpio"* respectively. On

17th November, the ABC re-started their Minors Club in Screen 1 and presented the first show free of charge.

A new manager, Mr. Alex Wright, took charge of the three screens and the tripling marked the departure of Mr. Frank Attoe. The latter had enjoyed quite a long association with the Black Country in several cinemas, while working for A.B.C. One assistant manager from this cinema moved on to greater things. Euan Lloyd became a successful film producer, making films like *"Shalako"* and *"The Wild Geese"*.

Like its fellow survivor, the ABC, Wolverhampton, it now has modern Philips projectors and sound, and although the tripling has changed the interior, the exterior has only been slightly modified by the presence of a modern canopy. Long may it occupy its dignified position in Town End Bank!

# FORUM THEATRE

## CALDMORE GREEN
### WALSALL                    Phone: 2618
Resident Manager — S. Francis Harvey.

# PROGRAMME

## for NOVEMBER, 1957

CONTINUOUS MONDAY TO FRIDAY
from 5-30 p.m.
SATURDAY from 2-0 p.m.
MATINEES : MON. & THURS. at 2-0 p.m.
SUNDAYS Continuous from 3-0 p.m.

Prices of Admission (inc. tax) :

Evenings 1/-, 1/6, 2/-.     Matinees 1/- and 1/6
Children under 14 (when accompanied by an adult)
9d. and 1/-.  Except Saturdays (after 3-30 p.m.)
Sundays and Holidays.

Book Your Appointment Now with
## JEAN ASH
MODERN HAIR DESIGNS
### 93 Caldmore Road, Walsall
Telephone: Wa'sall 2551
Hair Stylist & Eugene Permanent
Waving Specialist

## 8. The Caldmore Green Picture Playhouse later known as The Forum
*Caldmore Green*

Caldmore Green is one of those fringe areas of a town that neither belongs to the centre nor to the suburbs in the second half of the twentieth century. Yet once it must have had a confident identity of its own, perhaps to be compared with places like Blakenhall and Whitmore Reans in Wolverhampton, both of which supported their own cinemas.

The Caldmore Green Picture Playhouse unceremoniously opened some time in November or December 1915. The first show advertised in the Walsall Observer was *"Life's Highway"* which commenced on 27th December, but in the same issue of the paper as the advertisement was the report,

"......opened a few weeks ago, the Caldmore Green Picture Playhouse is achieving great success, and large audiences have been delighted with the atmosphere of cosiness and warmth which pervades the hall".

Manager Harry Parr was in charge of the cinema, which could seat up to eight hundred patrons. Its name was not quite such a mouthful when one remembers the name of the district is always pronounced "Karma Green". However it later abbreviated its name to Caldmore Green Picture House. Like many others, it boasted, throughout the twenties, that it had the finest screen in the Midlands and showed the "Best Selected Masterpieces". It also claimed that it was easily reached by tram from Darlaston and West Bromwich and may well have drawn patrons from a wide area.

It is not clear whether the cinema was purpose-built or converted from an existing building. The auditorium was at right angles to the foyer and main entrance which faced the Green. The auditorium had no balcony but the rear seats were separately raked in the "stadium" style. The projection room was approximately level with the screen.

On 14th April 1930 BTH sound equipment came into use, making Caldmore Green's little cinema the second in Walsall to introduce the "talkies". The following year it was acquired by Sheridan Film Services and changed its name to the Forum on 24th December 1931. The same company also acquired the Alhambra, Dudley Port, at about the same time. Later, both cinemas were transferred from Sheridan Film Services to S.T. Cinemas when Mr. Suffolk went into partnership with Mr. Thornton.

All went well for a time, but eventually events overtook the Forum. After the Second World War the Forum found itself very much "the last in line" and films had been seen at practically every other local cinema by the time they reached Caldmore Green. Mr. Suffolk opted for older films, that had the added virtue of being cheaper, but the resulting poor programmes drove patrons away.

In 1950 Mr. Suffolk appointed Frank Harvey as manager and gave him a month to study the cinema and report on its state. Frank Harvey had enjoyed a distinguished career in the projection rooms of the Odeon circuit. He had been at Wolverhampton Odeon from its opening in 1937 until coming to the Forum.

Little wonder he found the place very "run down" by comparison. Apart from recognising the results of poor programming, Frank Harvey also recognised the folly of charging five different prices for seats ranging from 1/6 to 3/-. The prices were also too high.

As it happened, Mr. Suffolk sold both the Alhambra, Dudley Port, and the Forum at the end of 1951, and the new proprietor allowed the manager to institute some reforms. The new proprietor was Horace Miller from Leicester. He booked better programmes and later passed that responsibility to Frank Harvey. Meanwhile, the latter had introduced a two price system, seats for 1/- and 1/6. Matters greatly improved straight away Even the family audience returned and queues were seen in Caldmore Green for popular films like *"Seven Brides for Seven Brothers"*!

Horace Miller then set about improving the Forum. He installed a new wide screen and new proscenium arch. A colour lighting system complemented the new silver satin curtains. The BTH equipment was removed and the latest G.B. Kalee 20 projectors with President arcs were installed plus G.B. Duosonic Sound. All the work was entirely carried out over one weekend between Saturday night and the Monday performance! With its fine modern equipment it could now legitimately claim "The Brightest Screen In The Midlands", and with its energetic manager, often present in the foyer, in the grand tradition, the Forum continued to prosper through that difficult era. Frank Harvey left in 1958 and Horace Miller sold the cinema to Vincent Wareing. It closed for a fortnight in June 1958, presumably coinciding with the change of ownership.

Vincent Wareing's excursion into the Black Country did not go well. As well as the Forum, he acquired the Palace, Great Bridge, and the Coliseum and Olympia Wolverhampton. Sadly, the Forum showed its last film on 28th May 1960. It closed with *"Northwest Frontier"*. Today, the auditorium is a warehouse for the Walsall Lithographic Company. The foyer became a restaurant but suffered a fire in 1979. The canopy and arched brickwork over the windows of the manager's office still suggest the presence of an ex-cinema.

## 9. The Rosum
*Leamore*

Half way between Walsall and Bloxwich the trams, and later the trolleybuses passed through Leamore. In the mid thirties, Edgar Summers, a local accountant, felt that this was an ideal spot for a super-cinema. It was to be called the Rosum, named after his wife, Rose Summers. To find the necessary funds, Edgar Summers joined forces with Captain Clift and the architect, Ernest Roberts, to form Rosumclift Cinemas Ltd.

Planning and construction followed very quickly. Legend has it that the plans produced by Ernest Roberts were identical to the plans of the Clifton, Wellington. The legend goes on to make this "fact" responsible for periodic flooding of the cinema's boiler rooms, as the Rosum was built on sloping ground, apparently quite different from the Clifton's site! Work began in December 1935 and the Rosum was completed in about eight months by J. & F. Wootton of Bloxwich. In fact, it was ready about ten days before the opening.

The building stands flush with its neighbours, with a portico over the street. The frontage was finished in

The Directors of

ROSUMCLIFT CINEMAS LIMITED

CORDIALLY INVITE YOU TO AN INSPECTION & THE OPENING OF

# ROSUM

LEAMORE • WALSALL

**MONDAY, 24th AUGUST, 1936**

white stone, now painted grey. Its simplicity reflected a "modern" style that was also to be found in the interior, but looked imposing when beautified by neon lighting. Above the three double swing doors the cinema's name appeared, occupying the position where the balcony foyer's windows were normally to be found on a Satchwell and Roberts cinema.

The auditorium, with its fine sweeping lines of plain plaster work by Bryan's Adamanta, held 808 patrons in the stalls and 392 patrons in the balcony. Turner's tip up seats were provided in three different shades of upholstery and the effect, looking back across the hall from the stage was a series of diagonal rows of each particular colour. Up in the operating room, the new "chief", Bill Lockett, who had come from the Grosvenor, found BTH projection and sound equipment. In nearly all respects it was a typical "Clifton" cinema.

Invitations were dispatched for the Rosum's opening on 24th August 1936. The ceremony was to be performed by Walsall's Mayor, Councillor Fletcher, and the Houston Sisters, the stars of the first film. At 5.30 p.m. on the great day the Houston Sisters had not arrived. The GPO provided a land line to loudspeakers in the auditorium and the audience could hear the Scottish accent of Renee Houston speaking from Leicester Square in London. "Hello Walsall", she said, "We are very proud that our picture has been chosen to open the Rosum".

The audience had to be satisfied with the presence on stage of Councillor Fletcher, Edgar Summers, Captain Clift and Ernest Roberts! In the audience was Pat Collins. The ceremony was followed by Mark Stone and Ida Barr, live on stage, and eventually the Houston Sisters' film "Happy Days Are Here Again" on the screen. A film was made of the opening and this was shown in the cinema on the next three anniversaries of the event. The film still exists today in Walsall Library's local collection.

Leamore's cinema was a success and fully justified Edgar Summers' hopes. Sometimes programmes enjoyed a local success for local reasons. For example, a film called "Black Diamonds" did well because the manager, Percy Rogers, exploited the local interest in coal-mining, and used tubs and track from a local pit to put on a promotional display. The Rosum also used its limited stage facilities to occasionally mount variety acts or bands to complement some films. The Great Nixon, who also visited the Regal, Wednesfield, came to the Rosum and stayed with Bill Lockett and his wife. They learned no secrets of his mind reading act.

The Rosum continued to prosper through the War, with female staff in the operating room. When Mr. Lockett returned in 1947 he was offered the ice-cream business! On Sunday 3rd October 1954 the Rosum introduced Cinemascope to Walsall with "The Robe". A few miles away in Brownhills the tiny Regent

56. The Rosum, 1936.

*(Author's Collection)*

had shown *"The Robe"* in July but nevertheless the Rosum led the field in Walsall.

Things began to decline in the sixties and Bingo was introduced on Tuesday and Friday nights for a time. The Star Group expressed an interest in buying the Rosum, but it took some time to agree to the terms of sale. Eventually the Star Group acquired both the Rosum and the Clifton, Wolverhampton. The last film was shown on 16th April 1966 and was *"Mary Poppins"*. As soon as the last film was re-wound, the contractors moved in to convert the interior for use as a full-time Bingo Club.

Bingo started on 21st April 1966 and has continued ever since. It became an EMI Bingo and Social Club in March 1975 and the auditorium is now bright and cheerful and the building well preserved. The canopy has gone, which further emphasises the plainess of the Rosum's frontage. The building still dominates Leamore, but excited patrons no longer cross the road and queue in the elegant trolleybus waiting shelter on the opposite side of the road. Nevermind, the last trolleybus ran in 1970. The Rosum's "double" in Wellington is still showing films.

## 10. The Rex and The Raj
*Stafford Street*

Indian films were first shown in Walsall at the Imperial in 1965 on Sunday mornings at the ABC. Their success led Surinder Kumar to investigate the possibility of creating a cinema specifically for that purpose.

In 1974 St. Patrick's Church Hall, Stafford Street, was acquired and planning permission was obtained to convert the building into a cinema. This revived the ancient tradition of converting such buildings into cinemas! A raked floor was installed, which pushed the rear seats well towards the ceiling and a small operating room was built over the entrance. Two ancient BTH machines came to life every Sunday until video enticed the audience away and shows were abandoned in 1981. It was called The Rex but the name did not appear on the building. I enjoyed one conducted tour of the building during the summer of 1980, which gave me the impression of time-travelling back to the fifties and venturing into a village "flea-pit".

In 1977 Tarsem Singh Dhami planned to build a four hundred seater cinema at Pleck on the site of the Bescott Petrol Station. It was an ambitious project which would have created a brand new purpose-built cinema as part of a community centre. It would have shown English language and Indian films but was continually opposed by Walsall Council. It would have enjoyed that most princely of names: The Raj.

## Bloxwich

Bloxwich was, for many years, in the Foreign of Walsall, and in terms of the history of recent local government, never enjoyed the kind of independence that Wednesfield experienced in relation to Wolverhampton. Nevertheless, it was a community that was proud of its own history and identity and tended to feel "separate" from Walsall.

Professor Wood brought his "animated pictures" to Bloxwich and presented them in the hall that had once

been the Sunday School behind the Wesleyan chapel in Park Road, in the early years of this century. He re-appears in the history of Bloxwich's cinemas later and joins the familiar names of the other men who showed films in Bloxwich: Thomas Jackson, Pat Collins and Oscar Deutsch!

## 11. The Electric Palace
*165 High Street*

The Electric Palace was opened by Alhambra Picture Palaces Ltd., a company established by Thomas Jackson to open Alhambra, Bilston, and this one in Bloxwich, following his first steps into the cinema business at the Strand in Whitmore Reans, Wolverhampton. It was a small hall, holding four hundred patrons, and it is not clear whether it was a conversion of an existing building or was purpose-built. The earliest show I have found advertised for the Electric Palace was for Monday 30th December 1912, when *"Romance of the Coast"* was being screened.

The cinema may not have been a great success, or the facilities simply inadequate, because it closed the following Spring for some improvements to be made! It re-opened on 12th May 1913, with *"Quo Vadis"*. The Walsall Observer reported,

"......Extensive alterations have been carried out in the building, and a balcony has been provided, no expense being spared to ensure the comfort of patrons."

From that date onwards shows were presented twice nightly, with matinees on Mondays, Tuesdays and Wednesdays. Seats cost 2d, 3d and 4d downstairs, or 6d and 9d in the balcony: a bewildering range of prices for a small cinema. Thomas Jackson formed a new company in 1913 called Wolverhampton, Walsall and District Cinemas and the Bloxwich Electric Palace became part of the empire of the new company.

Just after the First World War the cinema was sold to Pat Collins, who was making Bloxwich the headquarters of his fairground organisation at about the same time. It was also time when Pat Collins was acquiring various cinemas, including two others in the Black Country. The last film shown in the Electric Palace was *"The Tatters"*, screened on Saturday 3rd December 1921. It was then demolished to make way for Pat Collins's brand new cinema; the Grosvenor.

## 12. The Grosvenor
*High Street*

Pat Collins obviously wished to build a cinema of which he could feel proud in his adopted home of Bloxwich. His new cinema was to be called The Grosvenor, and was designed by Hickton and Farmer of Walsall, and built by J. & F. Wootton, at a cost of £12,000. While it was being built, Pat Collins showed films at the Central, as described later. Messrs. Hickton & Farmer had designed about thirty cinemas since 1910 and the Grosvenor was a very pleasing example of their work. The early twenties produced some very attractive Black Country cinemas even if the trade was going through uncertain times.

The frontage of the Grosvenor was treated in a classical style, finished in Hathernware terracotta. It

57. The Grosvenor, 1935.

*(Photo: John Maltby)*

58. The interior of the Grosvenor. 1935.

*(Photo: John Maltby)*

was built to hold a thousand patrons. Four swing doors gave access to a reasonably spacious entrance hall with staircases on each side to the balcony floor. It was opened on 11th December 1922 and Lady Arthur Grosvenor, of Chester, came along to perform the ceremony. Ironically, Pat Collins, who had become Walsall's M.P., could not be present. Lady Grosvenor praised her absent friend and admired the hall. The Mayor of Walsall, and Rev. Father H. McDonnell also spoke, and the latter expressed the hope that Pat would make his way to the House of Lords, to become Lord Bloxwich! The film that followed was *"The Three Musketeers"*, and the proceeds enabled £26.00 to be sent to Walsall Y.M.C.A.

The operators found themselves working in fairly cramped circumstances in a room at the back of the stalls, crammed between the staircases. Legend has it that tall patrons could cast a shadow across the screen! In 1929 Pat Collins appointed young Bill Lockett as third operator and today Mr. Lockett can remember the sound-on-disc system coming to the Grosvenor in July 1930. Western Electric equipment was used and *"Innocents of Paris"* brought the talkies to Bloxwich on 14th July.

Maintaining the arcs while setting up discs and dealing with reel changes every ten minutes made life difficult in the small operating box. Life became much easier in December 1931 when sound-on-film arrived and twenty minutes worth of film was put on one spool. The new equipment was inaugurated on Boxing Day with the film *"To Oblige A Lady"*.

Pat Collins continued to run the Grosvenor several years after selling his other two Black Country cinemas, but in 1935 he sold it to Oscar Deutsch and it became an Odeon. As an Odeon it survived the round of closures that put several old cinemas to death in 1956, but three years later it was sold to a Sunderland firm engaged in light industry. The company acquired the Picture House, Willenhall, at the same time. The last film *"Operation Amsterdam"*, was shown on 2nd May 1959, just before celebrations were being organised locally to celebrate the centenary of Pat Collins' birth.

The building has survived. For many years it became increasingly dilapidated, but about three years ago it was transformed. The original frontage has been given a face lift, but in essence has been preserved, and the premises are now operated as a discotheque-styled night-club using the name "Flix".

106

## 13. The Central
*Park Road*

Not long after the opening of the Electric Palace a local company was formed called the Bloxwich Picture Company. It was registered on 2nd June 1913, with a capital of £2,000. The directors were Samuel Wilkes, Jonah Wilkes, A. J. Wilkes, J. F. W. Binns and Jesse and Frederick Wootton, the builders. Many of the remaining shares were bought by the employees in Samuel Wilkes' lock works.

The company intended to build a cinema more or less on the site of Professor Wood's early shows, referred to earlier. In Park Road a large Wesleyan chapel, built in 1838, had been made redundant by the erection of a more modern chapel elsewhere. By extending this chapel backwards to include the Sunday school building visited by Professor Wood, it was possible to produce a cinema capable of holding five hundred patrons. A raked floor was put in and a small stage provided facilities for cinevariety. Naturally, the work was carried out by J. & F. Wootton.

As the Central Picture Palace it must have opened late in 1913 and one Harry Morris found himself managing the new rival to the Electric Palace. During 1915 and 1916 it was leased to Tom Wood and to some local people it is remembered as the Central, to others it is remembered as "Woods Palace". By the end of the War the original company seemed to have resumed showing the films.

It may have then closed for a short time because on 5th December 1921 we find that it was "reopened" by Pat Collins who wished to continue showing films in Bloxwich while the Grosvenor was being built. Pat Collins' shows continued for exactly one year and the Central closed just before the Grosvenor opened.

Pat Collins then used the Central as a store and a place where his fairground rides could be repaired. In 1937 it was sold to Bert Britain who converted it to a garage. Today, the premises are used by Mid Air equipment. The frontage of the cinema, which was basically the frontage of the original chapel, has remained almost unchanged. One interesting story concerning the Central tells of the tomb of two children buried beneath the central aisle when the raked floor was installed. They were the children of a Wesleyan minister, and they had died of diphtheria. When Bert Britain removed the raked floor in 1937 he discovered their grave. He had them removed and reburied in a more suitable place.

## Willenhall

Travelling anticlockwise around Walsall from Bloxwich one encounters the towns of Willenhall, Darlaston and Wednesbury. The development of the tramway system tied them to Walsall but they are not in any way "suburbs" of Walsall. Each has a distinct history of its own. Willenhall is particularly associated with the manufacture of locks and relishes the nickname "Humpshire" in memory of the locksmiths bent over their tasks. By the beginning of this century both Willenhall and Darlaston were "Urban Districts" each with a population of about 20,000. Cinemas were quickly provided to serve this population.

## 14. The White City
*Hall Street*

Soon after the passing of the Cinematograph Act Fred Redfern opened Willenhall's first cinema in a disused Catholic Church in Hall Street. It had been abandoned when the Catholics moved to a new church, but returned to life as the "White City". It had a balcony and claimed to be capable of holding 700 patrons.

Short films were punctuated with variety acts, some of which were organised as local talent competitions, with prizes for the performer who gained the loudest applause. Teddy Hall assisted Mr. Redfern as the White City generally did good business. It was unpretentious but was not particularly daunted by the opening of the Coliseum. The top of the picture at the Coliseum struck the low ceiling and the White City made much of this by claiming that their films were projected entirely on the screen! It seems to have closed sometime during the First World War, after the new Picture House had raised local expectations of what a cinema should be. The name is still a legend in Willenhall, although the building was demolished sometime ago, after further life as a steel stock-holding warehouse.

The White City was not Willenhall's only experience of early cinematography. Another hall was used for magic lantern shows and early films in Gomer Street. It was to be found next to the Falcon Inn and was possibly a former chapel. When A.P.P.H. opened their cinema in Stafford Street some local residents were careful to call it the *New* Picture House, to distinguish it from this older one. It seems likely, however, by that time films were no longer being shown in Gomer Street.

## 15. The Coliseum and The Dale
*Bilston Street*

The Coliseum was the first cinema in Willenhall worthy of being described as such! It was opened about 1913 or 1914 by Mr. H. Johnson, and used a barn-like building close to Dale House, the home of the Hinks Family. A smart foyer was built in which flowers and mirrors created a favourable impression on the patrons, but the single floored auditorium was still very barn-like and its low ceiling has already been mentioned. Not only was the top of the picture hitting the ceiling but the audience also seemed to suffer the noise from the projector. At first a pianist competed with the buzz from the machines but he was later replaced by a gramaphone.

The "Collie", as it was known, held about 400 patrons. It ran popular childrens matinees and Mr. Johnson distributed little conicle bags of sweets to his young customers paying a 1d on the benches or 2d for a seat. Each week one sweet bag contained a sixpence! Mr. Johnson's son acted as projectionist and a great time was had by all.

When the Picture House opened, the Coliseum was partially eclipsed, just as the White City had been. After the War Thomas Wood presented the programmes, advertising as Wood's Coliseum until July 1921. It was acquired by Herbert Anthony but Thomas Wood continued to advise and assist with the bookings. About 1925 a Mr. Samson tried his hand at running it for a year or two and then it passed to a Mr. and Mrs. Campbell.

59. The Dale, as photographed by Bennett Clark during the mid-thirties.

*(Photo: Wolverhampton Libraries)*

Mrs. Campbell was very business-like and ran the box office. It seems that they ran the Collie until its demise. The talkies arrive at the Picture House and the future looked bleak. Then the last member of the Hinks Family, a Mrs. Price, died and the entire estate, including Dale House and the cinema, were put up for sale. The Coliseum closed its trellis gate for the last time in 1930 or 1931.

The premises were purchased by John Tyler, a successful plumber and builder and decorator supplier in Willenhall. John Tyler, and his daughter Norah, were keen to build a brand new super-cinema on the site of the Coliseum and the malt-house at the back of Dale House. In the endless competition between each of Willenhall's successive cinemas this was to be finer than the Picture House and was inspired by Mr. Tyler's admiration for Wood's Palace.

Plans for the new cinema, the Dale, were therefore prepared by Mr. Hurley Robinson and it is believed to have been built by Messrs. J. & F. Wootton. To make good use of the site the Dale had to abandon the usual concept of a grand frontage and the entrance and foyer extended from the main auditorium towards the corner of Dimingsdale and Bilston Street, like a snake emerging from a basket. It held one thousand, one hundred and fifty patrons in an attractive auditorium that is relatively unchanged even today. The balcony held 275 patrons.

The Dale was opened on Monday 31st October 1932 with *"Viennese Nights"* in Technicolour and the wonders of Western Electric sound. The ceremony was performed by Councillor J. H. Harper, Chairman of Willenhall U.D.C. The entire proceeds of this matinee, nearly £51, were donated to the local Nursing Association. A packed cinema heard Councillor Evans of the Licensing Committe claim that the Tylers had created a cinema worthy of the richest corporations. John Tyler became a director of the Dunstall Cinema Company, and both cinemas were proud of their independence, though John Tyler did not live long to enjoy them.

The Dale passed to his daughter, Norah Tyler, but she died in 1945. The Dale was acquired by Messrs. J. L. and A. H. Brain who had just acquired the Avion cinema at Aldridge (26th September 1938 to 30th December 1967). The new owners left the Dale in the capable hands of the manager, Arthur Holland, who had come from Bilston's Theatre Royal.

The Dale and the Avion closed on the same day, 30th December 1967, with *"Lt. Robinson Crusoe"*. The closure also brought an end to Sunday shows of Indian films, organised by Tarsem Singh Dhami. It had outlived the Picture House and was a fine cinema. A few protests were made by local councillors about its conversion to a Bingo Club, but, nevertheless, it opened

60. The Picture House
*(Photo: Norman Tildesley)*

for Bingo on 16th February 1968.

Bingo is still being played in the Dale while this is being written. Despite some alterations, the auditorium and many details of the building still have a strong cinema-like atmosphere. It is well worth visiting.

### 16. The Picture House
*Stafford Street*

The cinemas built by A.P.P.H. were usually intended to introduce a grandeur and respectability to cinema-going in the towns they selected. In Walsall and Wolverhampton perhaps there was a middle class and affluent class of artisans ready to respond. Perhaps the situation in Willenhall was different. Whatever the reason, Willenhall's Picture House was relatively modest. It was small, only holding 736 patrons and was never quite finished!

The First World War had begun as construction was getting underway and the cafe and shops that should have complimented its frontage were never built. The entrance and foyer never effectively concealed the outline of the auditorium but patrons have told me that the interior was elegant and dignified. It opened on 19th April 1915.

After the War, in 1919, the Picture House was used to present local war heroes with clocks and watches as a token of the town's esteem. The male contribution to the War was reflected in the fact that the manager, Mr. Astbury, had to appoint a lady, Edith Johnson, as the chief operator. She remembers the cinema being called "the New'un" at the time.

As a result of A.P.P.H. being absorbed by its associate P.C.T. the cinema became part of a large national circuit, even if it was only a minor outpost of one. R.C.A. sound equipment was installed in 1929 and the first talkie in Willenhall is believed to have been *"Black Waters"*. One young lady who jumped the queue to get in to see it felt the picture was appropriately murky and could not understand where the sound was coming from! Through the thirties and forties, Willenhall was well served by the Picture House and the Dale, and queues were common.

By the mid-fifties, the Rank Organisation, who had inherited ex P.C.T. halls via Gaumont British, were beginning to close their smaller and older cinemas. The Picture House was a victim of the same "rationalisation plan" as the Odeon, Bloxwich. It closed on 2nd May 1959, with *"Storm Over the Nile"*. The same firm bought both cinemas.

Sometime later it was demolished, and a supermarket has now been built on the site.

## Darlaston

Darlaston is a typical industrial community of the Black Country. Until recently 85% of its working population was engaged in the manufacturing industry. Large firms like Rubery Owen and GKN dominated its well-being until recent unemployment has turned such a world "topsy-turvy". Ironically the centre of Darlaston has gone through its first major redevelopment just as jobs have disappeared. It is therefore difficult to visit Darlaston and imagine the busy factory-dominated town that existed as its first cinemas came into existence.

### 17. The Queen's Hall
*Willenhall Street*

As in other similar towns, films were first shown in Darlaston in the local "variety hall"; the Queen's Hall. The building was on the site of a Wesleyan Sunday School, or was a conversion of that building, and had been in business since the 1890's. "Animated Pictures" were presented between variety acts before the passing of the Cinematograph Act, and subsequently the Queen's Hall obtained a kine licence.

One elderly resident of Darlaston recalls that the films were projected from a make-shift platform erected above the paybox at the rear of the hall. He also recalls that the evening's show included variety acts, melodrama and films. Perhaps its greatest claim to fame is that Billy Russell, the Black Country comedian, worked there about 1910.

It is not clear who owned the Queen's Hall; one record says it was a Manchester firm, another says it was Rob Kennedy. Nor is it clear when the hall closed. Shows probably ceased at the end of, or just after, the First World War. If the Queen's Hall has any rival in claiming to show the first films in Darlaston, it would be Professor Wood. He probably visited the town once a year as his tour brought him through the Black Country.

### 18. The Picturedrome
*Crescent Road*

Darlaston's two pre-First World War cinemas opened within a few months of each other in 1911, and both have histories that have been relatively obscure and difficult to trace. The Picturedrome appears to have been purpose-built and was an imposing building. Its dome was a feature of the Darlaston skyline for many years and its white plastered frontage was most impressive. Its arch-roofed auditorium could hold up to nine hundred patrons.

The local magistrates issued a licence for the Picturedrome on 24th May 1911 and the cinema must have opened straight away, or in June. Although no record of the opening has been found, the Walsall Observer later mentions the cinema in connection with local Coronation festivities.

"On Monday (26th June) about 550 children attending the Central School visited the new Picturedrome in Darlaston where a special programme of pictures, including some fine films of the Coronation procession, were shown. The scholars thoroughly

61. The Picturedrome

*(Photo: from the Collection of Mr. and Mrs. Wooley)*

enjoyed themselves and further batches of children from other schools visited the Picturedrome during the week."

The new cinema became known as "the Drome", and was probably owned and run by a George Williams. In 1922 he sold it to Mr. Brettell of the Hockley Picture House Company, thus beginning the Brettell family's long association with cinema entertainment in Darlaston. Mr. Brettell and Mr. Olliver later formed Colmore Entertainments, running the Picturedrome for the rest of its life and building the Regal, and owning the latter to this day.

The Olympia just managed to introduce talkies to Darlaston ahead of the Drome, but Western Electric equipment was installed in the autumn of 1930 and the two cinemas competed on equal terms once more. In the end, the Olympia was the first to close! In the summer of 1956 the Picturedrome was refurbished by Modernisation Ltd., and the proscenium was widened to accommodate cinemascope and wide screen presentation. It certainly looked smart for its final battle for survival. Leslie Taff managed both the Picturedrome and the Regal in its final years.

Unfortunately, the Picturedrome closed on 2nd February 1959 with *"Escort West"* and *"Guns, Girls and Gangsters"*. The building was not demolished until the summer of 1963 and the site is now a car park. A short service road crosses the car park to the rear of the shops in King Street. In 1981 one of the three names being considered by Walsall Council for this road was Picturedrome Way. There is a Danilo Road in Cannock but I do not think any other Black Country road has been named after a cinema.

## 19. The Olympia
*Blockall*

The Olympia, known as "the Limp", also has origins clouded in mystery. The locally held opinion that it opened very shortly after the Picturedrome is borne out by a short report in the Express and Star, at the time of its closure, stating that the first film, *"Death Before Disaster"*, was shown on 15th October 1911. Unfortunately I have found no other documented verification of this.

Part of the site was once occupied by the Bell Street Chapel and the Trustees of this Chapel were given permission to sell the site in March 1910. A large "L" shaped building was erected, the short "base" of the "L" forming the entrance to the larger part of the building. It seems to have been erected by a Mr. Laycock who intended opening it as a skating rink. It never opened for that purpose, and in July 1912 a new company was formed by Mr. Laycock, and a partner, to take over the premises in the name of Olympia (Darlaston) Ltd., and convert the building to a picture palace. It is, of course, quite possible that films had been shown at the Skating Rink since the October of 1911. Before the new company was formed, an application for a kine licence had been turned down in March 1912, and structural alterations demanded. A composite version of the story would then suggest that films may have been shown at the Skating Rink from October 1911 to March 1912. It would then have closed for proper reconstruction as a cinema.

Whatever the truth about the early course of events, it is certain that in 1912 the local builder, William Taylor Lees, transformed the skating rink into a luxurious picture palace. The conversion was designed by Messrs. Joynson Brothers, a Darlaston architectural practice that had offices adjoining the Picturedrome.

In this form the Olympia opened on 19th October 1912. The Wednesbury Herald, published on the same day, described the building as follows:

"....the outside.....is pleasing but unobtrusive, and gives little idea of the extent of the interior. There is a large entrance hall containing a booking office and swing doors give access to a commodious lounge and refreshment buffet. This lounge is known as the Crush Hall and is one of the most striking features of the Olympia, being of considerable size, with a large lantern roof.... It is comfortably furnished and has a staircase leading therefrom to a cosy dancing room, built above the entrance hall.

.....The hall itself is a revelation, with its beautiful arched roof, gently sloping floor and general air of roomy comfort".

Bernard Williams, later a carpenter and joiner for W. T. Lees, was a choirboy at the time at All Saints Church. It was thought appropriate at the time that a new building should be given a parson's blessing, with full choral support. Mr. Williams went along as part of the choir, and with Sam Hampton conducting, they fulfilled this duty. Even an official blessing could not save the Olympia from the problem of subterranean fires. The cinema was built over some coal that was addicted to spontaneous combustion, possibly stimulated by the weight of the building above it.

In 1913 or 1914 the seats and flooring had to be removed and the whole floor was concreted over. The danger of "wild fire" became one of the legends associated with the cinema, but did not deter Pat Collins from acquiring the cinema at the end of the First World War. He may have been present at the opening of the cinema in 1912 but probably did not acquire it until venturing into the Black Country cinema business about 1919 with the Olympia and the Alhambra, Dudley Port.

For several years it was managed for Pat Collins by Walter Mould. It is known that Walter Mould took the staff of the Olympia for a grand outing to Llangollen by motor-charabanc on 8th August 1920. Pat Collins could not join the party but he helped pay for the trip!

By the end of 1926 it seems that Pat Collins wished to dispose of his two "old" Black Country cinemas. The Olympia was bought by C.D. Cinemas, the partnership run by Mortimer Dent and Joseph Cohen. Two years later the partnership was dissolved and most of the halls belonging to C.D. Cinemas were sold to A.B.C. As well as acquiring smart new cinemas like the one at Edgbaston, A.B.C. found themselves running a strange assortment of converted music halls and skating rinks — including the Olympia. A.B.C. installed sound, the R.C.A. system, in the summer of 1930, just ahead of "the Drome". For many years its capacity was quoted as 969 which made it slightly bigger than its rival, but, of course, both cinemas were outclassed by the arrival of the Regal in 1938.

Blockall is away from the centre of Darlaston and possibly the Limp successfully fulfilled a local need. A.B.C. certainly showed no predisposition to close it until the fifties. The cinema starred on the front cover of the A.B.C. staff magazine in June 1950 when a picture showed a group of A.B.C. staff and National Coal Board staff about to make their annual inspection of the state of the subterranean fire!

The end came very suddenly on 10th December 1955 with *"Thousands Cheer"* starring Gene Kelly. *"Calamity Jane"* starring Doris Day had been booked for the following week but an advertisement appeared stating that the theatre had "closed for redecoration and alterations". Whether there was any intention of re-opening it, or whether the subterranean fire was becoming too much to put up with, we will probably never know.

For a time the building was used as a car showroom but was derelict by the time it was demolished in the mid sixties. Walsall Council have redeveloped the area with new housing, after reassuring themselves that the problem of the subterranean fire has been resolved.

## 20. The Regal
*Pinfold Street*

A brand new super-cinema came to Darlaston at the end of the thirties, not promoted by Oscar Deutsch, who would have regarded Darlaston as too small, or by the Clifton circuit, but by Colmore Entertainments, who already owned the Picturedrome.

The chairman of Colmore Entertainments was Mr. C. O. Brettell, who had purchased the Picturedrome for his Hockley Picture Palace Co., in 1922. His fellow directors were his wife, who booked films for the company's cinemas, and Mr. V. Olliver, at one time associated with the Palace, West Bromwich. The Brettell and Olliver families had inter-married, and Mr. Olliver's son, John, managed the Picturedrome while the new cinema was being planned. Messrs. Brettell and Olliver had been instrumental in building the Tower, West Bromwich, but their other cinema activities had been in Birmingham. By 1938 they controlled a dozen halls.

Darlaston's new cinema was to be called the Regal. It was designed by Ernest Roberts, by now a bold exponent of the simple functionalism of the modern style. 193,000 bricks produced by the Bentley Hall Brick Company formed its massive rectangular walls. The frontage, in reconstructed stone, continued the emphasis on plain rectangular forms. The four pairs of double swing doors were well-recessed behind the building line, increasing the amount of shelter beneath the canopy.

The auditorium held 1043 patrons downstairs, and 372 in the balcony. Ernest Roberts had excelled himself with the design of the interior, and Bryans Adamanta had reproduced his bold flowing lines in plaster painted green, gold and rose pink. Horizontal shading lined the wall below the balcony level and near the ceiling an abstract "border" led from the curtained balcony exit right to the finely moulded ante-proscenium. The Wilton carpetting was green, black and old gold, matching the green appliqued curtains. When there were parted they revealed a festooned screen curtain in flaming gold. The seats were also upholstered in gold.

The Regal was built by J. & F. Wootton Ltd., and was possibly the last cinema they built. Equipment was supplied by Kalee Ltd., and Western Electric Mirrophonic sound system was installed. The "cherry on the top of the cake" was a Compton Theatrone electronic organ, a two-manual instrument that survived in the Regal until just after films ceased to be shown.

The opening took place on Monday 19th September 1938. Miss Thelma White, "the golden-voiced accordionist", appeared on stage, followed by a Micky Mouse cartoon on the screen. Then came a grand organ recital by Leslie Taff and the feature film; *"Make A Wish"*, starring the child-actor Bobbie Breen. It does not seem that any opening ceremony was performed.

The manager, John Olliver, had moved across town from the Picturedrome, but Leslie Taff, the organist, was given managerial responsibility fairly soon after the opening. The cinema became very much associated with Leslie Taff. During the War he broadcast many organ concerts for the BBC, some of which were made on the Regal's organ. He also organised Sunday concerts and variety shows, making good use of the stage and dressing room facilities. Patrons must have come from far afield to the Regal.

Leslie Taff devoted the rest of his career to the Regal, presenting films, playing the organ, organising shows and even a pantomime. Later he presented wrestling, Indian films and, finally, Bingo. When the Compton organ became unreliable and spares were difficult to obtain he could no longer play at the Regal, but after its removal in 1965 a Bird organ was installed to entertain the bingo players.

The Eastern Film Society, led by T. S. Sidhu, started by showing a few films at Wolverhampton's Wulfrun Hall in 1955, moved briefly to the Picturedrome and then to the Regal. The first Indian film shown at the Regal was *"Ladki"*, which played to an audience of 316 on 11th September 1955. The last Indian film was shown on 23rd June 1963 and the E.F.S. moved to the Alhambra, Bilston. By this time Bingo was being introduced on Tuesday and Friday nights and on Sunday afternoons.

The last film was a single performance on Saturday 1st February 1964. The main feature was *"Duel of the Titans"* starring Steve Reeves and Gordon Scott, supported by *"The Ringer"*. The next day Bingo began "full-time". For some unknown reason, it was called The Regent Cinema Bingo Club, unless the advertisement was misprinted.

Now, almost twenty years later, the Regal is still playing Bingo. Only minor alterations have been made to both the exterior and the interior of the building. It is managed by Leslie Taff's son and still owned by Colmore Entertainments.

62. The Regal, as a Bingo & Social Club. 1981.

*(Photo: Ned Williams)*

### Wednesbury

Wednesbury today is part of the Metropolitan Borough of Sandwell. No doubt I shall offend many by including it with Walsall. As a town of over thirty thousand inhabitants it obviously never regarded itself as part of *anywhere* else. Topographically it dominates the eastern half of the Black Country with its two churches standing proudly above the plateau and visible from almost *everywhere* else. As the M6 meets the M5, the motorist travelling northwards feels the eastern half of the Black Country closing in around him and those two churches are a signal to the Blackcountryman that he is nearing home. It is worth climbing the hill to the grimy stonework of St. Bartholomew's, or the red and blue brick of St. Mary's. Looking westwards, once upon a time across the roof of the Rialto, you can see Dudley Castle and the central ridge of the Black Country stretching from the Rowley Hills to Sedgley Beacon.

Wednesbury is at a crossroad, where Holyhead Road from Birmingham to Wolverhampton crosses the Dudley to Walsall Road which was once the beginning of a principle link between the Black Country and the East Midlands. The South Staffordshire Railway crossed the Great Western Railway at Wednesbury, and nearby the Patent Shaft and Axletree Company built their steelworks. All these things have gone; similarly Wednesbury no longer has a cinema, or a town hall.

As in other towns, Professor Wood used to bring his travelling show to Wednesbury during the first decade of this century and films appeared between variety acts at the local theatre; in this case the New Theatre Royal, which in 1910 changed its name to the Hippodrome.

No place of entertainment in Wednesbury really has a straightforward history and before we dismiss the Hippodrome as being part of theatre history it is worth noting that when H. J. Barlow's repertory company began to face declining audiences in the fifties, the Hippodrome did try showing films at the beginning of the week with live drama at the end of the week! The theatre disappeared twenty years ago.

### 21. The Kings Hall, The Borough Hall, and The Rialto
*Earps Lane*

The story of this institution is typical of the bizarre history of Wednesbury's cinemas. In 1860 a very primitive theatre was built in Earps Lane called The Royal. For a while it served as a kind of public hall and was hired to any touring show prepared to use it. In 1883 it was purchased by the Salvation Army but in 1909 they were able to move to a new citadel, and the building was sold to Benjamin Kennedy.

It was reopened about September 1909 as the Kings Hall. Ben Kennedy used this name for the hall at which he showed films in Birmingham. Together with Bosco's "Palace" in West Bromwich, it provides an example of films being shown regularly in permanent premises just before the Cinematograph Act. Variety acts were still used between films but the Kings Hall presented itself as a cinema. It was managed by Cinema Veteran, Charles Pindar. One young lad who helped Len Kelly, the operator, during the First World War, can still recall

113

the night that a bomb dropped on Wednesbury from a Zeppelin. He claims someone dived over the balcony when hearing the explosion.

Ben Kennedy seems to have relinquished some of his Black Country halls at the end of the War, including the Tivoli, in Tipton and the Kings Hall. It was sold to Messrs. Black and Hicks and substantially rebuilt to open as the Borough Theatre. It changed hands at least once more before being acquired by a Birmingham man, Mr. I. Kraines, who probably owned a building firm. He seems to have substantially renovated the place and then leased it to Mr. and Mrs. Jones of the Picture House, Princes End.

Newly adopting the name "Rialto", it opened under Mr. Jones' care on 24th October 1927. The first film was *"Nostromo"* and, in the freshly decorated hall, the audience enjoyed the film and the music of an orchestra led by Harry Stradd. The assistant manager of the Rialto from October 1927 to April 1930 was none other than Fred Leatham. He had left the keyboard at Princes End, was gaining experience of running a cinema and left to embark on an amazing career as a cinema proprietor, as described in Section One.

1930 was a hectic year at the Rialto. The cinema closed altogether for a month in the spring, reopening on Whit Monday, 9th June, with *"The Drake Case"* supported by a stage act, *"The Musical Monarchs"*. Sound was introduced with a special charity show on Sunday 2nd November of the same year. Mr. Kraines

reappeared in 1931 and set about rebuilding the place yet again. Possibly one reason for doing this was to improve the sound as it is believed that Mr. Kraines installed BTH equipment at this stage.

When it was closed on this occasion, on 27th June 1931, advertisements promised that it would be "much enlarged and vastly improved". This time Mr. Kraines managed to lease the Rialto to A.B.C. and they commenced business on 14th September 1931. They may have taken on the lease with a view to assessing the potential of business in Wednesbury. At first they retained the services of Mr. Jones. Quite what happened next is delightfully obscure. It is quite possible that A.B.C. decided not to continue running the Rialto and by 1936 or 1937 it had closed yet again. Mr. Kraines, although not apparently interested in running a cinema himself, never gave up. Another spate of major rebuilding began. In six weeks an imposing new frontage was built, believed to be designed by Ernest Roberts. A new stage and the latest type of glass-beaded screen were installed, as well as new seats for nine hundred and fifty patrons. The work was carried out for the new lessee, Cyril Joseph. On this occasion, Cyril Joseph called his enterprise Clifford Pictures.

The reopening, on Monday 15th August 1938, was a suitably grand affair. The ceremony was performed by Wednesbury's mayor, Councillor Charles Collins, but Charlie Kettle, from the Palace, opened the proceedings by introducing the new manager, Frank Ellis. Cyril

63. The Rialto, awaiting demolition in 1973.

*(Photo: Andy Rutter)*

Joseph told his guests, including Tom Wood, that the Rialto was now a "super-cinema" and everybody sat back to watch *They Gave Him A Gun* starring Spencer Tracy.

This restless cinema settled down to an undisturbed life under the control of Clifford Pictures until Cyril Joseph began dismantling his empire in the mid-fifties. The Rialto returned to the trustees of the estate of the late Mr. Kraines. With a nice twist of history it was now leased to Reay Wood. Tom Wood's son had found himself running the Savoy in Bilston and by leasing the Rialto he commanded enough seats to secure reasonable films.

He installed Cinemascope and tried to cope with dwindling audiences but admitted defeat on 30th March 1957 with *Somebody Up There Likes Me* starring Paul Newman. The following Monday Syncopating Sandy Strickland used the cinema to try to break the 134 hour non-stop piano playing record! As he broke the record the following Saturday, people paid a shilling to go in and see him do it. Ironically, every seat was taken.

The Rialto lay dormant for a time but a cinema with so many openings and closures was not beaten yet. On 10th November 1958 it was reopened by Neville Wright, with *Smiley*. It was redecorated again and Neville Wright boldly embarked on a six year lease. In the first year he prospered and installed the first non-carbon projector lamp in the Black Country into his machines. Somehow he managed to improve attendance, but as the new decade began, matters worsened. He kept the Rialto alive until 8th July 1961 and then organised a special farewell presentation with "something for all the family". The last programme began at 5.55 p.m. and included *Journey To The Centre Of The Earth* plus *Young and Dangerous* and other films, plus a live musical group on stage; *The Renegades*. Neville Wright made special presentations to two teenagers who had helped him run the cinema, Michael Griffiths and Vincent Docherty. This really was the last film show in Earps Lane.

As from Friday 21st July 1961 Miles Jervis operated his Midland Cinemas Bingo Club in the Rialto and this activity continued into the early seventies, by which time much of the housing in the area had been demolished. In 1971 the new ring road had to be bent to avoid the Rialto. Wednesbury Council were now the landlord but Miles Jervis' lease was still operative. Demolition finally caught up with the Rialto in June 1973. Earps Lane has completely disappeared under a newly landscaped grassy bank.

## 22. The Palace
*Upper High Street*

As films were proving successful in the rather unsatisfactory Kings Hall, it was not surprising that several local businessmen came together to build a proper cinema. They formed the Wednesbury Imperial Picture Company and the local architect, Mr. C. W. D. Joynson, drew up plans for a hall in Upper High Street to hold six hundred patrons.

Messrs. Summerhill and Jellyman built the new cinema, starting work in May 1912. The exterior was treated in white cement and was carried out in "free renaissance" style. The facade was crowned with a life-size female figure bearing an electrically lighted flare. It had a fully carpetted raked floor and scarlet plush tip up seats throughout. Every patron was guaranteed a perfect view of the screen. The Kings Hall still offered crowded benches and poor sight lines.

The grand opening took place on Monday 7th October 1912. Mr. Joynson presented the Mayor, Alderman Pritchard, with a silver key, and asked him to declare the cinema open. An "augmented orchestra" provided accompaniment to *The Man of the Wilds* and Edison's *Relief of Lucknow*.

As its full name was the "Imperial Picture Palace" it was sometimes known as the "Imperial" and sometimes the "Palace". In 1927 when Mr. Jones became manager and lessee of the Boro, as the Kings Hall was then known, Charles Pindar preserved his association

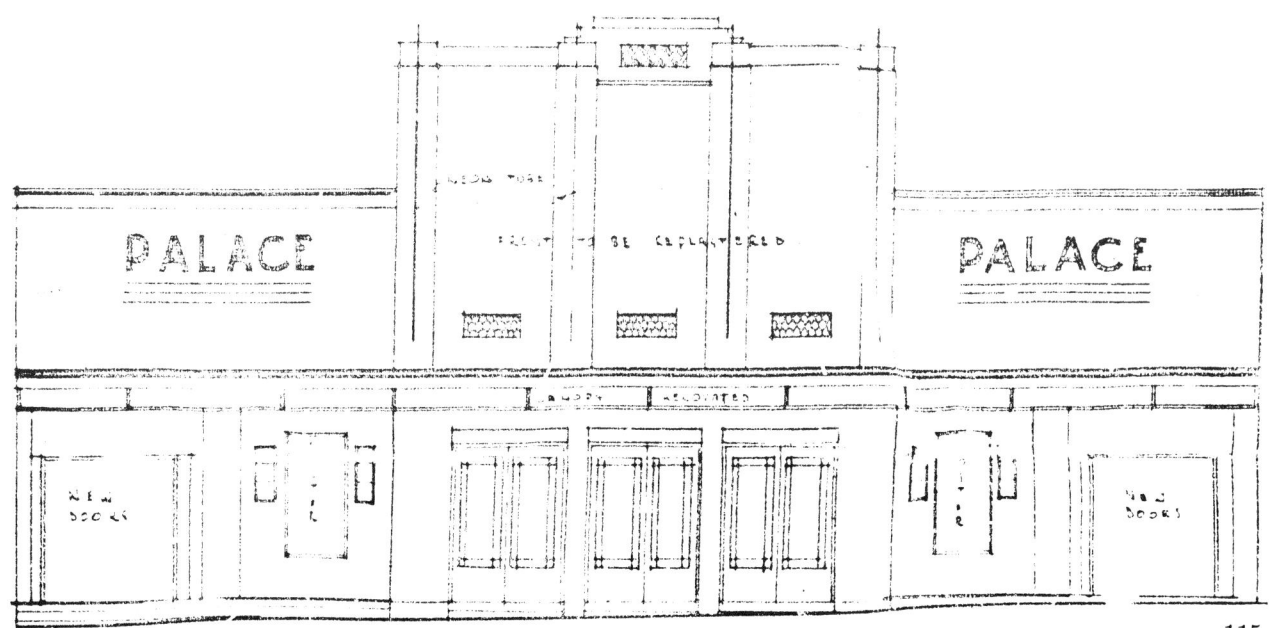

with Wednesbury by moving to the Palace, and stayed there until the first closure in 1937. Considering it was the town's first purpose-built cinema it had lost some of its prestige when the Picture House was opened. It was the last of Wednesbury's three cinemas to introduce sound, towards the end of 1931. The original building closed on 29th May 1937 with *"Not So Dirty"*. By then Thomas Wood had acquired a controlling interest in the Palace. His plans to reconstruct it unfortunately coincided with his retirement and the leasing of all his cinemas to Cyril Joseph.

Ernest Roberts had drawn up the plans for the new Palace. The former cinema was to form the crush hall to the new auditorium constructed at the rear of the original one. This would now provide accommodation for just over twelve hundred patrons. The construction work was carried out by J. & F. Wootton. The original entrance to the Palace was retained, but altered to give it a more modern appearance, and transformed by the effect of neon lighting. BTH equipment was installed.

The new Palace was opened on 27th September 1937 with Cyril Joseph, calling himself "Dual Pictures", as the host. Thomas Wood, now an alderman of Bilston, came along to pay tribute to the original Palace and to recall the even earlier times when he and his father had presented their travelling shows at the Town Hall. The cinema was declared open by Wednesbury's Mayor, Councillor Jack Smith and everyone enjoyed *"Gold Diggers of 1937"* starring Dick Powell and Joan Blondell.

The Midland Advertiser described the Palace as "The last word in modern cinema construction" and Charlie Kettle must have felt that he had not done too badly in coming from the mighty Tower in West Bromwich to manage the splendid "Palace". Both Cyril Joseph's cinemas in Wednesbury must have felt slightly overshadowed by the new Gaumont but the popularity of film-going during the War kept all three cinemas busy. During the War, Miss Fellows moved from the Rialto to manage the Palace while Charlie Kettle moved to the Olympia, Wolverhampton. Miss Fellows stayed until Cyril Joseph's lease expired in 1958.

Miles Jervis II replaced Cyril Joseph as the lessee of the Palace and tried to tackle the problem of declining audiences. Wrestling was presented on Wednesday evenings, but when this failed to gain popularity, bingo was introduced in the spring of 1961. The freehold of the building now belonged to G. H. Luce, a Wolverhampton businessman, but, while Miles Jervis was introducing bingo, the cinema was being sold to a Manchester firm of property developers.

Miles Jervis seemed reluctant to abandon his presence in Wednesbury, even if only to present bingo. By July 1961 he added a Sunday session of bingo at the Palace and had leased the Rialto to present Friday to Monday sessions of the game. By the end of the year he was persuaded to give up his lease on the Palace and the last film show was screened on 9th December, featuring *"Goliath and the Dragon"* and *"The Fourth Square"*.

On Monday 11th December 1961 the building was auctioned and the fittings were sold a few days later. Some demolition began and then ceased. The boarded-up remains of the Palace survived as an eyesore until wholesale demolition of the Upper High Street prepared

the way for development in 1964. Although not completed by him, it was Tom Wood's last cinema project in the Black Country. His son felt that it was a tragedy that such a fine and costly building lasted only twenty-four years.

---

### 23. The Picture House, The Gaumont later known as The Odeon and the Silver
*Walsall Street*

Perhaps a measure of the importance of Wednesbury was that A.P.P.H. chose the town as a site for one of their cinemas, or perhaps it was the loyalty to their homeland of a number of A.P.P.H. executives that prompted them to bring "wholesome amusement" to the Black Country.

The plans for the Wednesbury Picture House were drawn by the London architects Messrs. Atkinson and Alexander. The front elevation in Walsall Street, was carried out in Carra Ware and inside the presence of much polished wood panelling and tapestries gave the place a very luxurious atmosphere. Construction started in 1914 and was then suspended when the War began. Work was then resumed, but meanwhile rumours had apparently been spread that A.P.P.H. was a German company, all of which had to be strenuously denied when the cinema opened.

The Picture House was opened by the Mayor, Councillor Bishop, on 25th March 1915. The nine hundred guests, occupying every seat in the cinema, were welcomed by Mr. Newbould of A.P.P.H. who stressed that the company was British, that the Managing Director, Dr. Jupp, was from Walsall, and that the company was safely in the hands of South Staffordshire men. It was their nineteenth cinema to open. The first programme of films included *"The Man In The Street"*, *"Andy And The Redskins"* by Edison, *"The Middleman"* and a Keystone comedy *"The Face On The Bar Room Floor"*. Afterwards the Wednesbury Herald commented "......That such a building should have been provided in Wednesbury is a compliment to the town".

Like all A.P.P.H. cinemas, the one in Wednesbury later flew the flag of P.C.T. and then Gaumont British, but generally The Picture House had a less chequered history than the Palace or the Rialto. The Picture House introduced the talkies to the town on 11th November 1929 with Al Jolson in *"The Singing Fool"* on the R.C.A. system. (P.C.T. introduced sound at Dudley's Criterion on the same day).

Whatever its prestige or position in the pecking order of cinemas, the Picture House was still in Wednesbury. It therefore seems inevitable that it should close, be transformed, and reopened, at least once! On Saturday 8th January 1938 The Picture House closed with *"History Is Made At Night"* starring Jean Arthur and Charles Boyer. The local paper explained:

"The word went forth, the Picture House was to come down, only for a finer building to arise in far more glorious array on the site of the old one".

The replacement, the Gaumont, was designed by Messrs. W. E. Trent and W. S. Trent and W. S. Trent, assisted by H. L. Cheey of G.B.'s Architect's Department. The new "super-cinema" to accommodate 1594

64. The Gaumont, photographed from the roof of the
Public Baths, 1954.

*(Photo: Sandwell Libraries)*

patrons, was built in just over six months at a cost of
about £45,000. The Ideal Kinema claimed,

"......(it).....has achieved a standard of design, suitability, beauty and accommodation which will be
difficult to improve upon".

The facade was faced with cream faience slabs with a
thin blue tile insert to form regular squares. The building was dominated by a sixty foot high tower. The
large canopy and the tower were much enhanced at
night by the use of neon light.

The large entrance hall, with its peach coloured walls
swept the patron past the central paybox and down
steps to the main foyer, from which central doors led to
the stalls and side staircases led to the circle. The
auditorium, which tapered towards the screen, was
relatively plain, reflecting the contemporary realisation
that concentration should be directed towards the
screen. A simple diamond shaped pattern was carried
out in the plaster work, painted peach and blue.
Gaumont British Magnus projectors and the latest
Duosonic equipment were installed.

The Gaumont was opened by the mayor, Councillor
Collins, on Monday 10th October 1938, supported by
Graham Moffatt and Moore Mariott, who also appeared
in the feature film, *"Convict 99"* starring Will Hay.
Councillor Collins had already opened the new Rialto
during his year of office and on this occasion made
special mention of the work the construction of the
Gaumont had brought to local people. About one
hundred local men had been employed by McLoughlin
and Harvey, the contractors, and the structural steel-

work had been made by Rubery Owen at Darlaston.

Sidney Clulow, who had managed the Picture House,
was retained at the Gaumont, joined by several other
staff who had worked there many years. In two years,
the town's three cinemas had been completely renewed
and all could now settle down to compete with one
another and fight the local council on the question of
Sunday opening.

Perhaps it was inevitable that a cinema as fine as the
Gaumont should outlive its rivals. On the 9th March
1964, after the other two had closed, Wednesbury's
surviving cinema changed its name to the Odeon. By
then it was being managed by Tom Lloyd who had
watched his employer close Wolverhampton's cinemas,
and must have wondered how long life could continue
in Wednesbury. Like the Rialto and the Palace, the
Odeon enjoyed an unexpected extension to its life.

The Rank Organisation "closed" the Odeon on
Saturday 29th January 1972, but the cinema reopened
the very next day as the Silver. Odeons have not very
often been sold to anyone wishing to continue their
operation as a cinema, but in this case the Silver Cinema
Co. Ltd. bought the place and carried on. One of the
principal members of the new company was Tarsem
Singh Dhami, whose career is described elsewhere.

The Silver presented English language films six days
a week and Indian films on Sundays. The reprieve was
short. Ladbrokes purchased the cinema and continued
the shows until they obtained a gaming licence. The last
English language film show was on 18th May 1974,

featuring *"Easy Rider"* and *"Barry Mackenzie"*, although the last Indian film may have been shown a few weeks later

As a Ladbroke's Bingo and Social Club the building has survived and will hopefully continue to add its dignified presence to Wednesbury for many more years to come.

118

# SECTION FOUR　　THE CENTRAL VILLAGES

## Introduction

Today the Black Country is divided, for administrative purposes, into four large boroughs of about a quarter of a million people each. To accept their boundaries for the purpose of surveying local cinemas does not seem entirely satisfactory. To me the very act of lumping great chunks of the Black Country into these units seems contrary to the nature of the region, which as you travel through it seems to consist of many small units with strong local identities of their own. This "conurbation of villages" can be felt very strongly in the area I have chosen to call, "The Central Villages". Here we will look at the cinemas of Lower Gornal out on the western side of the Black Country, climb the central ridge to Sedgley, and descend from that ridge into the eastern half of the Black Country; into Coseley and Tipton. Even within that area many communities feel themselves to be quite distinct from their neighbours. A man who had grown up in Hurst Hill, a small community between Sedgley and Coseley, recalled the cinema going days of his youth when he could choose to walk to "Page's" or "Jack Darby's", or occasionally travel to Bilston to the Savoy. He would never have dared to venture into Bradley, however, for fear of the xenophobia of the local inhabitants!

The cinemas of this area were often small and certainly intensely local. As can be seen, they were often known by their nicknames. They are the most difficult to research from the historian's point of view and here you will find the greatest number of gaps in this book's narrative. None of them exists as a cinema today. Yet despite both these factors, they possess colourful histories that have become legends. As someone says to a newspaper proprietor in a John Ford Western, "If you don't have the facts, print the legend!".

## Lower Gornal

### 1. The Alexandra
*Redhall Street*

It is appropriate that our tour of the cinemas of the central villages of the Black Country should begin in Lower Gornal. The village, the legendary home of Aynuk and Ayli, maintained its Black Country character long enough to become a symbol of that culture. Two reasons, among others, may account for this. First its relative isolation, and secondly, the fact that the coal mining industry survived here, at Baggeridge Colliery, long after it had disappeared from the rest of the region. One of life's great experiences is to catch the 137 bus in Birmingham, Britain's "second city", and travel on an incredible tortuous journey through the Black Country until reaching the frontier of civilisation itself at Lower Gornal. Here the local dialect is possibly too strong to ask for directions, but the intrepid explorer will stagger up the hill until, in the most unlikely of surburban surroundings, he will come across the building that was once the Alexandra cinema.

Over a hundred years ago Doctor Hickin's Pit had worked the coal in the Redhall Road area, and later the travelling fair came to that part of Gornal and one local writer claims that illegal cock-fighting took place there. The man who brought the cinematograph to Gornal and chose to build a cinema in Redhall Street was Ernest Arthur Grenville Jones, an electrical engineer, who, at that time, lived in Pensnett. In March 1912 he registered a company called Alexandra Halls (Midlands) Ltd., with a capital of £500 and with three directors, himself, D. Jones and C. F. Webb. It seems that they hoped to own several cinemas.

Construction of the Alexandra must have proceeded quickly. It was a simple timber-framed building clad in corrugated iron. There seems to be no record of an exact opening date, but the Dudley Herald of 4th May 1912 records that the cinematograph licence had just been issued to the Alexandra and it can be assumed that it opened its doors as soon as possible after the granting of the licence.

The small hall held about five hundred people and was immediately successful. Many Gornal folk came twice weekly to see each programme and it became an established local social institution. It quickly earned the nickname, "The Bump", because of the noise from its slow-revving Crossley single cylinder gas engine which drove the generator in a shed at the side of the building. The stars of the silent screen became popular figures in Gornal, and the cinema itself produced its own legends: Uncle George, the drunken pianist, Ada at the cash desk, and Arlo, the chucker-out. One patron acquired local fame for laughing so much. His laughter apparently attracted further custom, so Jack Pugh was admitted free!

The "talkies" were about to bring Lower Gornal up-to-date in 1931, commencing Monday 31st August, but unfortunately a tragedy intervened. On the previous Thursday, 27th August 1931, Ernest Jones arrived at the cinema at about five o'clock to inspect the installation of the new "Imperial" sound equipment. Half an hour later, the operator, Francis Danks, from Shutt End, arrived and climbed into the operating room. By the time the first patrons were arriving, at about six o'clock, it was clear that something was going wrong as black smoke was pouring from the operating room. The fire itself seems to have started in the rewind room and although Ernest Jones and an assistant named Mr. Davenall, tried to extinguish the fire and rescue Frank Danks they failed.

George Ball, who lived nearby, also tried to rescue the unfortunate projectionist. Eventually he succeeded, after reaching the room via a ladder to a window. By then the fire was so intense that the Bilston Fire Brigade could not prevent the entire destruction of the cinema. Frank Danks died the same night at Dudley Guest

66. The Picture House, as a D.I.Y. store, 1981.

*(Photo: Ned Williams)*

Hospital. Ernest Jones was badly burnt but was determined to rebuild the cinema. Both men were non-smokers and the cause of the fire was never established.

"The Bump" was rebuilt and probably reopened as a sound cinema about 1933, but was now built much more substantially. Meanwhile, Ernest Jones also became associated with the Castle Cinema, in Dudley High Street, for a few years. In 1939 the cinema was acquired by Ken Jones and a Mr. W. H. Smith to be administered by Cinema Accessories Ltd., in other words; it had become a remote outpost of the Clifton circuit.

At some stage the new proprietors installed BTP sound equipment and every now and again it was refurbished in some minor way but essentially the Alexandra remained very unchanged and remarkably well supported, while other halls declined. By outliving places like the Regal, Wednesfield, it inherited seats from the larger cinema! I remember visiting the Bump in 1965. My companion and I had walked through the countryside from Pensnett to see *"Help"* and after the show a member of the staff presented my companion with the poster from the display case at the front of the cinema — perhaps in recognition of the fact that we were foreigners. It had been a noisy audience and everyone seemed to know one another, but the Beatles then seemed as popular in Gornal as Pearl White or William S. Hart had once been. As we walked back to Dudley via the dark windswept wastes behind Gibbons Brickworks one had a strong feeling of having just visited a remote oasis.

Alas, it all came to an end on 24th September 1966 with a screening of *"Those Magnificent Men in Their Flying Machines"*. The building later had a further burst of life as the Gay Throstles Club, but perhaps noisy football club supporters upset the sedate atmosphere of Redhall Road because the Club closed a few years ago, and since then the building has been boarded-up and is unused, its stark outline is still a feature of the hillside above the Gornal Wood bus terminus.

---

**YOUR LOCAL
CLIFTON CINEMA**
LOWER GORNAL (Alexandra) —
Those Magnificent Men in Their
Flying Machines (U) 5.20 & 8.00.

## Sedgley

### 2. The Picture House
*Dudley Road*

From Lower Gornal it is possible to climb the central ridge of the Black Country to Upper Gornal to join the main road from Dudley to Wolverhampton. At the point where Upper Gornal slides into Sedgley stood the Picture House, known to its patrons as "Jack Darby's".

Jack Darby was the licensee of the Leopard. He was a saddler by trade but came to this typical nineteenth century public house, with its own brewery at the rear of the premises, in 1905. At the time a large public hall stood next door, separated by a lane that took the trams to their depot behind that hall. The latter, known as "The Drill Hall", was built sometime in the previous century but our story concerns its twentieth century use.

It was turned into a cinema by a Mr. Lewis but, like "The Bump", its opening date is elusive. It seems likely that it opened late in 1911 or early in 1912. The earliest record I have found of its existence is a tiny note in the Dudley Herald stating that during May 1912 Mr. J. Lewis loaned the Picture Palace to local children for their spring pageant. About Mr. J. Lewis himself I have found nothing apart from the cryptic possibility that he may have later appeared as the proprietor/manager of a cinema in Wednesfield!

By the end of 1912 the cinema had been acquired by a Birmingham solicitor, Mr. Ernest Gilbert, who, with a friend, Fred Elvins, had registered the Midland Cinema Company on 27th November. They ran the Picture House for just over a year.

On 8th December 1913 Jack Darby took over. Along with his friends, Clifford Fellows and Joseph Eustace Fellows, he re-decorated the hall and "reopened" it. Jack Darby later acquired the Fellows Brothers' interests when they died. It was about the same size as the Alexandra and enjoyed a similar success. Possibly performances were quieter as the gas engine was at the rear of the cinema, and Sam Hartland's piano-accompaniments could be clearly heard.

Jack Darby retired from The Leopard in the mid-

65. The Alexandra, in retirement, 1981.

*(Photo: Ned Williams)*

twenties, and handed the Picture House over to his son, Howard Darby, in the early thirties. Howard Darby took a partner, a Mr. Holmes, in 1936 and set about bringing the Picture House up-to-date. A balcony was put in, which increased the hall's capacity to six hundred and thirty-one. A Western Electric sound system brought the talkies to Sedgley.

About the same time a brand new Clifton was being built in the centre of Sedgley, opening in May 1937, but this did not destroy the trade at the Picture House. In fact trade increased as the little cinemas had a reputation for warmth, and "order" was strictly maintained so that people could hear the soundtrack. The Clifton, like a few other super-cinemas, seemed cold and cavernous by comparison. During the Second World War the two cinemas shared the newsreels so relations between them cannot have been bad.

The Picture House carried on with its two programmes a week, two evening performances on a Saturday night and a children's matinee, often packed to capacity. Sometime early during the War a bomb dropped nearby and blew the neon-lighting off the front of the cinema. Howard Darby was in the A.R.P. (which had its HQ in the Tram Depot behind the cinema) and found the words "Picture House" torn off the front of the building. What did it matter? It was always known, and is still remembered, as "Jack Darby's". Just to cause a little confusion it was sometimes called the "Picture House and Hippodrome" in trade directories!

Mr. Holmes left the partnership sometime during the War and Howard Darby, and his wife, were left to run the place for the rest of its life. Although it was a small cinema they never regarded it as a "flea-pit". It was kept spotlessly clean by two sisters, Mrs. Britain and Mrs. Marsh, and the warmth and the atmosphere of an "orderly house" have already been mentioned.

During the troubled fifties Howard Darby still felt it was worth spending £4000 on re-decorating the cinema, replacing the Kalee projectors with new equipment capable of presenting cinemascope, and installing a wide screen. The remaining problem was one that always beset the independent exhibitor; one of obtaining films not already seen in Dudley or Wolverhampton,

modest trolley-bus journeys away, or at the Clifton. It was not possible to stay in business by endlessly reviving old favourites.

On 2nd January 1960 the chief operator, Jim Harrison, who had been there since the early thirties, projected the last show. The film was, *"The Mouse that Roared"*. Then came the problem of finding a future use for the building as various manufacturers could not obtain planning permission to use the place. In the end it had to be leased for retail use only, and since then it has been an interior decorating/D.I.Y. store, although its exterior has remained basically unchanged right up to the present time. However, all trace of emergency exit doors on either side of the main entrance has disappeared and no sign of its past as a cinema exists inside the building.

Like "The Bump" and "Pages", "Jack Darby's" is still a local legend and details of its past are still the subject of argument in The Leopard or at the Sedgley and Upper Gornal Labour Club. Maybe someone still possesses a monthly programme the Picture House used to issue, headed "What's On". Howard Darby claims they were the first to coin this title as a guide to forthcoming entertainment.

### 3. The Clifton
*Sedgley Bull Ring*

About a quarter of a mile from the Picture House the Wolverhampton Road reaches the centre of the village of Sedgley at The Bull Ring. I do not know when bull-baiting last featured as entertainment in the village, but in the nineteen thirties this seemed an ideal site to build a super-cinema. Like other cinemas being planned at the time, this cinema was to have a large car park available and, as well as serving the host-community, there was a feeling that the middle-class patron would drive to a cinema, and to be situated half-way between two large towns was as good as being in the centre of one of them!

Sedgley's Clifton was designed by Roland Satchwell, by then a member of the Clifton board, and was built by the Wolverhampton contractor, H. J. Amies and Sons Ltd. The basic steel and concrete structure was concealed behind a particularly handsome frontage carried out in cream faience with a low black dado. The use of a corner site was exploited by continuing the cream faience across the front of the cafe and shops that extended round the corner into Ettymore Road. The four entrances beneath the canopy formed logical continuations of the lines of the four large vertical windows of the balcony lounge. The windows featured attractive leaded glass. The Clifton therefore has a much lighter, and less fortress-like presence than Roland Satchwell's work at Penn, or Fallings Park.

Much of the Clifton's equipment and fittings was common to other cinemas on the circuit. In this instance 1091 patrons could be entertained in Turner's latest tip-up seats, 779 in the stalls, and 312 in the circle. (This figure was fourteen less than appeared in trade directories!). As usual, BTH projectors and sound equipment were provided in the lofty operating room and BTH Deaf Aids could be obtained at the pay box.

The Clifton was opened on Monday 17th May 1937 by Captain Clift himself, and the proceedings commenced at 2.30 p.m. After the Pathe News and a cartoon the audience enjoyed *"San Francisco"*, starring Clark Gable, Jeanette MacDonald and Spencer Tracy. Programmes were changed twice weekly, and during the first few weeks favourites like Will Hay, George Formby, Jessie Matthews and Tarzan all appeared on the new screen.

The first manager was Mr. H. W. H. Crane. He had been in the cinema business since 1915 and came from a theatrical family. He had already worked for six years at the Scala and Castle cinemas, Dudley, so had established many friends in the area. He left Sedgley two years later to manage the Clifton at Coseley, where he stayed until its closure. The manager most strongly associated with the Sedgley Clifton was Mr. Maxwell Gordon who arrived after the closure of his Clifton at Fallings Park and supervised the cinema through its sad decline. At the time of the Sedgley Clifton's opening he had been its young chief operator. One Saturday morning matinee about 1970 he allowed me to view *"Oh! Mr. Porter"* as the sole occupant of the circle while the children in the stalls below maintained the traditional disorder.

Along with other Cliftons, the one at Sedgley provided variety shows and pop concerts in the fifties thus keeping alive the tradition of live-theatrical use of cinema buildings, and, unlike some of its companions, it seemed to have a will to survive. When I first visited the Clifton, Sedgley, in the mid sixties, I found myself in a packed cinema enjoying a revival of *"Gone With The Wind"*. (Perhaps Clark Gable was popular in Sedgley!). However, by the mid seventies it seemed in a far less healthy state. It had outlived the Gaumont, Wolverhampton, and the Odeon, Dudley, but Bingo was being introduced for two nights a week.

By 1978 quite a few seats had disappeared, which added an extra bizarre quality to sitting in a very empty cinema. By the final show only 845 seats remained in use. In the April of that year the building was acquired by the Jarglen Company, and Maxwell Gordon and his eleven staff were given their notice. Dudley Licensing Committee transferred the Bingo licence to Jarglen commenting, "There were no objections" but when they announced their intention of going over to bingo

67. The Clifton, as a Bingo & Social Club. 1981.

*(Photo: Ned Williams)*

full-time some opposition was mobilised.

Although support for the films had dwindled to almost nothing, several local people opposed their total withdrawal, and I wrote a letter to Dudley's planning chief on behalf of the local Film Society but our protests had no effect. Jarglen were merely doing what had become inevitable, and at least have restored some social purpose to the building by running it successfully as a bingo hall.

The last films shown at the Clifton, Sedgley, were *"The Stud"* and *"The Anna Contract"* on Saturday 17th June 1978. Since then Bingo has been played seven nights a week without any significant changes having been made to the cinema, although I feel the old lady is beginning to show her age, as her faience begins to crack and letters drop from her name!

### Coseley

### 4. The Coseley Picture House
### (later known as The Cosy Cinema)
*Ivy House Lane*

Sedgley's cinemas are not far from the crest of the central ridge that bisects the Black Country. What could have been more romantic after an evening at the Clifton, than a stroll over Sedgley Beacon to admire the twinkling lights of the conurbation? Where the base of the ridge meets the eastern plateau beneath the Beacon, where the sea of lights begins, lies the village of Coseley. At one time, Coseley could have been divided into smaller communities, such as Roseville, Deepfields and Daisy Bank; small hamlets with a history of mining. When the New Birmingham-Wolverhampton Road was built in the twenties it bisected Coseley in general, and a local road known as Ivy House Lane in particular. In this lane was "Page's", Coseley's equivalent to "Darby's" or "The Bump", and contemporary with them.

William Page, a cabinet-maker from Walsall, decided to build a cinema in Coseley in 1912. He formed a partnership with a Mr. Cook and they gained planning permission for their project in December 1912. The cinema is often said to have opened in that year but construction did not proceed quite as quickly as that! Even so, Messrs. Page and Cook felt they were ready for business by the following March and applied for their licence. Four Coseley Urban District Councillors decided to make a prompt inspection of the place and one week later, at a meeting on 18th March, reported in favour of granting the licence subject to one or two suggested alterations being carried out. They made a second inspection four days later and the licence was issued. We can assume, therefore, that the Coseley Picture House, as it was then called, commenced business in the Spring of 1913. The name "Cosy Cinema" was not displayed on the cinema until after the Second World War, but everybody simply called it "Page's" anyway.

William Page lived opposite the cinema, and his son later lived in a bungalow built adjacent to it, so this close association with the cinema made its nickname inevitable. Mr. Cook's son-in-law later formed the other half of the partnership but he was bought out by Mr. Page, who ran it by himself until his death in the mid thirties, when the cinema passed to his son, William John Page.

William John Page had, in the meantime, taken over his father's cabinet-making and furnishing business in Walsall, although it seems that it was he who originally persuaded his father to build the cinema. W. J. Page's son, Victor Page, worked in his father's business by day and at his grandfather's cinema by night. Vic Page can still recall making the train journey from Walsall to Coseley, via Wolverhampton every night to assist his grandfather in the period following the First World War. He vividly remembers the sliding concertina gates at the front of the cinema, the little pay box in the porch, and the heat of the projection room. In the cramped re-winding room he used to assist Mr. Griffiths, the first operator at the cinema. In the best traditions of the business, the operator married the girl in the pay box, Ginny Oakley.

In those early days the front rows were bare benches, then upholstered benches, and tip up seats at the rear, and usherettes Lil Smith and Anna Beech, showed the patrons to their seats. Like many other cinemas, the Coseley Picture House used a gas engine to provide power for illumination, in the projectors, and the house lights, but the earliest projection equipment was hand-cranked, and some of the house lights were gas. Vic Page also had to fetch the films from Birmingham twice a week and carry the heavy cans of film from Deepfields station to the cinema. The shows usually consisted of a newsreel, a short comedy and then the feature, but serials like *"The Clutching Hand"* were also popular. The piano accompaniment was provided by a Mr. Cox, who was a painter and decorator during the day.

Children's matinees were presented on Tuesdays and Saturdays but the young patrons were not allowed to use the front entrance of the cinema. They stormed in from the side entrance and were by no means a quiet and docile audience. Even then the proprietors always

68 The Cosy, in its early days, when it was simply known as the Coseley Picture House.

*(Drawing by A. Hyde)*

had to be on the watch for "vandalism" and had to regularly check the screws in the seats!

Sound was installed in the early thirties, using Gyrotone equipment, and when popular musical films were being shown an ageing Mr. Page had to cry, "Standing Room Only". As some of the benches were replaced by more tip up seats the capacity of the little cinema fell from five hundred to four hundred. When William John Page took over he continued to modernise and improve the place and maintained the traditional personal approach to management, often standing near the pay box in evening suit and bow tie.

When the new Clifton, Coseley, opened in July 1939 trade was affected for about a month and then the old regulars started drifting back and business carried on briskly through the War years. In the 1940's a strong social scene existed in Coseley exploiting the two cinemas, dances at the British Restaurant, and refreshments at the old Hop And Barley. For a long time Arthur Grainger projected the films at the Picture House, and, in 1947, he was joined by a young assistant: fourteen year old Garton Hawkins who became a local legend as, "the little blackie in the operating room"! About 1950 W. J. Page sold the cinema to Messrs. L. Wilde and L. Poole and it officially became the Cosy Cinema.

Unfortunately, during the fifties the new proprietors were unable to keep up the payments on their private mortgage when the patrons drifted away, and the last film was shown sometime during 1957. The building was re-possessed by W. J. Page, now in his eighties and, like many other gentlemen in the same situation, he now found it was difficult to dispose of the place. As usual the local council refused planning permission for the building to be used for light industry or warehousing. The Ministry allowed Mr. Page to appeal against this decision at an inquiry held on 21st May 1959. The local residents supported the Council's view but it seems that the Minister upheld the appeal, on the grounds that the building had several years of useful life ahead and should be put to some use until the site could be redeveloped.

In the event it has become the Coseley Ex-Servicemen's Club, opened in 1961, and every now and again the residents of Ivy House Lane complain about parking problems and noise. (Compare with the subsequent history of "The Bump".). While this book was being written a Coseley councillor, Bob Griffiths, was dealing with a petition on the subject but in the meantime entertainment, of some kind, continues in the friendly atmosphere of Coseley's ex-cinema.

---

## 5. The Clifton
*Castle Street*

Coseley's cinema history follows the same pattern as Sedgley's. The small family-run picture house that had served the community since the early days of cinemas, found a new competitor with the arrival of a Clifton super-cinema in the late thirties. As in Sedgley, I feel the choice of this site had more to do with the emergence of private motor transport and the costs of building town-centre cinemas than with any inadequacy of the original cinema to serve its local community. True, Coseley's population was rising during the thirties, but

I feel the directors of the Clifton Cinema (Coseley) Ltd. were more struck by the potential of a site overlooking the main artery of the conurbation, the Birmingham-Wolverhampton New Road. Some lack of confidence in the identity of Coseley is betrayed by their description of the cinema as, ".....Erected on the outskirts of the Staffordshire town of Bilston."!

The site was only a hundred yards from the centre of Roseville; in effect, the centre of Coseley. It was built at the Dudley end of Castle Street and seemed to face the traveller making his way towards Wolverhampton along the New Road. The frontage was an impressive blend of brickwork with stone facing around the three windows, and three sets of double doors, reached by a small flight of steps. The pleasing harmony of this elevation was not equalled by the view of the side and back of the cinema that greeted the traveller coming in the opposite direction. Here the massive brick walls loomed over the blank spaces of the car park. The cinema's name in neon lights and a large hoarding advertising the programme did little to conceal how functional a cinema can be behind its facade when seen from this broadside view.

The building was designed by Roland Satchwell and erected by the Wolverhampton firm, Messrs. McKeand Smith and Company. It was built to hold 724 patrons in the stalls and 280 in the circle, but the capacity is usually quoted as 1050. Like other Cliftons it employed BTH equipment. Like the Regal in Wednesfield, it succeeded in giving its patrons an experience of luxury that few would have enjoyed in their own homes. Turner's tip up seats were upholstered in green, and the Super Wilton carpet was almost too good to walk on. When the finely designed proscenium curtains drew back they revealed a magnificent silver festoon curtain in front of the screen. Carpets and curtains were also supplied by W. W. Turner.

Since the opening of the Clifton, Sedgely, Leon Salberg had died, and Captain Clift was joined on the board of directors of this cinema by Messrs. Satchwell and Roberts, William Herbert Bull, normally associated with football, J. B. Share and C. W. Gray. The circuit now had over twenty cinemas operating in the Midlands and its opening somehow seemed less auspicious than the opening of the Regal, Wednesfield, in the circuit's infancy.

The opening took place on Saturday evening, 8th July 1939. The proceedings began with the National Anthem and then Ian Hannah, M.P., and Isaac Flavell, the Chairman of Coseley U.D.C. both said a few words. The latter was full of praise for the magnificent new building and stressed the educational value of the cinema to children. Ian Hannah felt there was something American about such a building. He added that he meant "American" in the best sense. A very British-made programme then followed consisting of *"South Riding"* starring Ralph Richardson and *"Oh! Mr. Porter"*, starring Will Hay, supported by Universal News. A special feature of the opening night was the free distribution of ice-cream!

The Clifton's new manager was Mr. Harry Crane, who had opened Sedgley's Clifton two years earlier. Apart from a period of service with the R.A.F. during the War, he stayed at the cinema for the entire twenty-four short

69. The Clifton, 1939.

*(Photo: Mrs. Charlesworth Collection)*

years of its life, witnessing the sad decline in trade after the War. He added his own personal touch to the cinema by introducing two large tanks of tropical fish to the foyer. He also regularly changed into evening dress to greet the patrons. When trade faltered in the fifties a few one-night shows were tried. The first of these was on Tuesday 24th February 1959, and starred Jimmy Young, but already the Clifton's days were numbered.

The Cliftons found themselves standing on sites that were valuable for "redevelopment". The one at Fallings Park closed after a mere twenty-three years of life in 1961, followed a year later by the Regal, Wednesfield. In 1962 a redevelopment company submitted plans to Coseley U.D.C. for a new shopping centre and bowling alley on the site. The plans were rejected but it seems that the cinema had already been sold, and its closure was by then inevitable.

The sad day came on 10th August 1963 when it closed with a screening of *"Nurse on Wheels"*, starring Juliet Mills. Mr. Crane told the local paper, "Every one will be able to laugh for the last time, it really is a very funny film". I doubt that the staff laughed very much, for, as well as Mr. Crane, three other members of the staff of fifteen had been there since the opening and the

rest had all been there for over ten years. As they stayed behind for a week or two to clear the building it must have been difficult to forget the happy years they had had together, and, ironically, the fate of their cinema still remained unknown.

Coseley's Town Planning Committee seemed to be having second thoughts about redevelopment after some discussions with Staffordshire County Council. On a new application the developers gained approval to build six shops, a supermarket with a bowling alley above them, and flats and car parks on the surrounding land. The cinema was demolished by the end of 1963 and the wholesale redevelopment of Coseley's central area began the following year. The bowling alley did not materialise.

## Tipton

As the reader will have gathered, while reading about the cinemas of Sedgley and Coseley, these "urban districts" were, in reality, amorphous clusters of many smaller communities. This pattern is repeated in the adjacent area that eventually became the Borough of Tipton. No doubt some Tiptonians had a clear sense of the geographical identity of their Borough, but to the outsider it could seem a baffling place, apparently without a centre, but one of those places one always traversed on the way to somewhere else! Tipton occupied a very central position in the Black Country and therefore its boundaries at some point touched just about everywhere else.

Six cinemas existed in the area, untroubled by invading Odeons or Cliftons and not really competing in any way with each other, such was the intensity of their relationship with very localised communities. Their history is often obscure but all of them are fascinating. The rebuilt Alhambra at Dudley Port was the nearest the area reached to producing a 1930's super-cinema, but probably the grandest cinema in Tipton was the Regent in Owen Street, an area with the strongest claim to being

the centre of Tipton. Not too far from the Regent was the Cinema in the High Street, a converted school building with a talent for survival. In quite separate communities, the Picture House, known later as The Bruce, served Princes End, the Victoria served Horseley Heath, and the Palace served Great Bridge. Not one of these places exists as a cinema today, and only one survives as a building. Tipton itself has vanished into the new Metropolitan Borough of Sandwell.

## 6. The Tivoli — The Regent — The Regal
## Owen Street

As Owen Street was the principal shopping street of the Borough of Tipton it is not surprising that the town's "premier" cinema was to be found there. The original building began life as a market hall, but on 30th May 1910 Benjamin Kennedy acquired approval from the Urban District Council for his plans to convert it into a cinema. The plans were drawn by Messrs. Scott and Clark. As with all "conversions" at this time, the work was accomplished very quickly and Mr. Kennedy was issued with his kine licence on 27th July 1910 and then presumably opened for business, although I have not

70. Owen Street, Tipton: The Regent just before its post-War alterations.

*(Photo: W. G. Langdon)*

been able to discover a precise opening date. Just before Christmas he was granted a stage licence, at first for a temporary period of three months, and the Tivoli was able to present films and variety.

The Tivoli is next heard of in mid July 1913 when plans, by G. Bowden, were approved for adding a raked floor to the auditorium. The U.D.C. minutes recorded that it would, "Certainly be an improvement". Apparently the Tivoli was a great success and I have been told the building was packed to capacity when the first Zeppelin raid struck Tipton and bombs dropped in Union Street. At the time it seems that it held about 1400 patrons, some of whom had a reputation for rowdiness.

Towards the end of the First World War, and immediately afterwards, the story of the Tivoli, and its successor, the Regent, becomes extremely complicated. It has been difficult to assemble the facts from the fragments of information available. Eventually the Regent was owned by Edgar Duckworth, son of the Lancashire cinema pioneer Joshua Duckworth. Some years later, Edgar's son, David Duckworth, told a local paper that they acquired the cinema directly from Benjamin Kennedy.

Other records seem to suggest that Benjamin Kennedy was neither proprietor nor operator of the Tivoli by the end of the War. It may have been operated by a Mr. Spittle and then acquired by Edgar Hounsell of the Midland Amusements Company. This Company also briefly acquired the Scala, Wolverhampton, in 1919 and then at the end of that year, sold both cinemas to Midland Entertainments Limited. Oscar Deutsch later held a controlling interest in Midland Amusements, when most of its activities were in Coventry, but his name is sometimes mentioned in connection with the Regent and the Scala. As I understand the fragments of information I have come across, Midland Amusements had shed both cinemas by the time he acquired his interest.

Midland Entertainments were certainly responsible for closing the Tivoli as from 1st January 1920 and for building its replacement. The Regent was not entirely new, but it was a very drastic "rebuilding" job. The contractor, a Mr. Edwards of Dudley, regarded it as extremely awkward. In fact the work was not completed for the opening. Bryans had to come and complete the plasterwork at a later date. The raked floor of the stalls had to be extended, a new balcony was installed, and an imposing new frontage was erected. Fifteen hundred new tip up seats were provided.

The Regent opened on Monday 16th August 1920 at 2.30 p.m. The opening was performed by the Chairman of Tipton Urban District Council, Councillor W. W. Doughty, who had his own cinema interests at the Victoria. He had been entertained beforehand with a ceremonial luncheon at the Black Cock, and joined the patrons, who had been admitted free of charge, for a screening of "The Gentlemen Riders" supported by "The Spiral of Death". At the evening performance the proceeds were donated to the local War Memorial Fund.

Midland Entertainments Limited also poses some mysteries. Some records state that it was a Manchester-based firm and therefore may have had something to do with Edgar Duckworth. However at the opening the company was represented by two directors; Messrs. Emmott and Hinchcliffe. Edgar Duckworth seems to have taken over from Midland Entertainments about 1924 and for the remainder of the twenties his name actually appeared as "the proprietor" on the Regent's advertisements.

Edgar Duckworth entered the business in 1903, when he was sixteen, and this just qualified him to be a Cinema Veteran. His expansion from Lancashire into the Midlands does not seem to have been very significant. Perhaps he is better remembered in Derby, where Duckworth Square is near the site of one of his cinemas.

The Regent became the Regal two weeks later than expected as can be seen from this invitation!

On June 14th modernisation was not complete at the New Regal Cinema
But now it is, and therefore

*Edgar and David Duckworth*

request the pleasure of the Company of

*Mr. Fellows and friend*

at the TIPTON Premiere of the Film of the ROYAL TOUR in

## CinemaScopE

# THE FLIGHT OF THE WHITE HERON
(TECHNICOLOR)

on MONDAY, JUNE 28th, 1954

*at the New Regal Cinema, Tipton*
(Owen Street)

at 2.30 p.m.
R.S.V.P.

Please bring this Card with you

In Tipton he ought to be remembered for organising Sunday charity shows for the local "Boot Fund". For example, when the Regent closed for a short time in 1930 to have Western Electric sound equipment installed, Edgar Duckworth "reopened" on Sunday 21st September with one of these concerts. He brought the Colne Town Board down from his Lancashire home to entertain the Tiptonians.

Meanwhile the local patrons eagerly awaited the events of the following day: the arrival of the talkies. Sound came to Tipton with "Paris", starring Jack Buchanan and "Smiling Irish Eyes" starring Colleen Moore. Soon afterwards the theatre was leased to the A.B.C. circuit. It was their only interest in Tipton and, until the opening of the new Alhambra, Dudley Port, its position as the town's premier cinema was unchallenged.

Early during the Second World War it seems that A.B.C. did not renew their lease and for a time the cinema was operated by the Marks Circuit of Manchester, a firm which was briefly interested in two cinemas in Wolverhampton in the early forties. After the War it seems that Edgar and David Duckworth resumed responsibility for running the Regent.

In December 1948 they replaced the existing sound system with new RCA equipment and put in new Ross projectors and arcs. From photographs it would appear that alterations to the operating room also took place and rather spoiled the frontage of the building. Further improvements were on the way. On 28th June 1954 the Regent became the "New Regal Cinema" and re-opened with a cinemascope presentation of "The Flight of the White Heron", a film of the recent Royal Tour.

In becoming the Regal the front of the cinema was given a facelift that successfully obscured the alterations mentioned above. A new canopy now supported a fin with "Regal" spelt vertically in neon lights on each side, placed in the middle of an arc-shaped facade that hid the protruding projection room. A slightly 1930's look was thus imposed on the centre of the building, the 1920 facade flanked either side of it and somewhere in the building some remnant of the original Market Hall probably existed! In its new form the Regal survived the fifties.

The end came on Saturday 3rd December 1960 with "Jazz Boat", starring Anthony Newley supported by "Kill Her Gently". David Duckworth had sold the cinema to Capital and Commercial Limited, a company that proposed redeveloping the site. The equipment was removed and then the empty building was left to the mercy of local vandals. By day children played in the shell of the building and by night it was visited by courting couples. By September 1961 scrap-dealers openly parked their horses and carts in Wood Street and raided the building for whatever they could find. Meanwhile the new owners complained that their planning applications were being kept waiting.

Eventually the sad remains of the Regent/Regal were demolished and new shops have been built on the site, but the sorry tale of decay and dilapidation lasting too long, and redevelopment being a long time coming, became a familiar story in Owen Street. At the time of writing some considerable redevelopment of the area has, at last, taken place.

## 7. The Cinema
### Tipton High Street

Tipton is sometimes called the Venice of the Midlands. At Factory Junction the Brindley and Telford levels of the Birmingham Canal Navigation are reunited and at Tipton Junction the line from the Dudley Tunnel meets the B.C.N. Leaving the Regent in Owen Street and heading for Dudley the traveller had to climb over the canal and pass through an area that might conceivably be regarded as Venetian to reach High Street. The area has been transformed in the past few decades but a few landmarks, like The Wagon and Horses, have stood long enough to give us some bearings.

About a hundred yards from the Wagon and Horses, on a site that is now a car park for Sedgley Steels, once stood "The Cinema". It never aspired to a more imaginative name. In the summer of 1913 an existing school on the site was converted into a cinema. The architect, A. T. Butler, of Dudley, drew up th plans for the conversion, and, as seen from the sketch, produced something that had the appearance of a cinema. At first it held four hundred and fifty patrons but as seating was improved this fell to just over three hundred.

I have been unable to trace the original proprietor, nor an opening date, but it seems certain that it was in business by October 1913, and at some time in its very early life it was owned by Messrs. Bradley, Nicholson and Beese. Its story successfully eludes the historian until the early twenties when Cecil Couper, of Brierley Hill, took it over as a distant outpost of his empire. He continued to operate it during the remainder of the silent era, his daughter sometimes providing the piano accompaniment. About 1930 Cecil Couper sold it to Fred Leatham who set about installing a sound system, using Gyrotone equipment. Fred Leatham then sold the

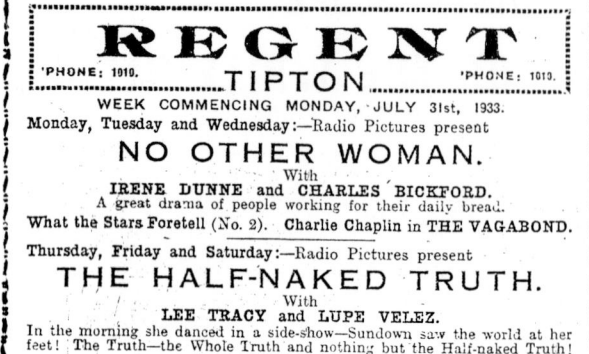

71. The Cinema, High Street, Tipton.

*(A drawing by Tony Wright based on the original architect's sketch of 1913 by A. T. Butler)*

place to his father, F. W. Leatham who ran it for a time in partnership with a Mr. Hinkinson. The latter was eventually bought out and it became very much a family affair. F. W. Leatham's other son, Leonard, was the operator, and later the manager. Although a modest cinema serving a very local clientele, it seems that it prospered through the Second World War.

Programmes changed twice weekly except under unusual circumstances. For example, *"Showboat"* was so popular it ran for a full week and returned later for a second run! I doubt the patrons appreciated that its director was born nearby in Dudley.

When F. W. Leatham died the cinema was shared by his four children but Leonard Leatham effectively ran the place. His stubborn refusal to abandon it probably accounts for its survival through the difficult times of the mid fifties. Leonard Leatham confessed to the local paper that audiences were often fifty or less. Ironically, I have sat in much smaller audiences in currently surviving cinemas!

Another irony, considering the decline in the 1950's, concerns Leonard Leatham's original intentions, after the War, of replacing the old converted-school with a brand new super-cinema. In 1949 he commissioned Roland Satchwell to produce plans for a magnificent

cinema that would have been called the Regal. Roland Satchwell's plans made ingenious use of the awkward site and the Regal would have held 837 patrons. The project compares with Mr. McDonald's similar proposals for the little cinema in Princes End.

Making obscure calculations from assorted hints and suggestions it seems that The Cinema showed its last film on Saturday 21st June 1958, saved from further agony by a Compulsory Purchase Order from the council. As at the Victoria, there had been a sudden switch to RCA equipment just before The Cinema's demise, but cinemascope was not installed. Leonard Leatham's modest little cinema faded away into obscurity a decade after he had dreamed of building something more grand.

## 8. The Alhambra
*Dudley Port*

The main road from Dudley to West Bromwich leaves the former town at the romantically named Burnt Tree Island and passes through three small communities on the eastern fringe of Tipton, each one supporting a local cinema. After a spectacular hump-back bridge over the Brindley level of the Birmingham Canal the traveller comes to a building that still looks like a cinema, and still proudly bears its name: The Alhambra. The road at

129

this point is called Dudley Port.

A quarter of a mile further on, the Telford level of the Birmingham Canal crosses this road on an aqueduct near the windswept station of Dudley Port and beyond this the traveller comes to Horseley Heath, home of the Victoria. Horseley Heath imperceptibly becomes Great Bridge, and between two more canal bridges the Palace was once to be found.

Returning to the Alhambra, its site, on a corner of Groveland Road and Dudley Port, was occupied at the end of the last century, by a Salvation Army Citadel. In the first decade of the century it had become the Alhambra Rink during the roller-skating craze. At a meeting of the planning committee of Tipton U.D.C. on 24th October 1910 a sketch was submitted to the committee to approve the conversion of the skating rink into a cinema. The committee insisted on seeing proper plans!

A meeting of the full council took place the next day and granted a kine licence to the "Dudley Port Skating Rink", and as usual in dealing with the cinemas of Tipton, the thread of the story then becomes difficult to follow. At a further planning committee meeting on 31st October, only one week later, the surveyor reported that proper plans had been submitted by Messrs. Stonehewer. The timber and galvanised corrugated iron structure was regarded as satisfactory but the plan was rejected as the provision of emergency exits was not thought to be satisfactory.

I do not know how quickly modifications were made, nor how quickly the Alhambra managed to become a cinema. Presumably it was towards the end of 1910 or the beginning of 1911. It is also not clear who was the original proprietor. The early history of the Alhambra is frequently associated with the name of Pat Collins, but, as will be seen, he entered the scene a little later. Having started its life as a cinema called the Alhambra, that name was dropped for a time and it became the Palace of Varieties. Jas Tyrer of Oldbury may have leased the place for a time, but for the duration of the First World War it appears to have been operated by Messrs. Round and Hipkins.

Certainly, by the time matters returned to normal, Pat Collins was definitely proprietor of the Alhambra and advertised the fact in the cinema's advertisements, reviving the original name. He ran it until December 1927 when he sold it to Miles Jervis I of Chasetown. The latter installed Frank Bills as manager and Frank stayed at the Alhambra through its first closure, rebuilding, changes of ownership and until its final closure while in the possession of Miles Jervis II!

Miles Jervis I must have continued to operate the cinema as a silent hall into the sound era and then, about 1933, sold it to Sheridan Film Services of Burton-On-Trent. The directors of this company were S. A. Suffolk, F. S. Suffolk, Fred Bailey and H. Armson. Mr. Suffolk's association with the Black Country included an interest in the cinema at Caldmore Green, Walsall.

The new owners demolished the old corrugated iron building, caring little for the patrons who liked to hear the rain pattering on the roof while watching "silent" films. The intention was to build a modern sound cinema, a precursor and mini-version of the super-cinema. During demolition they came across the original foundation stones of the Salvation Army Citadel and carefully returned them to that organisation, or to the people who had originally laid them!

Ernest Roberts was engaged to design the new building and William Jackson of Oldbury was contracted to build it. The result was very pleasing. Ernest Robert's apparent love of terracotta brickwork relieved with some work in patent stone worked well on a building of this size. Leaded lights, by E. Showell Trickett, were also a pleasing feature and the cinema's name in leaded glass survives to this day. It was built on the system that was then becoming established as the mode for building cinemas. Structural steelwork, by Rubery Owen, and reinforced concrete floors were now the order of the day. Externally, local bricks from Pratts of Oldbury, and internally, plasterwork by Bryan's Adamanta, disguised the straightforward functionalism of the building. One slightly old-fashioned touch was the atmospheric treatment of the interior, painted by George Legg. These murals depicted mountain scenes on the side walls. Rose pink curtains of oriental silk provided a touch of luxury, and naturally all the seats were upholstered tip-ups. Seven hundred seats downstairs were in brown plush, two hundred and twenty seats in the balcony were in green plush. Accommodation was later listed as 830.

The new cinema was opened on Easter Monday, 8th April 1935, with an official reception at 5.30 and the ceremony at 6.30 p.m. Frank Bills, the proud manager of the new building, introduced Fred Bailey, Chairman of Sheridan Film Services, who was on stage with Mr. Suffolk and William Jackson. The opening was performed by Councillor A. F. Welch, the Chairman of Tipton U.D.C. who said that he regarded the new cinema as part of the process of beautifying that part of Tipton. Unfortunately, Ernest Roberts was absent, due to illness, but everybody else sat back to enjoy Gracie Field's performance as "Grace Platt" in the film "Sing As We Go" specially written for her by J. B. Priestley. Music and songs reached the audience via an RCA Photophone system.

The Alhambra was now Tipton's finest cinema but its location was relatively poor. The Regent, then in the hands of A.B.C., was more centrally placed. The Alhambra hoped for trade from West Bromwich and Dudley as it was easy to reach from both places, but both towns had bigger modern cinemas of their own. Sheridan Film Services later became S. T. Cinemas, a partnership between Mr. Suffolk and a Mr. Thornton, still based in Burton. However, at the beginning of 1952 the Alhambra became the property of Miles Jervis II, the son of the man who had bought the original Alhambra from Pat Collins.

As stated earlier, Frank Bills continued to manage the place through all these changes. In the opening brochure he had stated,
"..... I will do all in my power to make this theatre so inviting, so cosy, that you will feel insidiously drawn towards it whenever you feel the need for amusement ..... I want your patronage regularly, consistently throughout the year."
How he felt as the audience declined in the fifties is not recorded. The new owner felt frustrated by the cinema's

location, and, by the end of that decade, by its six day licence.

Frank Bills had at some time served on the local council and sometimes gave people the impression that he resented the local authority's inspections and restraints. Nevertheless, they had to go "cap-in-hand" to Tipton Council and beg to be allowed to show films on the Sabbath. The Council delayed making the decision. While other local cinemas won the right (in Sedgley for example), and the Regent closed down, Miles Jervis waited two years for the issue to be resolved.

A public meeting was called for September 1961 and all the evils of film-going on the Sabbath were recited in public as if time had stood still in Tipton for fifty years. Only the Bruce and the Alhambra were still in business! The former had no intention of opening on Sundays and so the issue only affected the Alhambra. Very dramatically Miles Jervis was refused admission to the meeting on the grounds that he did not live in Tipton and Frank Bills braved the meeting alone to state the cinema's point of view. After all that, Sunday screenings were rejected. With a nice sense of irony Sunday Bingo sessions commenced at the Alhambra on 23rd October 1961 under the flag of the Midland Cinema Bingo Club. (The same flag was flown in Wednesbury).

The Bruce closed the following year leaving the Alhambra as Tipton's sole surviving cinema. A few yards from the cinema extensive road works began as the canal bridge was widened, and a final decline in the Alhambra's audience set in. The end came on 3rd August 1963 and the last film shown was "Sparrows Can't Sing".

The building still survives today as a warehouse for G. A. Nicholas Ltd. The pay box can still be seen in the tiny foyer and the staircase that used to go to the balcony and some plasterwork are still obviously cinema-like in that unmistakeable 1930's style. Details of the auditorium have been completely obliterated.

## 9. The Victoria
*Railway Street, Horseley Heath*

As our survey takes us to the remoter corners of Tipton the quest for information about the local cinemas becomes like looking for cigarette ash in a projection room. Perhaps this publication will encourage others to dig more deeply, if that is possible. Meanwhile the stories of the Victoria and the Palace seem somewhat sketchy.

Railway Street left the main road through Horseley Heath just beyond the Post Office. In 1859 the Primitive Methodists erected the Railway Street Chapel to hold a congregation of three hundred and eighty people. Early this century they moved to new premises, and on 21st February 1912 the planning committee of Tipton

72. The Alhambra, Dudley Port, as an electrical wholesaler's store. 1981.

*(Photo: Ned Williams)*

73. The Victoria in Railway Street, 5th August 1968, over ten years after the last film show.

*(Photo: A. H. Price)*

U.D.C. studied plans, drawn by Messrs. Scott and Clark, for converting the chapel into a picture palace. Approval was granted subject to exits being provided leading directly onto the street opposite the balcony stairs on each side of the building. It seems therefore that the small balcony was inherited from its days as a chapel, as was a mural of an angel! The balcony, which only contained about five rows of seats ended in two boxes, apparently popular with courting couples. (The cost of a box in 1945 was nine pence).

Once again no opening date seems to be recorded but presumably it was sometime in mid 1912. Its first licence was issued to a Daniel Darby in June 1912. The cinema seems to have been the property of William Wooley Doughty, a local councillor and J.P. He lived nearby in Horseley Heath Villa, and owned the Horseley Heath Hinge Works. He was a strict disciplinarian and took a personal interest in preserving order at his little cinema. He was also patriotic and liked to give away Union Jack badges between the films, and was philanthropic to the extent that during depressed times he sometimes sustained his audience with tea and biscuits or threw handfuls of pennies into the street!

When W. W. Doughty died his sole beneficiary was his housekeeper, Mrs. Smith, who thus became the owner of the Victoria. At the time the piano was played by Jimmy Jones and the second projectionist, Bill Wassell, had the nightly duty of re-whitewashing the plaster-of-paris screen. He believed it was the first of its type in Britain. Once a month he also had to clean an elaborate chandelier that was a feature of the hall. Leslie Taff began his distinguished career playing the piano at the Victoria.

How long Mrs. Smith remained the proprietor is not clear. A record exists showing that in 1932 it was sold by Messrs. Dixon and Hopkinson to a Mr. W. A. Webb, and that up until then it had remained a "silent" cinema. Mr. Webb refurbished the place and supplied new seats. More importantly, he installed the Classitone Sound System and on Boxing Day 1932, it was reopened as the Victoria Talking Theatre.

As it only seated three hundred patrons and served a very local community the Victoria never elaborately advertised its existence or announced changes of owner-ship. Its final owner, as a cinema, was Fred Leatham. It appears that he bought the cinema in the early forties. He was responsible for installing Gyrotone equipment, as used by his brother at The Cinema. As soon as the War was over, Fred Leatham tried to radically improve the Victoria. The original chapel had been just under fifty feet in length, but an entrance hall had been added, presumably by Mr. Webb, by extending another ten feet towards Railway Street. Now a thirty foot extension was tacked on to the rear of the building, and the floor level raised. At balcony level the building was extended towards the street to match the ground floor. Much improved, it re-opened on 14th April 1947 with *"Dodge City"*.

The improvements were a heavy investment to make at a time when the future was relatively uncertain. Fred Leatham was taking on a large mortgage at the

Victoria about the same time as he took on the Rex, Wolverhampton. His brother-in-law helped out for a time by running the Victoria and later his sister and her son helped at the Rex but they were difficult times. For one period Fred Leatham managed to organize a "swop" with Sidney T. Collett of Market Drayton's "Town Hall", called the Ritz by Fred Leatham. Mr. Collett met disaster at the Victoria, and Fred Leatham returned to it for its final battles. There was a last minute switch to RCA equipment and the installation of cinemascope but really the battle was lost and the Victoria "faded away" sometime in 1955 or 1956.

Mr. Leatham wished to convert the building to industrial use in order to pay off his mortgage but planning permission for the change of use was refused. Although it seems ironical today, Tipton's Town Clerk at the time insisted that Railway Street was a residential area. Mr. Leatham appealed against the Council's decision and the Minister's Inspector heard the sad tale of his £4,000 loss on the sale of the Rex, Wolverhampton. In 1958 the fact remained that it was a residential area, and no extenuating financial circumstances seemed relevant to the inquiry.

Two years later, in 1960, the Victoria was finally sold to Horseley Bridge and Thomas Piggott Limited and was used as a store for wooden patterns. During the following decade the residential nature of Railway Street suffered considerable demolition and by 1974 the Victoria was left standing in glorious, but dilapidated, isolation. The name "Victoria Palace" and some of the ornamental frontage remained. Suddenly, the building was demolished, Railway Street truncated, and the area redeveloped for industrial use.

## 10. The Palace
*Great Bridge*

Great Bridge is about half way between Dudley and West Bromwich, seems equally remote from each, and just as remote from the rest of Tipton, of which it was a part. The traveller from Dudley passing through Dudley Port and Horseley Heath is aware of coming to a place of slightly more importance as he comes across the large triangular road junction and a market place that suggests that Great Bridge once had a busy life of its own.

Canals and industry seem to completely surround this little commercial centre. For years the Kinematograph Year Books used to list Great Bridge as a separate place from Tipton, which might have been in recognition of its independence or simply a lack of certainty regarding its location! The most exciting way to approach Great Bridge, until 1964, was to arrive by train at either of its unbelievably antiquated stations. However, its cinema, the Palace, has a history stretching back to the days when the electric trams rolled past on their way to Dudley from Handsworth. Most of the history of the Palace seems very obscure. Only some of the small very short-lived cinema-halls of the Black Country give the historian a bigger headache than the Palace! Even when I have quizzed its patrons they say very little about the place itself.

In the days when steam trams struggled through Great Bridge it seems that the site of the Palace was occupied by a Toll House which became a barbers shop. This was demolished and a hall erected but whether it was specifically built as a cinema seems very doubtful. There is some evidence that it was an Odd Fellows' Hall. Whatever happened, by the spring of 1910 films were being shown there, a licence being issued by Tipton U.D.C. at the end of March. The licence was transferred several times during the next year or two, but The Palace is thought to have been actually owned by E. J. Crinnian.

It was a small hall with a total capacity of about 750, reduced to 629 by the end of its life. It had a small balcony, and an octagonal foyer with an entrance facing Slater Street. (The main auditorium ran parallel to Great Bridge rather than at right angles to it.). I assume that E. J. Crinnian remained the proprietor until the sound era. It seems that sound was installed by 1931, only a couple of years before the cinema was acquired by Cyril Joseph and his partners, this time using the name Storer Pictures. This was the first step taken by Cyril Joseph in forming his small Black Country chain of cinemas.

The little foyer, designed by Messrs. Gaskell and Chambers, may have been added by Cyril Joseph. He made similar improvements to the foyer and entrance at the Forum, Bradley. Even as late as the mid fifties various improvements were made to the Palace. For example, early 1955, none other than the Harry Weedon Partnership drew up plans for an improved projection box.

Storer Pictures (Cyril Joseph) ran the Palace until 1958 when it was acquired by Vincent Wareing, at the same time as he acquired the Coliseum and Olympia, Wolverhampton, also from Cyril Joseph, and the Forum, Caldmore Green. It seems a strange moment for someone to have embarked on a career of running four run-down Black Country Cinemas. However, no doubt they seemed irresistably cheap. When Vincent Wareing arrived, the Palace was using BTH equipment, but whether this was the original equipment installed in the thirties, I do not know.

Cyril Joseph had a large hoarding built at the side of the auditorium, facing the main road. Details of the programme were pasted up every week, but Vincent Wareing decided to save £15 a week by putting up a permanent poster. For the last two years of its life, this hoarding proclaimed, "Bring Your Alice To Our Palace".

Like other cinemas that had survived into the second half of the fifties there seemed, at the Palace, to be a dramatic decline in attendances at the end of the decade. Mr. Wareing blamed a budget after which a television could be obtained on payment of a single instalment rather than a third deposit. It seems that the Palace closed on 16th April 1960 with *"Valley Of Fury"*, starring Victor Mature.

At one time it seemed that the Catholic Church might have bought the place although Mr. Wareing thought it unadvisable to try and bring Christianity to Great Bridge at this late stage. They joked about changing the hoarding to read "Bring Your Alice To Our Chalice"! In the end, the site was purchased by developers, the Palace was demolished, and a parade of shops has been built there.

## 11. The Picture House — The Bruce
*New Hall Street, Princes End*

In another far-flung part of Tipton, the Dudley to Wednesbury Road made its way through Princes End. The Tipton/Coseley boundary ran along the centre of the main road at the time when Urban District Councils sat down to discuss the letters they had received from the County Council informing them of the Cinematograph Act and the delegation of power to issue licences to a very local level. New Hall Street is at right angles to that main road, opposite Bradley's Lane, which brought the Bruce closer to Coseley's cinemas than to the others in Tipton.

Leaving the main road, the Bruce was a small cinema to be found on the left-hand side of New Hall Street, although nothing is to be found of it today. Locally it is always said that it was originally owned by Joseph Pearson. He certainly owned it from the time of the First World War until 1922, but the original proprietor, according to the records was a Mr. B. T. Parsons. In July 1912 he submitted plans to the local council for the conversion of a chapel into a cinema. It opened as the Princes End Picture House on 18th November 1912.

Sometime early in its career as a cinema the frontage was heightened and the name "Picture House" appeared across the top of the facade. The apex of the original gable end can be seen rising above the centre of this facade in the illustration. The small entrance was flanked by boarded-up windows that were covered in boards advertising the programmes; Monday to Wednesday on the left, Thursday to Saturday on the right. This tradition was preserved even when purpose-built display cases, by Girosign, were added in 1948. In the early days five hundred patrons were squeezed into the building but when seating improved this was reduced to three hundred and fifty.

It was an unpretentious cinema in an unpretentious working class area but it had a magic all of its own. To the locals, its plain appearance earned it the nickname,

"The Brewus" or "Brew-House", as small out-buildings used for making home-made beer were called in the Black Country. It was therefore unique in the sense that its nickname eventually became its real name.

"The Brewus" or "The Pictures" served Princes End in the same way that the Victoria, or "Darby's" or "Page's," or "The Bump" all served their local communities. In 1920, while Joseph Pearson was running The Picture House, his position in Princes End was threatened by the proposed arrival of a new much larger purpose-built cinema. This would have been called The Victory and have had the advantage of occupying a prominent site in the High Street. It was promoted by Mr. Thornton and designed by Harold Tomkys, but never materialised. Mr. Thornton eventually appeared in Tipton as a partner to Mr. Suffolk in the acquisition of the Alhambra, Dudley Port. Joseph Pearson, unfortunately, went bankrupt running the Picture House and gave up the task towards the end of 1922, blaming the cost of films and the effect of unemployment on his takings.

He was followed by Mr. and Mrs. Jones who seemed undaunted by Joseph Pearson's problems and, in fact, they went on to make a great success of the Picture House, and even expanded their cinema activities to include leasing a cinema in Wednesbury for a while. They introduced Fred Leatham to the cinema business by asking him to play the piano accompaniment in silent days, and became local legends themselves.

The Picture House opened its doors seven days a week for a time because on Sundays it was used by the Rev. John Young, Minister of the New Hall Street Baptist Church, for talks and lantern-slide shows after evening service, and possibly some enthusiasts were there every seven nights of the week as one ex-resident of the street remembers seeing the same people going night after night! This period, in the mid-twenties, has often been recalled in letters to the local press and many people have written to me about it. I will quote one

74. The Bruce, Newhall Street, towards the end of the 1950's. (Note the original name still in the brickwork).

*(Photo: Mr. and Mrs. Woodroffe)*

letter, from Eddie Jones, recalling the fascination of Princes End's cinema:

"It was a very low small place, but heaven to us kids and the folks around. It had long hard benches at the front, more benches in the middle, padded and plush covered and rows of "select" chairs at the back with elbow rests: 3d, 7d and 9d in old money.

My mates and I would go to the Saturday afternoon show and Mrs. Jones would walk around with a very long cane to rap anyone misbehaving. Half way through the show a smoked glass slide was flashed on the screen. The writing on the smoked glass slide was scratched with a pin and on the screen was:—

Grand Talking Film Monday — Come Early.

Round about that time the talkies were just being installed around Birmingham. Comes Monday night we managed to get in, "standing up". The big picture came on accompanied by some scratchy music, and a man's voice trying to keep up with the man on the screen. I could hear one of my mates trying to stifle a laugh with his fist in his mouth. It was obvious we were being swindled. There must have been a man and woman and an old wind-up gramaphone hidden up there. Well, there were cat-calls of, "Change the Needle!" and, "Put a cowboy on!". After five minutes a woman in the film began to sing, in silence, and on went the scratchy record. Ironically, the song was called "Am I Blue", which did not fit at all.

Well, it finished up silent. We were disappointed but we had a good laugh. Funny, but Mr. and Mrs. Jones left early in the car.

Eventually the talkies did come and that episode was forgotten, or was it? There was always some comic in the audience that used to belt out, "Am I Blue" on suitable occasions".

Sound came to the Picture House on BTH equipment, but those benches lasted until after the Second World War! By such time Mrs. Jones had disappeared from the scene and the cinema was owned by a Mr. MacDonald who ran the place with the aid of his family. Legend has it that his son was named Bruce and that he thought his name was being given to the cinema when he heard it called "The Brewus". The legend of Robert the Bruce was evoked by a spider-motif that appeared on Mr. MacDonald's notepaper.

After the War, Mr. MacDonald had ambitious plans for the rebuilding of his little cinema. In the summer of 1947, the architect, Edmund Wilford, (of Lyttleton, Halesowen, fame!) produced plans for a magnificent new super-cinema. It would have held just under a thousand patrons and would have changed the face of Princes End. The project was dropped and Mr. MacDonald settled for a change of name.

The Picture House officially became The Bruce at the beginning of 1948, with its new name mounted on the front of the cinema to prove it. Internally it had been considerably renovated. The low tunnel-like single floored auditorium was transformed by removing old Tentest panelling and treating the exposed bare brick walls with rough cast and stippled, the base colour being pale green and the relief gold and red. The dado, to a height of six feet, was painted a purple red and varnished to give some feeling of warmth. Old gas-fired radiators were removed and some basic central-heating installed. The entrance hall was also improved. Thus renewed, the Bruce marched confidently into the post-War era.

When Mr. MacDonald Junior sold the Bruce to Mr. and Mrs. Woodroffe in 1953 it was still a very busy place. They found it was sometimes impossible to pack everybody in! They refurbished the Bruce again, using the services of Modernisation Ltd., of Sheffield, thus bringing the son of one of the pioneers of cinematography, Mr. Friese-Green, to this little cinema.

With a certain amount of pride the Bruce outlived the Regent, and even before 1960 had once proudly recruited two girls who had worked at the Regent. With trade falling at the Alhambra it seemed likely that the Bruce would be Tipton's last surviving cinema, even though it never advertised in the press nor expected to serve anyone outside Princes End.

If redevelopment threatened the cinema's existence it first seemed likely that such a threat would come from Allen's the nearest factory and employer of many of the patrons. However, it seems the Council had other ideas. One local legend tells that the place was deliberately set on fire to speed up its demise as Princes Enders would never have forgiven anyone personally responsible for depriving them of their little cinema.

It has been difficult to establish the facts. It seems that it closed after the Council refused to renew the licence. Some items from the cinema were stored in the house next door and on 31st May 1962 a fire was started by vandals amongst some cushions stored there. The fire caused some damage to the cinema itself, and soon afterwards it was compulsorily purchased by the Council.

No one, after exhaustive enquiries, seems to be quite certain when the last film was shown. The Tipton Herald, reporting the fire, said that the cushions had been in store since Saturday 26th May 1962. Possibly that was the date of the last film show at the Bruce; if not, it was probably during that month. Considering this is one of the few such cinemas where the opening date has been established, and considering that it lasted into the sixties, it seems amazing that the date of its last show can only be guessed — but that is part of the intriguing quality of the cinemas of the "Central Villages".

## AT Dudley's BIG 3

### REGENT

TWO GREAT 3-DAY PROGRAMMES.

Mon. July 24th, Tues., Wed.
EDNA MAY OLIVER
In
THE PENGUIN POOL MYSTERY.
Also
LEE TRACY
In
Half-Naked Truth.

Thurs. July 27th, Fri., Sat.
GEORGE (Night After Night) RAFT
In
Under Cover Man
Also
REGIS TOOMEY
In
STATE TROOPER.

### CRITERION

WEEK COMMENCING JULY 24th, 1933.

Monday, Tuesday, Wednesday
Gaiety! Melody! and Impudent Comedy!
HERBERT MARSHALL and SARI MARITZA in
EVENINGS FOR SALE
Also
Owen Nares & Benita Hume in
DISCORD.
GAUMONT GRAPHIC at Every Performance.

Thursday, Friday, Saturday
WARREN WILLIAM and LORETTA YOUNG in
EMPLOYEES' ENTRANCE
Also
Child of Manhattan.
With JOHN BOLES and NANCY CARROLL.

### EMPIRE

Mon., July 24th, for 3 Days.
MAE CLARKE and NEIL HAMILTON in
AS THE DEVIL COMMANDS.
A sensational Murder Drama that will thrill you.
Comedies & Interest Films.

Thursday, Friday, Saturday
BETTY ASTELL and CLAUDE ALLISTER in
That's My Wife.
Also JUNE CLYDE in
Thrill of Youth.

### CORONET

#### QUARRY BANK.

Prop.: QUARRY BANK CINEMA CO.   'Phone: 7210 BRIERLEY HILL.

#### WEEK COMMENCING AUGUST 21st.

Monday, Tuesday, Wednesday:—
TOM BROWN, H. B. WARNER, SLIM SUMMERVILLE
And
RICHARD CROMWELL
In

### Tom Brown of Culver.

One of the good pictures that matter—magnificent in theme, glorious in execution, packed with punches and fine sentiment.

Thursday, Friday, Saturday:—
The Picture for the Millions.
IRENE DUNNE, JOHN BOLES and a wonderful all-star cast in
Fanny Hurst's Great Novel:

### BACK STREET

The novel that set the country agog—now it is on the screen. Every bit as vivid and honest as the book itself.

SPLENDID SUPPORTING ITEMS WITH EACH PROGRAMME.

Continuous Monday to Friday at 6.20.  Twice Saturday, 6.20 and 8.30.
Matinees Monday and Thursday at 2.30.

*Although the mighty circuits penetrated the towns of the South West, as shown here where Gaumont British had acquired three of Dudley's cinemas, they left the smaller communities to the independents. The Coronet, one of Cecil Couper's cinemas, proudly served such places.*

The production of this section of the book has received assistance from Dudley Arts Council.

## Introduction

Dudley is the jewel in the Black Country's crown and is sometimes regarded as the region's capital. Dudley Castle stands on a hill that is part of the central ridge that divides the Black Country in two, and magnificent views are obtained from the top of the ruined keep. On a clear day you can see the Urals! When I came to live in Dudley twenty years ago I could not believe such a wonderful town could exist, and it was an ideal place in which to begin a discovery of the Black Country.

The area to the south and west of the Black Country has a character rather different to the region to the east of the ridge. In my opinion it is the best area in which to try and understand what forms the essential character of the Black Country. It is an intricate network of towns and villages clambering over ridges and into the vales of the rivers draining westwards to the Severn. Coal-mining, brick-making, and the iron trades have left their marks on almost every community.

Once again I have been compelled to ignore the boundaries established by local government reorganis-ation. The present Metropolitan Borough of Dudley includes most of the area covered in this section but I have also included the part of Sandwell that has crept over the ridge and absorbed Old Hill, Cradley Heath and part of Blackheath, all at one time part of Rowley Regis.

Here you will find a cinema for every taste: three Odeons, plus absorbed Odeons, Danilos, one Clifton, several striking independent super-cinemas and small obscure village cinemas of dazzling variety. Up until the mid fifties it was possible to see films in an unaltered nineteenth century Temperance Hall in the Lye, or a converted Market Hall in Kingswinford. If you were courting the Lyttleton provided double seats in both rear stalls and the circle in mini super-cinema surround-ings, or if you really felt brave enough to visit a cinema that normally enjoyed very local support you could venture into Quarry Bank, or Pensnett.

At the time of writing, one cinema survives in Dudley with two screens. One cinema survives in Stourbridge, and the Royal exists in Cradley Heath. I urge you to visit them while you can.

## Dudley

### 1. The Public Hall
*Wolverhampton Street*

The Public Hall started life as a Mechanics' Institute. Films were certainly shown there before the passing of the Cinematograph Act. From Christmas 1909 into the New Year Professor Wood was presenting a "Musical and Pictorial Combination", but he had decided, by that time, to settle in Bilston. It fell to another pioneer,

Irving Bosco, to be the first to present *regular* film-shows in Dudley, at the Public Hall.

During 1909 Irving Bosco had established a cinema in West Bromwich, but he had visited the Black Country long before that and may have presented travelling shows at the Public Hall. He was granted his kine licence on the day the Act came into operation: 1st January 1910.

He opened the Public Hall as a cinema on 31st January 1910, and his wife, Ducie Saunderson, sang between the films. His policy was to "keep one step ahead of Birmingham", and the Public Hall appears to have been a great success. Shows were presented twice nightly and the hall accommodated up to eight hundred patrons, a year later quoted as 630! Irving Bosco became a well known local personality and showed the usual showman's interest in raising money for local charities.

On 19th October 1911 he persuaded the Mayor, Dudley's M.P., and the Earl of Dudley, to attend a benefit show. The films shown are not recorded, but again Ducie Saunderson sang for the enthusiastic audience. Irving Bosco later expanded his empire but continued to present shows at the Public Hall until sometime in 1919, or possibly the summer of 1920. Films continued to be shown at the Public Hall by Edwin Griffiths but in 1922 his application for his kine licence was refused and he was told that the premises were not considered suitable for that purpose anymore.

On 22nd April 1922 Mr. Griffiths advertised, "This Hall is now to let as a cinema" despite his difficulty in obtaining a licence! In the event the Public Hall re-opened as a dance-hall on 27th November 1922. It later had a very prolonged existence as a derelict shell of a building, boarded up and waiting for death. Demolition has removed all trace of it and the area is now a public car park. Many old people in Dudley still recall the shows at the Public Hall, and its name is more frequently evoked than Dudley's other early cinemas.

### 2. The Colosseum
**(later known as The Gem, The John Bull, The Scala and The Plaza)**
*Castle Hill, Dudley*

Six kine licences were issued on 1st January 1910 in Dudley but the first purpose-built cinema did not open until almost the end of that year. It then suffered an eventful history, but at least it can be said that films are still, in 1982, being shown on the same site.

The Colosseum was created by John Maurice Clement (28th December 1840 — 25th February 1912). He is most well known as the founder, proprietor and manager of the Dudley Opera House, opened in September 1899. At some stage he had purchased "Lloyd's Circus" just round the corner in Trindle Road. He converted it into a theatre, using the name Colosseum, until its closure at the turn of the century. It later became a skating rink.

75. Castle Hill, about 1911:
The Colosseum, and the Opera House

*(Photo: Dudley Libraries)*

76. Castle Hill, 1981:
The Plaza, and the Hippodrome

*(Photo: Ned Williams)*

In 1910 he revived the name Colosseum for a small five hundred seater cinema built next-door to the Opera House. It was a "tin-shed" construction suitably disguised by an elaborate frontage. The "Grand Opening" took place on Christmas Eve, and from then on shows were presented twice nightly at seven and nine. Life did not run completely smoothly and it seems that it may have closed briefly in 1911, although Mr. Clement renewed the licence in 1912. He died in February 1912 and the cinema closed again.

It was reopened as the Gem on 15th December 1913 by George Lovatt of Wolverhampton, who had been unsuccessful in attempting to build a cinema in his home town. The opening programme featured *"The Battle of Gettysburgh"* and ladies were invited to attend free of charge at the first afternoon show. The advertising claimed that the Gem was "Dudley's Cosiest and Prettiest Picture House".

Even so, the cinema changed hands again nine months later, acquired by a John Nisbet, and yet again in October 1916 when it was acquired by a Mr. Cranston of Birmingham. (See Empire, Cradley Heath).

Mr. Cranston reopened on 2nd December 1916 with *"Infidelity"*, starring Theda Bara, and re-named the cinema "The John Bull". Another two years passed and the cinema changed name for the third time. On 17th December 1918 it became the Scala and was now in the hands of Ernest Davies, a local auctioneer and estate agent, who was also running the Opera House.

In 1920 Ernest Davies sold the Opera House to Benjamin Kennedy, but the Scala continued to change hands a number of times. By the mid twenties it was being run by Walter McMillan, who had opened the Castle Cinema in the old Temperance Institute, and, while both cinemas were in the same hands, Harry Crane gained some local experience of cinema management at both places that later stood him in good stead when he moved to the Cliftons at Sedgley and Coseley.

During 1931 the Scala seems to have been acquired, at last, by Benjamin Kennedy and underwent its final change of name to the Plaza. A few years later it was demolished to make way for Mr. Kennedy's new purpose-built super-cinema, but many people have happy memories of the place as the Scala, and have nostalgically recalled the perfumed deodorant of the scent sprays and its films in the "Blood Tub" tradition.

The new Plaza was quite different from its predecessor and illustrates how far its architect, Mr. Hurley Robinson, had adopted a functional approach to cinema design by the mid thirties. Its unadorned brickwork must have looked odd next-door to the Opera House, but about five months after the cinema opened the Opera House was burnt down, to be replaced by a new theatre designed by Mr. Hurley Robinson. The architect's sketch on the front of the silver opening brochure suggests that the original frontage was more effective than the present one. The cinema's name was more centrally placed and the largest brickwork flanks were relieved by monogram motifs. It would be interesting to know if they did ever appear on the cinema as built. The construction was carried out by Parsons and Morrin Ltd., of Edgbaston.

However plain its exterior, it was described as

"palatial" inside, and fifteen hundred patrons were said to be accommodated in the maximum comfort. The auditorium tapered towards the screen and this was thought to be good for acoustics. Sound was produced by Western Electric equipment.

The opening was held on Thursday 28th May 1936 and Benjamin Kennedy entertained the Council, the Town Clerk, and invited guests, to a presentation of *"Top Hat"* starring Fred Astaire and Ginger Rogers. Inspired by *"Top Hat"*, which was retained until the programme change in the middle of the following week, Mr. Kennedy advertised the Plaza as, "Joyously different to ordinary cinemas".

Benjamin Kennedy went on to open the new Hippodrome as the summit of his achievement, but died shortly afterwards in April 1939. His sons continued to run the theatre and cinema through the War years and into the fifties. On one side of Castle Hill stood the theatre, cinema and zoo. Opposite stood the Odeon. Both the Plaza and the Odeon entertained patrons from a very wide area.

Early in 1954 Miles Jervis obtained the Plaza from the trustees of the late Benjamin Kennedy's estate. He took Castle Hill by storm by installing cinemascope and advertising *"The Robe"* with a huge display that engulfed the Plaza's facade. Large queues developed of eager patrons, and no doubt the new screen format seemed to have come as the industry's salvation. *"The Robe"* opened on 14th June 1954 and was so successful it was retained immediately for a second week.

So successful was the Plaza that Gaumont British purchased it in autumn 1955 and thus, eventually, the Plaza and Odeon were united within the Rank Organisation. As time went on many people felt that Rank would be more likely to abandon the Plaza than the Odeon. They were wrong.

On 3rd February 1973 work started on twinning the Plaza; the first such conversion in the Black Country. The conversion cost £35,000 and was remarkable in that it was carried out without the Plaza ever closing. Both screens opened on Sunday 29th April 1973. Screen 1 which uses the old balcony and existing screen opened with *"The Triple Echo"*. Screen 2 opened with

"*Young Winston*". The two auditoria held 551 patrons and 199 patrons respectively, although I have seen slightly different figures quoted recently. Modern Cinemeccanica equipment has been installed.

The Plaza has outlived the Odeon and become Dudley's sole-surviving cinema. Long may its survival continue. I visited the Plaza frequently in the sixties and I will always remember one particular night. In the middle of "*Boccaccio 70*" the picture faded from the screen. There was much shouting and banging of feet. Then a tiny figure clambered onto the thin strip of a stage in front of the screen. He quelled the noise by waving his torch and shouting that there had been a power-cut but we should stay in our seats. This shadowy little figure then began telling jokes. Soon tears were running down our faces. When the film resumed we gave him a spontaneous standing ovation as he came up the aisle and disappeared.

### 3. The Opera House and The Trindle Road Rink

As stated in the previous section, John Maurice Clement ran a theatre in Trindle Road, called the Colosseum, during the 1890's. He presumably abandoned this interest when his magnificent Opera House opened in September 1899. The timber framed building in Trindle Road became a skating rink and seems to have enjoyed many and various uses in the field of popular entertainment. On 1st January 1910 William Harper obtained a kine licence for the rink. The licence claimed that a thousand people could be accommodated. It was renewed in 1911 and then lapsed. I imagine that films were occasionally shown in cine-variety programmes.

At the same time J. M. Clement obtained a kine licence, for the Opera House. Films had occasionally been shown there in 1909, and possibly earlier. They were used as a summer attraction. During the summer of 1910 twice nightly shows were presented at the "Opera House Picture Palace and Electric Theatre", invoking three names simultaneously to confuse later historians! The kine licence for the Opera House was renewed right up to the time of Ben Kennedy's arrival, but it is not known how much this was exploited. The story of the destruction of the Opera House and its replacement by the Hippodrome is described in the section on Ben Kennedy.

### 4. The Temperance Institute
### (later known as The Temple and The Castle)
*High Street*

Whatever went on at the foot of Castle Hill, Irving Bosco's real competitor was to be found at The Temperance Institute in the town centre. Like the Public Hall, it was visited by travelling shows and, therefore, already had established some identity as a "cinema" before the Act. From November 1909 until Christmas the Picture World Company were presenting their "animated films" in competition with Professor Wood at the Public Hall.

On 24th October 1910 the Crown Electric Picture Company commenced a season with their "Entirely new flickerless projectors". Their first programme included "*The Revolution in Lisbon*", "*Egypt in the Time of the Pharoahs*" and "*Range Riders*".

Exactly one year after Irving Bosco had established himself at the Public Hall, the first permanent film-exhibitor arrived at "The Temp". This was Howard Bishop, already successfully showing films in Netherton. He opened his "Pictureland" at the Temp Hall on 30th January 1911. A thousand people came to see a two hour show which included "*Sexton Blake*", and a colour film of Niagara Falls.

Howard Bishop loved the theatre, variety, concerts etc., and usually presented variety acts as part of his film-shows. He made great use of the tramway system by dispatching the performers to Netherton and bringing them back by tram. He usually presented shows twice nightly in Dudley and once nightly in Netherton. Later he juggled with the films themselves when he started shows in Cradley Heath. At least once he organised an outing to Kinver for all his patrons, who boarded the trams outside the Temp and enjoyed the rural virtues of the Kinver Light Railway. Not to be outdone by Irving Bosco he also organised benefit shows for charity. Howard Bishop was also proud that he had allowed a young violinist named Barrs Partridge to make his debut at Pictureland.

After the First World War the entire Temperance Institute was bought for £15,000 by a Mr. W. L. Moore, who intended turning it into a real cinema. Temple Cinemas Ltd., was registered in January 1920 and began the £7,000 improvement scheme. A lounge and cafe were provided in the basement and the auditorium, now reached by a flight of stairs, was raked and fitted with silk velvet tip up seats throughout. Axminster carpet added to the new feeling of luxury, and two new powerful Kalee projectors were installed.

It opened in May 1920 and Kine Weekly recorded that two thousand people attended the event. The licence permitted audiences of 690. Wilford Cheetam came from the Empire to manage the place, but by July was replaced for a time by Stourbridge's Harry Morris. For some reason the Temple was not a success. Its losses were blamed on "the depression". Shows ceased sometime in 1923 and the Temple Cinema Company was wound-up in the October of that year.

All was not lost, and, at the beginning of December 1924, a licence was issued to Mr. Walter McMillan to re-open the hall as The Castle. It reopened on 15th December 1924 with *"The Arizona Express"*, and advertised its orchestra directed by Leonard Singer. The identity of the new proprietors is somewhat obscure, but, at some stage Ernest Grenville Jones, of the Alexander, Lower Gornal, seems to have become associated with the Castle. From late 1929 it was managed for five years by Harry Crane, who later appeared at the Clifton, Sedgley.

At least it now enjoyed a more stable existence and kept itself up-to-date by installing British Acoustic sound equipment when the talkies arrived. It must have been rather over-shadowed by the splendid Regent when that opened a few yards away. However, its tasteful advertisements, featuring Dudley Castle, continued to appear regularly in the Dudley Herald until the end of April 1936. Whether it closed then, or continued a little longer, is very obscure. Only a few months earlier proposals had been made concerning a plan to double its size and improve the sound equipment.

It seems possible to me that its demise may be connected with the rebuilding of Mr. Jones' Alexandra but I have no evidence which could confirm it. The Castle eventually became a dance hall, with the cellar in use for a time as a roller-skating rink. It is now a Thoms' Superstore. When the building is viewed from the rear it is possible to imagine the outline of the Castle cinema!

### 5. The Empire
*Hall Street*

At the beginning of this century the original Victorian "Music Hall" seemed a thing of the past. If a town was modern and up to the minute it built a "Palace of Varieties" for the popular entertainment of the working classes! Such a building was erected in Hall Street for a Mr. Tom Prichard. On 3rd April 1903 he invited Dan Leno and the Mayor, John Hughes, to come along and lay foundation stones. It was Dan Leno's first visit to Dudley but he promised to return for the opening of the Empire.

Somewhat amazingly it was planned to have the theatre open at Easter, just a month away. The schedule was kept and on 6th May 1903 Dan Leno returned. He travelled down to Dudley in the morning, took part in the opening ceremony and the first matinee and then hurried back up to London to appear there. The theatre was far from finished at the opening. Ornamental plaster-work had not been applied and permanent upholstered seats had not been installed, but nobody complained.

The building was designed by a Dudley architect, Arthur Gammage, and held 1,100 patrons in the stalls and 900 in a huge steeply raked gallery. Part of the roof could be rolled back, and in the summer a little sunshine and fresh air were allowed to circulate before the matinee. Despite its popularity it seems to have changed hands a number of times, or possibly a variety of people leased the place. This is particularly true of the period following the passing of the Cinematograph Act. On 1st January 1910 none other than Irving Bosco obtained a kine licence for the Empire but does not seem to have shown films there himself for over two years. While he enjoyed success at the Public Hall a number of people tried showing films at the Empire. For example, towards the end of 1910 R. Colin was presenting "Colin's Famous Electric Pictures". Mr. Colin provided similar fare in Brierley Hill and West Bromwich. Cine-variety and pure variety tended to alternate until 6th January 1912 when the last live variety show was staged.

It began life as a full-time cinema on 8th January 1912 with a film called *"Fools of Society"*. The presenters were the Pantheon Syndicate. They renovated the Empire and experimented with various short-lived changes of name. By March it was advertised as "Under Entirely New Control" but was quickly in trouble again.

Irving Bosco took over on 8th April 1912. Bert Dawes, who had worked for Waller Jeffs, and for Irving Bosco at the Public Hall, became the manager, and some permanent order prevailed at last. A new electric projector was installed to replace the hand-cranked machine. For a few years it was known as "Bosco's Picture Pavilion" but by the end of the First World War it was the Empire again.

At the end of 1920 Irving Bosco sold his cinemas to a Nottingham-based syndicate led by E. C. Shapeero. A separate company was floated to run the Empire, but like other ex-Bosco-owned cinemas run by Mr. Shapeero, it was later sold to Denman Picture Houses which was a subsidiary of Gaumont British.

Mr. Shapeero's company installed back projection equipment in the Autumn of 1922, having built a little corrugated iron extension on the rear of the building to form an operating room. They gained a few seats in the auditorium by removing the existing operating room but by the thirties when people hoped for a little more leg-room and comfort the capacity came down to about thirteen hundred.

The Empire provided plenty of nostalgic memories for Dudley citizens. Some remember the Saturday afternoon matinees and the crowd of children who could

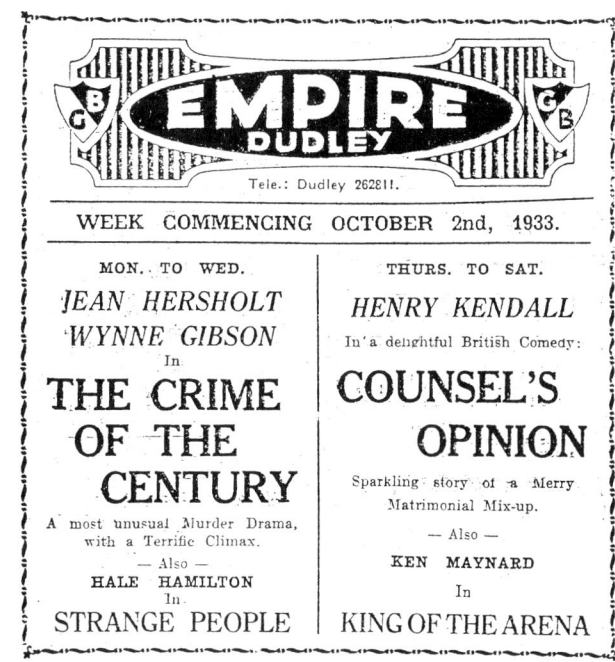

77. The Empire awaiting demolition.
*(Photo: Ned Williams)*

not afford one penny for admission. They gathered in Dudley Row and took turns at looking through a chink in the large exit doors. Patrons also remember the potted palms placed each side of the screen and the three-piece orchestra. In April 1922 the locally produced film *"Bladys of the Stewponey"* was given its Dudley premiere at the Empire, and later the same year they screened a film made in the Bean car factory, which was fairly close by.

Having acquired the cinema at the beginning of the sound era, Gaumont British set about preparing the Empire for the new medium. They abandoned Mr. Shapeero's back projection equipment and built a new projection room at the back of the balcony. At first the Cinephone Sound system was installed but later this was replaced by British Acoustic. Some variety acts were still under contract to appear at the Empire after G.B.'s acquisition and the screen had to be "flown" when these acts appeared on stage. This created problems when sound films were being presented and the large horn speakers had to slide into the wings when the screen

was flown! The first talkie was projected at the Empire by Abner Parker, who had previously been second operator at the Arcade in Worcester. It was the beginning of his long career in Dudley's cinemas.

For a time Gaumont British advertised the programmes of the Empire, the Regent and the Criterion together in one block: Dudley's "Big Three". However, G.B.'s three Dudley cinemas were hardly three of a kind, and I feel the Empire was always the "poor relation". An antiquated ex-Variety theatre, hurriedly built in 1903 was obviously going to be the first to be abandoned. The Empire closed on 2nd November 1940 with *"Let George Do It"*, starring George Formby, which seems an appropriate finale.

During the War it was used as a factory and warehouse, and for years was occupied by the Dudley engineers, Herman Smith. The peeling remains of the building survived until the beginning of the nineteen seventies. Following demolition, redevelopment was fairly slow, but today a brand new Tesco supermarket covers the site.

### 6. The Criterion
*Market Place*

The Criterion is presented out of chronological sequence simply because most people will think of the 1923 cinema rather than its almost forgotten predecessor that started showing films regularly even before the Empire. The Criterion, at the turn of the century, was a public-house which offered "Music Hall" entertainment in rather cramped conditions. It was run by Wally Davies' father, a fact which may have had some part in the hall finding its way to Sidney Bray.

A kine licence was issued to the Criterion Electric Theatre at the beginning of 1911. It could hold 253 patrons and is thought to have been the assembly room at the rear of the premises. As such it opened on 27th February 1911 with a programme that included *"Jerusalem and the Mount of Olives"* and *"The Little Mother"*. Admission to Dudley's "Most Up to Date Theatre" cost 3d and 6d.

At the beginning of 1913 it was much enlarged by extending the auditorium back towards the Market Place and building a proper entrance and pay box, with operating room above. Now that it was just a cinema, and nothing else, it managed to increase its capacity to 570. The kine licence changed hands several times and it closed briefly towards the end of 1913 to be re-seated and redecorated. It reopened on Boxing Day and from then on seems to have been in the hands of Benjamin Kennedy, until taken over by Sidney Bray. This was accomplished by the beginning of 1915 and marks the moment when Dudley's own cinema magnate established himself in his home town. His other interests were at Halesowen, Langley and Brownhills.

After the War Sidney Bray launched his ambitious plan to replace the Criterion with a fine new cinema. By building a large auditorium behind the existing cinema it was possible to continue business at the latter until about six weeks before opening. It could then be replaced with the crush hall entrance, and balcony level cafe for the new Criterion.

The Criterion Picture House (Dudley) Ltd., began raising their £40,000 capital in the Autumn of 1922. Sidney Bray's original fellow directors were F. J. Ballard (prominent in the industrial and civic life of Dudley and later associated with three other cinemas), A. J. Crump (the building contractor about to start building the cinema), W. Lloyd (an accountant), J. Mason (an industrialist) and Tom Hanson, the Dudley brewer.

The building was designed by Joseph Lawden, of Birmingham, and Howard Cetti of Dudley. The Dudley Herald told its readers, "The general trend of the design follows the lines of the Greek work of the Renaissance period". The huge hoardings across the front of the cinema were removed shortly before the opening and the public was suitably over-awed by the dignity of the facade. By everyone working up to the last minute it was possible to open on Saturday 17th November 1923, with a special presentation of *"Hearts Aflame"* and a locally made film of Mayoral Sunday celebrations. Viscount Ednam came along to perform the opening even though he was suffering from a broken collar bone acquired while hunting. The Mayor, Alderman Tanfield, and Corporation occupied the 1/3d seats in the balcony. Sidney Bray presented Viscount Ednam with a silver

78. The entrance to the Criterion, a drawing from the company's prospectus.

*(Author's Collection)*

paperweight made by Ivo Shaw of Dudley Art School. Horace Watson directed the newly formed orchestra and everybody felt confident that they were sitting in Dudley's finest picture palace.

Normal public shows started on the Monday and great claims were made about the Criterion's intention of showing film of a Japanese earthquake — "for the first time in Dudley". The Empire quickly organised a charity show on the Sunday and showed the same film while the Criterion was closed!

The Criterion was not so easily beaten. It could accommodate twelve hundred people in the greatest luxury Dudley had yet seen. Its cafe, open from 10 a.m. to 10 p.m., incorporating an American Soda Fountain, made the place a social centre and the kind of respectable establishment usually associated with A.P.P.H. Picture Houses.

Sidney Bray eventually handed the day to day management of the Criterion over to his brother, Clifford Bray, and the orchestra found a new popular leader in Stanley Pendrous. The orchestra also featured a Mustel organ. Nothing challenged the supremacy of the "Cry", as it was called, until P.C.T. announced their

intention of building the Regent. The approach of a large combine often upset the independent exhibitor. Clifford Bray decided to devote his energy to the Central in Stourbridge; Sidney Bray decided to make sure of his position in Halesowen by concentrating his energy on building a super-cinema there. He had just spent a large sum on rebuilding the Picture House in that town. By the time P.C.T. opened the Regent in September 1928, they had already acquired the Criterion through their subsidiary A.P.P.H., the previous year. P.C.T. were shortly to become a subsidiary of Gaumont British and by the end of the decade the Criterion, the Empire and the Regent were bedfellows.

Sound came to the Criterion on 11th November 1929 with *"The Glad Rag Doll"*, starring Dolores Costello, not far behind the Regent. The British Acoustic System was used. Despite the Regent, and later despite the Odeon and Plaza, the Criterion enjoyed a very central position overlooking a busy market place, it therefore deserved to survive. Its happy family atmosphere often attracted long terms of service. The Chief, Ab Parker, put in over twenty years at the Criterion and particularly remembers how "spick and span" his box was kept by his second and third operators, Beryl Byfield and Iris Robinson. In total Ab Parker worked over thirty-five years for the Company.

The end came suddenly in 1956 after the Rank Organisation had threatened to close theatres if the Government did not abolish entertainment tax. They rationalised the circuit by closing the oldest halls in towns where they had several screens. The Cape Hill

Electric and the Criterion both closed on 29th September 1956. The last film at the Criterion was *"Reach for the Sky"* starring Kenneth More. As Ab Parker laced up *"Reach for the Sky"* for the final performance he, and the manager, Mr. Toole, must have found it ironical that the film was playing to a packed house and had done terrific business throughout the last week.

The property was later sold to Broadmead, supplying radio and electrical goods. Only the entrance to the cinema was converted into the shop. The auditorium, stripped of its seats, continued to exist as a giant warehouse. The frontage is still to be seen today, now part of the Wigfall's chain of shops, but the auditorium was demolished in the autumn of 1980 and has now been replaced with a furniture store facing King Street.

When I visited the auditorium in June 1980 I was amazed to find the ornamental plaster work still intact. Elaborate, but dusty, cornucopia were abundant. Four grinning faces peered down at me from the plaster work of the proscenium arch. A quarter of a century had passed since the last patrons had sat there enjoying the exploits of Douglas Bader.

## 7. The Regent
### (later known as The Gaumont)
*High Street*

The Regent was one of those cinemas built just as the silent era was coming to a close, and just as the new decade was about to produce a new taste in simplicity in cinema design. It was designed by W. E. Trent, and built by Messrs. McLaughlin and Harvey in eight months. A large sweeping "stadium" style auditorium was provided to accommodate sixteen hundred patrons. The front of the theatre was treated in white stone and an iron and glass canopy, cleverly lit, made it most impressive. This effect was lost over the years as the canopy was replaced, and the shops which shared the frontage became a greater distraction.

The auditorium, crush hall and entrance featured relatively "modern" plaster work, painted in delicate blends of mauve, blue and ivory. Stage facilities and dressing-rooms were provided, plus space for a large orchestra and, of course, a Wurlitzer organ. Considering the whole affair was a P.C.T. enterprise, a surprising number of local people found work there, particularly from the Criterion! Stanley Pendrous came to conduct the orchestra, Beatrice Holmes came as cashier, and Mr. H. Godwin Longthorn arrived as manager. He must have been a gentleman who specialised in opening new halls. He opened the Criterion, and the Majestic, Cradley Heath, but never stayed at a newly opened cinema for long.

The Regent was opened on Monday evening 3rd September 1928 by that cinema-minded Mayor, Councillor F. J. Ballard. There was not enough space to accommodate everyone who wished to be there. Twenty-two year old John Howlett opened the Wurlitzer while the packed house waited for the Mayor to make his speech. There followed quite a variety of entertainment, short films, vocal solos, organ interludes, and an orchestral "turn". The feature film was *"The Magic Flame"*, starring Ronald Colman and Vilma Banky.

79. The Regent/Gaumont as a Top Rank Bingo & Social Club, 1981.

*(Photo: Ned Williams)*

People certainly travelled from far and wide to hear the new organ, and a year later they flocked to hear sound as *"The Singing Fool"* introduced the talkies to Dudley in August 1929. Western Electric equipment was installed. Organists moved about frequently at that time, gaining experience and reputations, and a number of famous men appeared at the Regent briefly: Reginald Dixon, Leslie Taff, really orchestral pianist at the time, Sidney Wallbank, Harry Farmer, Norris Bosworth and Clifford Baggott. Even after the opening of the Odeon many patrons remained loyal to the Regent because of its organ. One also has the feeling that the Regent had a kind of personality and intimacy that some of the supers that followed lacked, despite its size.

On 25th November 1935 James Whale's *"Bride of Frankenstein"* began a six day run after a long publicity run-up. It was billed as "Dudley's own thriller, directed by Dudley's own director". It had been banned by most surrounding authorities, but Dudley Watch Committee decided that local patrons over the age of sixteen should be allowed to see a local man's work! Perhaps the wonderful scene in which the monster is introduced to his bride and her resulting scream was a more exciting cinematic event than Al Jolson singing to his mother a few years earlier.

By the end of the thirties the Gaumont British presence was clearly established in the advertising, uniforms and monthly programme leaflets but the name "Regent" remained in use until 1950. While it was officially known as the Gaumont for the next decade, as with most such name changes, the force of

tradition was too strong, and most people still label it "the Regent" in their memories.

At the end of the War, Bill Greaves took over as manager and during the settled period that followed many employees put in long periods of unbroken service. Three sisters, Beatrice, Freda and Margaret Morton worked there for many years. A good example of the kind of devotion to be expected from the staff was to be found in the Chief of Staff, Fred Hewitt, who looked very smart in his Gaumont uniform. He had been a carpenter and joiner. He had taken a temporary job at the Criterion and then stayed there over six years. While he was there he built a new sales kiosk which he installed at the Odeon, Blackheath. It was constructed entirely from re-cycled scrapped display materials. When he came to the Gaumont he made another one! The last resident organist at the Gaumont was Stanley Harrison, who worked there from 1947 to 1951, and later went to the Majestic, Cradley Heath.

When the little Savoy in Netherton died just before Christmas in 1960, Bill Greaves hoped that Netherton cinema-goers would come to the Gaumont. Perhaps he had no idea that his own cinema would close seven months later. I am sure he could never have anticipated how little attention the closure of Gaumont was going to receive. The Dudley Herald gave the Savoy a front-page obituary, the Gaumont's passing was ignored!

The last film show was on Sunday 16th July 1961 and consisted of a one-day showing of *"Man of the West"* starring Gary Cooper, plus *"Submarine Seahawk"*. Not a moment was wasted in turning the premises into

80. The Wurlitzer at the Regent/Gaumont was played at the cinema, by then a Bingo hall, for the last time on 23rd February 1969. A Cinema Organ Society recital included performances by S. Tovey, John Bee, etc.

*(Photo: John Sharp)*

a Bingo and Social Club. It opened eight days later, on Monday 23rd July, as the Top Rank Bingo Club. So far, it has continued to operate in this capacity for twenty-one years.

At some stage there was talk of reviving the organ, but by the early seventies this was regarded as an impossible task. Replacement parts seemed too costly or even impossible to acquire. Many of its six ranks of pipes had been stolen. Even the cost of trying to remove the remains for scrap seemed daunting. An organ enthusiast from Peterborough, Mr. Roy Mosley, purchased it in 1975 and no doubt the proprietors heaved a sigh of relief.

Preservationists are never daunted, as railway enthusiasts who have heard of Barry Scrapyard will testify, and the Regent's 2 manual, 6 unit Wurlitzer has been lovingly restored at Peterborough Technical College. It was reopened on 8th March 1981 by John Mann. It was hoped that John Howlett himself would venture out of his semi-retirement to perform the ceremony. Unfortunately he was prevented from doing so by ill health. He sent a recorded message to the gathering, admitting his great affection for the organ. "I've seen it since its restoration and felt as if I was meeting an old friend", he said.

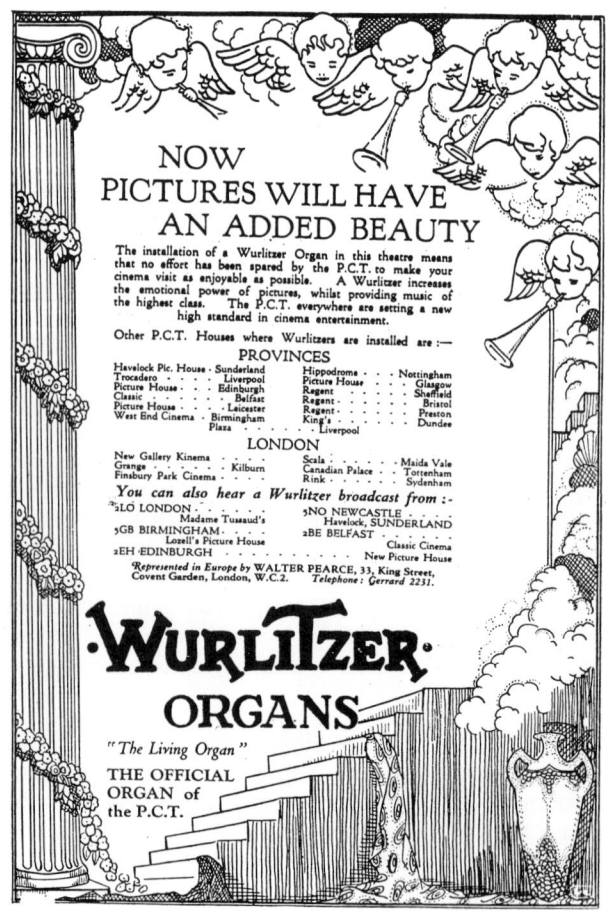

81. The Odeon in July 1937.

*(Photo: John Maltby)*

### 8. The Odeon
*Castle Hill*

The last cinema to be built in Dudley represents what many people believe to be the zenith of cinema design: a late thirties Odeon designed by the Harry Weedon office. This particular Odeon seems to have been the work of Budge Reid. Its strong stylistic simplicity is just as impressive as those Odeons with their fins and towers.

A site was found on Castle Hill directly opposite the Plaza. The cream faience treatment of the Odeon's frontage stood face to face with the huge unrelieved brickwork facade of the Plaza and, in my opinion, proved the more attractive. The only disadvantage that the Odeon appears to have suffered is that the rising ground of Castle Hill somewhat buried the impact of this frontage. It looked as if the building had sunk into the hillside, coyly hidden behind some ornamental gardens. (It was best seen from half-way up the chair lift in Dudley Zoo).

It was built by Housing Ltd., of Blackheath, who also built the Wolverhampton and Kingstanding Odeons. It is reputed to have cost about £31,500. It held 1,876 patrons, 1,234 in the stalls and 642 in the circle. Like other Odeons it was fitted with BTH equipment.

The Odeon was opened on 28th July 1937 by Dudley's Mayor, Alderman J. Hillman. After his speech there was a musical interlude provided by the Band of the First Battalion, Royal Scots Regiment, followed by a charity collection on behalf of the Dudley Guest Hospital. The the films began with *"British Movietone News"* and a cartoon. The feature was *"Beloved Enemy"* starring Merle Oberon. Mr. and Mrs. Deutsch attended the opening although such events were now becoming rather numerous.

The first manager was Charles Crathorn, who apparently later became a radio and television personality. The first chief, Harry Willis stayed at the Odeon for years. The two men had worked together before at the Odeon, Blackheath. Even one of the patrons was so loyal he became an unpaid member of staff! This was Fred Hemmings, who had visited the Odeon every week since the opening, and, at his own expense, offered to look after the ornamental garden in front of the cinema!

The size and architectural grandeur of the Odeon immediately established it as the town's major cinema. It exuded a confidence that led you to believe that it would last forever, even when surrounded by competition. From then on its history was simply one of stability and success, punctuated with anniversaries and a few special events. In 1941 the Minor's Club began and attracted over a thousand members.

At the end of 1952 two new BTH projectors were installed. Work began after the last show on Saturday night, and the Mayor, Alderman A. M. Silcox came in on Monday to switch them on! The Manager,

Mr. Alexander, described them to the local press as "the very latest thing". Perhaps this was ironical in view of the success of cinemascope across the road at the Plaza two years later. Of course, cinemascope came to the Odeon eventually.

By the time the Odeon was preparing to celebrate its twenty-first birthday, in 1958, Donald Pass was the manager. He ordered a 150 lb. cake to be made by the Dudley Co-Operative Society with a replica of the cinema on top. In order to find a film with a suitable title, he acquired Carol Reed's *"The Key"* direct from the Berlin Film Festival.

In the sixties, after many cinemas had closed, it was still possible to find queues at the Odeon and one had the feeling that its patrons still came from a very wide area. It was best to arrive early to be sure of even finding accommodation in the cinema's spacious car park. When the Plaza was twinned at the beginning of the seventies people began to wonder about the future of the Odeon but business, to an outsider, seemed good. The Saturday Morning Club still had eight hundred members. The last children's matinee was presented on 8th February 1975.

The Odeon closed completely on 22nd February 1975 with the popular musical *"Oliver"*. It was rumoured that the building was going to be pulled down and replaced with an office block. While a few people began to insist on the architectural interest of the building it remained boarded-up and unused. Dudley Council rejected Rank's application to demolish it.

In 1976 an unlikely purchaser materialised who was willing to conserve the building and put it back into regular use, not as a cinema, but as a Kingdom Hall. The Jehovah's Witnesses have certainly extended considerable love and attention to their Odeon, both internally and externally. When they moved in they found the seats had been removed and, therefore, had to buy 1,600 seats from Rank! The conversion, renovation, rewiring etc., cost about £40,000 and makes an interesting comparison with some of the splendid Bingo Club conversions. The work has made the auditorium very bright and colourful without being gaudy. The Jehovah's Witnesses themselves seem so pleased that they sell a souvenir set of post-cards of their work! Interesting touches abound. The mock orchestra pit has become a baptismal pool. The projection suite has become residential accommodation and the one-time flag-pole has been replaced by a bird table that, for a time was delightfully at odds with the well-preserved facade, but it has recently been discreetly resited.

82. The foyer and pay box, Odeon, 1937.
*(Photo: John Maltby)*

The most interesting living proof of the power of cinema traditions to survive is to be seen at a meeting at mid-day on Saturday. Packed lunches are brought into the auditorium on trays swinging from the shoulders of well-groomed volunteers. If only the lights were dimmed you could still imagine that ice-creams were on the way and the main feature would be following some exciting trailers.

## Netherton

Although a part of Dudley it seems quite wrong to think of Netherton as a suburb of Dudley in the way that Stone Cross might be a suburb of West Bromwich, or Penn a suburb of Wolverhampton. Netherton is an industrial village with its own identity, and complex character. When I arrived in the Black Country in 1962 I had never heard of Netherton but I soon found myself visiting the place again and again, to explore tow-paths, the Netherton Tunnel, Cobb's Engine House and all the wonders of Windmill End and Withymoor Basin. Netherton is enclosed in a huge horseshoe of the Dudley Canal, and the highest point within that horse-shoe is crowned with the parish church in which can be found some remains of the organ from the Odeon, Stourbridge. The entire hill and church looked, during the sixties, as if open-cast mining would obliterate them, but the landscape has been restored.

All around Dudley the Parish Churches stood on hills, safely within sight of one another, but remote from the industrial activity and social life of the villages below them. Non-conformists and publicans brought their services much closer to people's work and homes, and a bustling community was to be found on either side of the main Dudley to Halesowen road. Until ten years ago here one could find places like the incredible shop of Emile Doo, now removed to the Black Country Museum, and drink the home-brewed ale of the Old Swan, now much acclaimed by CAMRA. A few yards away is the Netherton Arts Centre, the home of the Dudley Little Theatre. This is where films first came to Netherton.

## 9. The Institute
### (known as Pictureland and the Imperial)

The Netherton Institute was a large public hall built at the end of the last century, after the Countess of Dudley had carefully laid the foundation stone on 5th July 1883.

On 1st January 1910 Howard Bishop obtained a kine licence for film shows in the public hall of the Institute. At first these were irregular, presumably dependent on when the hall could be booked for that purpose. These shows were advertised as taking place at the "Picture Palace, Netherton". By the end of the year it seems that Mr. Bishop had managed to acquire a more permanent lease and regular shows began on Monday 14th November 1910. The advertisement announced that Jesse Hackett, a celebrated local vocalist, would be present at the opening of the Electric Pictureland.

"Pictureland" was the name used by Howard Bishop not only at Netherton, but also at the Temperance Institute in Dudley and the Working Man's Institute in Cradley Heath. Locally people preferred to call it "The Stute", and later the nickname "Bungies" became so popular that it became a legend.

Howard Bishop provided all the services one would expect from a cinema operating in its own premises. The children's matinee was particularly popular and the usual rules prevailed: a penny downstairs, twopence in the small balcony. The man taking the money used to shout, "Tak 'im back, 'e ay five", and try and keep order. If the film broke or a reel had to be changed the noise of stamping feet and whistling usually brought Mr. Bridgewater out of the library next-door to appeal for silence. At some point Mr. Bishop himself usually came on stage and banged the floor with a broom handle until the audience was silent. He would some-times announce that the following week everyone would get two free comics! After the show several tons of monkey-nut shells had to be swept up before the evening's performance.

Throughout the twenties Pictureland continued to present films in Netherton although the shows at the Temperance Institute in Dudley had finished at the end of the War. Mr. Bishop was able to obtain seven year leases on the hall in Netherton. It held about seven hundred patrons, including a few in the balcony. The floor of the hall was un-raked and is presumably little changed today.

By the end of the twenties business had declined and Howard Bishop joined forces with Cecil Couper to bring the hall up-to-date by installing sound equipment. It is believed the Morrison system was used. Now a sound cinema, the name was changed to the Imperial, and it is thought to have opened as such about 1932.

In the event Howard Bishop died shortly afterwards and his son, Charles Bishop, took his place. By this time the hall could only be obtained on one year leases and there was always some uncertainty regarding the future of the Imperial. The result was the building of the Savoy, which opened in August 1936 but that did not lead to the immediate closure of the Imperial.

When Charles Bishop took over his father's interest in the Imperial, his wife began working in the cash desk during the afternoons to learn about the business. She undertook the task of learning everything, including operating the machines, and stoking the boiler. All this knowledge was later put to good use at the Savoy!

For the two or three years that the Savoy and the Imperial were both open Mrs. Bishop used to organise the matinees at the Imperial then leave it in the hands

of the staff while she went to open-up the Savoy. By the War the Imperial had closed but I have been unable to trace any date for a final show or details of the last programme. In recent times the "Stute" has become the Netherton Arts Centre. Its stage is regularly used by Dudley Little Theatre. The projection room beneath the balcony has occasionally been used to present 16 mm. films, but "Bungies" has really been relegated to the world of local legend.

## 10. The Savoy
*Northfield Road*

As stated above, the Savoy partly grew out of Mr. Bishop's dissatisfaction with the terms on which he could obtain the hall in the Institute. But seen in terms of Mr. Cecil Couper's career it was a logical part of his 1930's policy of building purpose-built sound cinemas in Black Country villages, a process he had started in 1933 at the Coronet in Quarry Bank.

Mr. and Mrs. Charles Bishop and Mr. and Mrs. Cecil Couper formed the directors of the new company: Savoy Cinema (Netherton) Ltd. Stanley Griffiths of Stourbridge designed the building and it was built by J. M. Tate of Cradley Heath. It was built behind the Institute in Northfield Road. Five shops faced the road and the entrance to the cinema was reached by a grand flight of steps, and a covered shelter was provided for waiting patrons across the Recreation Street end of the building. There was no balcony and the five hundred and ninety patrons were accommodated on a single raked floor that sloped against the natural slope of the hill on which the cinema was built! A fairly modest nameplate over the entrance and a small sign advertising the current programme were the only adornments to the overall "snowcreted" surfaces of the building.

The Savoy was opened on Wednesday 26th August 1936 at 7.30 p.m. by Councillor Hillman, Mayor of Dudley. (Later during his term of office he opened the Odeon, just by way of contrast!). It was floodlit for the occasion. For the opening evening only *"Naughty Marietta"*, starring Jeanette MacDonald and Nelson Eddy, was booked but for the rest of the week *"First A Girl"*,

starring Jessie Matthews, was screened. Ironically, the patrons in Netherton seemed to prefer American pictures which gave the proprietors many headaches when trying to fulfil quota regulations. They were an audience who wanted plenty of film for their money, and generally wanted plenty of "action" in the films. Mrs. Bishop cites the Gaumont British News as an example of something too intellectual for the Savoy!

The art in running the Savoy successfully lay in persuading the patrons to wait for the films to arrive and not sneak off and see them earlier in Dudley. The Savoy also boldly advertised its shows alongside those of its big rivals in Dudley itself without any of the modesty of some Black Country village cinemas. The Savoy assured its patrons that it was the home of good family entertainment.

After the War the equipment was modernised and the Chief, Tommy Willetts, found himself in charge of an RCA LG220 sound system coupled to Ross GC1 projectors, replacing the Morrison sound system favoured by Cecil Couper. The Savoy survived the first winds of change that began to blow through the industry in the fifties. Even in 1958 business was good during the school holidays, and when suitable programmes could be booked. Cinemascope had been installed to keep the cinema up-to-date.

The Savoy never opened on a Sunday and ran two programmes per week throughout its life. Many of the regulars expected to occupy the same seat everytime they attended, including one fat lady at the matinees who regularly occupied two seats. Everything was efficiently supervised by Mrs. Bishop, and everybody could have "lived happily ever after", but the end of the fifties changed everything and by the end of 1960 they felt they could no longer fight a losing battle.

The Savoy closed on Christmas Eve, 24th December 1960 after wishing everyone a Happy and Prosperous New Year! The last programme consisted of *"The Iron Sheriff"* and *"Hidden Fear"*. Mr. Bishop was interviewed by the Express and Star, and the Dudley Herald gave the Savoy's closure front page headlines. Few other similar cinemas closing at roughly the same time received

84. The Savoy, decorated for the Coronation in 1953.

*(Photo: Mrs. Bishop)*

any attention at all, the Savoy must have been "special" after all.

The building has remained standing and will soon have been "closed" for as long as it was open as a cinema! It is now a carpet warehouse.

## Harts Hill

### 11. The Harts Hill Limelight Cinema
*51A Vine Street, Harts Hill*

Half way between Dudley and Brierley Hill is the village of Harts Hill. Ribbon development on the main-road and the growth of housing estates before and after the last War have obscured the identity of such small communities. But in the early twenties Harts Hill was quite distinct from neighbouring Holly Hall, or Woodside, and fields separated them. In the other direction the railway and The Earl of Dudley's Iron-works separated Harts Hill from Brierley Hill. Harts Hill managed to straddle the boundary of Worcestershire and Staffordshire!

Industry followed the mining of coal in the form of a glassworks, replaced by the Dudley Drop Forging Company, and ironworks, replaced by Hill and Smiths. Opposite the "Dudley Drop" were Cartwright & Paddock, who employed a versatile engineering fitter named John Henry Revill.

John Henry Revill (1881 — 1965) was a local man who built his own house behind numbers 49 and 51 Vine Street. To amuse his children he would show them films in the living-room of this house, projecting from outside the house through the window. From these humble beginnings grew Harts Hill's little cinema.

With the help of his nephew, Leslie Ball, Mr. Revill built himself a cinema on the land adjacent to his house. It was a brick shed-like edifice with two entrance/exits in the side wall and a small operating room at one end. It appears to have cost just under £100 to build, and about as much again to equip. (At 1920's prices!). Mr. Revill recorded every single item of expenditure from two shillings and sixpence paid for five dozen brass wood-screws to thirty pounds for an Ernemann Bioscope and twenty pounds for a Dreadnought Bioscope.

The Dudley Council issued a kinematograph licence for the premises on 30th August 1921 and it is to be assumed that Mr. Revill opened his cinema as quickly as possible after that date. The licence allowed 103 patrons to occupy the building but audiences may have sometimes been twice that size! All the front seats were benches but there were about twenty-four tip ups at the back. Seats were 2½d and 4d, later rising gradually to 3d and 6d. The screen was high up on the end wall of the building and lost the two top corners with the slope of the roof. The plastered brickwork inside was gaily painted.

It was operated very much as a family affair. Leslie Ball helped to project and was a genius with the gas engine used to generate power. Mr. Revill's wife, Mary Elizabeth, ran the pay box and pasted up the local advertising hand-bills. Their daughters worked on the gramophone used to provide musical accompaniment.

Outside work, life in Harts Hill had consisted of visiting pubs or chapels, of which there were plenty of both, playing football or racing pigeons. When the Limelight opened in 1921 life gained a new dimension. The cinema was a great success in the local community, and a tribute to the versatility and enterprise of John Henry Revill. In Harts Hill and Holly Hall today old people can recall the shows vividly. Serials like *"The Monkey's Paw"* and *"The Count of Monte Cristo"* were popular even though they seemed old then! Mr. and Mrs. Revill recorded many of the films shown in their own note-book and listed their own stock of "stand-by films".

Like other cinema proprietors they ran a popular Saturday matinee performance, and the shop at the front of 49 Vine Street did a roaring trade in sweets. Sometimes their takings at the matinee appear to have been greater than at the evening performance! Versatile Mr. Revill even printed his own hand-bills and letter-headings, and advertised his cinema on a large hoarding on the far-side of the main Dudley-Brierley Hill Road.

Originally they used one projector and screened a slide while changing reels, but later bought a second movie projector. They also extended the cinema at some stage. The approach was along a "drive" next to 49 Vine Street, where a small wooden pay box was erected. Mrs. Revill sat there, in splendid isolation from the auditorium. From the drive, patrons turned right

85. The Harts Hill Limelight Cinema: a low winter sun shines into the camera in January 1982 as the photographer tries to record the view of the tiny cinema surrounded by visual obstructions on all sides! Maud Revill and the author pose outside the small door that leads into the rewind room and up into the operating box.

86. An old Ernimann projector stands in the operating box. Over forty years have elapsed since it last sprang to life, and over fifty years since it was last in regular use. It brought the wonder of the cinema to Harts Hill for less than a decade but it is to be hoped that it might yet return to life.

*(Both Photos: Tom Hetherington)*

by the shed housing the gas engine and walked past the Revill family's house to the cinema.

It seems that the Limelight closed at the end of 1929. By then the talkies had arrived in Dudley, Mr. Revill's family were growing up and the audience may have dwindled. Mr. Revill later used part of the auditorium to keep his collection of tropical fish. One night during the Second World War he coaxed the gas engine back into life and managed to revive a projector to show a few films to his daughter and her husband, and then all was quiet once again.

The absolutely amazing thing about the Harts Hill Limelight Theatre is that it has remained in existence right up to the time of writing this book! I visited the premises in January 1982, over fifty years after its closure. It was one of the most astonishing events connected with my research into this subject. The screen was still on the wall, the projectors were still in the operating box. The gramophone was still in the auditorium — once filled with the sound of the Destiny Waltz and the Skaters Waltz. Reels were in their place in the rewind room, and the engine room and pay box still stood where they had always been. One tip up seat, the Limelight only had about two dozen, was still in the auditorium.

It is to be hoped that the Limelight can be preserved.

## Brierley Hill

In the middle of the nineteenth century a descendant of the original line of the Barons of Dudley was enjoying the process of becoming an industrialist by supplying raw materials, and fuel, for the activities of local ironmasters. Then, about 1855, he decided to make iron himself and his agent began the task of building an ironworks at Round Oak. His success possibly influenced Queen Victoria in creating a new peerage. In 1860 he became the first Earl of Dudley. Thus Round Oak Steelworks has always locally been known as "The Earl's".

The town that grew up alongside "The Earl's" was Brierley Hill. The main street runs from the steel works to the parish church along the crest of the hill that gave the town its name. Along this street were once to be found Brierley Hill's cinemas.

Cinemas were also to be found in the surrounding villages; Quarry Bank, Wordsley, Kingswinford and Pensnett. Two buildings still exist as Bingo clubs, one in Brierley Hill and one in Pensnett, but showing films in this area is now as much a part of history as digging for coal, puddling iron, shaping fire-bricks, forging chains or filling sausages.

Town Hall. *Brierley Hill.*

## 12. The Queens Hall
*High Street*

Brierley Hill's Town Hall contained a large assembly hall capable of holding eight hundred people on the ground-floor and the gallery. In 1910 this was leased to Mr. R. Colin for his presentations of film and variety. The same gentleman, at various times, had presented similar shows at the Empire, Dudley, and the Hippodrome, West Bromwich.

On 27th May 1912 the same hall reopened as "The Queens Hall", having been refurbished. The Lessees were now Pooles Perfect Pictures. They had also established themselves at the Kings Hall, in Stourbridge. Their first programme in Brierley Hill included *"The Charge of the Light Brigade"*. Admission was 3d and 6d, and twice nightly programmes were changed every Monday and Thursday. The manager was Cecil Couper.

Cecil Couper has been introduced in the first section of this book. He adopted Brierley Hill as his home and devoted the rest of his life, apart from army service, to local cinemas. About a year after arriving as manager, he took on the lease himself and made a great success of running the Queens Hall.

Although not a purpose-built cinema it enjoyed a long life. It survived into the sound era, by installing Morrison sound equipment and had the honour of introducing the talkies to Brierley Hill on 3rd February 1930, a month ahead of the Picture House. *"The Singing Fool"* was projected for the first three days of the week, and *"Sonny Boy"* for the following three days. They were projected by Harold Roberts.

Cecil Couper's son-in-law, Harold Roberts, learnt the business as an operator at the Queens Hall before taking on the Coronet, Quarry Bank in 1933, and it is not clear how much longer into the thirties the Queens Hall survived. All the indications are that it survived almost until the Second World War, apparently being run by a Mrs. Lamb who had graduated from the Palace. Mr. Couper's daughter is of the opinion that when her mother finally abandoned the lease the local council were at a loss to know what to do with the hall!

## 13. The Palace
*High Street*

Not far from the Queens Hall, on the opposite side of Brierley Hill High Street, was the Palace. It was a timber framed corrugated iron building behind the Horseshoe Hotel. Variety and melodrama were popular at the Palace, usually referred to as "The Blood Tub", and it is thought that Cecil Couper acquired it just before the First World War.

It was never one hundred per cent wholeheartedly a cinema but after the War it did show films much more regularly and advertised its programmes as far afield as Stourbridge and Tipton. In the mid-twenties, when Cecil Couper also took on the Olympia at Wordsley, the Limp and the Palace sometimes shared films.

The original building was damaged by fire sometime in the mid-twenties and was rebuilt more substantially of brick. It was reached via a passage-way from the High Street, the entrance being an arch with the pay box in the centre. Mr. Lamb projected the films, while Mrs. Lamb acted as cashier, assisted by Bernard Gash. Later

153

the variety artistes, Kitty and Alfred Stewart came to help the Coupers run their various enterprises and Kitty Stewart played the piano at the Palace.

Sound was never installed at the Palace and it is thought that it had returned to variety entertainment by the time of Cecil Couper's death in 1937. It seems to have "faded away" towards the end of that decade, and no trace of it exists today.

### 14. The Kinematograph Hall
*Dudley Road*

The Kinematograph Hall, Dudley Road, almost next-door to the Round Oak Steel Works, and opposite the future site of the Danilo, appears to have opened in February 1913. Local residents remember it as "The Tin Shed", but information on the place has been very hard to find.

It seems to have been owned by Mr. D. W. Priest and was large enough to accommodate six hundred patrons. Most puzzling of all is its demise. It seems to have closed by the end of the First World War.

88. The Picture House becomes the Odeon, 14th April 1936, with a new canopy and an "Odeon" name board over the original name.

*(Photo: John Maltby)*

### 15. The Picture House (later The Odeon)
*High Street*

Brierley Hill's great claim to fame is that it was the home of the first cinema built by Oscar Deutsch; not his first Odeon, which came later, nor his first cinema, which had come earlier, but the first actually built for him. Oscar Deutsch joined forces with a local solicitor, Alfred Hawkins, to form the company to build the Picture House, and the architect was another local man: Stanley Griffiths from Stourbridge.

It was described as being in the "Assyrian Style", but was a fairly modest frontage by Odeon standards. The auditorium was set back from the High Street, and parallel to it. The frontage that greeted the patrons was merely the entrance to the pay box and crush hall.

It was opened by Thomas Williams, the Chairman of Brierley Hill U.D.C. on Monday 1st October 1928 with *"The Ghost Train"* plus *"Woman on Trial"*. Not to be outdone, Mr. Cooper presented the Ramon Navarro *"Ben Hur"* at the Palace on the same evening! However, the Picture House was the grandest cinema yet seen in Brierley Hill. Perhaps over-awed by its size, local people had worried about the safety of the balcony, but the manager, Mr. A. C. Swift from the Grosvenor, Bloxwich, assured everybody that it was safe.

The Picture House began life with an orchestra led by a local composer, and pianist, Harold Hunt, but obviously the silent era was drawing to a close. The

Picture House installed BTH equipment and opened for sound on Wednesday 12th March 1930 with *"The Rainbow Man"* proudly proclaiming:

> "The only complete All British "talkie set" in this district — Made and assembled in the Midlands by Midland Engineers".

The name "Picture House" was replaced by "Odeon" in January 1936. The original name was covered rather than removed, and was thus exposed again when the cinema was demolished. As it was smaller and slightly older than most Odeons, although younger than some of the halls absorbed by the circuit, it had the feeling of being a fairly remote outpost. In August 1951 when it was featured in "The Circle", the house magazine of the circuit, the Manager had taken a day off and the young chief operator, Tom Roberts, had acted as the cinema's ambassador! They concluded that it was "small but cosy".

One small claim to fame on the mighty Odeon circuit for Brierley Hill's cinema was that it had once been the responsibility of the circuits youngest-ever manager. Donald Pass was eighteen years old when he became manager at Brierley Hill. He started work there when it was the Picture House, way back in 1930, as a re-wind boy, and returned as manager when it became the Odeon. He later managed the Odeons at Stourbridge and Dudley.

In the fifties Rank began to close cinemas like Brierley Hill's, and early in 1959 rumours abounded that it was to be included in a forthcoming auction. In the event the auction did not take place but the Brierley Hill Odeon was certainly up for sale. It was acquired by Stan Bastock, a trader at Brierley Hill's Market Hall. It closed without ceremony or comment on 25th July 1959 with *"Idle on Parade"*, only having outlived the Forum, Pensnett, by a couple of months, and leaving the Danilo as Brierley Hill's sole surviving cinema. A Fine Fare supermarket now exists on the site.

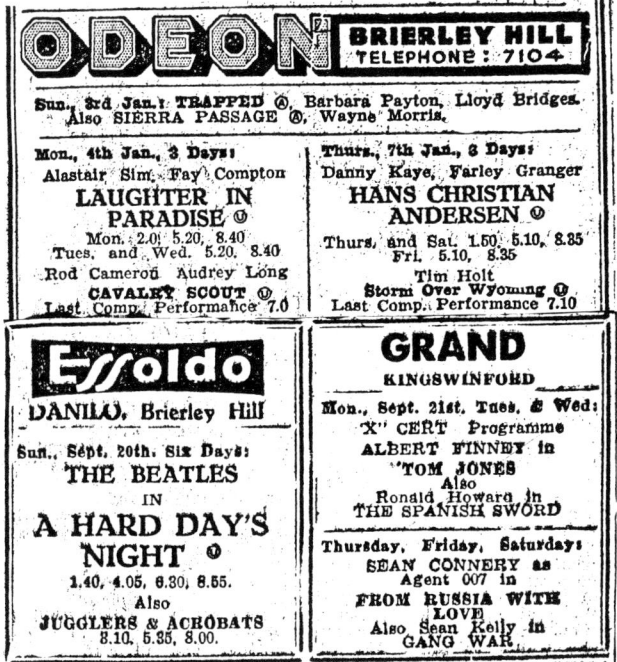

## 16. The Danilo
*Dudley Road*

Brierley Hill's only genuine super-cinema was the Danilo. Danilo (Brierley Hill) Ltd., was registered on 4th October 1935 with two directors; Mortimer Dent, and John Benton, of the Turks Head, Brierley Hill. It is thought to be designed by Ernest Roberts, and was built by William Jackson of Oldbury. It was a twelve hundred seater and, when new, must have seemed the most impressive building ever erected in Brierley Hill. It was equipped with sound by RCA.

It was opened on Monday 21st December 1936 by the Earl of Dudley, in the presence of George Formby, who was currently appearing on stage in Birmingham. The Earl of Dudley actually arrived just too late to make his opening speech and found that his son Viscount Ednam had deputized for him! George Formby had sung a song, and music had also been provided by the band of the Sixth Battalion of the South Staffordshire Regiment. Mr. R. H. Morgan, the Stourbridge M.P. who was interested in cinema matters, was present but Mortimer Dent seems to have been very self-efacing at these ceremonies. The first feature film shown was *"The Lady Consents"*, and proceeds from the event were divided between the Dudley Guest Hospital and Corbett Hospital.

Whatever the pretensions of the Odeon, the Danilo, through size and modernity, was the town's most prestigious cinema. Muriel Morgan who went to work there as an usherette, from the Coronet, Quarry Bank, found herself working in a team of eight. The girls wore made-to-measure uniforms and it was the kind of place where brass buttons had to be polished. She remembers *"Love is a Many Splendoured Thing"* running for three weeks at the cinema and people queueing to see it several times. The usherettes never grew tired of the film either, nor weary of the audience crying.

Mortimer Dent occasionally visited the Danilo, usually accompanied by two large dogs, but ten years after it opened, the Danilo, along with the others on the circuit, was sold by Mr. Dent to Mr. Southan Morris' S.M. Super Cinemas Ltd. In turn it passed to the Essoldo Group but the name Danilo was retained until the end. As part of a large circuit, management seemed to change fairly frequently and no one particular named individual seems to have become well known locally through his work at the Danilo.

From 1959 onwards it was the only cinema left open in Brierley Hill, but I found it a rather impersonal and slightly run-down cinema when I visited it in the mid sixties. We went to see *"How The West Was Won"* and after the film had started we were annoyed not only by the three-lens process in which the film had been shot, which created a very distorted picture, but also a large mark across the picture suggesting the operator had left part of his bacon sandwich in the gate of the machine. When I complained I was told that it was a stain on the screen and the effect would be there throughout the film!

By then Essoldo Ltd. were already trying to obtain permission to operate Bingo. Dudley Council at first refused to grant permission but after an appeal and a

89. The Balcony Lounge. Although the window in the background still exists in the 1980's, the atmosphere in this picture belongs firmly to the 1930's. Hidden lighting and simple decor replaced the chandeliers, murals and fussy look that would have been popular in a 1920's cinema.

90. The screen's view of the auditorium shows the triumphant arrival of "Art Deco" to Brierley Hill. Note the simple patterns on the plasterwork of the side walls and the light fittings.

91. The foyer of Brierley Hill's Danilo introduced the patrons to the prevailing house-style. Note the Danilo mat in front of the pay box!

*(Photos 89-91: William Jackson)*

92. The Danilo, ready for opening, December 1936.

*(Photo: Collection of William Jackson Ltd.)*

public enquiry in 1967, permission was eventually obtained.

The Danilo showed its last film, *"The Graduate"* on 22nd February 1969. The facade, at entrance level, has been modernised with black and white tiles totally lacking in sympathy with the great expanse of brickwork that created the "Danilo-style", but generally the exterior of the building has survived into the eighties without a great deal of alteration.

Wordsley

### 17. The Olympia
*Brierley Hill Road*

To the West of Brierley Hill lie the villages associated with the glass trade, Amblecote and Wordsley. The Clifton circuit planned to build a cinema in Amblecote during the thirties, and actually acquired some land to do so, but a cinema did not materialize. Wordsley, on the other hand, had supported a cinema of its own since before the First World War.

The Olympia, Wordsley, was the property of Anthony Bailey. He owned a brewery in Brewery Street,

now called Brierley Hill Road. Later he made mineral water. But in 1912 he converted part of the premises into a cinema. It held about six hundred patrons and had stage facilities and dressing-rooms.

The Olympia opened on 23rd December 1912, presenting programmes of cine-variety. It closed again from June to August Bank Holiday 1913 for re-seating and was then leased to Benjamin Kennedy for six months. After that it seems to have settled down and was looked after by Mr. Bailey for the next decade. During this time the early pianist, Charley Matthews, had been followed by the violinist, Lena Wood. She became well known and attracted a large following.

About 1922 Anthony Bailey suffered a heart attack, and early in 1923 he sold the Olympia to Cecil Couper. On the day the cinema changed hands a special presentation was made to Mr. Bailey by Lena Wood. Cecil Couper's background enabled him to continue the traditions of live variety at the "Limp", as it was known locally. Cecil Couper had installed Morrison sound equipment in the Olympia by the autumn of 1931, but it is not clear what film was the first talkie shown in Wordsley.

93. Anthony Bailey stands outside the Olympia.

*(Photo: Dudley Libraries)*

The cinema had a habit of changing hands about every ten years. In 1934 it was taken over by Fred Leatham, this time in association with Eldon Firmstone. Mr. Firmstone, who lived nearby in Wordsley Manor, was an accordianist and cinema organist. He built his own private cinema at the Manor, at about the same time.

The restless Mr. Leatham stayed at the Olympia until about 1940 and then it was sold to a Mr. Bullock. Again there seems to have been some change of equipment, and for the rest of its life the cinema used the Worthytone system. Mr. Bullock tried hard to run an orderly house and had a like-minded chucker-out named Mick Masters. The latter ran the children's matinee and even during the Second World War found himself wading through monkey-nut shells after every performance to replace screws missing from the seats! One gentleman who was a child in Wordsley at the time can remember saving sixty-five pounds of waste paper to earn free admission to *"Gasbags"*, starring the Crazy Gang.

Mr. Bullock ran the Limp through the fifties until it became impossible to go on. The last film, *"Maracaibo"*, starring Cornel Wilde, was screened on 16th May 1959. (A fortnight before the closure of the Forum, Pensnett). Mr. Bullock sold the premises to a neighbouring die-casting firm.

The building was not demolished until 1969. (During demolition an 1858 foundation stone was uncovered). The site is now a car park, and looking back from the 1980's it is not only difficult to imagine films at the "Limp", but even more difficult to imagine its successful pantomimes and variety shows.

Kingswinford

## 18. The Grand
*Market Street*

Kingswinford seemed a smaller village than Wordsley in the days when cinemas were young. The electric tramway had linked Kingswinford with the outside world towards the end of 1900 but the journey to Brierley Hill meant a change of car at Brettle Lane or Scotts Green and it is difficult today to imagine how "separate" such communities once felt. Brickworks, fire-clay mines, desolate pit banks etc., all once separated the little village of Kingswinford from its neighbours.

In Market Street, on the road southwards to Wordsley and Stourbridge, stood a Market Hall. Just after the First World War a group of local businessmen led by the builder and timber merchant, Mr. Charles Coulson, decided this building would be ideally suitable for conversion to a picture palace. They were inspired by the success of other local cinemas, and invited Thomas Cooper of Blackheath to join them to provide some expertise. Together they formed Elysian Pictures.

It was planned that the Grand should open on Boxing Day 1919 but unfortunately it was not ready in time. It opened on Monday 5th January 1920, and the first programme included a five reel feature film, *"The Claw"*. Seats were 3d, 4d, 9d, and a one shilling, and the Grand featured an "orchestra", which was unusual for a place of its size where a trio would have been as much as could be expected. The pianist was James Hough, who later became manager for a time.

Like many small cinemas in the more "remote" parts of the Black Country its history is relatively obscure. It did not advertise regularly in the press, although occasionally special shows were mentioned in the Dudley Herald or sometimes the Stourbridge County Express. For example, on 11th May 1920 a free show was presented on *"The War Work of the Church Army"*. In February 1924 the Canadian National Railway was recruiting for emigrants with a free showing of *"A Land of Opportunity"*, but of the early fortunes of the Grand itself, one can learn very little.

It seems that by 1924 things were not going too well. All but Saturday shows may have been suspended for a few months. Elysian Pictures then seem to have decided to open again on a six day basis and appointed George Corbett as a manager for a time. Mr. Corbett tried to exercise some showmanship. When he screened *"The White Rose"*, his daughter, in her new silk dress, presented a paper white rose to every patron as they arrived. He was very artistic and was able to make his own posters to advertise the shows.

Sound was first introduced to the Grand, about 1930, on Edison Bell equipment but once again, the cinema seems to have run into difficulties. This time a Mr. Russell came to the rescue. Mr. Russell had previously been involved in travelling cinema shows in North Wales. He had come to the Midlands to install sound equipment in a cinema in Redditch. He came to the Grand to re-equip the cinema to a better standard and manage the place.

He removed the old bench seats, installed RCA equipment and much refurbished the place. The Grand re-opened once again about 1935. Almost immediately he seems to have been given a lease on the 650 seater hall which was to run until about 1948. Mr. George Corbett was still around, and joined forces with Mr. Russell to print publicity material.

Mr. Russell died in 1937 and his wife assumed responsibility for his company. Selected Cinemas Amalgamation Ltd., and for running the Grand. It was difficult keeping the Grand going through the Second World War, but with the help of the chief, George Gregg, Mrs. Russell ran the Grand until the lease expired. It then closed once more.

The situation was resolved on this occasion by Thomas Cooper taking over Elysian Pictures and his son set about refurbishing the cinema yet again for another reopening. Two Kalee 12 projectors were installed, with B.A. sound and its last lease of life began about 1950. Once again the chief, now Ken Waterhouse, took a large part in running the Grand. It somehow survived the testing years at the very end of the fifties.

Thomas Cooper died in 1961 and the Grand continued to operate while the estate was settled. Remarkably, this took three years and the final show at the Grand did not take place until 26th September 1964. The cinema closed with *"From Russia With Love"*. Even then the building remained empty for a time while rumours circulated about its redevelopment. Two months later the owners still denied that the site was for sale, "for the time being". Having just "faded-away" the building was eventually demolished and a new set of shops built on the site. The position of the cinema is now occupied by a branch of Boots.

94. The Grand, shortly after closure.
*(Photo: County Advertiser)*

95. The Forum as a Bingo & Social Club, 1981.

*(Photo: Ned Williams)*

## Pensnett

### 19. The Forum
*Commonside*

Pensnett was much closer to Brierley Hill than Wordsley or Kingswinford, but like the latter two villages, it existed in a strange hinterland of brick-fields, old iron-works, pit banks and derelict land. The area has gradually been tamed in the twentieth century, covering all traces of the past with the relentless extension of successive waves of suburban sprawl. The centre of modern Pensnett developed on the main Dudley-Kingswinford Road, along which the electric trams first ran in December 1900, but the village also traditionally straggled along Commonside towards the back of Brierley Hill. It was here that Cecil Couper built the last of his "mini-super-cinemas" of the 1930's.

The Forum was built on land near the Queens Head on Commonside, on ground that had been the Victoria Football Ground. It was designed by Stanley Griffiths of Stourbridge and was built by J. M. Tate of Cradley Heath, like its predecessor on Mr. Couper's "circuit", the Savoy, Netherton. It held five hundred and fifty patrons on a single floor and was a simple straight-forward building with just a hint of grandeur to make it feel "cinema-like".

The Forum opened on Wednesday 20th January 1937: the last cinema to open in the Brierley Hill area. It was opened by J. T. Higgs, Esq., President of the Midland Counties Mutual Benefit Society, and apparently a well known local citizen. He made the usual remarks indicating that entertainment should try to be healthy, up-lifting and educational! Some more fitting remarks were made by Andrew Cooper who proclaimed,

   ....."The people of Brierley Hill ..... are indebted to Mr. and Mrs. Couper, and the directors of the firm, for several reasons. They had not built any huge cinemas, but what they had done was to erect buildings suitable for the district, the working man and his family, and the working man's pocket!"

This was greeted with loud shouts of "Hear! Hear!" and there were further cheers when Andrew Cooper pointed out that 1937 was the Silver Jubilee of Mr. and Mrs. Couper's arrival in Brierley Hill.

The audience then watched *"Evergreen"* starring Jessie Matthews and Sonnie Hale. This was only presented as an opening show. The following night *"Queen of Hearts"* starring Gracie Fields, began a three day run. The proceeds from the first show were sent to the local hospital committee and everybody felt satisfied that Pensnett had arrived on the cinema map in fine style.

Cecil Couper was not present. He was very ill and was to die in a London Nursing Home later during 1937. The directors of the Pensnett Forum were Mrs. Couper, Harold Roberts, the Couper's son-in-law who ran the Coronet, and a Mr. J. H. Hobson. The Forum was equipped with Morrison sound, which seemed generally favoured by Cecil Couper.

After Mr. Couper's death the Forum was usually looked after by Kitty Stewart, an old friend of the Coupers who had played the piano at the Palace and helped run the Olympia. Local legend has it that she could never bring herself to like the local dialect and local children used to infuriate her by asking, "Any sates?". "How do you spell that?" she used to reply. There is even a very distinctly local way of pronouncing the name "Forum", in which the emphasis is transferred to the second syllable.

About 1946 the Forum was sold to Fred Leatham. After acquiring the Rex in Wolverhampton, in August 1947, Fred Leatham asked Fred Ward to help him run the Forum. Fred Ward had worked for him as a manager at the Victoria, Horseley Heath. It appears that Fred Leatham favoured the RCA sound system, and this was installed at the Forum, as well as the Victoria and the Rex.

On 24th August 1952 Fred Leatham took over the Plaza in Dover and sold the Forum to Fred Ward and Ray Eggington. Mr. Eggington had worked as "Chief" at the Rex, having previously worked at places like the Coliseum, Wolverhampton, and the Alexandra, Lower Gornal. The same two gentlemen still own the building today — thirty years later.

Like most small cinemas, it suffered a drastic decline in its fortunes at the end of the fifties. A coffee bar was installed upstairs, and there were often more people in the highly successful coffee bar than there were in the cinema.

The last film was shown on 30th May 1959, "The Sun Also Rises", starring Tyrone Power. Messrs. Ward and Eggington then put in a maple dance floor, and the Forum enjoyed a successful life as a ballroom for a couple of years. After that Bingo arrived and has stayed ever since. The Essoldo group, who present Bingo a mile away at the Danilo, have just taken on the lease.

Its survival as a Bingo Club, an oasis of bright light and social activity in Commonside, has preserved the building as a monument to Cecil Couper and his brave belief in building little village cinemas at a time when everybody else believed in the super-cinemas. No converted chapels for Quarry Bank and Pensnett — they had purpose-built cinemas of which they could be proud.

---

Quarry Bank

## 20. The Coronet
*High Street*

Quarry Bank retained its individuality and the essential character of a Black Country industrial village up until very recent times. It seems only yesterday that we used to visit Noah Bloomer's factory to watch hand-made chains being made just as they had been made for the past two hundred years. But the chain shop has closed and new estates are now being built around Quarry Bank to transform it from a village to suburbia.

Quarry Bank's first and only cinema was one of Cecil Couper's purpose-built mini-cinemas of the thirties. It was designed by A. L. Horsburgh of Birmingham. The plans were approved in July 1932. It was built by Messrs. Batham and Beddall of Brierley Hill. The four directors of The Quarry Bank Cinema Company, formed to run the Coronet, were Mr. and Mrs. Couper, their daughter, Irene, and her husband, Harold Roberts.

It was opened on 22nd February 1933 and every one of its five hundred seats was occupied by six o'clock. Many more people arrived and were unable to obtain seats! The ceremony was performed by Mr. J. E. Dunn, who was President of the Quarry Bank Hospital Carnival Committee, and the proceeds were given to that committee. The film presented was "The Cuban Love Song" but that was only presented for the one night. A normal three day run followed of "New Moon", a Drury Lane Musical starring Lawrence Tibbett and Grace Moore.

It was a small cinema, with no balcony, despite originally offering seats at four prices, between four-pence and a shilling. The frontage featured three vertical windows that gave an impression of there being a balcony but this was misleading. The two sets of double swing-doors in the centre of the facade were flanked by small shops. As in other Cecil Couper cinemas, Morrison sound equipment was installed but after the War this was replaced with the RCA system when some new Kalee II projectors were installed.

It was very much Harold Roberts' cinema. He had worked for his father-in-law at the Queens Hall, and presented the first talkie in Brierley Hill a few years before coming to the Coronet. He was well-liked by staff and patrons and a happy family atmosphere flourished at the Coronet throughout its life. For a time three sisters worked at the Coronet: Nelly Horton in the cash box in the main entrance, which led to the cheap seats, and Muriel Horton was an usherette. Muriel married Tommy Morgan who had started work as a page-boy, later worked at the Queens Hall, and then became an assistant operator at the Coronet. Various chief operators came and went, including Don Weston, George Horton and Jack Fletcher (who was Muriel Horton's brother-in-law!). Harold Roberts, of course, could project the films himself if necessary, but such was his popularity that Tommy Morgan would go back in later years to help him out if required.

In places like Cradley Heath Sunday-opening has never prevailed, even to the present day. However, the Coronet took advantage of Sunday-opening in Brierley Hill, after a campaign fought by the Odeon and Danilo, and opened seven days a week after the War.

One feels sorry for Harold Roberts as the nineteen-fifties brought the problems of declining audiences and even vandalism. In 1959 the Olympia, the Forum, and even the Odeon, all closed within the Brierley Hill area. His wife died about the same time. It seemed unlikely that Quarry Bank's little cinema could survive much longer.

Mr. Roberts put on the Coronet's final show on 20th February 1960: "The Mouse That Roared", starring Peter Sellers, supported with "Good Day For A Hanging". The Coronet had lasted twenty-seven years. Mr. Roberts' problems were not yet over. He applied for planning permission to convert the building into a factory and the application was refused. He then planned to convert it into a car showroom but again the application was turned down. The building changed hands several times before being demolished in January 1967 to make way for a petrol service station, which survives on the site today.

## 21. Some Brierley Hill Mysteries

The Kinematograph Year Books are obviously fallible however anxiously a researcher might wish them to be otherwise. Every now and again they seem to produce a cinema that has no other existence except between those attractive red covers, but such entries leave a question mark in the historian's mind. Two questions arise in relation to Brierley Hill.

In 1928 and 1929 the Kinematograph Year Books recorded the existence of the Market Place Picture House in Brierley Hill. It was said to be owned by Nottingham Pictures Ltd., a company associated with Mr. Shapeero. This gentleman ventured into the Black Country when acquiring cinemas like the Empire, Dudley, and Electric, Cape Hill, from Irving Bosco, at the beginning of the twenties. Is it possible that he planned to build a cinema in Brierley Hill or is the entry in the Year Book a mistake?

Almost throughout the twenties the Year Books credited Kingswinford with two cinemas: The Grand and "The Picture House". Sometimes the latter was said to be owned by a Mr. M. Cooper. One possibility is that both entries were referring to the Grand, or maybe it was just a misplaced entry.

One of the most intriguing mysteries of all concerns the possibility that Pensnett may have had a cinema long before Cecil Couper built the Forum! The only tiny shred of evidence of this appears in a letter in a Tipton Herald of January 1912. The letter is from Albert Edwards, sometime manager of Picture Halls at Dudley Port and "one at Pensnett". We must assume that a manager of a Picture Hall would know where his building was located, but few other hints have been found of the existence Albert Edwards' "one at Pensnett"! Such "hints" of its existence that I have encountered link Pensnett's ghost-like cinema with a chapel at Tansey Green, and with Jasper Tyrer of Oldbury! Cinema-lovers who like unresolved mysteries should proceed to Brierley Hill and look for these three cinemas.

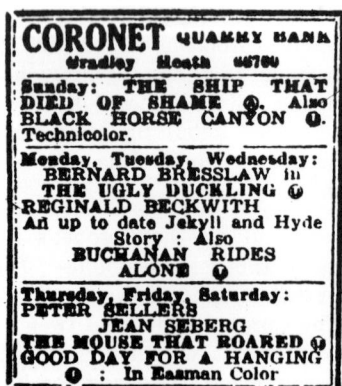

The advert for the last show at the Coronet gave the reader no clue that this cinema was about to close. Cinemas usually seem to have been rather coy about announcing their demise.

## Stourbridge

Stourbridge occupies the extreme south western corner of the Black Country, and like Wolverhampton and Walsall, it is part of the Black Country by association rather than a geological definition concerning underlying coal measures. Once Stourbridge was a market town of rural North Worcestershire but during the nineteenth century its industrialisation was rapid. Because the glass industry has survived until the present day, it is often regarded as one of the principal industries of the area. The truth is, that by the middle of the nineteenth century, Stourbridge was dominated by the iron trades.

The iron trade not only industrialised Stourbridge but also transformed the neighbouring villages of Lye and Wollescote, along the Stour Vale. The opening of the railway from Stourbridge Junction to Birmingham in 1867 not only served this area but also eventually turned Stourbridge and some of the towns of the Stour Vale into a dormitory of Birmingham in a way that was unknown in other parts of the Black Country.

By the beginning of this century industrialisation, transport, and housing development linked Stourbridge completely with the Black Country. Like its neighbours, the town first encountered moving pictures at Pat Collins' fairground or at the travelling shows presented at the Town Hall by Pooles of Gloucester and Professor Wood. In fact, Professor Wood continued to visit Stourbridge Town Hall until 1913, by which time he was permanently established in Bilston. At the Alhambra films could be seen during 1909, just before the passing of the Cinematograph Act, and the Kings Hall then rapidly established itself as the principle home of film entertainment before the First World War. Stourbridge then added a new cinema representing each epoch of cinema history until four cinemas served the twenty thousand inhabitants of Stourbridge at the beginning of the Second World War. The Scala arrived in the first flush of post First World War cinema building, the Central arrived at that glorious moment at the end of the silent era when every major cinema had an organ and an orchestra and quivered with anticipation of the coming of sound. The Danilo represented the following decade and the modern super-cinema. Meanwhile the Kings Hall had built a new "super" around itself. The four major cinema-buildings of Stourbridge survive, and ironically the earliest of the four is the sole survivor as a cinema!

Meanwhile, the story of the cinemas of The Lye is the typical story of Black Country village cinema. The small cinemas, that had successfully served the community since the earliest days, were challenged by a Clifton during the thirties. By the mid-sixties The Lye was without a single screen, leaving behind a nightmare for the cinema historian to try and unravel.

The cinemas of Stourbridge and The Lye are the only Black Country cinemas to have received the attention of a historian committing himself to print! In 1952 Chris Gittings, better known as Walter Gabriel of The Archers, researched the history of local cinemas and theatres and nearly thirty years later his work was published as a booklet by Dudley Teachers Centre. Chris Gittings, therefore, deserves to be recognised as a pioneer of local cinema history.

## 22. The Alhambra
*Off the High Street*

Behind an inn called The Coach and Horses was an area known as Barlow's Yard. During the early nineteenth century this area was used by travelling showmen, and eventually the "Theatre Royal" was established there, although the theatre may have been no more than an outbuilding or barn adjoining the yard. The Alhambra was built there, probably in the 1880's, by the travelling theatre company of Bennett and Patch.

By the end of the last century the widow, Mrs. Patch, was running the small wooden theatre until, upon her death, it was acquired by Douglas Phelps. Mr. Phelps was an actor who had tired of his nomadic life and decided to settle in Stourbridge and run a permanent theatre. From 1900 to the First World War he brought opera, melodrama, musical comedy, and variety shows to the stage of Stourbridge's tiny theatre.

On 21st April 1909 Douglas Phelps presented films at his theatre; "Phelps Picture Plums": *"The Grand National Steeplechase of 1909"*. During the following weeks films of football matches and the Boat Race were presented, as supporting attractions to programmes of variety acts. He used one hand-cranked, lime-lit, projector and by the Autumn of 1909 was advertising it as "Phelps Alhambrascope". The following year, when a kine licence was required before such entertainment could be offered, mains electricity was brought down Stourbridge High Street and the Alhambra became "Phelps Electric Theatre".

Douglas Phelps joined forces with Alfred Wall who had introduced cinematography to The Lye during 1910, and together they opened The Empire for the sole purpose of showing films. The Alhambra continued to offer theatrical presentations, but the Empire seems to have been fairly short-lived, and by 1912 the Alhambra was very much involved in showing films again. "Phelp's Famous Electric Pictures" presented *"The Tale of Two Cities"* from 12th August 1912 onwards and this seemed to mark the Alhambra's return to the cinema business, and to serious competition with The Kings Hall.

As the Kings Hall emerged as the victor, the Alhambra presented fewer and fewer films. However, some of the films shown at the Alhambra would be of considerable interest today as they were shot in Stourbridge, often featuring visiting variety artistes. After the First World War very few films were shown at the Alhambra. An exception was the Canadian Pacific Railway's film that also appeared at the Grand, Kingswinford, in the early twenties.

Douglas Phelps briefly flirted with films again in 1922 when he introduced back projection for a series of film shows that commenced on Bank Holiday Monday 7th August 1922. Shortly afterwards the Alhambra was acquired by George Ray and he continued film shows for a time in 1923 while waiting to obtain a licence for further theatrical use. For the next five years George Ray ran the place as a theatre. When the building was condemned in 1929 he had enthusiastic plans to build a new playhouse but the recent opening of the Central Cinema nearby showed that theatres could no longer expect to lead the field in popular entertainment. The Alhambra closed its doors on 6th April 1929.

## 23. The Empire
*Duke Street*

As stated in the previous chapter, Douglas Phelps, of the Alhambra, joined forces with Alfred Wall, of The Temp in The Lye, to provide Stourbridge with a hall entirely devoted to showing films. They acquired an old brewery warehouse in Duke Street, and converted it into the Empire.

At three o'clock on 3rd October 1910 the Empire had a grand opening, and thereafter presented twice nightly film shows. Mr. Weaver, who had played the piano at the Alhambra, accompanied the films at the Empire, and Chris Gittings recalls the auditorium as being very long and narrow, but provided with a raked floor. In his notes on local cinemas he recalls the smell of oranges, and the girls who dispensed, not only the oranges, but a range of refreshments including chocolates and ginger-beer.

Possibly the Empire was not quite the success Messrs. Wall and Phelps had hoped for. After a few months it closed. It "reopened" on 17th December 1910 with shows presented by the Motiograph Picture Plays Syndicate and in the following year changed name to the Empire Picture Palace and then the New Picture Hall. It may well have closed by the end of 1912, but the Motiograph Syndicate later reappeared at The Temp in The Lye.

## 24. The Kings Hall
*New Road*

Messrs. Pooles of Gloucester regularly visited Stourbridge Town Hall with their travelling Myrioramas. After the passing of the Cinematograph Act they looked for premises in which to provide permanent regular film shows. Sometime during 1911 they decided to acquire the skating rink in New Road. This had opened as recently as 23rd October 1909 and was managed by Harry Wharton. The large corrugated iron building, completely transformed, was opened on 6th November 1911 for "Pooles Perfect Pictures" and "Vaudeville". A cockney named Teddy Day was taken on as the operator and he took charge of the Imperator projector, and the gas engine that was installed to provide power.

A Mr. Talbot was given the job of commissionaire and was sent out, in a smart uniform, to woo customers from the Alhambra. Within a few months of opening an arrangement was made with the owners of Longcroft Buildings in the High Street to use a passage from the High Street to New Road as an entrance to the cinema. Mr. Talbot could then face Frank Gittings, the Alhambra's "barker" in a nightly battle in Stourbridge High Street. The Kings Hall somehow managed to secure better films than the Alhambra and Frank Gittings had to sing the praises of his employer's programmes by describing them as "Slightly bent, but not broken!".

Ironically Frank Gittings' brother, Percy Gittings, sometimes worked for the Kings Hall. Brotherly loyalty should have inspired him to support the Alhambra, but in his time Percy had been a champion roller-skater in the rollerdrome that was now a cinema and therefore maybe he felt his heart was in New Road. Percy Gittings sometimes provided sound effects for the silent films. For example during a film called *"Curse of War"* one

96. The Kings, September 1956, just before the take-over by Rank.

*(Photo: Dudley Libraries)*

scene featured an aeroplane being started up. Percy Gittings started up his motor cycle behind the screen with perfect synchronisation! During those early days only a piano, usually played by a Mr. Hull, provided the accompaniment but after the War an orchestra was engaged.

The Kings Hall was fairly large, and claimed to be able to seat one thousand five hundred patrons. In the theatrical tradition the most expensive seats, costing sixpence, were at the front, and for twopence one could sit in the balcony! The seating was later re-organised when the ground floor was provided with a proper rake, with a reversed rake just in front of the screen.

When the Scala opened in 1920 the Kings Hall faced competition of an entirely new order. To compete with the Scala's orchestra, the Kings Hall engaged a proper orchestra of its own, led by Norris Stanley. Before the War Stourbridge had seen the "Battle of the Barkers", now the town enjoyed the competition between the rival cinema orchestras! There was also some rivalry between Harry Wharton and Harry Morris, the two cinema-managers, although they later changed places!

Although the Kings Hall was unimpressive from the outside it had quite a beautiful interior. Large hessian murals draped the walls, and together with the silk lanterns hanging from the ceiling, gave the hall an oriental atmosphere. Pooles' staff had smart uniforms and there was considerable pride in working at the Kings Hall. It had vanquished the Alhambra, had stood

up to the Scala and, at the end of the twenties, was ready to compete with the new Central. As soon as part-sound films, using the Vitaphone system, with sound-on-disc, were available the equipment was installed at the Kings Hall. However, by 8th July 1929 RCA equipment was installed and the Kings Hall brought proper "talkies" to Stourbridge with "In Old Arizona".

The Kings Hall enjoyed good acoustics. Every Monday morning the Chief sat in the auditorium while the second operator ran the newly made-up programme through to check the timings and the sound settings. During the thirties the Chief was James Powell and towards the end of the decade the position passed from father to son when Bernard Powell took over. The latter worked at the Kings Hall while its new replacement was built around it.

The rebuilding of the Kings Hall was quite an amazing venture. The new super-cinema, to be called simply the "Kings" was designed by Stanley Griffiths, the only cinema the Stourbridge architect and writer designed for his home town. It was ingeniously planned so that the red brick shell of the building could be built over and around the original corrugated iron building. The Kings Hall then closed for a very brief period while the old structure was demolished inside the new, and the interior decoration completed. The main contractor was Joseph Hickman and Son of Brierley Hill and Mr. K. Friese-Green took responsibility for the interior, including the curtains and lighting. The new seating

164

could accommodate eighteen hundred patrons, making it the town's largest cinema, and was arranged in stadium-style. The operating room was unfortunately low in relation to the highly-raked rear seats of the auditorium and it was possible for patrons to stand in the projector's beam!

Everything which had made the old Kings Hall a great success was retained in the new Kings: Simplex projectors, RCA sound equipment etc. Even so, the Chief, Bernard Powell, had to admit that some of the great intimacy and atmosphere of the original cinema was lost. The cinema also suffered from having a frontage facing the rather anonymous backwater of New Road, rather than the High Street. The frontage, therefore, relied for its effectiveness on a separate entrance hall and some prominent neon lighting. Once in the main building a spacious foyer led to a massive staircase rising to the stadium "balcony" and a large leaded-light window gave this foyer an atmosphere of some grandeur.

The grand opening was planned for Monday 4th September 1939 at 3 p.m. The Mayor, Councillor J. A. Mobberley, was invited to open the cinema and enjoy *"The Little Princess"* starring Shirley Temple, in glorious Technicolour. Unfortunately War was declared on 3rd September and all cinemas closed for a short period. The opening ceremony had to be indefinitely postponed, but normal shows were allowed to start on the following Saturday in Stourbridge and perhaps it is, therefore, more realistic to think of the Kings opening then, 9th September 1939. Black-out regulations meant the neon lighting which was to be such a feature of the new Kings remained switched off. It was not switched on until April 1949, nearly ten years later!

Harry Morris was followed at the Kings by Mr. Rothery-Ellis, who had managed the Opera House and Hippodrome, Dudley, for Benjamin Kennedy. He ran the Kings as if he was running a live theatre and with a confidence that suggested the Kings still thought itself better than the Odeon or Danilo.

Eventually the realities of the post-war World must have made it apparent that a town the size of Stourbridge could not support four fairly large cinemas. The Kings tried to preserve its superiority and, in the fifties, was the first cinema in town to present cinemascope. On 1st October 1956 the Kings was purchased by the Rank Organisation and it seems that the sole purpose of the purchase was closure and elimination of competition. Ex-Pooles staff naturally felt it would make more sense to close the Odeon and retain the Kings but I doubt if that was ever considered.

The Kings closed on Saturday 22nd June 1957 with *"Time Without Pity"* starring Michael Redgrave, supported by *"Fort Petticoat"*, starring Audie Murphy. The Circuits Management Association, (The Rank Organisation), put a notice in the local paper stating:

"We regret to announce that due to the high Cinema Tax this theatre will be permanently closed after business today. The Management would like to thank Patrons for their past support!".

The property was sold to Samuel Johnson, the coach hire firm who may have only used the car park. Since then it has changed hands several times and lost all signs of ever having been a cinema. The huge red-brick building has recently been a furniture store, but appears to be closed and out-of-use at the time of going to press.

## 25. The Scala
### (later known as the Savoy and ABC)
*Lower High Street*

The original Kings Hall may have established its dominant position as a cinema by the First World War but as soon as the War was over a local company was formed to provide a new purpose-built cinema in Lower High Street. The chairman of the Stourbridge Picture Playhouse Ltd., was George Parker of Birmingham and the Birmingham architect, Joseph Lawden, produced the plans.

Work commenced in September 1919 following the demolition of some old malt houses, and the construction was carried out by a local builder, A. H. Guest Ltd. The auditorium, designed to hold eleven hundred patrons, was treated in a classical style with fluted pillars decorating the side walls. The exterior, which has remained little changed over the years, is very attractive. Again the treatment is classical, with pillars flanking the entrance, and the brickwork above the entrance enhanced by the surrounding terra-cotta Hathernware tiling.

The Scala was opened on 11th October 1920 by Isobel Elsom, who was starring in the first feature film to be screened; *"The Edge of Beyond"*. Miss Elsom appeared to be rather nervous although she was rapturously received by the audience. Everyone of the eleven hundred tip up seats were taken! In the event the main speech was made by Stourbridge's Deputy Mayor, Arthur Moody.

The Manager of the Scala was Harry Morris, and the orchestra was led by Charles Bye. The competition between these gentlemen and their counterparts at the Kings Hall has already been mentioned. The Scala settled down to a routine of two programmes a week at prices that ranged from 1/3d in the balcony to 5d in the front stalls. The latter were reached from an entrance in Queen Street.

A settled existence seemed to come to an end with the closing of the silent era. During the thirties the Scala appears to have changed hands a number of times. When Western Electric equipment was installed and the first talkie screened on 12th May 1930, *"The Sky Hawk"*, the cinema was owned by a Mr. G. Hunter. By April 1936 it was calling itself the "New Scala" and appears to have been acquired by a group of Birmingham businessmen headed by B. T. Davis and H. Yoward. The same gentlemen were about to open a new super-cinema in Wolverhampton, the Penn.

At the beginning of the War it was acquired by Fred Leatham after he had sold the Olympia, Wordsley, to Mr. Bullock. All this changing hands came to an end in September 1942 when it was acquired by A.B.C. By this time it must be remembered that the Central had become an Odeon, and the Kings and Danilo had provided Stourbridge with two very modern super-cinemas. The Scala now seated less than a thousand patrons and had become the smallest of the town's cinemas.

It was re-named the Savoy on 20th September 1943 and like the other "Savoys" has since become the ABC. When Eric Johnson arrived in 1961 to manage the

cinema the staff felt he had been sent to see if it was worth keeping open. The fifties had ended with Stourbridge's cinemas reduced to three.

As it turned out, Eric Johnson's stay at the Savoy had a positive effect on the future of the cinema. Ironically he died in June 1978 just before work was finished on completely refurbishing his cinema, by which time it was the only cinema surviving in Stourbridge. Eric Johnson's death, at the age of 57, brought to an end a career that had begun with him joining ABC as a page-boy forty-five years earlier.

During his career at Stourbridge the Savoy/ABC had come close to closure at least once. In 1974 EMI had agreed to sell the cinema to Ladbrokes subject to an application to run the place as Bingo Club being approved. A great deal of local protest was generated and strong objections were raised when the application for a gaming licence was heard. Most of these protests were not considered relevant by the Court but, nevertheless, the application was turned down.

Ken Waterhouse, who had managed the Lyttleton,

Halesowen, from 1964 to 1974 told the press on 21st May 1974 that he was prepared to make a realistic offer for the cinema. The following year it was rumoured that the Classic Group was interested in purchasing the ABC. After this it was probably a relief to Eric Johnson that EMI seemed reconciled to keeping the cinema and, in 1978, started refurbishing the interior.

After Mr. Johnson's death Tim Williamson arrived to take up the post of manager. Coming from the large ABC in Walsall he was most impressed to find long queues outside the little Stourbridge cinema, now reduced to holding 750 patrons. Over twenty thousand patrons came to the refurbished ABC to see *"Grease"* in 1978.

The ABC is now one of the few remaining Black Country cinemas. Despite Tim Williamson's positive style of management its services have been further curtailed. Only the seats in the stalls are at present in use, reducing its capacity to 453. Saturday morning matinees ceased on 5th July 1980. Even so it is a cinema that is well worth visiting. The strong colours of the

98. The Central, 10th December 1937, after acquisition
by Oscar Deutsch.

*(Photo: John Maltby)*

167

1978 re-decoration have not robbed the hall of its 1920's atmosphere. Up in the operating box the operators, Tom Watkins and Janet Bruton work with ancient Ross GC3 machines that still use carbon arcs for illumination, and, as stated earlier, the exterior of the ABC is well preserved. It will be a sad day for Stourbridge if the ABC is forced to close its doors in the eighties.

At the time of going to press the ABC is presenting single evening performances only, except during school holidays. The "Chief", Vic Court, retired from the ABC just as this book was going to press. He had worked at this particular cinema for twenty-eight years.

### 26. The Central (later the Odeon)
*63 High Street*

As the national circuit, P.C.T./A.P.P.H. closed in on Dudley during the latter half of the 1920's, Sydney and Clifford Bray of the Criterion decided to sell out and concentrate their energies on the smaller towns of Halesowen and Stourbridge respectively. Clifford Bray set about forming a company to build a new cinema in Stourbridge, along the same lines that his brother had used to build the Criterion, Dudley.

99. The organ, stage, and auditorium of the Central, 10th December 1937. Note the introduction of Art-Deco light fittings and the orchestra pit replaced by a rockery!

*(Photo: John Maltby)*

F. J. Ballard became the chairman of the new company and local, Dudley based, companies and businessmen participated in the venture. Land was acquired in Stourbridge High Street consisting of part of the Old Fair Ground and part of the site of the old Conservative Club. This gave the cinema a narrow frontage to the High Street itself. The building was designed by the Dudley architects, Messrs. Webb and Gray, and was constructed by the Dudley firm of A. J. Crump. The latter had his headquarters opposite the home of Sydney Bray, in Aston Road, and had been associated with the building of the Criterion. It was originally designed to hold fifteen hundred patrons, 900 in the stalls and 600 in the balcony.

During 1929 work proceeded quickly on the Central, and made local news when one of the balcony girders being swung into position from the High Street, slipped and struck several erectors, sending them flying to the ground. A. J. Crump's foreman, George Underwood, was largely responsible for seeing that the cinema was completed in time for the opening.

The Central was built at one of those moments in history when stylistic developments in cinema design were at a crossroads. In many respects the traditional

theatrical conventions were incorporated into its design. For example the balcony had a horseshoe shaped front that extended almost to the proscenium arch. The ornamental plasterwork reproduced classical columns on the side walls and at either side of the screen, as favoured by the Scala, planned ten years earlier. In the centre of the orchestra pit a £4,000 Compton Organ was installed. It was a three manual, ten unit, organ and John Howlett was invited to open it.

The grand opening took place on 16th May 1929 with a film called *"Love's Crucifixion"*. In the absence of the Mayor of Stourbridge the ceremony was performed by the well known Stourbridge citizen, Ernest Stevens. As it happened, Alderman F. J. Ballard who opened the proceedings in his capacity as Chairman of the Company provided a "mayoral" presence as he was Mayor of Dudley at the time! Alderman Ballard stressed that, although the Central opened as a silent cinema, the company would keep abreast of any developments in the provision of sound. Meanwhile an excellent orchestra was provided under the leadership of Mr. Barrs Partridge, the Cradley Heath musician who had come to the Central from Birmingham's West End. And, of course, there was the Compton Organ. John Howlett had worked at two other cinemas since opening Dudley's Regent in the previous September. Alderman Ballard was full of praise for the young men at Webb and Gray, and for A. J. Crump's construction work, and Ernest Stevens was presented with a silver replica of the key to the cinema as a momento of the occasion.

Within just under a year of opening the original Simplex projectors found themselves being fitted with sound heads and Western Electric equipment was installed. Talkies arrived at the Central on 7th April 1930. For a short time the orchestra was retained to provide live musical interludes. Clifford Bray appears to have played some part in promoting the Central, at Kidderminster and both cinemas had much in common. (The history for the Kidderminster Central is detailed in Mercia Bioscope No.7).

Clifford Bray, as General Manager of the Company, and day-to-day manager of the cinema became a popular genial figure in Stourbridge. The proceeds from the first performance had gone to the Corbett Hospital and Mr. Bray continued to act as a fund-raiser for local charities by organising special shows at the Central. By the mid-thirties he began to suffer the effects of ill health. He died, aged 52, on 23rd April 1937 and a short time afterwards the Central was acquired by Oscar Deutsch. In January 1938 it adopted the name "Odeon". A few art-deco style light fittings were introduced to try and impose the Odeon style on the rather old-fashioned auditorium.

By comparison with the new Kings and the Danilo, opened in 1939 and 1940, the Odeon had an intimate atmosphere that made it a very pleasant cinema to visit. When more modern seating was installed, reducing its capacity to about eleven hundred, it seemed even more comfortable and cosy.

Like other Odeons, it ran Saturday morning matinees and the organ continued to be played by "Uncle Ken" at these events well into the post-war era. The organ was broken down and removed in 1958 and some parts of it are to be found locally in Netherton Parish Church.

Because the Odeon survived the sixties it seemed to have a kind of permanence that made the announcement of its closure, in 1973, come as something of a surprise. Perhaps the fact that only the five hundred seats in the balcony were being used should have warned us that the writing was on the wall.

The last show was presented on 16th June 1973. The programme consisted of a revival of *"Bonnie and Clyde"* supported by *"Blind Terror"*. The Chief, Joe Jones, had been at the Odeon for eighteen years, but that was a short time compared with the record of the commissionaire, George Crowther, who had been there thirty-four years, almost as long as it had been an Odeon. One interesting detail concerning the last show serves to illustrate how short the lifetime of a cinema could be. Among the people who had paid 44 new pence to see the last film was Sydney Ryder, who had paid 6 old pence to see the first film in 1929.

The shell of the Odeon still exists and anyone seeing it from the back as they drive round Stourbridge Ring Road could easily think it was still a cinema. (Incidentally back views of the Kings and the ABC are also obtained from the circumnavigation of Stourbridge's amazing one-way inner ring road!). In the High Street the entrance and canopy of the cinema still exist, but inside the building has been transformed into a department store for Owen Owen.

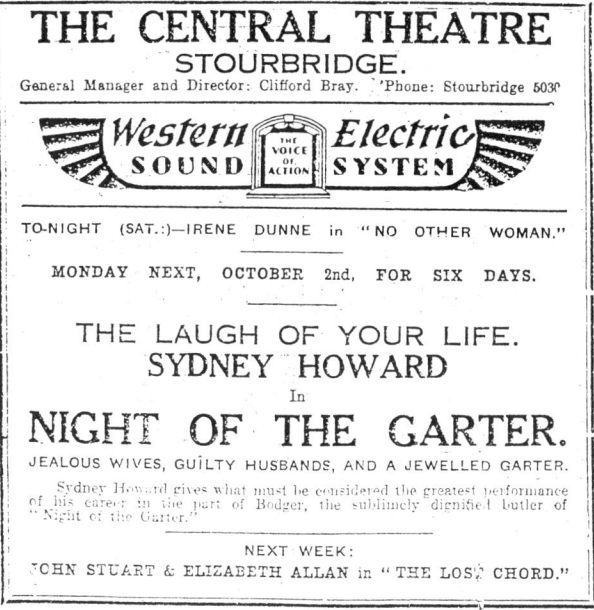

## THE CENTRAL THEATRE
### STOURBRIDGE.
General Manager and Director: Clifford Bray. 'Phone: Stourbridge 5030

**Western Electric** SOUND SYSTEM
THE VOICE OF ACTION

TO-NIGHT (SAT.):—IRENE DUNNE in "NO OTHER WOMAN."

MONDAY NEXT, OCTOBER 2nd, FOR SIX DAYS.

THE LAUGH OF YOUR LIFE.
## SYDNEY HOWARD
In
# NIGHT OF THE GARTER.
JEALOUS WIVES, GUILTY HUSBANDS, AND A JEWELLED GARTER.

Sydney Howard gives what must be considered the greatest performance of his career in the part of Bodger, the sublimely dignified butler of "Night of the Garter."

NEXT WEEK:
JOHN STUART & ELIZABETH ALLAN in "THE LOST CHORD."

## 27. The Danilo
*Hagley Road*

The last cinema to be built in Stourbridge opened during the early part of the Second World War. Arriving on the scene so late, it represents the ultimate achievement of Ernest Roberts in producing cinemas in the modern style. It was also the last Danilo cinema to be opened by Mortimer Dent. It seems that he may have hoped to build up a circuit of about twenty cinemas. The seventh, at Stoke-on-Trent opened after the War began and it looked at one point as if work on the eighth at Stourbridge would be halted by the difficulties in obtaining essential materials. As it happened, it opened about six months later than expected, and no further Danilo cinemas were built.

100. The impressive brick facade of the Danilo, June 1940.    *(Photo: Collection of Keith Skone)*

Ernest Roberts designed the building to accommodate just under fourteen hundred patrons; 970 in the stalls and 410 in the balcony. The front elevation was carried out in rustic brickwork with stone dressings and heavy stone cornices. The five tall windows rising above the deep canopy had stained and leaded glass panes, admitting light to the balcony lounge. The four foot high letters of the cinema's name mounted above the stone cornice were made of stainless steel and could not be outlined in neon lighting due to black-out restrictions! The cinema was built by William Jackson of Oldbury.

The steps up to the five pairs of entrance doors made the building seem very large and dignified from Hagley Road and once through those doors the patron found the interior treated in fine modern style. Concealed lighting and abstract designs in the fibrous plaster-work flattered a huge rectangular ante-proscenium. The forty-three foot wide stage was guarded by bright stage curtains and festooned screen curtains, all of which could be lit with varying effects.

The latest Ross GC projectors were installed and sound was supplied by RCA Photophone apparatus, much favoured by the Danilo circuit. If completed before the outbreak of War such a fine cinema would have enjoyed a very grand opening. In the circumstances the Danilo opened without ceremony on Whit Monday 13th May 1940 with *"At the Villa Rose"*. A sign of the times was that the programme included "All the latest War pictures and news".

The staff, in their smart emerald green Danilo uniforms, greeted the patrons, but due to the War there was a rapid turnover of staff which made the Danilo somehow more anonymous than the other Stourbridge cinemas, and less a part of the local community. It was the least-talked-about hall whenever I talked to Stourbridge people about their cinemas.

At the end of the War it passed from Mortimer Dent's control to the circuit of Mr. W. Southan Morris, and a decade later it became part of the Essoldo group. From February 1957 onwards it was advertised as, "The Danilo — An Essoldo Theatre". In the sixties the Essoldo Company seems to have been fairly interested in Bingo, and they closed the Danilo on 21st December 1963 to perform a very rapid conversion to Bingo. In fact they re-opened for that purpose on 27th December!

The Danilo had closed with *"The Yellow Teddy Bears"*, a film about teenage pregnancies, and *"The Terror of Doctor Hitchcock"*. Its twenty-three year life as a cinema, has now almost been matched by its life as a Bingo hall. It is now a Mecca Bingo and Social Club, and fortunately much of the character of the building is well preserved. If you are lucky when you go there to play Bingo you may meet Harry, who once worked there as an operator. He was interviewed and appointed by Mortimer Dent himself and worked in most of the Danilo cinemas.

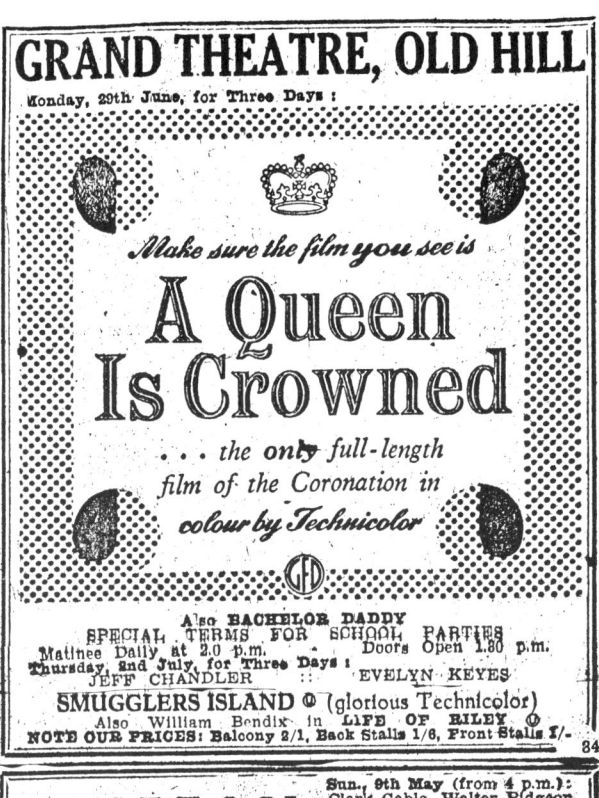

# GRAND THEATRE, OLD HILL

Monday, 29th June, for Three Days:

Make sure the film you see is

## A Queen Is Crowned

...the only full-length film of the Coronation in colour by Technicolor

GFD

Also BACHELOR DADDY
SPECIAL TERMS FOR SCHOOL PARTIES
Matinee Daily at 2.0 p.m. Doors Open 1.30 p.m.
Thursday, 2nd July, for Three Days :
JEFF CHANDLER :: EVELYN KEYES
SMUGGLERS ISLAND ⓤ (glorious Technicolor)
Also William Bendix in LIFE OF RILEY ⓤ
NOTE OUR PRICES: Balcony 2/1, Back Stalls 1/6, Front Stalls 1/-

84

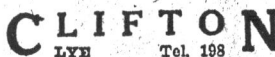

**CLIFTON** LYE Tel. 198

Sun., 9th May (from 4 p.m.):
Clark Gable, Walter Pidgeon in COMMAND DECISION ⓤ and Full Supporting Programme.

Monday, 10th May, 3 Days:
Duncan MacRae, Jon Whiteley
**THE KIDNAPPERS** ⓤ
5.25, 8.30
Stephen McNally, Julia Adams
THE STAND AT APACHE RIVER ⓤ
(Tech.) 7.5

Thursday, 13th May, 3 Days:
Marilyn Monroe, Jane Russell
**GENTLEMEN PREFER BLONDES** Ⓐ
(Tech.) 5.25, 8.30
Howard Duff, Helene Stanley
ROAR OF THE CROWD ⓤ
7.5.

---

**TEMP CINEMA, LYE**

Sunday, 9th May (From 4.0 p.m.):
MOON ⓤ, Robert Mitchum, Barbara Bel Geddes, ARMOURED CAR ROBBERY Ⓐ, Charles McGraw, Adele Jergens.

Monday, 10th May, 3 Days:
**OUTLAW WOMEN** ⓤ
Cinecolor
Marie Windsor, Richard Rober
THE FLANAGAN BOY Ⓐ
Barbara Payton, Frederick Valk

Thursday, 13th May, 3 Days:
Jean Simmons, Stewart Granger, George Sidney, Deborah Kerr, Charles Laughton
**YOUNG BESS** ⓤ
Technicolor
Full Supporting Programme

---

## BLACKHEATH

**REX**

Monday, 10th May, 3 Days:
That Great Epic
**THE CONQUEST OF EVEREST** (Tech.)
Also John Frazer in
GOOD BEGINNINGS

Thursday, 13th May, 3 Days:
John Wayne in
**WAKE OF THE RED WITCH** ⓤ
Also Ethel Barrymore in
KIND LADY

**KING'S**

Monday, 10th May, 3 Days:
Alec Guinness, Yvonne de Carlo
**THE CAPTAIN'S PARADISE**
Also Douglas Fairbanks Jr. in
THREE'S COMPANY

Thursday, 13th May, 3 Days:
Susan Hayward in I'D CLIMB
THE HIGHEST MOUNTAIN
(Tech.) Also Patrick Knowles in THE STRANGE CASE OF DR. X, Ed. M CAPTAIN VIDEO, Vengeance of Vultura

*Advertisements from the early 1950's for the cinemas of Stourbridge and the Stour Vale. The Danilo, Odeon, Kings and Savoy regularly competed for an audience but the smaller cinemas such as The Temp, and the Grand, Old Hill, sometimes advertised, sometimes did not. Advertisements therefore cannot always be relied on to help the historian locate a final show, as in the case of the Rex, Blackheath.*

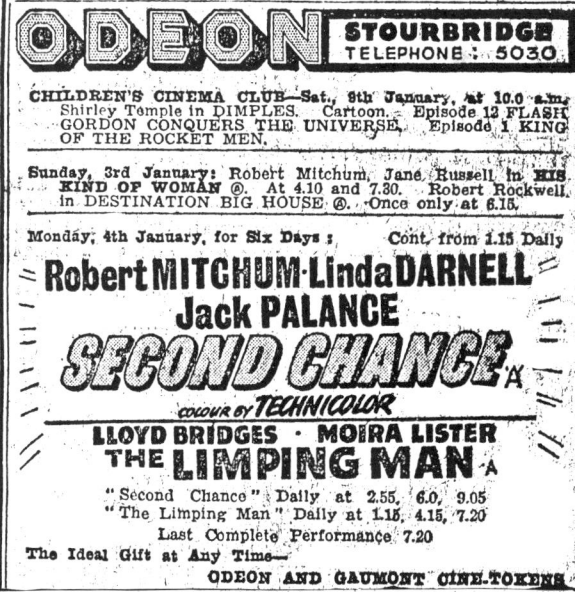

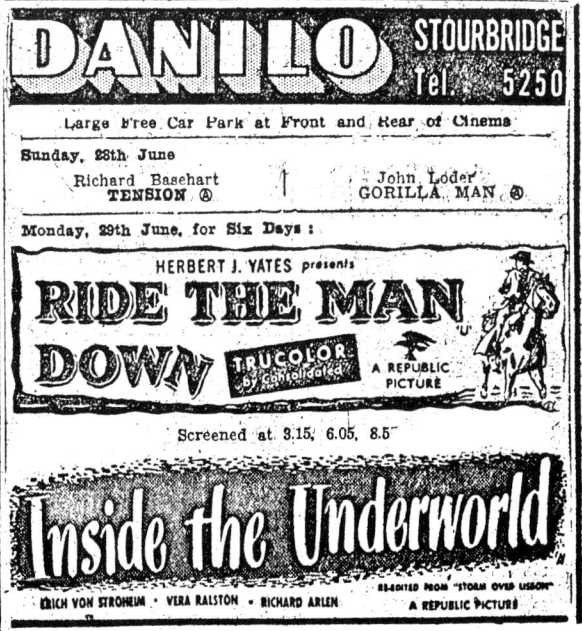

## The Lye

Working our way eastwards from Stourbridge, the towns on either side of the Stour Vale form the southern boundary of the Black Country. Just outside Stourbridge we come to The Lye, a community of about thirteen thousand people, who usually included the definite article in the name of their town.

As in other small industrial communities of the Black Country that enjoyed an existence independent of the larger towns, it has been very difficult to assemble a reasonably complete history of the local cinemas. The Vic and the Temp both seemed to "come and go" more than most! Indeed, they are the Rosencrantz and Guildenstern of the local cinema scene; infuriating minor characters that are each often confused with the other! My story of The Lye's cinemas, therefore, differs from other published versions of the story. My research leads me to insist that the "Palace of Varieties" was the name given to Alfred Wall's operation in the Temperance Hall and not a separate place that later became the Victoria.

### 28. The Temp
### (Also known at one time as the Palace)
*Church Street*

A Temperance Hall was built in The Lye in 1874, having been designed by the Stourbridge architect, Joseph Morris Gethin. During the first decade of this century concerts and variety shows were presented in the hall. A man named Alfred Wall seems to have tried showing films there.

On 16th April 1910 Alfred Wall opened the hall as the Lye Palace of Pictures and Variety, having obtained a permanent lease on the premises, and having had the place converted for such a purpose by Safety Bioscope Ltd. He told the press,

> "This London company has fitted out a number of London theatres and halls, and the pictures seen at Lye will be of the same standard as seen in the Metropolis".

It is difficult to imagine what form the conversion took as The Temp did not seem particularly cinema-like even many years later! The ground floor was not raked and the balcony seemed chapel-like. Possibly it was a question of fitting a projection room that satisfied the requirements of the Cinematograph Act. For years the "box" at The Temp was little more than that, it was a tiny wooden structure hanging on the wall of the building!

Originally it held about 550 patrons, later this figure seemed to increase by a hundred, later still it decreased by a hundred. Alfred Wall later joined forces with Douglas Phelps and opened the Empire in Stourbridge, but after that his name disappears from the scene. The Motiograph Picture Playhouse Syndicate who took over the shows at the Empire also seem to have presented shows at the Palace by the beginning of the First World War.

By the middle of the War, when it was still known simply as the Palace, a Mr. T. Brookes was presenting cine-variety at the hall. After the War he was followed by Will Pritchard, a local carpenter. In the mid twenties the lease was obtained by Mr. J. Entwistle.

Mr. Entwistle was a local grocer who had opened his first shop about 1906 and built up a small chain of stores in the area. He ran The Temp, as it was called from then onwards, for thirty years and is still fondly remembered in The Lye. The trustees of the Temperance Society kept a watchful eye on the lessee of their hall but Mr. Entwistle earned the affection and respect of everybody. One patron claimed that he went to The Temp to enjoy a chat with Mr. Entwistle, rather than to see the films. He was devoted to his cinema, having acquired an interest in films from a brother-in-law who was in the business.

Music was supplied by "a first-class orchestra", and sometimes title songs were sung by Jesse Hackett. The stage was still used, and Cedric Hardwick made one of his earliest public appearances there. When Sir Cedric Hardwick returned to The Lye to open the community's

101. The Temp, note the obvious projection box and the less obvious lettering "Temp Cinema", on the brickwork, above the "arrow slit". Summer 1969 — two years before complete demolition!

*(Photo: H. Cartwright, Collection of Dudley Libraries)*

first carnival he begged Mr. Entwistle to be allowed to take his wife to see The Temp!

Mr. Entwistle installed Gyrotone equipment, and brought the talkies to The Lye on 28th July 1930 with *"Voice of the City"*. The supporting film, *"Parade of the West"*, was silent. After the War, in 1949, he installed the latest Mirrophonic Sound and his advertisement claimed, "Always A Good Show". It had to be: not only did the Trustees have to be satisfied, but The Temp was next-door to the Police Station, and many a policeman sought relaxation in the cinema.

It seems that Mr. Entwistle managed to continue running The Temp until 2nd June 1956, when he presented *"The Prodigal"*, starring Lana Turner. The following day the place was used for a talent contest and then the place appears to have remained dormant.

The Temp reopened on 6th May 1957 with *"Calamity Jane"*. The person who had decided to run The Temp at this late stage was a Mr. Pointon, from the Garden Cinema, Bewdley. He rented it from Mr. Entwistle who still held the lease but its new life was short. It seems to have closed for the final time on 25th November 1957 with *"At War With The Army"*, starring Jerry Lewis and Dean Martin.

The building stood for another decade. I remember coming across it in the mid sixties, when the seating was still in place and vandalised projection equipment was rusting away in that odd little projection box. The Church Street area of the Lye has now been re-developed. Although everybody was stunned when the Temp closed it has now passed into the world of fading local legends.

## 29. The Victoria
*High Street*

As stated earlier, my research indicates the Palace was the name given, at various times, to the Temp. The Victoria was quite a different matter. It was a brand new purpose-built hall, and was never known by any other name, apart from the abbreviated form: the Vic. It was originally the brain-child of Joseph Heathcock, and was erected very quickly in the last two months of 1913.

The auditorium was clad in corrugated iron, but it had an imposing frontage built of brick, treated in plaster, that survived almost unchanged for half a century. The stalls were properly raked, although it maintained the theatrical tradition of putting the best seats, the individual tip ups, at the front. It had a proper balcony decorated with simple ornamental plasterwork. Eight hundred patrons could be accommodated. The architect, Hugh E. Folkes, of Stourbridge, had surely demonstrated that the "tin shed" type of cinema/theatre was capable of some elegance.

The Victoria was opened on 5th January 1914 by County Councillor J. T. Worton, a local draper. He recalled the past amusements of Lye residents, in particular cock-fighting and bull-baiting. He did not believe man existed only to work and sleep, so he was very pleased that Joseph Heathcock had provided The Lye with a proper theatre.

Joseph Heathcock, who had been connected with seaside pier entertainment for over twenty years, presented an opening programme of films that included

102. The Victoria Hall — as new. *(Photo: Dudley Libraries)*

103. The auditorium of the Victoria Hall — best seats at the front and inadequate blackout! *(Photo: Dudley Libraries)*

*"Tapped Wires"*, *"A Surprise Encounter"*, and *"Twixt Love and Fires"*. Music was provided by an orchestra led by Mr. H. Duffell. Seats were 2d, 4d, 6d, and 9d, with the best seats at the front.

By the autumn of 1915 Edward Lucas and Walter Williams from Cradley Heath were running the Victoria, and two years later Jack Arnold was presenting plays there plus films as part of variety shows. His regime at the Vic seems to have lasted into the twenties, a decade in which I have been unable to trace the cinema's fortunes.

From November 1931 to April 1934 Sidney Bray was showing films at the Vic, then the story becomes confusing once again. Mr. Russell, previously mentioned in connection with the Grand, Kingswinford, may have shown films there briefly. According to Chris Gittings' history of local cinemas and theatres it was closed for a few years before the Second World War until opened for a short season of variety by a Wordsley-born playwright named Charles Hatton. At the beginning of the Second World War it was being used by Lye Entertainments Ltd., again for film and variety.

From then on the story becomes confused and patchy once more. Several local people have suggested that the last film was shown there in the very early fifties. The building survived and continued to enjoy a varied and unpredictable career. By the beginning of the sixties it was being used as a rollerdrome and dance hall and probably even flirted with Bingo before demolition caught up with it in 1964.

## 30. The Clifton
*High Street*

After the turbulent history of The Temp and the Vic it is relaxing to consider the straightforward story of the Clifton. Perhaps the only puzzle is the question of why the Clifton circuit built a luxury super-cinema in The Lye? However, when one considers the location of the other Black Country Cliftons at Sedgley, Coseley, Wednesfield and Fallings Park, it can be seen that the company favoured village sites and presumably felt that providing car parks would lure patrons from the larger towns.

The Clifton at The Lye was planned by Roland Satchwell. In my opinion his plan lacked the elegance of his work at Sedgley and Coseley, possibly because the front elevation did not exploit the effect of tall vertical windows above the canopy. However, it was treated in faience and was perhaps more "modern" than Roland Satchwell's other Black Country cinemas. The three double entrance doors were flanked by shops and the auditorium took advantage of the falling ground on the site. It did not, therefore, tower above its surroundings.

It was built by B. Whitehouse and Sons Ltd., whose only other cinema work in the Black Country was at the Warley Odeon. Internally it was a standard Clifton cinema, in other words BTH projection and sound equipment was installed. It was built to accommodate just over a thousand patrons, 726 in the stalls and 280 in the balcony. It was, therefore, the smallest Clifton

104. The Clifton, as illustrated in the opening brochure, 1937.

*(Photo: Mrs. Charlesworth Collection)*

in the Black Country.

The Clifton opened on 8th February 1937 with *"Under Two Flags"*, starring Ronald Colman, Claudette Colbert, Rosalind Russell, and "a cast of ten thousand". The opening ceremony was performed by R. H. Morgan, M.P., a man who had been present at so many other local cinema openings.

At the opening, the Manager was Mr. A. U. Morris, and the operator was Jim Davis, who was being groomed for management of the Regal, Wednesfield. Later operators included Bernard Powell, who had previously worked for Gaumont British and Pooles, and Vic Court, who retired from the ABC, Stourbridge, in March 1982. The operators at the Clifton often had to provide technical assistance to Mr. Entwistle across the road at the Temp.

From War-time onwards the Clifton opened seven days a week unlike the cinemas of Cradley Heath, and also presented children's matinees on Saturday afternoon. As well as the Sunday show, the Clifton changed programmes twice weekly even in the early sixties.

As stated above, its life was uneventful. Cinemascope was installed in the fifties, and by the end of the decade it had outlived the Temp and the Vic. However, it still suffered a decline in its fortunes. In 1964 wrestling was presented on some nights as an alternative to film. The end came on 7th August 1965 with *"The Patsy"*, starring Jerry Lewis, supported by *"Robinson Crusoe on Mars"*.

Fortunately the building still exists, and today is in use as a market hall. A level floor had to be installed and the auditorium's interior destroyed but the basic exterior of the building has not been substantially changed.

## Cradley Heath

In each of the towns surrounding the Stour Vale the local cinemas were dominated by the efforts of one man; in Cradley Heath it was Walter Williams; in Halesowen, Sidney Bray; in Old Hill, Benjamin Priest; in Blackheath, Thomas Cooper.

Cradley Heath has a long association with the iron trades of this part of the Black Country, namely the manufacture of hand-made nails and hand-made chain. Life in Cradley, on the opposite bank of the Stour, at the turn of the century has been vividly described by the late Cliff Willetts in his books, *"When I Was A Boy"* (published by Dudley Teachers Centre), and life in an industrial village was far from idyllic, and almost totally lacking the amenities associated with twentieth century urban life. Cradley Heath seemed more "civilised", the growth of its late Victorian housing that followed the coming of the railway, and its High Street reflected a greater material prosperity. In Cradley Heath, theatres and cinemas became part of life on the northern slopes of the Stour Vale.

### 31. The Palace

It is difficult to say with certainty who showed the first films in Cradley Heath but it seems likely that the honour fell to an obscure little cinema in Spinners End, between the Vicarage and the G.W.R. Goods Yard. The building still exists today just to tantalise the historian who can find out so little about its past.

It may have been presenting cine-variety at the time of the passing of the Cinematograph Act. Walter Williams' son felt it was in business before his father started showing films at the Central, and that was in 1910. A brief report in the Dudley Herald of 20th May 1911 mentions that Sam Williams was continuing to put on good films and variety acts at the Palace, but the name normally associated with the Palace is Mr. W. Barnes. Locally it is sometimes still referred to as "Barnes' Palace".

Just one isolated advert in a Dudley Herald of 3rd February 1912 proudly claims that programmes of films and variety at the "New Palace" were presented twice nightly and patrons were advised that, "Trams pass the door"! Mr. W. Barnes claimed to be the proprietor and the manager was D. E. Barnes. From Mr. Barnes' licence application in August 1913 we learn that he could accommodate two hundred and fifty patrons in his Palace.

How long it continued to exist I do not know. I imagine that it closed sometime during the First World War. It seems that Walter Williams purchased its projector and possibly some of the benches.

## 32. The Central

At the turn of the century Walter Williams was a gentlemen's outfitter, who had premises in Cradley Heath High Street. He was fascinated by the world of theatre and variety, and eventually by cinematography and still photography.

Early in 1910 he rented a hall that had been used as a roller-skating rink behind the Empire known as The Empress Skating Rink. He opened this as the Central.

It could accommodate about eight hundred patrons and had an entrance in Foxoak Street, where it adjoined the Salvation Army Barracks, and a narrow entrance reached from Newtown Lane. The original opening date is obscure but 25th September 1910 was advertised in the press as a "Grand Re-opening".

In 1912 Walter Williams planned a new "Central Picture Hall", but this became the Royal when it opened early in 1913. He does not however, seem to have closed the Central immediately because he renewed its kine licence in August 1913.

## 33. The Royal
*Bank Street*

As mentioned above, in 1912 Walter Williams decided to build a brand new purpose-built cinema behind his premises in the High Street. The site was originally occupied by the chain shops associated with these premises in earlier times. The original front entrance of the building faced Bank Street, a small side-street from Cradley Heath High Street.

Behind the usual concertina metal gates, steps led up to two entrances on either side of a central box office. At that time the auditorium was a single floor and the entire building, including the stage, occupied an area that now forms the auditorium alone. Even so it was claimed that it could hold nine hundred and fifty patrons. (Cradley Heathens must have expected a squash whenever they sought entertainment).

105. The Royal, as seen from Bank Street. Note the huge fly tower, the emergency exit from the balcony and the new entrance (extreme right of picture). 1981.

*(Photo: Ned Williams)*

176

106. The Simplex projectors in the small operating room behind the rear stalls.

*(Photo: Mrs. Williams)*

107. Walter Howard Williams posed next to a machine that would still be showing films nearly forty years later!

*(Photo: Mrs. Williams)*

The Royal Electric Theatre opened on 3rd February 1913 with the famous film of the life of Christ: *"From the Manger to the Cross"*. Four prices of admission ranged from fourpence to a shilling, but later these were reduced. After the first show variety acts were included between the films, presented on a very temporary stage with a proscenium arch made of canvas. The relatively large stage and fly-tower were added after the War.

Walter Williams always took a very personal interest in running the Royal, and did not install a manager. He made films himself of local scenes, such as workers leaving local factories, and showed these at the Royal. Apart from the proprietor, a few other people made a name for themselves at the Royal, including Mr. Barrs Partridge who went on to the Central, Stourbridge and, eventually the City of Birmingham Symphony Orchestra. As he was a Cradley Heath man, the Royal was proud of the fact that he had played the violin for a time at the local cinema. On 23rd December 1923 the chief operator, Harry Johnson, distinguished himself with his prompt action in dealing with a film fire. In an incident that many operators encountered every now and again, he tore the burning film from the machine and extinguished the fire with only a brief interruption to the performance. He was also well known locally as a champion ox-roaster! Joe Cockin was well known as the chucker-out but his other duties included stoking the

boiler. One day he was found dead in the firebox door.

It seems that the circle was added sometime after the First World War, possibly at the same time as the stage and fly-tower were built. The Royal added sound when the talkies arrived but had to put up a notice stating, "Silence while the talking pictures are on", as the patrons were used to explaining the story to each other and commenting on what they saw! The major updating of the Royal came in the late thirties when it was decided to build a new entrance in the High Street. The plans were drawn by Clarence Bloomer, and were approved in November 1936. The work was completed in time for a grand reopening on 29th August 1938 with *"Heidi"*, starring Shirley Temple.

The new entrance, and various alterations made at the same time, brought the Royal up to a new standard. British Acoustic Duosonic Sound was installed, plus new festoon curtains, modern chandeliers etc. The owners claimed that this had nothing to do with competition from the Majestic! Apparently the Royal did not suffer any great fall in attendance after the opening of its new rival. Even so the Royal had installed its own small organ for a time, played by Nelson Dingley, as if they acknowledged that William Sykes was establishing a powerful reputation at their nearest rival cinema.

Walter Williams was helped in running the Royal

and Empire by his son Walter Harold Williams, and by his daughter who worked in the pay-box at the Empire. However, towards the end of the War he decided, with the family's agreement, to sell the Royal.

On 30th June 1945 the Royal was sold to Howard Lee, but within a year or two of acquiring it, Mr. Lee died, and his daughter, Isobelle Dorsett has run it, on behalf of the trustees, ever since. The Royal has thus proved itself to be one of the great survivors of the cinema business. It has outlived the Majestic and all the other surrounding cinemas. Once the last in line to receive new films due to "barring", the Royal has survived into an age when such considerations are almost irrelevant.

In the long battle to survive, Mrs. Dorsett, and her son Michael Dorsett, have tried many experiments to encourage business at the Royal. A Saturday Morning Film Club for children was operated for a time, and, as recently as March 1976, Sunday night variety shows were tried. Sunday-opening has never come to Cradley Heath and so the cinema operates on a six-day licence. However the variety shows were presented as club-nights and for sixty pence members could enjoy monthly shows. It was the first use of the stage for variety for fifty years! The stage had not been used for any purpose at all since one week in 1945 when the local Operatic Society had last mounted their show on its boards. The experiment was short-lived.

More recently the entrance and foyer have been converted to an amusement arcade and fruit machines and space-invaders provide "somewhere to go" for young Cradley Heathens. The balcony has now been closed but three hundred people can be accommodated in the stalls and now reach their seats from an entrance in Bank Street. History turns full circle! Two ageing Simplex projectors grind away in the original operating room at the back of the stalls and while waiting for the film to start it is interesting to look around and wonder

what might date from 1913, from the twenties, or the late thirties.

I have enjoyed several memorable visits to the Royal. One Sunday afternoon, 25th January 1970, myself and my fellow members of Uralia Films of Dudley, went to see the premiere of a 16 mm. film called "Amber", made and presented by "Film Group 32", another bunch of local amateur film-makers! The Royal was packed, even the Mayor of Warley, Councillor Harold Jackson, was present. The thirty minute horror film was well received, and it seemed fitting, even then, that the Royal should be the scene of such an unusual event. On another occasion I sat in the balcony one Saturday night and saw a cat walk across the stage in front of the screen. Such bizarre moments are seldom witnessed in mighty Odeons and all who love little independent cinemas should make at least one pilgrimage to the Royal before it is too late.

In November 1979 a planning application was made to Sandwell Council to turn the building, or the site, into a supermarket or "market hall". There was opposition from other local traders but the planning committee approved. With the strange momentum the Royal possesses, it is still showing films at the time of writing. However, the study of local history should warn us that nothing can ever be taken for granted. Perhaps we should already be campaigning for the preservation of the Bank Street facade with its elegant legend: "Royal Theatre".

108. The Royal, the 1938 entrance in Cradley Heath High Street, 1981.

*(Photo: Ned Williams)*

## 34. The Empire

*High Street*

The Empire was opened, as a theatre, on 11th September 1893, thus illustrating that Cradley Heath had sufficient urban aspirations by the end of the nineteenth century to support a theatre. It may have only been a brick facade that concealed a large corrugated iron auditorium but it had a certain grandeur inside that impressed the local population. Huge stone angels, holding lights aloft, stood one each side of the proscenium, and even the brick frontage was treated with plaster to create a stone-like surface.

It is said that some melodramas were taken so seriously by the local chainmakers that they would wait outside the theatre for the villain, and actors needed police protection. At one time it was owned by a Mr. Moreton, but by the time Walter Williams was showing an interest in bringing film and yet more variety entertainment to Cradley Heath, it was owned by Mrs. Susie Cranston and managed by Sidney Cranston. Whether they were any relation to the M. J. Cranston that ran the John Bull in Dudley in 1916, I do not know.

The Empire held a kine licence and, during the spring of 1913, for example, Douglas Phelps of the Alhambra, Stourbridge, had his films shown there amongst the variety acts. During the First World War the Empire was acquired by Walter Williams. It "re-opened" under his management on 14th February 1916 and continued presenting melodramas and variety for a short time. Walter Williams then closed it until he could modernise and reconstruct it to be re-opened as a cinema. The projection equipment was already installed, and even as a cinema, it then presented cine-variety, so really very little changed. Mr. Edward Lucas came up from the Victoria at Lye to manage the Empire for a time, and it seems to have flourished up until about 1937 or 1938. Possibly it closed when the Walter Williams decided to modernise the Royal.

Certainly it had closed by the time the Royal's new entrance opened in August 1938. Although variety had flourished at the Empire, it closed as a cinema. (Ironically, sound at the Empire was acoustically better than at the Royal. An interesting point concerning sound at the Empire was that shortly before the talkies arrived films were presented with sound effects provided by a man with a gramophone just beneath the screen. His synchronisation was always better in the second performance than during the first.). The building appears to have remained standing until after the Second World War, but no-one I have spoken to seems to be sure of when it was demolished.

Today a car park next to the Holly Bush Inn occupies the site of the Empire and it is difficult to imagine the hall where the famous striking lady chain-makers once held their meeting.

## 35. The Institute

**(Also known as Pictureland)**

The Workers Institute was opened by the Countess of Dudley on 10th June 1912. The trustees of the Institute included Mary MacArthur of the Anti-Sweating League, who had led the striking women chain-makers in 1910. The fact that they had found a voice and a new confidence was reflected in the building of the hall. It seems that, when planned in 1911, it was to be the Women Workers Institute, funded by women in the Trade Union Movement.

However, it seems that building the Institute had proved expensive and the large hall was leased to Howard Bishop to help repay some of the costs involved. Quite when Mr. Bishop began using the hall for his "Pictureland" is not clear. Like the other Pictureland in Netherton, it was usually known locally as The Stute, but a sign saying "Pictureland" was put up over the side-door. Films, particularly serials, were often shared between the two concerns and travelled backwards and forwards between Netherton and Cradley Heath on the trams.

The twice nightly programmes began with a two-reel silent comedy that was actually shown in silence. The pianist, one was a Harry Raybould, would arrive to accompany the feature. The serial always came last and then the hall was cleared for the second house. In some respects the Cradley Heath "Stute" seems to have been more cinema-like than Netherton. For example, it appears that the floor was raked. However, it never went sound, unlike Netherton, and it seems to have closed in 1933, a few weeks after the opening of the Majestic.

Towards the end it had become a paradise for sky-larking by the local children and the chucker-out, Mr. Hartland, appears to have had to work hard to maintain order. Mr. Bishop tended to look after the shows at Netherton, and therefore, Harry Wild looked after Cradley Heath's Pictureland for him.

Later the hall was used for boxing, and later still, after the floor was levelled, billiard tables were installed. The building still survives in 1982, half a century after the last film show.

## 36. The Majestic
### Cradley Road

The real proof that Cradley Heath was no forgotten backwater of the Black Country came in 1933 with the opening of a very elegant super-cinema: the Majestic. The Majestic Cinema (Cradley Heath) Ltd., was a company of local men led by Dudley's Alderman F. J. Ballard, whom we have already encountered in connection with the Criterion, Dudley, and the Central, Stourbridge. Since being in the chair at the opening of the Central in 1929, he had also been involved in building the Central, Kidderminster, opened on 5th October 1931. The invasion of Dudley by P.C.T. does not seem to have deterred him from investing in independent super-cinemas, or made it difficult to find other local businessmen to join him in such ventures. On this occasion the architect joined the Board, plus "outsiders" like Mr. J. H. Male of the well-known local haulage firm and two other local councillors, Messrs. Millward and Frost.

The Majestic was designed by Messrs. Webb and Gray of Dudley, who had designed the two "Centrals". It was built by J. M. Tate and Son, a local contractor, and made good use of its site in Cradley Road, not far from the Five Ways, which had become the centre of the town. Due to the narrowness of Cradley Road it is impossible to stand back and appreciate the symmetry of its facade. The central entrance was flanked by shops and they have encroached upon the impact of its canopy and the beautiful stained glass leaded lights of the windows of the balcony crush hall. The most beautiful window, by T. W. Camm of Smethwick, is in a relatively obscure side wall, but when driving up Cradley Road from the Stour's valley at night, it can still be seen in all its glory. This window, and the others in the front of the building make a visit to the Majestic imperative.

The Majestic was built to hold fifteen hundred patrons, just over a third of which were in the balcony. The auditorium was fan-shaped, and treated in a modern style when compared with Messrs. Webb and Gray's earlier work. The plaster-work was carried out by the West Bromwich firm of John Malin and Company. From the start it was purpose-built for sound, using the Western Electric system, and the building enjoyed good acoustics. The Majestic was proud of its up-to-date projection suite, fitted with Ernemann III machines fitted with Zeiss lamps and lenses.

One of the most important features of the Majestic was its organ. It was the only Christie organ to be found in the Black Country, apart from Eldon Firmstone's instrument at Wordsley Manor, and was a three-manual, ten unit instrument. Of course, all this should be written in the present tense, as it is the only Black Country cinema-organ to still reside, alive and well, in its original location. At the opening the sight of the organ console rising on its pneumatic lift in the centre of the orchestra pit absolutely astounded the audience.

The "inauguration" of the cinema, as the event was called, took place on Monday afternoon, 27th March 1933, in a packed hall. Alderman Ballard made a few opening remarks and then handed over to Councillor D. M. Chapman, Chairman of Rowley Regis U.D.C., to perform the opening ceremony. After two short films an organ recital was given by the new resident organist, William Sykes. The afternoon ended with the British feature film, "The Flag Lieutenant", starring Henry Edwards and Anna Neagle. The proceeds were donated to the Cradley Heath Friendly Society and the local Carnival Committee.

The cinema's manager, at the time of opening, was Mr. Godwin Longthorn, who had also opened the Criterion and P.C.T.'s Regent, but after a short time

109. William Sykes at the console of the Christie Organ, picked out in the spotlight. Above one of his home-made slides is projected onto the screen.

*(Photo: Mrs. Drinkwater)*

110. The Christie organ at the Majestic — the only Black Country cinema organ still operating in its original home.

*(Photo: Mrs. Drinkwater)*

111. The Majestic, from the architect's sketch in the opening brochure.

*(Author's Collection)*

William Sykes was appointed Manager as well as organist. William Sykes' career is described elsewhere. He worked at the Majestic from 1933 until 1958 and was largely responsible for its success. As a manager he maintained reasonable prices without any increase until the War, and fostered many links between the cinema and the local community. As a musician he educated the musical tastes of the Cradley Heathens.

As Mr. Sykes' organ interludes began the page-boy would come on stage with the title of the music printed on a large card. The console would rise into the spotlight, and slides, made by Mr. Sykes, were projected onto the screen above him. The organ interlude between films was always treated as an integral part of the programme; it was not just a matter of playing before the programme. His work during the War is recorded in the chapter on organists.

As independent cinemas, both the Majestic and the Royal suffered from barring practices after the War. For a super-cinema the Majestic faced an early decline in its fortunes and when Stanley Harrison took over as organist and manager after William Sykes' retirement the cinema seemed to be fighting a losing battle. The organ itself became less and less used and a sign of the desperate search for an audience came when wrestling was introduced for a time on Wednesday evenings. The cinema was too "majestic" for Cradley Heath in the sixties and the inevitable closure came on 2nd November 1963. The last programme consisted of *"Jumbo"*, starring Doris Day, and *"Kill or Cure"*.

The "cure" for the Majestic was Bingo, and it re-opened as the Majestic Casino on 7th November. The

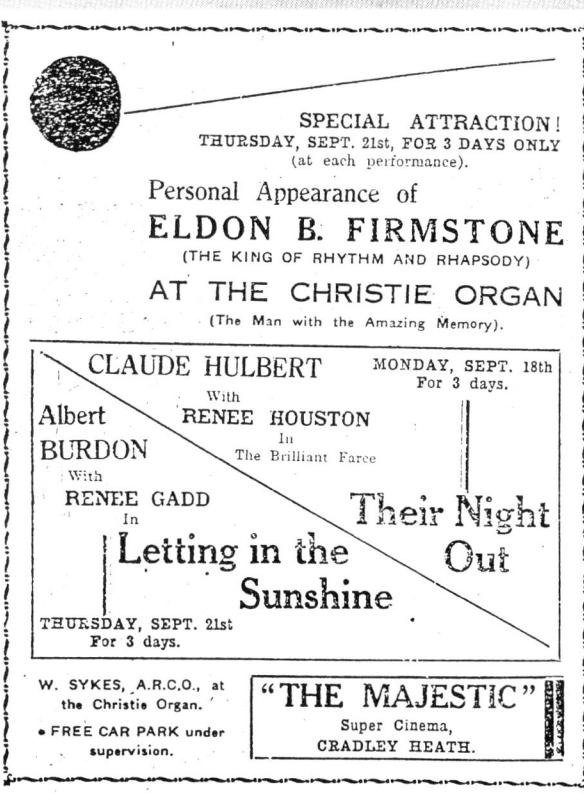

**SPECIAL ATTRACTION!**
THURSDAY, SEPT. 21st, FOR 3 DAYS ONLY
(at each performance).

Personal Appearance of
**ELDON B. FIRMSTONE**
(THE KING OF RHYTHM AND RHAPSODY)
**AT THE CHRISTIE ORGAN**
(The Man with the Amazing Memory).

CLAUDE HULBERT            MONDAY, SEPT. 18th
              With              For 3 days.
Albert    RENEE HOUSTON
BURDON              In
              The Brilliant Farce
  With
RENEE GADD                    *Their Night*
    In
*Letting in the*                *Out*
        *Sunshine*
THURSDAY, SEPT. 21st
For 3 days.

W. SYKES, A.R.C.O., at        "THE MAJESTIC"
the Christie Organ.            Super Cinema,
● FREE CAR PARK under          CRADLEY HEATH.
supervision.

*During the Majestic's opening year Eldon Firmstone made a brief appearance on the Christie organ. His flamboyance and jazzy style could not have been a greater contrast to the style of the cathedral-trained resident organist: William Sykes. It was Eldon Firmstone's only appearance in the Black Country apart from in his own cinema built in Wordsley Manor. (See chapter on the Olympia, Wordsley).*

council had privately discussed acquiring the building but quietly dropped the idea. With the idiosyncrasy the reader may have come to expect of Black Country cinemas, the Majestic did briefly present films again after its "closure". These films took the form of Saturday morning matinees, introduced in January 1964, and operated until the kine licence expired. Six hundred children attended the first show, which hardly filled such a large cinema, but was good house for a cinema that had just decided its future lay in Bingo.

The story does not end there. Mel Edwards took over the organ and fully restored it over a period of three or four years with the co-operation of the lessees, Star Bingo. By 1973 it could be played once again and became a feature of Friday evenings at the Bingo Club. The Majestic is now used as a Bingo Club by Jarglen Ltd., and some alterations have been made to the stage area and proscenium but, as mentioned earlier, the basic architectural features of the building, including the windows, are still worth seeing.

## Old Hill

Visitors to the Black Country who believe what they read on official signs will have noticed that in recent times Old Hill has ceased to exist. It is now part of Cradley Heath, in Warley, in Sandwell! Not so long ago the population of Old Hill was slightly larger than that of Cradley Heath, but perhaps an indication that the place was doomed to obscurity, was the fact that it only ever enjoyed the services of one cinema.

### 37. The Grand
*Halesowen Road*

The "Grandowd'ill" should be pronounced as one word as far as those local people who knew the place are concerned. For them the place has become a local legend, but for the historian the Grand is poorly documented.

Everyone associates the Grand with Benjamin Priest, and the nut and bolt manufacturing business that still exists just behind the cinema. The Benjamin Priest, who founded the original firm in 1854, was the grand-father of the Benjamin Priest associated with the cinema. The latter was born in 1881, in Old Hill, and entered the family firm after completing his education. He seems to have developed an interest in the theatre, and later in the cinema, that led him to build the Grand. Whether it was purpose-built or converted from an existing building is not clear but, at the time of opening, it definitely saw itself as both theatre and cinema.

The Grand opened on Bank Holiday Monday, 4th August 1913, with members of the local council in the audience. They sat down to watch a programme of variety acts, which included the screening of Part One of a film called *"Our Navy"*. Part Two was screened the following week!

During the War Benjamin Priest met a factory inspector who had been an actor, James Broadhurst. It is said that it was he who introduced Ben Priest to the possibility of filming the Reverend Baring-Gould's novel, *"Bladys of the Stewponey"*. This heavy Victorian melodrama, written in 1897, had plenty of cinematic possibilities and Ben Priest, as soon as the War was over, formed his own production company to make such a film. James Broadhurst earned himself a part in the film.

*"Bladys"* went into production in 1919, directed by Lionel McBean, and photographed by Arthur Kingston, both of which received praise for their work. The finished film ran for an hour and a half, and was given a press-preview at the Grand on 18th September 1919. Although the filming had created quite an interest locally when the crew and cast descended on Kinver, the finished product does not seem to have caused so much excitement. After showing it at the Grand, Ben Priest did find a national distributor for the film but whether it was a great financial success seems extremely uncertain. It appeared at Black Country cinemas but was not strongly exploited for its local connections. It came to the Empire, Dudley, for example, for three days in 1922 without special attention.

The operator at the Grand when *"Bladys"* was first shown was Leonard Morgan. He worked at the Grand until 1946 and remembered the film being kept at the cinema. It is thought to have disappeared during structural alterations in 1958.

In the years following the production of *"Bladys"*, the Grand still presented variety as the major part of its programmes. Films seemed to have a stronger future with the prospect of adding sound and towards the end of the silent era Ben Priest expanded his cinema interests to include the Grand and Futurist at Kidderminster. For many years he also ran the Kinema at Kinver.

Western Electric equipment was installed at the Grand, and the talkies came to Old Hill on 5th December 1932 with *"Tarzan, the Ape Man"*. From then on it was mainly used as a cinema, although the stage was used by Cradley Heath Operatic and Dramatic Society on occasion.

For many many years the manager of the Grand was George Smith. He was there so long that he saw three generations of his patrons come to his cinema. He was a manager in the great tradition; smart and well dressed. always present to attend to the patrons. He had been an operator at the Royal, Cradley Heath, before going to the Grand, and at the latter he stayed until closure.

Early in 1950 advertisements started proclaiming, "Big Live Shows Coming Shortly". The last film was shown on Saturday 18th March 1950, *"The Small Black Room"*, starring Jack Hawkins. The following Monday live shows started. They only appear to have lasted for about a year, but during that time there were several incidents on stage which attracted the attention of the National Press.

The Grand then languished, unused, for a time, during which Ben Priest died on 23rd May 1954. He was buried at Kinver. His company was anxious to use the Grand as a warehouse and sought planning permission to do so in 1956. The council rejected the application on the grounds that Old Hill needed recreational facilities. In 1958 the company, therefore, submitted new proposals which involved using the ground floor as a warehouse, and using a first floor as a "public hall".

About 1960 it was sold by the Priest family and Mr. J. Regan converted the building to a dance hall; The Plaza Ballroom. The original facade, which included two shops as well as the cinema's entrance, was now obscured by a completely new frontage, designed by no less than Hurley Robinson and Son.

It enjoyed some success as the Plaza Ballroom, but in 1970 Halesbury Enterprises Ltd., applied for a Gaming Licence and the Plaza became a Bingo Club. It still survives in this role in 1982. The auditorium, which held just under nine hundred patrons, is now unrecognisable but the exterior, behind the Hurley Robinson frontage, is a reminder of the Grand as a cinema.

On a side wall a painted sign on the brickwork has almost weathered away, but a message concerning the price of the tip up seats is still just about discernable.

## Halesowen

On the Worcestershire banks of the Stour Vale, on the southern-most border of the Black Country lies the town of Halesowen. The town has a long history, particularly an ecclesiastical history associated with Halesowen Abbey. The survival of court rolls for the manor and for the borough have enabled a detailed history of medieval Halesowen to be constructed. Unfortunately the much more recent twentieth century history of the town's cinemas has not been so well documented!

Halesowen's own Francis Brett Young described the area as, "A bewildering mixture of beauty and squalor", a description that could be applied to almost any part of the Black Country from 1800 to the present day. Industry encroached on Halesowen via the Stour Vale, through which the Dudley Canal, and eventually the railway, passed. The sweated iron trades, such as the manufacture of nails grew up in the villages south of Dudley, Netherton, Old Hill and on to Halesowen, and as this cottage industry declined factories grew up manufacturing tools such as scythes and spades, and the holloware trade. Until recent times the Stour Vale was dominated by the large factories of Walter Somers and the Halesowen Steel Company. Today new industrial estates carry on that tradition.

One man dominates the history of Halesowen's cinemas; Sidney Bray, who came not from the town itself, but from Dudley. He left no legend behind him to compare with Professor Wood in Bilston or Cecil Couper in Brierley Hill, yet he created one of the nicest Black Country cinemas; the Lyttleton, a super-cinema in the modern style reduced to the human proportions that were a realistic response to the entertainment needs of Black Country communities.

## 38. The Drill Hall

In the County Advertiser for 28th January 1911 appeared the claim, "Electric Pictures will be shown for the first time in Halesowen". They were to arrive on Monday 30th January, and the man who had leased the Drill Hall to show them was Sidney Bray, from Dudley. His brother-in-law, Wally Davies was in charge of the box office and was almost knocked over in the patrons' stampede to obtain seats! Mr. Bray himself stood outside shouting, "Two, Four and Sixpence, this way!".

Programmes were twice nightly, six days a week, except for one Tuesday each month when the Masons used the hall. At a Masonic Meeting Sidney Bray

encountered a Mr. Harvey who became the chief operator. Mr. Harvey worked at the Drill Hall until moving to the Cosy Corner, where his son, Lawrence Harvey, started work as the rewind boy. The latter worked for Bernard Bray when the Picture House closed, thus illustrating the "family" nature of working for the Brays.

Ironically Sidney Bray was not really the first to show films at the Drill Hall. It had been used earlier by travelling film-shows. For example, on 20th December 1909 it had been used by Messrs. Gale and Polden, of London, to present a one day show of "animated pictures" on military subjects. However, Sidney Bray's shows at the Drill Hall were on a permanent regular basis.

What is not very clear is how long the Drill Hall was used as a cinema. It was certainly going strong after the First World War, when Bert Holden went there as the pianist, and he and Lena Wood on the violin used to accompany the films. There was also a time when the Drill Hall used to share serials with the Grand, Old Hill. The Manager had to take each episode over to Old Hill after it had been shown at the first house in Halesowen, and later bring it back for the second house. One night the film caught fire at Old Hill and the second house at the Drill Hall never saw that episode!

It seems likely that the Drill Hall was closed when the new Picture House was opened in 1927, or when Sidney Bray took over the Cosy Corner. Like several other Black Country halls, the Drill Hall claimed that the Black Country comedian, Billy Russell, made his debut there!

## 39. The Kings Hall (later the Cosy Corner)
*Peckingham Street*

The Dudley Herald for 20th May 1911 records that Mr. Barnes of Smethwick had applied for permission to convert the Golden Cross Inn, Peckingham Street, into a Picture Palace. This may have been the Mr. Barnes associated with the little cinema in Spinners End, Cradley Heath. Whether this materialised as the Kings Hall is not clear, particularly as people who remember the place always talk of it being converted from a gospel hall, where a Mr. Butler had once presented magic lantern shows on religious subjects.

Whatever its origins, the Kings Hall seems to have been Halesowen's second cinema, and shows continued there until towards the end of the First World War. After the War it was purchased by Percy Dyche, a name associated with various cinemas in Birmingham, and whose only other venture in the Black Country was at the Beacon, Smethwick.

William Jackson, the building contractor from Langley, lavishly reconstructed the Kings Hall for Mr. Dyche and it re-opened at the end of 1920, or the very beginning of 1921, as the Cosy Corner. To live up to its new name it had plush tip up seats to hold four hundred and thirty patrons, plus Axminster Carpets. It was managed by Frank Robbins.

Almost immediately, William Jackson assumed control and ownership of the Cosy Corner. It was not his only venture into the cinema business as he also ran the Regent, Langley, for a time. In July 1922 he appointed Will Tyrer as manager, and from then on the

Cosy Corner prospered. Mrs. A. Lee of Halesowen, vividly recalls those times. Her mother and her sister worked there as usherettes and always looked very smart in their black dresses and white aprons. Mrs. Lee writes;

"Mr. Will Tyrer did a lot to liven things up, as he used to say. He introduced variety acts on stage such as conjuring or songs. Sometimes Will's own wife, who was a singer, would entertain the audience before the film started. I remember the queue stretching up to the top of Peckingham Street on Saturday nights, long before the doors were due to open. If there was a good performance on, there would be buskers outside the cinema, or the organ-grinder with his monkey".

Will Tyrer's success at the Cosy Corner caused trade to decline at the Drill Hall, and the latter introduced variety acts in order to compete. The Cosy Corner also had a good three-piece orchestra of drums, violin and piano. Wilf Hollyhead, who worked there for twelve months in 1923 as an operator, also recalls Will Tyrer's management. While he suffered the cramped conditions of the operating box, he had to admit everything there was of the best for the patrons. He recalls that during wet weather they used to put sheets over the stair-carpets in order to keep them clean!

At the end of the silent era the Cosy Corner was acquired by Sidney Bray. Although he had introduced

talkies to Halesowen at the Picture House he continued to run the Cosy Corner as a silent cinema. The pianist Bert Holden who had moved from the Drill Hall to the new Picture House in 1927 was now moved to the Cosy Corner, where he had to provide solo accompaniment to the film. Lawrence Harvey, who was trained at the Cosy Corner by his father, the "chief" at the time, has already been mentioned in the chapter on the Drill Hall. His wife, Lilly, worked at the Cosy Corner during the evening and in the local button factory by day. When the Cosy Corner closed she went to the Picture House!

The survival of the Cosy Corner into the sound era is curious. It seems likely that Sidney Bray, after his departure from the Criterion, Dudley, was keen to consolidate his position in Halesowen. Rather than modernise the Cosy Corner it seems that he wished to replace it with a brand new sound cinema, or, failing that, to build a brand new cinema elsewhere in Halesowen. The latter is what eventually happened.

By 1934 the Cosy Corner was no longer considered "structurally suitable for public exhibition" by Supt. Mobbs in his report to the licensing magistrates. The tiny operating and rewind room was particularly inadequate. At the beginning of March 1935 the kine licence had to be renewed and these objections were raised again. Sidney Bray protested that he was willing to extend the operating room and build a fire-proof rewind room but what he really wanted to do was build a new cinema.

The licence was renewed for nine months only, on Mr. Bray's undertaking that he would build a new cinema. Later in the year Mr. Bray found difficulty in securing land for a new super-cinema and in August he asked for an extension to the licence for the Cosy Corner and promised that he would spend £800 improving the place. His application was turned down so we must assume that the Cosy Corner closed at the end of 1935.

The premises were later converted to a Ladies' Clothes Shop but have totally disappeared as Peckingham Street has shared in the radical redevelopment of Halesowen's town centre. A pedestrianised Peckingham Street still exists and Woolworths have a store on the approximate site of the cinema.

### 40. The Electric Theatre
### (later The Picture House)
*Stourbridge Road*

Halesowen Cinemas Ltd., was registered on 25th July 1913 and it is thought that this was the company that built the Electric Theatre in Stourbridge Road. It was a corrugated iron, timber framed building, and had a seating capacity of nine hundred. This was not a venture launched by Sidney Bray, but by the Rose brothers of the Halesowen Steel Company. The four Rose brothers were named General, Major, Captain and Baron. Presumably the last named had most to do with running the cinema because it was known locally as "Baron's". It appears to have opened in 1913.

Sidney Bray seems to have acquired it in the early twenties, but then disaster struck. In the early hours of Thursday morning, 14th February 1924, fire mysteriously broke out in the cinema. A Mr. Garnet Clift, whose

112. A grand flight of steps up to the Picture House, the only known photographic record of this cinema.

*(From the Postcard Collection of Peter Barnsley)*

bedroom overlooked the cinema, raised the alarm and the local fire brigade, led by Captain Binfield, was on the scene within minutes. Fanned by strong winds the fire blazed furiously and it was five hours before it was completely extinguished. The building was completely destroyed, except for a brick-built shed that housed the gas engine and generator. Apparently the fire had not started in the operating box, and the operator arrived on the scene and managed to retrieve the films before the fire reached them! Another local legend tells that the film being shown that week was called *"Mighty Like A Rose"* and local wags claimed it was now "Mighty Like A Ruin".

Sidney Bray had to find a way of replacing the Electric Theatre and more than three years passed before the Picture House was completed in its place. The new building was designed by Halesowen architect, Stanley Beech, and was built to accommodate nine hundred patrons in a brick auditorium. It was built by J. M. Tate and Son.

The Picture House opened on Monday 12th December 1927 with the film *"Second to None"*. Seats were 1/- and 9d in the balcony; 6d and 4d in the stalls. A full orchestra was provided, featuring Bert Holden from the Drill Hall. It has already been recorded how Lilly Harvey came to the Picture House from the Cosy Corner and later Sidney Bray asked her to persuade her husband to leave the Rex, Blackheath, and join the staff as the chief operator. He did so and stayed there until its closure.

The Picture House was the smartest cinema Halesowen had yet seen, and two years later had the privilege of introducing the talkies to the town. BTP equipment was installed and *"The Singing Fool"* arrived at the Picture House on 25th November 1929. After the Second World War Gaumont British Kalee projectors were put in, and a G. B. Sound system.

When Sidney Bray died in 1940, the Picture House and Lyttleton passed to his son, Bernard Bray, who also inherited the partnership with "Uncle Wally", Wally Davies, at the Brownhills cinema. It was a straightforward matter for the two men to concentrate on running the three cinemas as before; Wally Davies in Brownhills, Bernard Bray in Halesowen. Both men were interested in aircraft and worked with the Halesowen Air Training Corps throughout the War. Wally Davies built his patent trainer for the Corps.

Bernard Bray ran the Halesowen cinemas successfully, but like most other independent cinema proprietors times proved difficult during the latter half of the fifties. He was interviewed by the Express and Star in April 1958 and in view of the difficulties at the Picture House, seemed anxious to sell it. A Mr. Brown, who had bought the Cosy Corner for his clothing business had been interested in buying it for use as a factory, but apparently planning permission had been refused.

There was a brief experiment in presenting wrestling in September 1961, but six day film presentation prevailed for the last few months of operation. (The Picture House had never opened on a Sunday.) After Bernard Bray's death it was possibly a relief to find that the Council wished to acquire the building in order to widen the Stourbridge Road.

The Picture House closed on 9th December 1961 with *"Pirate of the Black Hawk"*, and one of my favourite "Z" films, *"Invasion of the Hell Creatures"*. The building was not immediately demolished, and during the mid sixties the Council leased the building to the Scala Bingo Club. Eventually it was sold to the Conservative Club who demolished it to provide space for a car park. The road was never widened.

---

## 41. The Lyttleton
*Hagley Road*

Halesowen's cinema history reached its zenith in the construction of the Lyttleton. In my opinion this was the ideal Black Country cinema. It had all the glamorous trappings of a super-cinema, but was built on a scale that seemed appropriate to the size of a Black Country community. Undoubtedly it was built by Sidney Bray to keep Gaumont British out of Halesowen, but it was really his son's cinema. Bernard Bray kept the Lyttleton under his personal supervision from the opening until his death.

At the conclusion of the story of the Cosy Corner we last encountered Sidney Bray searching for a site for a new super-cinema! A site was found at Hasbury, in "surburban" surroundings, on the Hagley Road, now eclipsed as a main road by Manor Way. For some reason unknown it was not designed by a local architect, but by Edward Wilford. He produced a cinema that held just over a thousand patrons, with an attractive frontage in rustic brick and contrasting faience. The balcony lounge windows extended the vertical lines of the four sets of double doors beneath a very rectangular canopy. On the left hand extreme of the facade a large fin carried the name of the cinema in neon light. Neon lighting, and flood-lighting, made the Lyttleton very attractive at night, even at the end of its cinema career.

It is said that William Jackson expected to build the Lyttleton, but the lowest tender was supplied by Mr. J. Felton, who had rebuilt the Regent, Brownhills, when it had been acquired by Sidney Bray and Wally Davies. It was certainly going to be a struggle to build the Lyttleton and costs had to be kept as low as possible while

113. The Lyttleton, as built, in 1938.
*(Photo: John Felton)*

114. The balcony lounge at the Lyttleton, an independent cinema in the modern style. 1938.

*(Collection of John Felton)*

providing as fine a cinema as possible. The bricks used to build the auditorium came, second-hand, from the demolition of Her Majesty's Theatre in Walsall. It was built using the established practice of putting up structural steelwork and filling in with brick and concrete. The main girder arrived by rail at Rowley Regis and had a difficult journey by road to Hasbury!

John Felton calculated that he built the Lyttleton for £6,480. When it came to equipping the place everything was hired from Gaumont British rather than purchased outright. This included everything from the seats to the Gaumont Eclipse projectors and the British Acoustic Duosonic sound system. A pleasing sense of luxury was provided in the auditorium, the plaster-work painted in autumnal tones and concealed lighting used effectively.

The Lyttleton opened on Monday evening, 11th April 1938 with the film, *"Farewell Again"*, starring Flora Robson. The ceremony was performed by Alderman Downing, the Mayor of Halesowen. Sidney Bray said that he felt quite a veteran, having presented films in the town for twenty-seven years, and he was glad his son would be looking after the new cinema. The official party posed for a photograph, reproduced in the chapter on the Brays, and when it was reproduced in the County Express the paper told its readers "The cinema has been built regardless of cost". As it happened this statement was true in a way other than in which it was intended.

Bernard Bray ran the Lyttleton successfully. During the War it prospered as a result of the patronage of soldiers stationed nearby, and after the War it prided itself on keeping up-to-date. For example it was quick to install cinemascope. Its champions claim that it was the first to do so in the Black Country but I do not know if that is true.

After Bernard Bray's death in 1961, his wife, Edith Bray, ran the Lyttleton but it was not an easy task. When the Grand, Kingswinford, closed in 1964 Ken Waterhouse came to the Lyttleton. At the Grand he had been a chief operator with managerial responsibilities and his versatility and enterprise helped the Lyttleton survive. He fought hard to preserve the dwindling family audience, and the balcony at the Lyttleton continued to attract this audience providing one could maintain order in the stalls.

By the early seventies, Bernard Bray's daughters were running the Lyttleton. It was busier than it had been in the early sixties but companies interested in promoting Bingo Halls were prepared to offer high prices. The Lyttleton was sold to Ladbrokes in the autumn of 1973, but it continued to operate as a cinema until the company obtained a gaming licence the following summer. Ken Waterhouse found himself working for Ladbrokes with the prospect of Bingo approaching.

The Lyttleton closed on 1st June 1974 with *"The Intelligence Men"* plus *"Bless This House"*. The conversion proceeded with great haste, but the new proprietors did not touch the operating room, they simply truncated all the wiring! It was more important to provide new heating and new lighting as Bingo Clubs are invariably brightly lit.

After all this, Bingo was not a great success at the Lyttleton. So much so that the story of this cinema takes a surprising twist. Ladbrokes decided to show films again on four nights of the week, from Friday to Monday. This brought Sunday-opening to Halesowen for the first time.

Restoring cinema facilities to the Lyttleton was not easy. The screen had been removed in October 1975 and now formed the screen in the Shenstone Theatre, in Halesowen's new library. It is still being used today by the Halesowen Film Society. Three operators, Harry and George Siddall, and Steve Sidaway, had to collect equipment from all over the Midlands. Lights came from the Gaumont, Wednesbury, owned by Ladbrokes, chandeliers and a clock came from the Odeon, Stourbridge, and a new second-hand curtain came from Villa Cross.

Although the projection equipment existed, re-connecting it was a nightmare, and circuits were traced by making one's way along the plaster-work with a magnet to detect the metal conduit. It re-opened at the beginning of January 1976.

At first it was difficult to obtain a supply of suitable films, but Ladbrokes took showing films seriously, and even introduced Saturday morning matinees for children. Alas, during the summer, just as good programmes were being booked, Ladbrokes decided to make financial cutbacks and it was decided to abandon the film operation at the Lyttleton.

The second and final closure was on Monday 27th September 1976 with *"The Poseidon Adventure"*, plus *"How to Steal A Diamond"*. The three operators who had put so much work into their task were heart-broken. The projection equipment was removed and "given away" and Bingo returned, but apparently still without great success.

Eventually the Lyttleton was sold to Harry Whitehouse, a Birmingham businessman who successfully runs Bingo at the Avion, Aldridge. He brought success to Bingo at the Lyttleton and it still exists today. The exterior is still attractive, although shorn of some of its details.

Unfortunately I only visited the Lyttleton once but it introduced me to courting-seats, which I had never encountered in London. The last such seat in the Black Country existed in the Royal, Cradley Heath, but in 1982 none remain in use.

Please note: A photograph of Sidney Bray, Wally Davies and the official opening party at the Lyttleton on 11th April 1938 appears on page 23.

## Blackheath

Blackheath has two faces. When approached from Quinton via Long Lane, passing the Odeon, it seems a suburb of Birmingham. When approached from Dudley via Rowley Regis it seems part of the Black Country. Administratively it was part of Rowley Regis and, therefore, today it is part of Sandwell.

The Kine Year Books usually listed Blackheath's cinemas in with those of Birmingham. This book restores them to the Black Country and puts on record the work of Thomas Cooper.

## 42. The Picture Palace
*Cardale Street*

The first cinema in Blackheath was the Picture Palace. It opened on Saturday 9th July 1910, when scenes from the life and funeral of Edward VII were included in the programme. Seats were sixpence and threepence, children were charged twopence. In its advertising it claimed to be, "The first cinema in the Midlands. and the finest". It was certainly not "first" in the historical sense!

It was managed by Mr. T. Kimberley, and probably operated in converted factory premises. It was still open at the end of 1912, but after the Pavilion opened in 1913, Thomas Cooper bought out the Picture Palace and closed it. It became a bakery and later a factory again.

## 43. The Pavilion
*High Street*

The first purpose-built cinema in Blackheath was provided by Thomas Cooper. It seems that he owned the land at the time, and the cinema business seemed to be booming, therefore, he built one in the last four months of 1912. The Electric Picture Pavilion opened on 4th January 1913, with a programme that included *"Fire At Sea"*.

Following his success with the Pavilion, Thomas Cooper built a cinema typical of each of the cinema-building eras. The Kings arrived in 1923 and the Rex in 1938. When the latter opened, the Pavilion closed, but the story did not quite come to an end.

The building remained unused through the War years but after the hostilities Thomas Cooper planned further use for it. In 1948 plans were drawn by N. Hadley and Son to convert the Pavilion into a News Theatre. When this seemed too limited a use for the premises it was re-conceived as a multi-purpose ballroom.

It was re-opened in this capacity in May 1951 with a Staffordshire County Police Ball. However, as well as accommodating three hundred dancers, it was also hoped that plays and films would be presented there. The projection room and balcony seating were retained. A start was made in 1952 on installing new equipment and removable seats were made so that it could still be a News Theatre three or four nights a week. Then the idea was dropped.

A Cee Jay supermarket now occupies the site, almost opposite the Post Office, but the exterior outline of the auditorium can still be clearly seen from The Causeway, running behind the High Street.

## 44. The Kings
*Long Lane*

After the First World War Thomas Cooper decided to build a larger, more impressive cinema. Like others at the time, he felt slightly uncertain about the future of the business and, therefore, built the hall as a fully equipped theatre.

Unfortunately details of the architect and builder have not been found. It was certainly an imposing building, although the entrance was fairly modest. The Kings opened on Monday 2nd April 1923 with *"Dick Turpin's Ride To York"*. As a reflection of its size and importance it had an orchestra of six or seven musicians.

Despite the theatrical facilities, it was dedicated to showing films. It seems that it was only used as a theatre for about five weeks of its entire life! It was used a few times by a local amateur operatic society and once T.C. Pictures ran their own pantomime for a week.

Edibell Sound equipment was installed, and on 31st March 1930 the talkies arrived in Blackheath with *"The Broadway Melody"*. Its position in the town remained unchallenged until the Odeon opened in 1934. Thomas Cooper decided to fight back by building his own super-cinema; the Rex. Consequently the Kings slipped into third place.

Ironically the Odeon was the first to close, perhaps reflecting the relative obscurity of its location. But if the Odeon could not survive long into the sixties, what chance did the Kings stand? The last show advertised in the County Express was for 3rd November 1962 when the beautifully elegiac *"Guns in the Afternoon"* was shown, but it seems that the Kings may have continued in business for anything up to another two or three years. (Local supporters of the Rex state that it closed during the winter of 1964/5 with *"The Absent Minded Professor"*.)

It would be nice to think *"Guns in the Afternoon"* was the final picture because Randolph Scott and Joel MaCrea symbolised the kind of films that could endear the Kings to its patrons. Obviously Mr. Cooper put his best films in the Rex, but the "B" Westerns that ran at the Kings were more "popular" in a perverse kind of way.

Today the premises are used as a Bingo and Social Club in the auditorium, and as an amusement arcade in the entrance foyer.

## 45. The Rex
*Halesowen Road*

As stated in the previous chapter, the arrival of the Odeon, in Long Lane, in 1934 upset Thomas Cooper's local monopoly of cinema entertainment. In building the Rex in Halesowen Road he re-asserted his position as the Rex was much closer to the centre of Blackheath.

The Rex was designed by Sidney H. Wigham, a Birmingham architect, and was built, by J. M. Tate and Sons, to accommodate fourteen hundred patrons. Its fortress-like solid brick presence is only relieved by six vertical windows at the balcony level. The four windows of the balcony lounge do not continue any verticals established at entrance level and it does not, therefore, enjoy the pleasing symmetry of some Satchwell and Roberts cinemas. Perhaps its regality was established by the stone window surrounds and cornices. Its name was certainly chosen to recall the royal associations of the local authority's name; Rowley Regis.

An organ chamber, and console pit in front of the stage, were provided but no organ was installed as Thomas Cooper was of the opinion that patrons came to see films, not hear music! The auditorium was finished in warm tones of russet and rose du Barry in shaded plaster bands, above a green and black dado. Kalee II projectors were installed but in about 1946 they were moved to the Kings, and were replaced with Kalee 12 machines. The British Acoustic sound system apparently did not suit the Rex and was eventually replaced with hybrid equipment that worked better.

The Rex opened on Sunday 25th September 1938 with a special charity concert. Films commenced the following day with *"Owd Bob"* starring Will Fyffe.

189

116. The Rex, as a Bingo & Social Club, 1981.
*(Photo: Ned Williams)*

As with other cinemas that opened just before the Second World War, its history was fairly uneventful and involved no major changes of structure or ownership. Small details changed, for example a larger screen was installed mid-week during the showing of *"Genevieve"* in the early fifties, but generally the Rex enjoyed a quiet life.

The general decline in cinema business caught up with the Rex in 1968. On 6th July of that year it closed with a screening of the controversial film, *"Ulysses"*. The Rex advertised it as "The Film Sensation of All Time"! The chief operator, Bill Birch, who had also managed the cinema for the past eleven years, was sorry to leave. He had been in the cinema trade for twenty-two years and still hoped that he would find another job in that line.

The Rex was leased to a company who turned it into a Bingo Club but even now, fourteen years later, it still retains much of the appearance of a cinema, particularly in the fully-seated balcony. It is said that the projection equipment has remained up in the operating room as if waiting to return to life.

### 46. Odeon
*Long Lane*

During the period between the opening of the first Odeon at Perry Barr, and the opening of the Warley at the end of 1934, Oscar Deutsch had cinemas designed by a variety of architects without clearly establishing a recognisable house-style. After 1934 it was a different story, but Blackheath's Odeon belongs to that early stage of the development of the Odeon circuit.

The Perry Barr Odeon, in its strange Moorish style, had been designed by Stanley Griffiths, whose name will now be familiar, and Horace Bradley, an architect favoured by the Hewitsons in Smethwick. Stanley Griffiths was commissioned to design the Blackheath Odeon and produced something quite different to the cinema being built at the same time a mile or two away at Warley.

The long auditorium running parallel to Long Lane featured a cinema entrance in the centre of the side of the building, flanked by shops. The entire side wall, entrance and shops were finished in striking cream faience with black borders. When new, the effect was stunning, as can be seen in the photograph. The Art-Deco influence was strongly felt in the design of the leaded glass windows, and particularly in the abstract, but very geometrical, decoration of the interior. The auditorium contained 1,232 seats and was a striking exploitation of the stadium style, used again by Stanley Griffiths for the Kings at Stourbridge. It was built by Housing Ltd., and, like other Odeons, was fitted with BTH equipment.

117. The Odeon, when new, in 1934. (And as still exists today in general outline).
(Photo: John Maltby)

118. The stadium-style interior of the Odeon, 1934.
(Photo: John Maltby)

The Odeon opened on 20th October 1934. Two local councillors shared the opening ceremony. Alderman J. B. Downing, Chairman of Halesowen U.D.C. made the first speech in which he praised the beauty of the cinema and pointed out that 1,200 houses had recently been built in the area surrounding the cinema. He was supported by Alderman B. Hobbs, the Mayor of Rowley Regis. Mr. R. H. Morgan, the M.P. for Stourbridge, and a veteran of cinema openings added a few remarks.

Up in the operating room Harry Willis laced up the first films, including *"The Rise of Catherine the Great"*, starring Douglas Fairbanks Junior, and Frank Harvey began to familiarise himself with BTH equipment to prepare himself to open the Warley in six weeks time. Both men became veterans of Odeon openings, and Mr. Harvey later distinguished himself as manager of the Forum, Caldmore Green. It is interesting to reflect on the fact that Oscar Deutsch opened seventeen cinemas in 1934!

The manager was Charles Crathorn who had come into cinemas via the world of dance hall management. He had cultivated an "Uncle Charlie" personality to attract junior patrons at one of his previous appointments, which proved useful in establishing the children's club at this cinema. He later managed the Odeon, Dudley.

Compared with town-centre Odeons, the one at Blackheath seems to have led a quiet backwater existence. It had a large car park and presumably hoped to serve more than the immediately local surrounding area, but it was possibly over-shadowed by the Warley Odeon and the Danilo at Quinton.

It claims to have been the first Odeon to introduce a Children's Club but apart from that I have learnt little about its twenty-six years of life.

It closed on 19th November 1960 with *"Wild River"*, and then stood empty for a long time. In 1962 the idea of turning it into a bowling alley was considered, and Bingo was tried from 10th February 1967 onwards. Its most exciting further lease of life came when it was turned into a ballroom, but ballrooms are not popular with local residents and presumably they have found life quieter since the building became retail premises.

At present it is a D.I.Y. supermarket run by the B. & Q. organisation. The exterior is preserved in general outline, and even the leaded windows survive. The Art Deco tiles are obscured by paint and the original harmony of the "frontage" is lost. Virtually nothing of the cinema interior still exists.

## Introduction

On 1st April 1974 the County Boroughs of West Bromwich and Warley amalgamated to form the new Metropolitan Borough of Sandwell. I have avoided using the name Sandwell in the title of this section simply because the name is still a puzzle to people living outside the Black Country. Even the explanation leaves people puzzled as the creation of Warley was the result of earlier reorganisation, and names like Smethwick, Oldbury, Rowley Regis etc. are still better understood. At the same time West Bromwich had absorbed Tipton and Wednesbury.

Once again it is best to forget current boundaries and regard this section as dealing with the south eastern quadrant of the Black Country, an area partly bordered by Birmingham. The proximity to Birmingham, and the topography, give this area an atmosphere that is quite different to the other parts of the Black Country. In the part of this area furthest from Birmingham, the industrial villages have not quite merged to form a solid conurbation but close to the border, along the fringes of Smethwick I feel the Black Country atmosphere is lost. Some of the cinemas, in practice, belong to suburban Birmingham although technically built outside the city.

## West Bromwich

It is difficult to imagine the scattered selection of industrial hamlets that turned into West Bromwich during the past two centuries. Probably the coming of Telford's road and the Birmingham Canal brought the forges, furnaces and foundries of the iron industry together and began the modern development of the town. When the Great Western Railway arrived in 1854 the population had already risen to 35,000, seven times its size at the beginning of the century. When the cinemas arrived in this century they found themselves in a town with one of the most "linear" of Victorian High Streets, stretching for almost a mile from the clock in Dartmouth Square to the clock in the tower at Carters Green. The cinemas built within that area are described first, in chronological order. Two cinemas, however, were built further afield, at Hill Top and Stone Cross; they are dealt with separately.

### Central West Bromwich

### 1. The Hippodrome/Olympia
*High Street*

The Hippodrome opened on August Bank Holiday

Monday, 1906. It was a large corrugated iron theatre with an attractive frontage facing the High Street at the Carters Green end of the town. Variety was presented at the Hippodrome and gradually films were introduced between the acts. The proprietor was R. Colin, who also presented film and variety at the Empire, Dudley, and Tivoli, Brierley Hill. "Colin's Famous Electric Pictures" were a feature of entertainment in West Bromwich by the time the Cinematograph Act was law.

However, in 1911, he seems to have sold, or leased, the building to Benjamin Kennedy. The name appears to have changed to the Olympia in 1914. A new company, West Bromwich Olympia Ltd., had been registered in September 1913, and appears to have partly rebuilt the theatre in time to re-open as the Olympia on 1st June 1914.

Just after the First World War it appears to have suffered a fire and possibly remained closed until its demolition during the summer of 1922. It always renewed its kine licence, but probably Mr. Kennedy continued Mr. Colin's policy of presenting variety, films, and frequently, mixtures of both. It has two claims to local fame. First, people remember a huge balloon that was tethered to the place, when new, but which sailed away one day when the cable snapped. Secondly, the tin roof, that produced so much noise when it rained, once collapsed under a weight of snow!

## 2. The Palace
### (usually known as the Queens)
*Queen Street*

The Hippodrome/Olympia was really a theatre that flirted with the new medium. The town's first cinema was undoubtedly the Palace, and, although not purpose-built, I would regard it as the first cinema to open in the Black Country. The building had been Josh Bailey's printing works but was converted to a cinema by none other than Irving Bosco. It opened on Saturday 23rd January 1909, almost a full year ahead of the great burst of cinema-opening activity. As the "Picture Palace", its first programme included *"Rifle Bill"* and many and varied short films. It was managed by Irving Bosco's brother, James Bainton, and probably Irving's wife appeared there to provide song accompaniment to some of the films.

Irving Bosco introduced "benefit shows" at the Picture Palace, just as he did later at Dudley's Public Hall. In February he held a show to raise funds for the local hospital, at which the Mayoress, eleven year old Miss Edith Field, was presented with a bouquet. Later, she, and her brother Charles Field, worked at the cinema. Edith sold penny toffee bars from a tray and Charles worked in the pay box, or, if necessary, in the operating box, where a hand-cranked Pathe projector struggled to present the films without too many fires!

The name "Queens" seems to have been adopted about May 1910, perhaps to avoid confusion with the new purpose-built rival in the High Street, the Electric Picture Palace. Certainly the Queens was quick to compete on any front imaginable. When the new cinema advertised its bright coal fire installed in its lounge the Queens claimed, "N.B. The Hall Is Comfortably Warmed". During the summer of 1911 it closed for a week to be re-seated and to have better use made of its space, after which it claimed, "N.B. The Coolest Hall In The Midlands!".

It thrived on the "penny and a pass" system of filling its seats and advertising its shows, and by enterprising programming. For example in December 1910, the first Christmas after its rival had opened, the Queens presented *"Puss In Boots, plus Pictures"*, and in the January: *"Sleeping Beauty plus ten Pictures"*.

Irving Bosco seems to have parted with the Queens earlier than his other Black Country cinemas. About the time of the end of the First World War it was sold to Thomas Leach, who rebuilt the place into the basic form which survived until 1969. Increasing its capacity from about 800 to 1200. With the aid of his brothers, and brothers-in-law, Tom Leach built up quite a circuit of local cinemas, and in West Bromwich both the Queens, and the St. Georges, were eventually leased to the F. J. Emery circuit, sometime in the 1930's. By then, of course, it was a sound cinema, using British Talking Pictures equipment.

During the Second World War the Queens appears to have declined. Its seating capacity dropped to a thousand which suggests that F. J. Emery was more generous in the space allowed per patron than Tom Leach. Local folk tales abound concerning rows in which some seats were missing altogether, and unsuspecting patrons fighting their way along the row to a non-existent place! Possibly the usherettes knew no better, and again local legends suggest a high turn-over of such staff in the early forties. The Queens became known as "The Banger" and "The Bug and Blanket".

In July 1946, along with the other cinemas that formed the estate of the late Tom Leach, the Queens was sold, by auction, to Miles Jervis II. This marked a change in its fortunes. Miles Jervis II persuaded Mr. Emery to relinquish the lease, and began to improve the Queens. First of all he installed a more effective sound system (British Acoustic), and added new G.B. Kalee G K 18 projectors.

About 1949 Miles Jervis II improved the frontage of the Queens with a new, longer canopy and, in 1952, Modernisation Ltd. were invited to refurbish the interior. Miles Jervis found that the Queens was the most successful of his Black Country cinemas and it became his headquarters for a time, as well as the scene of his innovations. A "Synchro" screen was successfully tried at the Queens and, in 1956, automated projection was introduced. At first, the chief operator, Peter J. Evans, was proud of the new equipment but in the course of time it turned out not to be very successful. It was, however, the fore-runner of more successful systems.

In 1957 Miles Jervis acquired the Kings and became even more firmly established in West Bromwich. The Kings was much more impressive than the Queens but the latter showed no sign of immediate retirement. By the mid sixties, however, its future looked less secure. I visited it once in 1965 and a dismal programme, (*"The War Game"* plus *"Four in the Morning"*) perhaps made the cinema seem more dismal than it really was. Possibly even then it was realised that redevelopment would force its closure.

119. The Queens, in the mid 1940's, before the canopy was extended etc.

*(Photo: Collection of Miles Jervis)*

The Queens showed its last regular programme on Saturday 5th April 1969, closing with the magnificent Vincent Price film, *"Witchfinder General"*. The Queens was used on Sundays for the presentation of Indian films, organised by Tarsem Singh Dhami and his colleagues, and these shows continued. Mr. Dhami recalls these shows as being extremely successful and remembers having to rush to the Kings to obtain further supplies of ice-creams to feed his packed house.

The council compulsorily purchased the Queens from Miles Jervis and it was demolished in the August of 1969. Mr. Dhami claims that the demolition contractor came along to start work while the last Indian film show was still taking place!

"The Banger", the Black Country's first cinema on a permanent site, had lasted sixty years. Following its demise, life returned to the Imperial and plans were being formulated for a brand new cinema to perpetuate the tradition of film-exhibition established in West Bromwich by Irving Bosco way back in 1909.

3. The Electric Palace
(later known as The Palace)
*High Street*

The chapter on the Electric Palace, Walsall, has already introduced Electric Picture Palace (Midlands) Ltd., a company that set out to build half a dozen purpose-built cinemas in the area, and who opened their second hall in West Bromwich. It was built, near the junction of Paradise Street and the High Street, to accommodate 1200 patrons, and was designed by Messrs. Hickton and Farmer. The main entrance was originally in Paradise Street.

It opened at three o'clock on Whit Monday, 16th May 1910. Mr. Simpson, the manager, entertained his first patrons with eleven films concerning the life and recent death of Edward VII —

"No better selection of pictures could be made for the opening week, for tragedy in various forms, the romantic, and the comic phases of life are all represented".

Continuous performances were presented from 3.00 p.m. to 10.30 p.m. and it was described as, "A pretty as well as a cosy theatre". A rivalry grew between the Queens and the Palace, but it seems the latter genuinely offered more comfort and luxury.

Towards the end of 1912 the cinema became the property of United Electric Theatres but the current manager, Roland Lea, retained his post, and during the following year saw the Palace improved with the addition of a new entrance. On 27th October 1913 this new entrance, in the High Street, was opened and Roland Lea booked the best films he could find to celebrate the occasion, including *A Message from Mars"*.

The High Street facade was lavish indeed. The

195

Midland Chronicle recorded that,
> "The Cornices and Griffins adorning the palisters are an exact replica of those used in decorating the great London Opera House".

The work was done by John Dallow and Sons and made great use of Messrs. Doulton's tiling. Unfortunately no photograph of the Palace seems to exist.

Thomas Jackson of Wolverhampton acquired both the Palaces, Walsall and West Bromwich and, after the First World War, stressed the quality of music to be found at both. In 1920 a new musical director, Owen Moore, was appointed and advertisements claimed the Palace had, "..... One of the best orchestras in South Staffs". In addition Fred Diggle performed on the two-manual Mustel Organ.

Following Thomas Jackson's financial troubles in 1923 the Palace was probably administered by Mr. Thompson, the official receiver of the Midlands Counties Circuit. It was managed by Percy Norton, from Wolverhampton. In the autumn of 1930 it was sold to the Hockley Picture House Company, previously encountered in the Black Country at the Picturedrome, Darlaston. Mr. V. Olliver ran both the Palace and the nearby Imperial for this company until both cinemas were brought under the control of Messrs. Griffin, Wilson and Bassett. In turn Arthur Griffin's company, Griffin Cinemas Ltd., ran the Palace.

These changes of ownership only concerned the building itself as the freehold belonged to Horton Estates of Birmingham. The site was right in the centre of town and yet somehow the Palace never seems to have quite dominated the town's cinemas as one might have expected. Percy Norton used to advertise it as, "The super cinema with super productions", but it always seems to have been eclipsed by its rivals. As it only held about nine hundred patrons perhaps it did not quite deserve to be recognised as a "super". It

introduced sound by Western Electric on 16th December 1929, with "A Dangerous Woman", but the talkies had already arrived in West Bromwich at the Plaza.

Under the control of Griffin Cinemas it prospered with its colleague, the Imperial, during the Second World War but as business declined it seemed redundant. It is not surprising, therefore, that the Palace should abandon the cause when its lease expired in 1957. It closed on Saturday 28th September 1957 with "The Lonely Man", a western starring Jack Palance. Horton Estates then redeveloped the site and, compared with its old rival, the Queens, the Palace seems forgotten. Arthur Griffin still maintained the Imperial, nearby, until ending his association with local cinemas in 1963.

---

### 4. The Imperial
*Spon Lane*

A group of local West Bromwich men assembled to form the Imperial Picture Palace Company after watching the success of the Queens and the Electric Palace. They engaged local architect, Albert Bye, to design their cinema, and employed local builder, Messrs. Dallow and Son, to construct it, on a site next to the Dartmouth Hotel in Spon Lane. Other local firms were used wherever possible, including Messrs. Mallin and Co., who produced the fibrous plasterwork, and Messrs. Chance Brothers who provided glass tiles that were used to decorate the foyer.

The thirteen hundred seater cinema was built in approximately two months and was well and truly worthy of its name. The facade consisted of four shops facing Spon Lane, with the cinema's entrance in the centre. The whole facade was extremely decorative, and was dominated by the figure of Electra bearing an electric torch above the porch. (Echoes of the Wednesbury cinema of the same name!). The auditorium, set back behind the shops and the facade, also presented a highly decorative appearance as seen from Spon Lane, and claimed to be one of the first buildings in the town to have an asbestos slate roof! Inside luxury and ornate decor prevailed. A raked floor, and upholstered tip up seats throughout housed the audience before the large screen surrounded by amazing ornate plasterwork.

120. The Imperial, 4th March 1973, enjoying a new lease of life while the new Kings was being built.

*(Photo: Terry Cresswell, C.T.A.)*

The Imperial Picture Palace opened on 8th April 1912. Patrons were greeted by the manager, H. P. Mears, and entertained by an orchestra led by Ralph Powell. However the "official" opening did not take place until 17th April, when the Mayor, Councillor Kenrick came along to perform the ceremony and see a programme that included *"A Question of Seconds"*. As the official party left the cinema they were filmed and the results were later screened.

Despite being such an impressive place, the Imperial was almost completely rebuilt after the First World War. Only portions of the original side walls of the auditorium were retained. The building was brought forward to a facade in Spon Lane that extended to the full height of the cinema. Once again the architect was Albert Bye and he described the style of his new Imperial as "Georgian". Pillars, balustrades, palisters, etc., were all treated in a striking white glazed terracotta, with intervening panels of purple brick. It was vulgar, highly eclectic and to a perverse cinema-lover, wildly beautiful!

A proper balcony could now stretch across the lengthened and heightened auditorium, replacing the small corner "boxes" that had existed before, and was reached by an oak-panelled staircase. New seats were upholstered in royal blue velvet. The ceiling was panelled and decorated with owls and bats flying overhead. The doors were draped in black velvet curtains trimmed in amber, and the usherettes wore dresses to match the curtains! The orchestra pit was moved to the side of the screen, rather than in front of it, and Mr. F. Rigby became the new musical director.

The £25,000 reconstruction was completed in time for a grand re-opening on 2nd March 1921, when a one-day screening was presented, followed by *"Aylwin"* on the first three days of normal shows. The company may have paid a lot more than originally intended, but nevertheless felt satisfied. The directors of the Imperial Company were George Arthur Griffin, William J. Wilson, Bill Bassett (the footballer) and Edgar Hounsell (previously encountered at the Scala, Wolverhampton, and Regent, Tipton). Mr. Griffin, the father of Arthur Griffin of the Dart Spring Company, had been interested in making films and made one production which resulted in Sax Rohmer suing him for "pinching" the story!

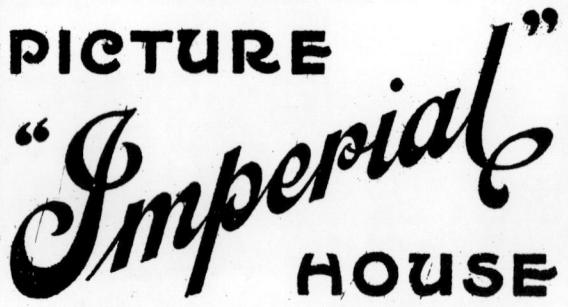

In the early thirties the Imperial appears to have been leased to Mr. V. Olliver of the Hockley Picture House Company. He ran both the Imperial and the Palace until launching the Tower, at Carters Green. While at the Imperial he installed Western Electric sound equipment. After his departure it presumably returned to the original owners, and then, after Mr. Griffin's death in 1938 it passed to Arthur Griffin. Thus it was to Arthur Griffin that Miles Jervis went in 1963 to acquire the Imperial. Griffin Cinemas showed their last film, *"Blood on His Lips"* on 28th September 1963, and the Midland Cinemas Bingo Club opened its doors on 24th October. But the Imperial was now owned by a man dedicated to showing films so the story does not stop there.

On Easter Monday, 7th April 1969, the Imperial made a triumphant return to life as a full-blooded cinema. The Queens had closed on Easter Saturday and the manager, Bruno Tomana, crossed the High Street to open a transformed Imperial. Bingo had ceased six weeks earlier and Modernisation Ltd., had arrived to completely refurbish the place. Eight hundred bright red super armchair seats, 1380 yards of new luxury carpet and a new Perlux screen went into the auditorium. New sound and projection equipment was supplied by Rank Audio Visual and John Wood, long ago a manager of the Imperial, became the new "chief". The £20,000 conversion from Bingo back to films was celebrated with Rex Harrison's *"Doctor Doolittle"*.

I visited the Imperial several times in the early seventies and was really impressed by the place, particularly by the gleaming white exterior, little changed since 1921, apart from modern signs. (See illustration). While the Kings was being replaced the Imperial preserved Miles Jervis' cinema-presence in the town, and, unfortunately it closed on Friday 27th June 1975, the day before Kings I and II came to life.

It was purchased by the Council for demolition in

order to complete the road improvements associated with the redevelopment of the area, but I cannot help feeling that the destruction of that facade was a sad loss. *"Breakout"*, starring Charles Bronson, was the last film to flicker across that six year old screen in the fifty-four year old building.

### 5. The St. George's
*Paradise Street*

The first cinema in West Bromwich to open after the First World War was not a grand purpose-built place like Woods Palace or the Kings, Blackheath. It was a very old building, and the act of converting it to a cinema actually unearthed a box of one hundred year old coins! It may have been a Wesleyan chapel and a school somewhere in its long history, but, in 1859 it was established as the Public Hall. It served as a public meeting place until 1875 when the new Town Hall was opened, but continued to be used for occasional concerts and meetings until 1891. Then it became a wire works!

After the War a company was formed to convert it into the St. George's cinema by Mr. A. A. James. He already owned the place as a factory, and is alleged to have already had interests in at least three Birmingham cinemas. Work began at the beginning of 1920 and somehow a reasonable auditorium to seat seven hundred patrons was created in the old building. The decor was described as being in a, "rich dark Italian style", featuring hand-painted panels in "Arabesque style". A St. George and dragon motif was supplied to reflect the cinema's identity.

The St. George's opened on 26th July 1920, under the management of Harry Jordon, and with an orchestra led by Mr. Westworth. Programmes were presented in separate performances rather than continuously. Mr. James had organised a private gathering on the day before, a Sunday, in order to show the place to friends and guests. I have no information on films shown on either the Sunday or the following day.

Only one month later adverts appear in the local paper announcing a re-opening on 21st August, "Under

New Management" and that phrase was frequently repeated in its advertising. It closed altogether for four weeks in summer 1922, re-opening on 4th September with another new manager: William Singer. One of these early changes probably marks the acquisition of the St. George's by Thomas Leach, although in a Midland Chronicle report of 28th January 1944 it is claimed that Mr. Leach had owned the cinema from the start!

While owned by Tom Leach a BTP sound system was installed, (his other cinemas used the same equipment) and, along with the Queens, and the Savoy, Oldbury, it was eventually leased to J. F. Emery. Together with those cinemas it was acquired by Miles Jervis in 1946.

Miles Jervis II never lavished attention on the St. George's as he did with the Queens. Apart from using it as a place to put on a second week run of a particularly successful film, he seems to have regarded it as fairly redundant, and possibly too overshadowed by the Kings on the opposite side of the road. He did remove the BTP equipment, which he disliked, and replaced it with a G.B. Duosonic system. Perhaps it is not surprising to discover that the St. George's was an early casualty. It appears to have closed on 18th June 1955 with a Swedish film called *"Unmarried Mothers"*, advertised as "......a vital message to every young woman"!

This was not quite the end of the story. Mr. B. K. Puri persuaded Miles Jervis to allow him to use the cinema to show Indian films. It reopened on Sunday 24th September 1955 as the Krishna Cinema. A packed house watched *"The Savage Princess"* and similar shows followed for about thirteen weeks.

The last film was therefore shown at the end of 1955 but the building was not demolished until August 1962, leaving a few local legends to survive into the eighties. Several people have recalled a "chucker-out" at the St. George's who did his job in reverse. People were frightened to pass him outside the cinema as he was known to press-gang passers by into the cinema!

## 6. The Sandwell Cinema
*Sandwell Road*

At the other end of the High Street, near Carters Green, another "conversion" produced West Bromwich's second cinema to open after the First World War. An old chapel, dating from 1812, complete with graveyard, had lain derelict and unused in Sandwell Road for some time.

It appears that it was bought by a Mr. J. Hughes and converted to a cinema. An entirely new frontage was built in front of the ex-chapel and the latter was converted to an auditorium capable of accommodating nine hundred cramped patrons. The Sandwell Cinema was opened by the Mayor, on 24th August 1922 although the event does not seem to have been reported. Will Smith, from Liverpool, was the new manager.

All does not seem to have gone well, and in February 1924 Albert Smith, of West Bromwich, took control of the cinema and, with his wife's help, tried to revitalise the cinema with promotional advertising gimmicks and local premiers. His advertisements continued to appear in the Free Press until early 1925 and then all was as quiet as the graveyard adjoining the cinema. Children who had made their way through the graveyard to reach the entrance to the cheap seats grew up to tell legends of a manager absconding with cash, and cashier, but I have been unable to find out any factual information about the Sandwell's demise.

For another quarter of a century the building remained derelict again, served a short life as a Council store and was then demolished in the mid fifties.

121. The Sandwell Cinema: a drawing by Tony Wright based on a poor photograph of the building taken long after its demise as a cinema.

## 7. The Empire (later known as The Plaza, the Kings and the new Kings)

*Paradise Street*

Just before the First World War Benjamin Kennedy set out to provide West Bromwich with a first class purpose-built theatre, in the town centre. The Olympia, at Carters Green, was too far from that centre and presumably not really grand enough. Plans were drawn by Messrs. Wood and Kenrick and the £10,000 theatre was built by Messrs. Dallow and Sons. The Empire opened, as a theatre holding 1800 patrons, on Whit Monday in June 1914.

The reason that it appears here, between the details of the Sandwell and the Tower, is that its life as a cinema did not begin until 1927. In that year it was leased to C.D. Cinemas, the partnership between Mortimer Dent and Joseph Cohen. They reopened it as the Plaza Super Cinema on 26th September 1927. Then, and for the whole week, the Plaza presented *"Love Me and the World Is Mine"*, with Jesse Hackett singing the title song and Mr. Grainger leading the new orchestra.

The claim to be a "super cinema" was justified as the place had been redecorated and re-seated with eleven hundred plush tip up seats. As with many theatre-conversions the operating room was very high and the screen had to be tilted, but the theatrical atmosphere became a very positive quality at the Plaza, and later the Kings.

122. The Kings, 4th March 1973, shortly before closure, demolition and replacement with a brand new cinema.

*(Photo: Terry Cresswell, C.T.A.)*

By 1929 C.D. Cinemas had sold out to the A.B.C. circuit and the new lessees were glad to acquire a position in West Bromwich. They installed BTH sound equipment and ran the Plaza until they were able to acquire The Tower at Carters Green. With A.B.C.'s departure in 1936, the lease reverted to Ben Kennedy just at the time he was preparing to open his own brand new Plaza in Dudley.

Ben Kennedy continued to use the Plaza as a cinema but was surrounded by competition from the surrounding four cinemas, let alone the Tower.

After the War the Plaza returned to its former way of life as a theatre. In the post-War era that was not an easy option and the place declined. Like the Hippodrome, Dudley, and Royal, Bilston, the Plaza found that *"Strip, Strip Ahoy!"* (a navel revue!) and the *"Phyllis Dixie Show"* attracted some patrons but led many others to "write off" the place completely. It was rumoured that the Clifton Circuit may have been interested in acquiring the Plaza, but Miles Jervis II beat them to it.

The grand final show, as a theatre, was presented on 2nd February 1957. It was called, *"Thanks For The Memory"* starring Hetty King, Randolph Sutton and Billy Danvers, a fitting farewell tribute to "Variety". Miles Jervis then started work on the theatre's second conversion to a cinema. He rebuilt the projection room and equipped the theatre for cinemascope. He re-seated the stalls, redecorated, and gave the exterior of the building a facelift. A modern canopy was erected and, after much correspondence with the Council Planning Department, the facade was transformed at night with a flood of neon lighting, by Claudgen Neon Signs.

It opened again, this time as the Kings, to complement the Queens, on Monday 11th March 1957. *"Between Heaven and Hell"* was presented in Cinemascope, and its future as a cinema seemed bright. As stated above, the theatrical atmosphere served to heighten the experience of visiting the Kings and my memories of the place seem bathed in bright red and gold even in the mid sixties when other converted theatres, like the Clifton, Wolverhampton, seemed much the worse for wear. Local amateur operatic society shows were performed at the Kings so the stage did still see very occasional use.

When substantial redevelopment threatened the Kings, only Miles Jervis III's determination to continue in the cinema business saved the day. Unfortunately the original Kings had to go, but the hard fought battle to make sure there would be a replacement was won. The Kings was expected to close on 10th March 1973, but its life was extended to 28th April when it finally closed with *"The Aristocrats"* and *"The Legend of Young Dick Turpin"*. As patrons we were re-directed to the amazing revived Imperial, while the Kings was demolished and construction of its successor began

**EXCITING ANNOUNCEMENT!
OPENING SATURDAY, 28th JUNE
'KINGS' No. 1 and No. 2 CINEMAS
(KINGS THREE TO OPEN SHORTLY)**

The new Kings was to be a purpose-built triple screened cinema, the only entirely new cinema to be built in the Black Country since the War. It was designed by Keith Davidson and Partners and is as plain as the Imperial and old Kings were ornate. It was built by Costain Construction Ltd., of Coventry and the interior decor was by Modernisation Ltd.

On 28th June 1975 the first two screens were opened. Kings I, with 320 seats, presented *"Shampoo"*, and Kings II with 280 seats presented *"The Yaguza"*. Kings III, the largest auditorium, with 442 seats, opened on 20th July 1975 with *"The Godfather, Part 2"*. Rank Audio Visual supplied new Cinemeccanica equipment, and as before, renewal and innovation have seen technical modifications made in the last seven years. Recently large horizontal platters have been installed in the operating rooms to bring the Kings right up-to-date.

The new screens opened during a heatwave and business was slack, but matters improved and the Kings can be recommended if you like to see your films in a well patronised cinema. It can also be recommended for the advantages of seeing films in purpose-built auditoria. (Not a "botched conversion" beneath the balcony of a fifty year old "super"). It boasts a bar with colour television! And programming that often provides the Black Country with its only genuine variety and choice. Long may it continue to do so.

## 8. The Tower
### (later known as the ABC)
*Carters Green*

The Tower, or "the Bloody Tower", as it was known to its rivals, was a super cinema in a class of its own. It still dominates the street scene at Carters Green, where the clock tower itself had once dominated a major Black Country tramway junction, although, at present, the building is dilapidated and out of use.

The Tower was promoted by, and built for, West Bromwich Cinemas Ltd. The directors were V. Olliver, who already had strong connections with the town as a result of managing the Palace and the Imperial, W. H. Onions, a Birmingham cinema entrepreneur also connected with the Warley Cinema and the Clifton, Stone Cross, and Mr. and Mrs. C. O. Brettell. The Brettells, and Mr. Olliver had established the Birmingham based "Piccadilly Circuit" and ran the Piccadilly itself in Sparkbrook, the New Palladium, Hockley, the New Imperial, Moseley Road and, in the Black Country; the Picturedrome at Darlaston. Later they built the Regal, Darlaston.

They engaged Harry Weedon to design their new super-cinema and Cecil Clavering imposed the style on it that he had helped Harry Weedon develop for the Odeon cinemas. It seems that Oscar Deutsch may have considered joining the venture but appears to have disliked the location. Therefore, despite its appearance, it never had anything to do with the Odeons.

The site was not cleared until May 1935 and the huge cinema was built very quickly, completed by J. R. Deacon Ltd., in seven months. It had originally been conceived as a 1560 seater, but extra land became available just before construction began and it was enlarged to hold 2000, 750 of which were accommodated

in the circle. Due to the simplicity of its design, it is its size that made it so imposing. The huge facade was treated in biscuit coloured faience, above a base of black faience tiles. Four small pillars dividing the flight of steps that extended across the entire frontage were similarly treated, as can be seen in the photograph. They originally supported little shrubs! Above the balcony lounge windows the name sign provided essential relief to the huge area of faience. Without it the building has looked rather bare and ugly. A huge foyer, elegant stair-cases, a cafe in the balcony lounge, all impressed the patron long before he or she entered the auditorium which was bathed in blue and gold. All the fibrous plasterwork was in the Modern style and concealed lighting was cleverly employed.

In the centre of the "orchestra pit" was the illuminated console of the three-manual, ten unit, Compton organ, mounted on a lift. The organ itself was in a basement beneath the stage. Up in the operating suite Kalee projectors were installed, and sound was by Western Electric. The owners felt it was better equipped and more genuinely sumptuous than the Odeons. Charlie Kettle was appointed as manager, and Leslie Taff was appointed organist, coming to the Tower from the Gaumont, Birmingham.

It might be expected that such a magnificent super-cinema would be given a civic opening but Mr. Olliver and the Brettells did not seem to go in for such things, although a lavish souvenir brochure of the Tower's opening was produced. Business commenced at 6 p.m. on Monday 9th December 1935. A Laurel and Hardy short, a Walt Disney Cartoon, and Gaumont British News started the programme. Then Leslie Taff rose into the spotlight on the illuminated console of the organ. The organ had on "Electrone" attachment, and the audience was told,

"With it sounds of unprecedented and surpassing beauty, which have never previously been heard by the human ear may be created."

The main feature was that magnificent Hitchcock film, *"The 39 Steps"*, starring Robert Donat and Madeleine Carroll.

The Tower's independence did not last long. A.B.C., who had cultivated a presence in the town at the Plaza, bought out the directors in the following year, and gradually installed their own staff. As part of a major circuit it had the advantage of visits by film-stars, expensive and elaborate promotions and publicity campaigns, and its size and grandeur no doubt gave it some importance on the circuit but I have often wondered if A.B.C. found being in Carters Green was not quite the same thing as being in the centre of West Bromwich. People from Oldbury and Wednesbury have told me that they visited the Tower when they wanted to go somewhere "posh", but less people in West Bromwich have mentioned it!

From War-time onwards its history consisted of anniversaries, at least one of which was celebrated with a huge cake that was an accurate model of the cinema, and details like the inauguration of the A.B.C. Minors' Club in June 1946. Among the stars that come to the Tower were Old Mother Riley, who came on 17th May 1952, and Richard Attenborough who came along on 3rd April 1948 to promote *"Brighton Rock"*.

In March 1951 RCA High Fidelity Sound was installed. Ten years later, in July 1961, it dropped its name, the Tower, and simply became the ABC. I visited it once, in the mid-sixties, to see *"Morgan, A Suitable Case for Treatment"* but I am ashamed to admit that the building made no impression upon me. By then the organ had gone. A farewell concert had been held on 14th November 1965. Leslie Taff returned to play on it, plus Mel Edwards, but it is believed that Trevor Bolshaw played it for the last time before it sank back into the pit. It was bought by Arthur Large, who unfortunately died soon afterwards, but the organ has been restored and is now to be found at Marston Green Hospital.

The Tower/ABC closed on 28th December 1968, with *"Hot Millions"*, starring Peter Ustinov. It reopened as an EMI Bingo and Social Club on 18th January 1969. As the seventies have progressed its exterior has grown increasingly shabby and the Bingo Club has now closed. The entrances are boarded-up and the faience is cracking. Once again the clock tower is the smartest feature of Carters Green.

124. The Hill Top Cinema, being used as an Agricultural Division store by the Dart Spring Company, shortly before demolition. Note the bulldozer arriving on the left!

*(Photo: May Siviter)*

## Outer West Bromwich

### 9. The Hill Top Picture House
### (also known as the Rex)
*Hill Top*

The Tower, at Carters Green, represents the northern boundary of central West Bromwich. From there Telford's road made its way through small villages that have since become industrialised but their names still stir the imagination: Swan Village, Guns Village, Black Lake and Hill Top. The latter's name is self explanatory, and from the crest of the hill good views are obtained of Wednesbury. Despite the view, Hill Top belongs to West Bromwich.

Two West Bromwich men, Messrs. Bellingham and Jackson, formed a company, with the intention of bringing the cinematograph to the village community of Hill Top. It was no hurried conversion, but a proper purpose-built 750-seater cinema. It was designed by Howard Tipler and was certainly unique in style and appearance! The frontage was finished in a strong red terracotta brick, with a tunnel-like arch round the main entrance, flanked by shops. For many years the words, "The Regal Academy of Reel Art" were inscribed on the surface of this arch. The interior decor was originally carried out in chocolate and gold. It was equipped with a "Reflecta" screen and Motiograph projectors. It cost about £20,000.

It was opened on Wednesday 27th July 1921, six months later than intended. The first manager was Vincent Hopcroft, who had managed cinemas in Leicester and Merthyr. At the opening there was a full orchestra but subsequently the accompaniment was provided by a piano alone for several years.

# PLAZA SUPER CINEMA

### (Late EMPIRE),
## WEST BROMWICH.

GRAND OPENING MONDAY, SEPTEMBER 26th, at 2.30.
CONTINUOUS from 2.30 to 10.30.

### ALL THE WEEK.

*First presentation of one of the biggest Screen Masterpieces of the year based on the popular Song-Ballad :*

## LOVE ME AND THE WORLD IS MINE.

Never in the history of filmdom has such a stupendous cast of players been assembled in one production, including
MARY PHILBIN, HENRY B. WALTHALL, NORMAN KERRY, BETTY COMPSON.

| | |
|---|---|
| **Monday, Tuesday & Wednesday.** Also on the same programme the first Chinese production, shown by special request to Her Majesty Queen Mary, **THE LEGEND OF THE WILLOW PATTERN PLATE.** | **Thursday, Friday and Saturday.** Also on the same programme **MANAN LESCAUT** adapted from the well-known play starring LYA DE PUTTI. |

MR. JESSE HACKETT will sing the Ballad, "LOVE ME AND THE WORLD IS MINE."
**HEAR GRAINGER and his SELECTED ORCHESTRA.**

# HILL TOP PICTURE HOUSE,
### WEST BROMWICH.

## GRAND OPENING, WEDNESDAY, JULY 27th,
### 5.30 p.m. to 10.30 p.m.

### The Only Hall of its kind in the Midlands.

**PERFECT PROJECTION combined with COOLNESS, CLEANLINESS and PERFECT CONTENTMENT.**

# HILL TOP PICTURE HOUSE

Trams to Wednesbury stop near the doors.
Circular Route and Stone Cross-Hill Top 'Buses stop at the doors on request.

### Re-opening after Renovations, Monday next, Jan. 2nd.

Under the entirely New Management of the Lessees, the Reel Academy, Ltd.
Directors: His Worship the Mayor (Coun. H. Bellingham) & S. Jackson, Esq.
Manager: Councillor A. Guest.

**Monday, Jan. 2nd, for Three Days:—EMLYN WILLIAMS in**

## DEAD MEN TELL NO TALES.
Also FULL SUPPORTING PROGRAMME.

**Thursday, Jan. 5th, for Three Days:—CHARLES LAUGHTON in**

## VESSELS OF WRATH.
Also FULL SUPPORTING PROGRAMME.

Matinees Mondays and Thursdays at 2.30. Evenings Continuous from 6.
Children's Saturday Matinees at 2.30.
THE FAMILY HOUSE AT THE TOP OF THE HILL.

| Imperial Picture House | The Palace Cinema |
|---|---|
| **WEST BROMWICH.** | **WEST BROMWICH.** |
| **Week Commencing January 2nd:** FOR SIX DAYS. **THE CRAZY GANG IN A MAGICAL COMEDY.** NERVO & KNOX. FLANAGAN & ALLEN NAUGHTON & GOLD. ALASTAIR SIM — IN — **ALF'S BUTTON AFLOAT** (U) THE WHOLE SHOW IS A RIOT. YOU'RE GOING TO LAUGH PLENTY WHEN YOU SEE IT. ALSO FULL SUPPORTING PROGRAMME. | **Week Commencing January 2nd:** Double Feature Programme FOR SIX DAYS: **BREAK THE NEWS** Featuring **JACK BUCHANAN, MAURICE CHEVALIER, JUNE KNIGHT.** A Picture with hectic action, Drama and Comedy. **WILL HAY In—** **GOOD MORNING BOYS** (A) |

Advertisements that tell the story of West Bromwich's cinemas: The Empire becomes the Plaza, the Hill Top Picture House opens and re-opens, and the Imperial and Palace shared a column while both were owned by Griffin Cinemas — superlatives are found for every occasion and the Plaza even invents a new word: "filmdom"!

How long Vincent Hopcroft stayed is not clear, as the owners soon leased the cinema to Tom Leach. For most of the first half of its life it was managed by Joe Robbins, believed to be Tom Leach's brother-in-law. (He had previously managed the Queens for Tom Leach).

A picture of the Hill Top cinema in those days was given to me by Bill Priest:

"On entering was the pay box, on each side were steps leading to the 9d and 6d seats. The 4d seats were reached by a passage-way that came out half way down the hall. The cheap seats were wooden benches in three rows with two central gangways, but the "posh" seats were ordinary tip-ups. It was a single storey building with no balcony.

At one time my three aunts; Kate, Dolly and May Cooper had taken the tickets, which I also did for a spell. We were paid 9d a night and 6d for a matinee, and most weeks we had to ask for our wages. The orchestra was just a piano until one Saturday night it was announced that the Bijou Orchestra would be an added attraction. This consisted of piano, violin and drums. On Monday nights the back row of the wooden benches was where the young mothers brought their babies, and out would come their breasts to feed them. Some thought they were shameless hussies but I didn't think so.

As I write I can still smell the tang of orange peel and the scent of those atomizer sprays, and can still recall the flickering gas jets. When the flame went down the fans were turned on to clear the air. Things got bad towards the end of the silent era. I remember seeing "The Lash of the Law" when there were only two of us paying customers in the 4d seats.

However, finally the cinema was converted to BTH sound and from then on we saw mainly Paramount films".

Poverty-row "B" westerns and strong melodramas were successful at little cinemas like the one at Hill Top. The stars of these films are still loved and remembered by patrons like Bill Priest, half a century later.

Tom Leach seems to have ended his lease on the Hill Top Cinema at the end of 1938. It then closed for renovations and re-opened on 2nd January 1939. The original owners appear to have formed a new company, the Reel Academy Ltd., to run the cinema. H. Bellingham was now the Mayor of West Bromwich, and a fellow councillor, A. Guest, became the new manager. The re-opening was therefore performed by the Mayor, or the proprietor, depending on which role Councillor Bellingham saw himself taking. Just to confuse everybody he also assumed the role of an attendant and, grabbing a torch, escorted several patrons to their seats.

The cinema now aspired to greater respectability and advertised itself as "The Family House at the top of the hill". Male attendants were replaced by female usherettes dressed in attractive light blue uniforms with beige facings. Some time after this it began calling itself the Rex, although exactly when is not clear. It was certainly known by that name in 1944 when it was purchased by Arthur Griffin. He formed a separate company, Arthur Griffin Ltd., to run the Rex rather than incorporate it with Griffin Cinemas Ltd. As soon after the War as

possible he put up a neon sign saying "Rex".

It was successful for a time but audiences declined quickly in the mid fifties and it operated for two or three years at a loss. It appears to have survived until December 1960 when it probably closed with "The Vikings". It seems impossible to be more precise about this. The building was sold to the Dart Spring Company for use as a stores. The rather bizarre building stood for at least another fifteen years. About 1976 it was sold to David Siviter of Dudley Street Motors Ltd., and was demolished to make way for an extension to his premises.

## 10. The Clifton
*Stone Cross*

Stone Cross, between West Bromwich and Walsall, rapidly developed between the Wars as a surburban residential area. It seems that W. H. Onions, having been "bought-out" by A.B.C. at the Tower, Carters Green, came to the area in search of a site for a new modern super-cinema. He was joined by Captain Clift, who became the company's chairman for a time, by Ernest Roberts, who was to design the cinema, and Edgar Summers, previously encountered at the Rosum at Walsall.

An old smithy that previously occupied the site was demolished and Messrs. J. and F. Wootton constructed the new super-cinema using the established methods exploiting a steel super-structure and concrete. The auditorium was capable of holding 896 patrons in the stalls and 306 in the balcony, in green upholstered tip-up seats. The modern plasterwork was finished in pastel shades of silver, pink and orange. Like other Cliftons, it used BTH equipment. The exterior of the auditorium was finished in red brick and, due to its position on a small hill, its massive presence can be seen from afar. The entrance and crush hall were greatly extended from the auditorium and had their own striking curved facade, adjacent to some shops.

The Clifton was opened on Saturday 16th July 1938, with a special one night showing of "Whoopee" starring Eddie Cantor. The opening ceremony was performed by the British film actress, Miss Valerie Hobson. She was given a film-star's reception by crowds outside the new cinema and by the capacity audience within. Her latest film, "The Drum" was to be shown at the Clifton shortly. Regular three-day programmes began the following Monday with "Return of the Scarlet Pimpernel".

The manager, when the cinema opened, was Philip Cleife, and the chief operator was Jimmy Edwards. The latter stayed at the Clifton for almost its entire life. Like other suburban Cliftons it had a fairly short and uneventful life but there were several slight changes in its ownership. At some stage W. H. Onions ran the Clifton independently of the Clifton Circuit, that is, without the services of Cinema Accessories Ltd., and it was managed for him by Ernest Highland.

The Clifton had one dressing room and an 18 feet by 40 feet stage but the only record I have found of this being used was during March 1958 when amateur variety acts were supplementing the films. Perhaps this was a sign of the times! The following year when

Mr. Onions was objecting to his rate assessment he publicly complained that his cinema often had to wait six months to screen popular films, by which time they had been seen in West Bromwich, Wednesbury and Walsall. An independent exhibitor starved of films, losing patrons, and isolated in the suburbs faced many problems.

Eventually the Clifton was brought back under the wing of the "circuit", now administered by Theatre Administration, but its days were numbered. Bingo was introduced on Thursday nights, surrounded by three programme changes per week. Occasional Sunday morning shows of Indian films were presented by Tarsem Singh Dhami and his colleagues.

The closure came on Saturday 7th March 1964, with *Doctor No*, starring Sean Connery in the part of James Bond. Regular sessions of Bingo commenced the following Tuesday, run by Harry Whitehouse, of the Lyttleton and Avion. During this period, 1964 – 1968, Tarsem Singh Dhami's Indian film shows were presented more regularly on Sundays.

In 1968 the Clifton was acquired by Ladbrokes, and they are still operating the Bingo and Social Club there at the time of writing. It is a very smart club indeed and much of the decor of the cinema is extremely well preserved. The shaded plaster band round the balcony and extending to the very rectangular ante-proscenium is still a feature of the decor, as is the concealed lighting system above the site of the rear stalls, housed along the main balcony girder. The 1930's murals have vanished from the crush hall but the place is still worth a visit.

## Oldbury

Oldbury's relationship to West Bromwich, reminds me of Bilston's relationship to Wolverhampton. It was the little "urban district" next door, very heavily industrialised, but without the civic history to be able to compete with its larger neighbour. Places like Oldbury and Bilston became boroughs in the thirties and were inevitably swept aside in later local government re-organisation. Yet as a child growing up in London I had heard of Oldbury long before I had heard of West Bromwich thanks to Accles and Pollock's memorable advertising on the tube trains!

From the New Road Oldbury seems to be totally dominated by the tube works, chemical works and the engineering industry, but somewhere among the factories enough people lived to support several local cinemas despite the fact that the major circuits ignored the place!

Recalling life in Oldbury before the War a local resident explained that the Palace was the town's best cinema, or, at least, the most respectable. The Picture House was dark, menaced by cobwebs and never seemed clean, but it was cheaper and you could make as much noise as you liked! On Saturday nights Mother and Father would make for their regular seats at the Regent, Langley, making sure they arrived in good time, but a teenage girl in Oldbury would live in the hope that a young man would materialise and say, "Meet you outside the Tower!".

125. The Stone Cross Clifton in use as a Bingo & Social Club in 1981.

*(Photo: Ned Williams)*

206

126. The Palace as a Bingo & Social Club.
*(Photo: Chris Clegg)*

## 11. The Palace
*Freeth Street*

Oldbury has returned to life in recent times with the building of the Savacentre. (So called because it has saved the centre of Oldbury?) The new development obscures the site of Oldbury's first cinema: The Palace.

The story begins at The White Swan, popularly known as "The Museum", in Church Street. In 1910 the licensee was Jas Tyrer and Music Hall entertainment had long been provided at the White Swan. He applied to make alterations to the building in order to show films, but before doing so he acquired a seven year lease on the premises in Freeth Street. (For subsequent events in Church Street; see "The Grand").

Now established in Freeth Street, Jas Tyrer spent £350 converting the new premises into a cinema. The conversion was designed by G. Bowden, of Smethwick, and was carried out by H. Banner. The Palace opened, a week later than intended, on Monday 7th November 1910, with a programme that included *"Lady Helen's Escapade"* and *"Fun on the Tom-Tom"*. It was managed by the proprietor's son, Billy Tyrer, later to manage the Cosy Corner, Halesowen, and various Odeons, including the one in Bilston.

A cryptic report appears in the Weekly News for 14th September 1912: Jas Tyrer denies that his cinema is to close and assures everybody that he now has a fourteen year lease. He then adds, "I have recently taken over similar places of amusement at Dudley Port and Pensnett". The former refers to the Alhambra during a chequered period of its early history, but the latter is a great mystery. (See Mysteries of Brierley Hill). It also marks the beginning of a confusing period of this cinema's history.

In 1913 it appears to have been operating as the Cosy Picture Palace. By 1915 it was "Tyrer's Palace" and the proprietor was Mrs. Tyrer. On 17th April 1916 it re-opened as the Premier Kinema, having been reconstructed for a Mr. G. H. Gosling. It seems that a balcony was put in at this time, with accommodation for 85, and 345 tip-up seats were installed downstairs. The work was carried out by a Mr. Bailey, and the Premier Kinema opened with *"Whom the Gods Would Destroy"*.

It closed yet again in 1917 and reopened on 13th August 1917 as the Palace Theatre, with *"East is East"*. Some continuity is implied by the fact that the proprietors were Premier Cinemas Ltd. By the end of the year another change had taken place and it became the Palace of Varieties, controlled by Joe Day.

After all these changes some stability was restored towards the end of 1919 when it was acquired by Charles H. Dent. Eventually he replaced the original building by erecting a brand new cinema behind it. This was a much larger hall, capable of holding just over a thousand patrons, and had basic stage facilities incorporated in its design. I have not discovered who was the architect but it seems that the builder was William Jackson.

The "New Palace", opened on Easter Monday, 9th April 1928, with *"The Phantom of the Circus"*. It was managed by C. H. Dent's son, John Marshall Dent. The following year the new cinema brought the talkies to Oldbury on 9th December 1929 with *"The Trial of Mary Dugan"*. The better known *"Broadway Melody"* ran for the second half of the week. BTP equipment was used.

Having extended his cinema interests to the Black Country it seems that Mr. Dent looked around for further possibilities of expansion. In 1933 Mr. Hurley Robinson produced some plans for him for a cinema in Warley but the scheme was dropped when the Warley Cinema materialised. However, in the spring of 1935 it became possible to acquire the Regent at Langley, and from then on John Marshall Dent ran both cinemas. Mr. Dent retained an interest in live "Variety" and sometimes the cinema insisted on being called "The Palace of Varieties".

When film business declined Variety still seemed an alternative. The Palace closed on Sunday 30th April 1961 with a one day showing of *"The Private War of Major Benson"*, starring Charlton Heston. The adverts claimed that it was closed for, "Repairs and Renovations". It reopened later as the Palace Variety Club but gradually forsook Variety for Bingo. In the early seventies it was acquired by the Noble Organisation, who continued to run it as a Bingo Club for a few years until it was demolished. For a while it had dominated the devastated approach to Oldbury from Brades Village and then it seemed to vanish overnight.

## 12. The Picture House
### (later known as the Savoy)
*Birmingham Street*

Following Mr. Tyrer's success in bringing the cinema to Oldbury, others tried to emulate his example. In the Spring of 1911 Alfred Griffiths applied for a licence to show films at the Portway Hall, the matter was adjourned and presumably failed. Albert Bradley acquired the Market Hall next to the canal bridge in Birmingham Street and was granted a licence to show films there at the end of April.

Using the name, Picturedrome, the ex-Market Hall appears to have opened as a cinema on 1st May 1911. Jas Tyrer had opposed both licence applications, but from now on he had to accept competition. Such a state of affairs may not have lasted very long as the Picturedrome ceased advertising in July. It appears to have closed in order to be rebuilt to make it more like a cinema. Messrs. Harper and Sons carried out the work

and by the time they had finished it could hold 400 patrons.

It reopened as the Picture House on 25th November 1911. A Mr. Sam Leonard came from Lancashire to run the place, but it is not clear for whom! The anonymity of the new undertaking suggests that possibly Thomas Leach had acquired it, the Picture House was certainly his by the First World War. Sam Leonard continued to present the twice nightly shows of *"Animated Pictures & Comedy Acts"* for a time but Mr. A. Robbins, another of Mr. Leach's brothers-in-law eventually replaced him.

During the mid-twenties the Picture House was entirely rebuilt to the plans of Mr. Way Lovegrove. He produced a building of relatively considerable height in order to accommodate more than one thousand patrons on a fairly small site. Miles Jervis II later complained that the seats were extremely close together and even a person of average height was forced to squeeze into his seat sideways. Even the operators worked in cramped conditions. Wilf Hollyhead recalls working there in a tiny room barely six and a half feet high and lacking adequate ventilation. Despite all its faults, the facade was quite impressive as can be seen from the illustration.

The "new" Picture House opened in 1926, three years before the "new" Palace. When the latter installed BTP sound equipment the Picture House did the same thing, introducing talkies on 27th January 1930. Towards the end of the thirties it was leased to F. J. Emery and generally seemed run-down compared with the Palace. On becoming part of F. J. Emery's circuit it seems to have become the Savoy.

In 1946 Miles Jervis acquired the freehold, and then the lease. He had few illusions about the Savoy and was not particularly impressed with Oldbury as a town in which to show films. Miles Jervis found that the auditorium was so lofty that it was impossible to keep warm and the acoustics were terrible. He installed BA equipment and added extra speakers including special dimensional speakers to face the balcony but to no avail.

Perhaps it is not surprising that the Savoy closed on 22nd March 1958, by which time Miles Jervis was much committed to West Bromwich. Jack Palance starred in *"I Died A Thousand Times"* on the final night, but the first half of the last week had paid tribute to cinema

127. The Picture House as rebuilt for Tom Leach.

*(Photo: Collection of Chris Clegg)*

history with a revival of *"Gone With The Wind"*. After the cinema had closed a notice appeared on the entrance doors exclaiming:

"Closed — At least until the result of the budget is known".

The budget produced a small cut in entertainment tax but apparently it was not enough to persuade Miles Jervis to reopen a cinema for which he had no particular liking!

The Savoy was sold to the Midland Electricity Board but a decade later people were complaining that it had ceased to be used and was becoming an eyesore. It seems that Warley Council purchased it towards the end of the sixties and it was demolished in May 1970.

## 13. The Grand
*Church Street*

Oldbury's least known cinema was to be found next-door to the White Swan in Church Street. (The pub still exists at the time of writing). As explained in the chapter on the Palace, Jas Tyrer had managed the White Swan during the first decade of this century and the place had incorporated a "music hall" for some time. In 1912 the Wolverhampton And Dudley Breweries Ltd., proposed separating the entertainment facilities from the public house by building a purpose-built hall alongside it. Plans were produced by Frank Jones.

On 17th December 1912 Ben Kennedy applied for a music and singing licence for the hall and it was granted. Presumably as soon as possible after that date he opened the hall, calling it "The Tivoli". It seems to have become

the Grand when it was reopened on 15th February 1915 by a Mr. W. H. Vaughan. He included films between the variety acts and claimed, "Our aim is respectability". I am not sure whether this deterred patrons or attracted them, but Mr. Vaughan had intended the latter and had gone to some trouble to refurbish the hall and decorate it in the flags of the allies. Mr. Vaughan ran the Grand until the early twenties.

In 1923 the proprietors had become Messrs. Redfern and Stoddard. They owned a Birmingham typewriter firm but ran cinemas as a sideline. They had one in Coventry, and, for a time, one in Willenhall. By a twist of fate the Grand was managed for them by Jas Tyrer until February 1924. The Grand carried on until at least 1926. No-one seems sure when it closed, or ceased showing films, but it seems to have well and truly faded from the Oldbury scene by the time the talkies arrived in 1929.

## Langley

Langley sits above the Eastern Boundary Fault, where the Ten Yard Seam suddenly drops to a depth beneath the surface that originally put it out of reach. To the southeast of this fault towns like Smethwick are not part of the Black Country according to the geological definition! Langley grew rapidly after the building of the Titford Canal and the opening of the Langley Forge. The Forge premises, the Canal and other interesting buildings, like the Maltings, still exist but the area has been transformed many times. When I first encountered the Regent cinema it stood almost alone in Crosswells Road as if Langley had been mysteriously removed from around it.

## 14. The Langley Palace

The first cinema in Langley was the result of an early venture by Sidney Bray. Films were shown in the hall of the Langley Institute, which had been built as a Temperance Hall in 1875. The shows may have started as early as 1910, and legends tell of films being made featuring local people and being shown at the Institute Hall. All the facts seem obscure but it seems certain that from 1913 onwards Wally Davis was running the place for his brother-in-law. It seems likely that he returned after the First World War and may have presented films in Langley until taking control of the Palace, Brownhills, in 1924.

The Institute Hall then seems to have been taken over by Mrs. B. L. Clamp, and the kine licence was renewed in her name up until 1931. I am not even certain when it was first called "the Palace". The earliest advertisements I have seen using that name date from summer 1927.

The Palace was still showing films three nights a week in December 1930 and had apparently experimented with "sound-on-disc", but seems to have admitted defeat with the coming of the sound era. For some reason it was known locally as, "The Snob" and one legend that still survives in Langley concerns the female "one-man-band" that accompanied the films for a time. Apparently she played six instruments at once — better than a "Bijou Orchestra"!

## 15. The Regent
### (later known as the Astra and the Milan)
*Crosswells Road*

After the First World War the Langley Cinema Company was formed to provide the community with a proper purpose-built picture house. Among the directors were Dr. Broughton, a leading local public figure and member of Worcestershire County Council, William Jackson, who was about to build the cinema, and Abel Round, a Birmingham architect who designed it, and Edward Bayliss.

Dr. Broughton performed the official opening at a ceremony held on 26th January 1920, and the first film was, *"Out of the Shadows"*. It seems that William Jackson, the builder, had made the major contribution towards creating the cinema by actually building it and was probably paid in shares, thereby taking control of the cinema and the company. It was known simply as "The Langley Cinema".

It did its best to keep up with the Oldbury cinemas even when they were renewed as the twenties went on. The talkies arrived in Langley four months after coming to the Picture House. *"The Rainbow Man"* opened on 7th April 1930.

Perhaps the success of the talkies convinced William Jackson that the cinema business had sufficient future to make it worth rebuilding the Langley Cinema on a grander scale. It closed on 27th May 1933 with *"After the Ball"* and rebuilding started straight away. The original balcony was enlarged, a new ceiling supplied, a new loung and cafe put in, and a new impressive frontage was erected. This has looked austere in recent years but in 1933 was relieved by an elegant canopy and by the cinema's new name across the top of the facade. Obviously the work was done by William Jackson, and proceeded very quickly.

Thus renewed, the auditorium could hold 1200 patrons and was internally decorated in rich cream and pale green. New sound equipment by British Acoustic was installed, and Langley now had a cinema that could easily compare with the two rivals in Oldbury. From now on it was to be called "The Regent".

The Regent opened at 3 p.m. on 4th September 1933. William Jackson welcomed everybody from the stage, accompanied by Edward Bayliss and F. S. Sandover, the General Manager. Mr. Sandover later left the Regent to take over the West End, Whitmore Reans. Mr. Jackson regretted that Dr. Broughton could not be present, and declared the cinema open. The first programme featured *"Just My Luck"*, starring Ralph Lynn.

128. The Regent, Langley, in 1980.
*(Photo: Ned Williams)*

Barely two years later, in April 1935, the Regent was acquired by Mr. Dent and therefore joined forces with one of its Oldbury rivals; the Palace. From then on it seems to have survived successfully and uneventfully until circumstances changed almost thirty years later. Its first closure came on 14th August 1965, when "I've Got A Horse", starring Billy Fury, was shown, supported by "Carry On Teacher".

From that date onwards its history is as obscure and as complicated as that of any tiny pre-First World War cinema. Charles Dent's son, John Marshall Dent, first converted the Regent into a Variety Club and began for a week's trial run in that capacity at the beginning of November 1965. Over the next four years it opened and closed as a Variety Club several times.

In the end Mr. Dent seems to have decided that business was better as a cinema. New luxury seating was intalled, a new wide screen and stereo sound. On 19th July 1969 it reopened as the Astra, with "The Magnificent Seven". It must have closed yet again because on 30th July 1970 it had a further reopening. This time it was decided to abandon the family audience and provide "adult films" on a club basis. Mr. Dent told the local paper that he thought the Astra would replace the late Prince's, Smethwick!

Mr. J. M. Dent died later in 1970 and the Palace and the Regent/Astra had to be sold. Tarsem Singh Dhami considered purchasing it but decided not to. It was eventually bought by Mr. Gupta, best known in the Black Country as a garage proprietor, but the story is still far from simple as he then leased it to a number of people.

On 3rd November 1973 it reopened at 10 a.m. to present a children's matinee featuring "Submarine X—1" and "Thunderbirds 6". Then all was quiet until the next day, Sunday, when "A Clockwork Orange" hit the screen. Once again it had been re-seated and redecorated, only holding 650 patrons, and Kalee 21 projectors were installed, having previously been in the Dale. We visited it early in 1974 and were very impressed with its bright cleanliness, the personal courtesy of the staff and its determination to survive. One surprise was that it was now calling itself the Regent once again! Surrounded by a demolished Langley, the staff told us that they hoped Brummies would drive out to the Regent to catch up with popular films they might have missed in the city.

The last English-language film was probably shown in February 1976. It then adopted the name, the Milan, and enjoyed some success in presenting Indian films. In fact Binesh Patel, one of the lessees, was "overwhelmed" by the Milan's success. In February 1978 the Milan was ordered to close by the Sandwell Health Department until various improvements were made. It seems that the problems were overcome and that films continued to be shown until the end of 1979 or beginning of 1980.

In March 1980 the Council approved an application to turn the cinema into a clothing factory from Mr. M. Lall. When I started work on this book a month later the work on conversion had started and I do not think there will be any more re-openings in Langley.

## Smethwick

I have already cast doubts on any claim that Smethwick might belong to the Black Country, but as it was definitely part of South Staffordshire, as distinct from Birmingham, I think we can overlook the fact that the ten yard coal seam does not lie just beneath its surface. If people wish to include Telford's Galton Bridge in their Wonders of the Black Country, who am I to exclude Smethwick's cinemas?

Cinemas, and theatres, in Smethwick became synonymous with Edward Hewitson and his sons. However, the very first purpose-built cinema in the town was provided by Irving Bosco. For a time the Hewitsons and the Bosco-Baintons were next-door neighbours in Smethwick. Good neighbours might prefer their cinemas to be dealt with separately rather than from an overall chronological point of view. Therefore this section is divided into four sections: the cinemas of Edward Hewitson, the cinemas of Irving Bosco, the two "other" cinemas of Smethwick, and finally the two cinemas on the Birmingham border.

## The Cinemas of Edward Hewitson:

### 16. The Town Hall: Pictureland.

Following the passing of the Cinematograph Act at the end of 1909 most towns witnessed some hurried opening of cinemas. In Smethwick matters proceeded more slowly. Edward Hewitson was manager of the Theatre Royal in Rolfe Street at the time and may have experimented with showing films there in Variety shows, or as late evening special events.

By the end of 1911 it seems that he had decided that showing films was a viable proposition. After a special benefit performance held at the Theatre Royal in his honour, he left to show films in the Town Hall. These shows began on 25th March 1912 and were advertised under the name of "Pictureland". The Cape Hill Electric was already in business, and the Skating Rink in Windmill Lane started showing films the following month, but the Town Hall was located in the centre of Smethwick, and having established himself there, Edward Hewitson began planning something more ambitious: The Prince's Hall. Pictureland closed when the new cinema opened.

The former Town Hall is now used as a Public Library and therefore it is still possible to visit the location of Mr. Hewitson's "Pictureland".

### 17. The Prince's Hall (later the Prince's)
*High Street*

While his film shows were running successfully at the Town Hall, Edward Hewitson organised the construction of a purpose-built cinema. He commissioned F. J. Gill to design the building, and Messrs. Dallow and Son to build it. It was erected on the site of the old Post Office. Only a narrow entrance actually presented itself to the High Street, but a reasonably large auditorium was constructed to hold 950 patrons in tip up seats on a raked floor.

The Prince's Hall opened on Thursday evening 19th December 1912, in the presence of the Mayor and leading townsfolk. Patrons paid 3d, 6d, 9d or 1/- to see a programme that included "Jasmine" and "Fire at Sea".

129. The Prince's, October 1980.

*(Photo: Ned Williams)*

One or two local people can still recall the popular Saturday afternoon children's matinees. The hall was usually packed and halfpenny nougats were sold in great numbers. When Miss Washington, the pianist, arrived she was always greeted with deafening cheers.

From these beginnings Edward Hewitson's empire gradually expanded. By the end of the silent era it no doubt seemed old fashioned and therefore it was replaced with something more modern. It closed on 27th April 1930 with *"The Wright Idea"*. William Jackson, the builder, moved in to erect its successor.

The Prince's was designed by H. G. Bradley and is one of those fascinating cinemas caught in a transition period, reflecting something of the twenties, heralding something of the thirties. Mr. Hewitson told the press, "The whole building, in fact, expresses the modern spirit of architecture, that there shall be no beauty without use, and nothing useful that is not beautiful".

A faience-treated facade crowned in a pediment and featuring ornate leaded windows may not have struck some people as pure modernism. Once again a narrow entrance led to a huge auditorium hidden by neighbouring shops. The new Prince's could accommodate 1500 patrons in some luxury. The latest BTH equipment was installed, but the talkies had already arrived at other local cinemas by the time it opened.

It opened on 26th December 1930, Boxing Day,

with a film called *"Dynamite"*. A feature of the Prince's was the two manual, five unit, Compton organ. The instrument was opened by Wilfred Southworth. Six years later, however, it was moved to The Empire.

Although more modern cinemas later opened in Cape Hill and Bearwood, the Prince's was central Smethwick's premier cinema throughout its life. It was very nearly destroyed in the Second World War when a land mine almost landed on it. Sam Smith's foundry, just behind the cinema was hit, throwing a length of steel girder into the air which came crashing down through the roof and ceiling of the cinema. The Prince's closed for a short time for repairs and the girder has been "preserved" to this day as a souvenir.

After the War Edward Hewitson's son, Geoffrey Hewitson, was not very keen on installing cinemascope so he put in an extra large 42' x 21' screen instead. Even so "scope" had to be installed eventually. The Prince's was still busy enough in 1966 to warrant spending money on redecoration and re-seating. The 360 seats in the circle were replaced and 300 removed from the stalls to make it more spacious. A short time afterwards a massive programme of house-clearance in the area near the Prince's suddenly removed the local patrons to distant parts of the borough. Attendances dropped drastically overnight.

The Prince's closed on 27th June 1970 with *"Carry*

212

On Cruising" and "Carry On Teaching". Geoffrey Hewitson sold it, at what he considered to be a bargain price, to Nirmal Singh Sanghera. It reopened in April 1971 and was a very successful and profitable cinema for its new owner. Although basically committed to presenting Indian films, the Prince's did show some English language films during the week again, for a time. By the end of the decade it was only in use at weekends, and closed about February 1980. At the time of writing it stands forlorn and deserted awaiting some new use.

## 18. The Majestic
*Bearwood Road*

Having provided central Smethwick with the Prince's Hall it seems that Edward Hewitson turned his attention to Bearwood. Next-door to the headquarters of the Midland Red Omnibus Company he found a site to build the Majestic. By this time the First World War was underway and little seems to be recorded about its construction or design. It was probably built by William Jackson. It accommodated 1000 patrons in the stalls, and 336 in the balcony.

The Majestic was opened on 7th February 1916 by the Mayor, Councillor G. E. Ryder. The first feature film shown was *"The High Road"*. The cinema was particularly proud of its orchestra, led by Herbert Povey, which was described as, "Second only to the one at the Scala, Birmingham".

The Majestic was to experience two more "openings" during its otherwise uneventful lifetime. It closed for a month in 1939 while a new frontage was built on the theatre in an attempt to modernise it. The new front elevation was designed by Roland Satchwell. It was carried out in black, primrose and green Vitrolite, which was not quite as strong as it sounds. Primrose predominated with narrow bands of green, while black only appeared at the base of the facade. The work was completed by William Jackson. New BTH equipment and a new screen were installed. It reopened in this form on August Bank Holiday Monday, 7th August 1939 with *"Little Tough Guys in Society"*.

Twenty years later the cinema business was going through hard times. The Majestic quietly closed on 21st February 1959 with *"What Lola Wants"*. The ground floor of the cinema became a Market Hall and later a ballroom, but that was not quite the end of the Majestic. By the mid seventies the Majestic and the Midland Red Depot were owned by a property company hoping to undertake wholesale redevelopment of the entire site. Apparently to help prevent vandalism they wished to find someone to lease the cinema for eighteen months, the first six months "rent free"! Michael Flook acquired planning permission to create a small 250 seater cinema using the former circle.

As "The Studio" it opened on 31st March 1977 with *"Gumball Rally"* and *"Lets Do It Again"*. Recent events are not necessarily easier to research than ones long past and Michael Flook and "the Studio" seem to have faded away within a year without leaving me the date of the final show.

The auditorium was demolished at the end of 1978 and the frontage followed early in 1979. Nothing remained by March 1979.

## 19. The Coliseum
*Bearwood Road*

Relatively little documentation on the Coliseum seems to have survived. It was promoted by Ben Kennedy's company that had opened the Smethwick Empire in 1910, but was a much more modest building. It was designed, again by Mr. Bowden, to hold a mere 875 patrons on a single floor. From the photograph reproduced here it would seem that the projection room was added later.

Ben Kennedy applied for a kine licence in April 1911 and when his application came before the magistrates it met incredible opposition. Witness after witness, including Edward Hewitson, claimed that there were already sufficient places of amusement in the area, and then local churchmen stood up to cast doubts upon the propriety of such entertainment. Despite all this it seems that the licence was granted and that the Coliseum

120. The Majestic, 19th June 1960.

*(Photo: Mr. Jones, Sandwell Libraries)*

213

131. The Coliseum in 1929. Note on the extreme left the construction of the Windsor is going on behind the hoardings.

*(Photo: S. Smith, Sandwell Libraries)*

quietly opened soon afterwards.

Despite Mr. Hewitson's views on the abundance of cinemas and theatres in 1911, he seems to have been happy to acquire the Coliseum in 1917, and show films there for the rest of the silent era. Towards the end of the twenties Edward Hewitson decided to build a brand new super-cinema in Bearwood Road — on the opposite corner of the Dunsford Road junction to the Coliseum. At first the "replacement" was to be called the "New Coliseum", but it materialised as the Windsor.

The Coliseum closed on Saturday 27th September 1930, to make way for the Windsor's opening on the Monday. The last film shown was a Ken Maynard Western called *"The Phantom City"*. Eventually the building was sold to the Staffordshire Territorial Association, but was not used by them. In more recent times the site has become a garage.

## 20. The Ring Palace
*Oldbury Road*

This little-known cinema was in West Smethwick not far from the railway station of that name. It was originally owned by George Devey, but whether it was purpose-built, or was converted from an older building is not clear.

The Ring Palace opened on Saturday 27th March 1915

214

and offered, "Warmth, Comfort and Civility", as well as screen entertainment. It was taken over by Edward Hewitson two years later, March 1917, apparently simply to buy-out any opposition, although the Hewitsons seemed to look down on their acquisition and dismissed it as a "flea-pit". Mr. Peake was sent along from the Prince's Hall to run the place and for a time it was re-named the "Picture Playhouse".

By the end of 1917 it advertised itself as "The Palace", which was very confusing as Oldbury's "Palace" was going through numerous minor changes of name at the same time. By the end of the War both settled on calling themselves The Palace! To the locals there was no problem — it was always called "The Ring".

The Ring's finest moments ironically came just as it was about to close. When the Prince's Hall closed to be rebuilt the orchestra was transferred to West Smethwick! By the beginning of 1931 when all neighbouring cinemas were presenting talkies, The Ring stressed in its adverts: "The only house for silents with an orchestra".

The light on the screen faded and the orchestra took their final bow on 5th March 1932 with a showing of *"Motherland"*. After standing empty for a time the building became a warehouse, but has long since disappeared without trace.

132  The Ring Palace in August 1934, after closure.
*(Photo: F. Parkes, Sandwell Libraries)*

## 21. The Empire
*St. Pauls Road*

The Empire Theatre Company, under the chairmanship of Ben Kennedy, opened the Empire on 5th September 1910. The building was designed by the local architect, Mr. G. Bowden and was conceived as a theatre. In other words a large audience was accommodated on three levels and its stage facilities were fairly generous. The seating capacity before the First World War is quoted at various figures between 1400 and 2000! The facade, described as "free-renaissance style" survives to this day and feels "theatrical". It was built by John Dallow and Sons.

Ben Kennedy held a kine licence for the Empire and certainly films were presented there early in the theatre's life. About 1915 it seems to have passed to Messrs. Black and Hicks, who continued to present cine-variety. The same gentlemen took over the Kings Hall, Darlaston from Ben Kennedy. Contrary to other published accounts of this theatre's history, I do not believe it was acquired by Edward Hewitson until 1922. It seems that he purchased it for £14,350 at an auction on 22nd September of that year.

At that time it was said to have 1334 seats and eighty-seven years of its lease to run. It seems that Edward Hewitson may have reopened the Empire three months later for more cine-variety, but in 1924 he set

about considerably altering the theatre to make it a full-time cinema. The extensive refurbishing and the new cinema equipment warranted a ceremonious reopening on 6th October 1924, by Smethwick's Mayor, Alderman Betts. The opening feature film was *"Scaramouche"*, accompanied by an orchestra led by Caradoc Davis. The variety tradition could not be broken and the opening also featured *"Henriette and Selina"* on stage. Alan Hewitson, Mr. Hewitson's son, became the manager.

Like the other halls in the group, when sound arrived the Empire installed BTH equipment, and then went one stage better by adding an organ. The two manual, five unit Compton organ from the Prince's was installed at the Empire, with an additional unit. It was opened by George Hunt,, and remained in its new home until 1959 or 1960. It was then removed to Holly Lodge Grammar School.

The Empire's position among Hewitson Theatres was somewhat reduced by the opening of the new Prince's and the Windsor, and finally by the modernising of the Majestic. Perhaps if the Second World War had not come along the Empire might have been next on the list.

As it turned out it was an early casualty of post-War problems. It closed on 13th April 1957 with *"Too Bad She's Bad"*, starring Sophia Loren, plus *"Card of Fate"* starring Gina Lollobrigida. The building became a hardware and D.I.Y. store. For years the stage stored

215

scenery for an amateur theatrical group and the elegant leaded glass canopy reminded people of the building's past. It still stands, proudly bearing its name, the canopy modified, its red brickwork much painted, but still unmistakeably a one-time place of entertainment.

## 22. The Windsor
### Bearwood Road

As stated earlier, the Coliseum closed as its successor, the Windsor, opened. The Windsor was an entirely new theatre and was the summit of Edward Hewitson's achievements. Once again Mr. Hewitson called upon the services of the Birmingham architect Horace Bradley, and the builder, William Jackson. Mr. Bradley designed a super-cinema that was attractive from all elevations, as opposed to the dull rectangular box that looked splendid as long as one looked at its frontage! The exterior was finished in stone and rusticated brick and the entrance faced the corner of Dunsford Road and Bearwood Road rather than the latter only. The curved corner entrance, enhanced by an elaborate canopy bearing the hall's name, was particularly attractive, and crowned with a stunning turret and dome. Leaded glass windows abounded and even the dome featured leaded lights that illuminated the balcony lounge just above the cafe.

The 1750 seater auditorium featured decorative plaster-work in white, gold and cream plus two huge murals on either side of the organ grilles. A simple rectangular proscenium enclosed a large screen, up to forty feet wide if required, and there was a 60' x 25' stage and full dressing room facilities. Seats were upholstered in old rose velvet, carpets were rose and mauve, and the curtains were old rose and green. As with the new Prince's, owner and designer both felt their hall was "modern", but really its charm was its exploitation of the features of the "traditional" 1920's picture palace.

Naturally the Windsor was built as a sound cinema from the out-set, and BTH equipment was installed in its relatively spacious operating room. It opened with Kalee No. 8 projectors. The Windsor also featured an organ; a Compton three manual, eight unit instrument, and the actual organ loft was placed above the stage, the grilles forming an arc between the proscenium and the ceiling.

The work should have been completed by August but the opening was delayed one month. The Windsor was opened on Monday 29th September 1930 by the Mayor, Sam Smith, the proprietor of the foundry behind the Prince's. The first programme featured, *"Chasing Rainbows"*, starring Charles King and Bessie Love. The

216

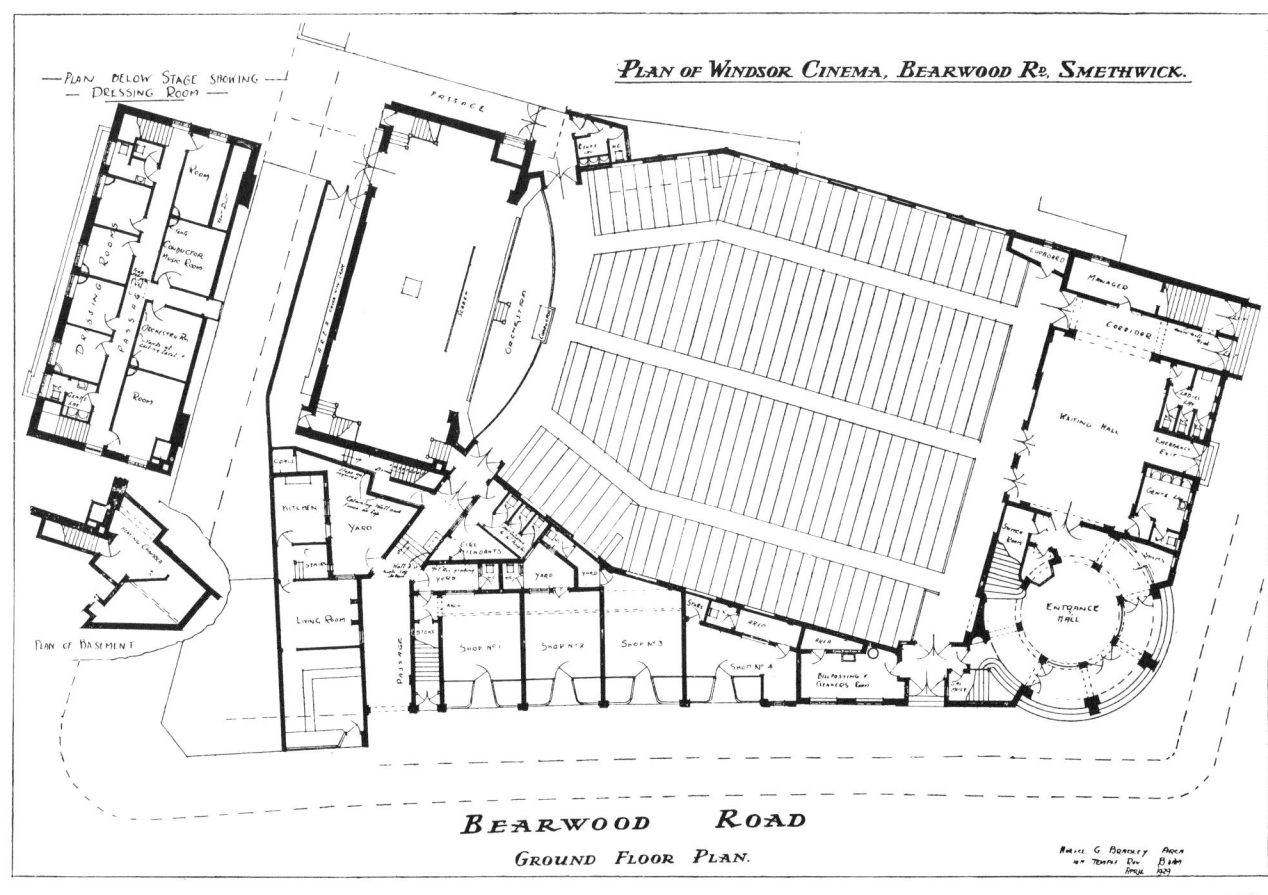

Horace Bradley's plan for the Windsor, seen below, made ambitious use of the corner site. Even in the 1980's, as seen above, it is an impressive building.

THE
NEW
WINDSOR

BEARWOOD'S
LATEST
TALKIE
THEATRE.

On 24th September 1930 *The Bioscope* published a supplement to mark the completion of the Windsor, which was then produced as an opening brochure for the cinema. Interior features, such as the Highland-scene murals, the organ grille above the proscenium and the curtains were pictured on this page.   *(From the Collection of Geoffrey Hewitson)*

organ was opened by Reginald Maynard.

The Windsor became the headquarters of the Hewitson group, and of course its flagship. Even so its history ran curiously in reverse. Many buildings that had opened as theatres, closed as cinemas. The Windsor was contrary. Variety acts were gradually added to some film shows and after the War films were abandoned altogether in favour of revues and variety shows. Many stars that are now well known made early appearances on the stage of the Windsor.

Towards the end of its life, Geoffrey Hewitson presented repertory by a resident company from 1957 onwards. With its grand opening as a cinema long forgotten the Windsor closed on 6th February 1960 at the end of the run of the Christmas Pantomime: *"Mother Goose"*. The organ was removed and is now in Oxley Parish Church, Wolverhampton.

For three years the Windsor stood empty until a Mr. Osborne spent £100,000 turning the building into Bearwood Ice-skating Rink. It was successful and popular for a time but closed in that capacity on 18th March 1973. The building then stood empty for another seven years, in which various plans were put forward for its use. These plans included re-opening as an ice-rink, conversion to supermarket, temple, disco and Bingo Club. All were turned down.

One more spectacular rebirth took place. Four local men, Albert Higgs, Alan Harrod, Arnold Deakin and George Grainger looked at the building in 1978, formed the Windsor Club (Bearwood) Ltd., and set out on a brave and ambitious plan to reopen the Windsor as a "night spot". Only the vandalised shell of the original building remained and even that was in a sorry state. Nevertheless the transformation was accomplished and the Windsor Club opened on 5th September 1980 with Duggie Brown on stage.

The new owners were very conscious of their opening almost coinciding with the original opening fifty years

earlier, and that some of the stars they had booked, such as Frankie Vaughan, would be making their second appearance in Bearwood. As I started work on this book I was pleased to see the Windsor smartened up and return to life. It seemed a good omen. Unfortunately the Windsor Club was short-lived and now the building stands empty again. What can its beautiful leonine gargoyles look forward to?

The Cinemas of Irving Bosco :

Edward Hewitson's cinemas in Smethwick remained his, or his sons', property until their closure. Irving Bosco's two ventures in Smethwick passed to other people and eventually into the same major circuit, but they are "his" in the sense that he opened them.

### 23. The Cape Hill Electric
*Cape Hill*

The Electric was the first purpose-built cinema in Smethwick and very much a product of the Black Country rather than Birmingham! Irving Bosco's activities centred on Dudley at the time and his new cinema was designed by the Dudley architects, Messrs. Gammage and Dickinson, and built by the Dudley builders, Messrs. Oakley and Coulson. (Mr. Coulson later became involved with the Grand, Kingswinford). Its opening was reported in as much detail in the Dudley Herald as in the Smethwick Telephone !

Smethwick was in the middle of Coronation celebrations by the time Irving Bosco's cinema was ready to commence business and his first programme included films of that event. Local citizens were told to, "Bring the little ones to see the Coronation". The opening took place on Monday afternoon, 19th June 1911. The Mayor of Smethwick had a seat in the balcony and came to the stage during the interval to make his speech.

135. The Cape Hill Electric, 16th June 1957, almost a year after closure.

*(Photo: J. H. Harvey, Sandwell Libraries)*

The Cape Hill Electric held 680 patrons at the time, and slightly fewer as years went by. A "Ladies Tea Room" originally adjoined the balcony. Irving Bosco was anxious to make it clear that he was solely interested in presenting pictures. There were no variety acts. At first there were three shows daily at 3, 7 and 9 o'clock, and manager Chas Herrick was left in charge of the place. In order to live up to its name the cinema frequently acknowledged the source of their "electricity" — the Birmingham and Midland Tramways Committee!

Along with Irving Bosco's other cinemas, the Cape Hill Electric passed to Mr. Shapeero in 1920 and then to the Gaumont British subsidiary Denman Picture Houses Ltd. One of their managers, Ken Jones, left to go to the rival Grove cinema and rose to the position of General Manager of the Clifton Circuit. The cinema was equipped with British Acoustic sound equipment.

Neither Mr. Shapeero, nor G.B., nor the Rank Organisation ever seemed to feel any desire to change the Electric's name to anything more modern and one is given the feeling that it was rather a backwater as far as these large organisations were concerned. To its staff it was "small and friendly", to Rank it was probably considered small and old fashioned and it was therefore abandoned in autumn 1956 when the company closed a number of such halls, including the Criterion, Dudley.

The last show, on 29th September 1956, featured *"Angels One Five"*, starring Jack Hawkins. The building was demolished completely and now offices stand on the site.

## 24. The Rink
### (later known as The Gaumont)
*Windmill Lane*

On 4th September 1909 a large skating rink opened in Windmill Lane. It was promoted by a company formed of local businessmen and was designed by local architect, G. Bowden. It was a timber-framed building clad in corrugated iron but was built on too large a scale to be dismissed as a "tin shed". From the outside it seemed to be finished in a half-timbered effect.

In 1912 it was acquired by Irving Bosco. He overhauled and reconstructed the building, and installed 1500 seats. It opened as the Rink Picture House on 8th April 1912 with a programme that included a Western, a Comedy and a documentary about wild birds that was in colour.

Along with the Cape Hill Electric, it passed to Mr. Shapeero, of Nottingham, in 1920, and then to Denman Picture Houses of Gaumont British. The latter closed the cinema and began to demolish it in November 1929. The contractor moved onto the site on 15th December and work furiously began on a brand new cinema. Within six weeks two hundred tons of stell, provided by Braithwaites of West Bromwich, were erected and the outline of the cinema could be seen. One or two aspects of this outline were reminiscent of the original Rink!

The new Rink was designed by W. T. Benslyn. A plasterer who worked on the building, for Bryans Adamanta, told me that Mr. Benslyn had won the commission in competitive circumstances, and his

winning interior design had been inspired by ideas produced by his young daughter! Both the interior and exterior of the new Rink were, and are, splendid. The curved brickwork of the frontage, one hundred and twenty feet in length, is relieved by impressive window surrounds in Portland stone. One of the most interesting features of the facade is the use of ornamental stone peacocks, all of which are excellently preserved. The Architects Journal described it as, "Modern in appearance, with a suggestion of the Italian Renaissance".

A large foyer and generous crush halls anticipated large audiences and the staircases to the balcony greeted patrons with huge murals painted by the scenic artist, Frank Barnes. The huge auditorium held 1,300 patrons in the stalls, and 650 in the balcony. The side walls featured elaborate collonaded Moorish arches cleverly lit with concealed lighting. British Acoustic sound equipment was installed, and a Compton three manual, nine unit, organ with the console mounted on a lift.

Somehow the entire building was constructed in seven months, which was considered as a Midlands record for a building of such size. When it opened it brought the talkies to Smethwick, two months before the Windsor, and eight months before the new Princes. Although Smethwick's three new super-cinemas opened within such a short time of each other they really served quite different areas.

The Rink, "The Wonder Talkie House", was opened on 7th July 1930 by Smethwick's Mayor, Councillor Sam Smith, and the programme featured *"Flight"*; "the screens all talking pageant of the air". Leslie James, who was resident for the entire first week, opened the new organ and patrons filled those acres of seats for 6d in the stalls, and 9d upstairs.

At the risk of offending supporters of other Gaumonts, I feel that the Rink was the finest Gaumont cinema in the West Midlands, but I also feel that I know its colleagues in Wolverhampton and Wednesbury much better. I do not even know if building the Rink on such a lavish scale was ever justified. It has the grandeur, and "confidence" of the later Odeons, and also something of their anonymity!

The Rink became The Gaumont in 1949 and five years later celebrated its twenty-fifth anniversary with an appearance of a local children's choir, accompanied by Reg Johnson on the organ, and with film star Bill Owen cutting the Gaumont Cake. I am sure no-one could then have believed that such a cinema would cease showing films within a decade.

The Gaumont closed on 1st February 1964 with *"Bitter Harvest"* and *"Tiger Bay"*. Apparently the closure came as quite a shock to the manager; Jim Gower. He had recently been chosen as the circuit's top manager in the West Midlands for his work in publicising the cinema and promoting films! In fact the Gaumont had recently retained *"From Russia With Love"* for two weeks, such was local demand. Poor Mr. Gower had come to Smethwick from the Odeon Dunstall which had eventually become a Bingo Club. He had operated Bingo sessions three afternoons a week at the Gaumont, but had never expected complete apostacy.

Apparently patrons could hardly wait to get their

136 The original Rink, photographed in May 1929.
(Photo: W. H. Elvis, Sandwell Libraries)

137 The new Rink. 1930.
(Photo: Kevin Wheelan Collection)

"eyes down". Full-time Bingo began on 13th February 1964. When I visited the present Top Rank Bingo and Social Club last year I met one lady who had been there every night since the opening. I doubt whether any member of the staff could even make such a claim! The establishment is extremely well kept and Mr. Benslyn's interior provides a palatial environment that is well worth visiting. The proscenium arch, balcony seats and walls of moorish arches still exist.

The Rink's organ is also preserved and since 1961 has been in use at Quinton Parish Church. A picture of cinema organists assembled outside the Rink is included in Part 1.

138. The Rink, as it is today: a luxurious setting in which to play Bingo.

*(Photo: Ned Williams)*

The others:

## 25. The Beacon
*Brasshouse Lane*

The Beacon seems remote from central Smethwick, let alone the rest of the Black Country, but I like to think that perhaps its name has some local significance. The promoter of the cinema was Percy Dyche, a Birmingham man connected with other cinemas in the city, but whose only other excursion into the Black Country appears to have been briefly at the Cosy Corner, Halesowen.

The Beacon was designed by Harold Scott and built by T. Elvins. The following description appeared in the Smethwick Telephone:

"The new house has a dignified simplicity both without and within. Nondescript ornamentation is entirely absent; the whole building gives a delightful impression of beauty and spaciousness. The colour-scheme represents a beacon, though sunset colours are also suggested. The green carpet and deep blue curtains edge the bronze of the lower walls, that merge into russet-red and amber, while the ceiling is mottled sky blue".

Mr. W. E. Lawrence J.P. opened the Beacon, on Monday 30th September 1929. He was joined on stage by Percy Dyche, James Hill J.P. and the local vicar, Rev. F. K. Roberts. The programme included *"Give and Take"* and *"The Politic Flapper"*. The auditorium held just under a thousand patrons at 4d and 6d in the stalls, 9d and 1/- in the balcony. The projection room contained Ernimann Imperator 200 machines, and the orchestra pit contained a small ensemble directed by H. J. Miller. Mr. A. S. Anderton was General Manager.

The year after the Beacon opened Smethwick's three super-cinemas opened their doors, but the Beacon's isolation probably enabled it to serve a quite distinct community. (The "other side of the tracks"?). It kept abreast of the times by installing Western Electric sound equipment and, in 1932, claimed to be the first cinema in Smethwick to put on matinees for the unemployed. They were admitted for 3d. It also offered three programmes per week at a time when other cinemas offered two.

Sometime early in the 1930's the cinema became part of the County Circuit, which, in turn, was absorbed by A.B.C. The latter collected quite a few ancient or obscure Black Country cinemas! It managed to outlive their Palace, Walsall, and Olympia, Darlaston, but closed on 15th February 1958, with *"The Lady And The Tramp"*.

The Beacon was sold, for £10,000, to Mohammed Firdar, and he spent another £15,000 modernising, re-decorating, and re-seating the place. Even a new screen was installed. It reopened, showing Indian films, on 3rd November 1962. In the following years it was leased to various people, but at least it survived. It closed for a short time in 1978, by which time it was only open four nights a week. The manager, Ragbir Singh carried out various improvements demanded by Sandwell Council, and business resumed.

It was very much on its last legs when I first visited it in the summer of 1980, and I was not surprised to learn that it had closed by the end of that year. Another casualty of the video revolution; the building is now a clothing factory.

## 26. The Grove
*Dudley Road*

The Grove virtually stands on the border of Birmingham and Sandwell. To me it has always seemed to have less a claim to be included in the Black Country than the Warley and Danilo, Quinton, both of which also occupied sites virtually on the border, but the compulsion to be comprehensive has forced me to include it!

The site on the corner of Grove Lane and Dudley Road was first seen as a potential location for a super-cinema by Sol Levy. It was surrounded by a densely residential area and the little Cape Hill Electric was regarded as unequal to the task of serving this community. The project was taken over by the Grove Cinema Company under the chairmanship of George Parker. More significantly, two of the principle directors were Sidney Clift and Leon Salberg and their interest in the Grove can be seen as the starting point for the creation of the Clifton circuit.

139 The Beacon, coming to the end of its life as an Indian cinema. 1980. *(Photo: Ned Williams)*

140 The Grove, not long before final closure, 1981. *(Photo: Ned Williams)*

The huge 1700 seater cinema, designed by Roland Satchwell, was far bigger than the Cliftons later built in the Black Country "proper", perhaps reflecting the trend already established at the new Rink: the nearer to Birmingham, the bigger the super-cinema. Ken Jones left his job with Gaumont British at the Cape Hill Electric and moved into the mighty Grove. From the position of manager he rose to be General Manager of the entire circuit.

The Grove opened on 22nd August 1932 with "Arsene Lupin", starring Lionel and John Barrymore. The ceremony was performed by Chairman George Parker, last mentioned in this book in relation to the company that promoted the Scala, Stourbridge. Unlike later Clifton cinemas that favoured BTH equipment, the Grove opened with sound by Western Electric.

Due to its position out on the frontier, little of the history of the Grove seems to have been recorded by the local press in Smethwick. Its "presence" gradually emerged once other local cinemas closed! By the nineteen seventies the newly formed Borough of Warley included not only the Princes, in what had been the heart of the town, but also such diverse and far flung cinemas as the Grove and the Royal, Cradley Heath.

In keeping with the Grove's gradual "movement" towards the Black Country, 9th April 1978 it was sold by the original company to Tarsem Singh Dhami, the Bus Inspector from Wolverhampton. He inherited a cinema that had remained remarkably unchanged since the thirties. Lloyd-Loom chairs still stood in the balcony lounge and display cabinets etc. still had an unmistakeable Art Deco appearance. Cinemeccanica equipment had been installed the previous year so at least the Grove was technically up-to-date. He showed English language films during the week and Indian films on Sundays.

In the following year the remaining audience seemed to gradually melt away. The last regular film presentation, featuring "Happy Birthday to Me", took place on 24th October 1981. Sunday shows had been presented by various lessees and specialist martial-arts programmes had tried to make a last stand, but without success. The very last Indian film was screened on 14th November 1981. I last visited the Grove on 7th November and a magnificent historical epic from the Bombay studios was playing to half a dozen people. At the time of going to press the Grove is up for sale.

The Birmingham Border

## 27. The Warley
### (later known as the Odeon)
*Hagley Road West*

The Warley Odeon, as it was generally known, stood symbolically at the "Gateway to the Black Country". A Blackcountryman returning from Birmingham felt "at home" once he had passed the massive cinema that stood at the junction of the Hagley Road and the Birmingham-Wolverhampton "New" Road, even if the real Black Country air could not be breathed until passing under the railway bridge at Langley. In the 1930's this site was located within the boundaries of the Borough of Oldbury.

The original company that set out to build a cinema on this site included Sidney Clift and W. H. Onions. Their involvement presumably accounts for the fact that Roland Satchwell was the original architect. At some stage the company seems to have run into financial difficulties and Oscar Deutsch was invited to join the scheme. He became the chairman of the company and the Warley played an important part in defining the emerging Odeon style. The main elevation was designed by Cecil Howitt, but of greater significance was the fact that Harry Weedon was asked to plan the interior. Harry Weedon engaged Cecil Clavering to actually come up with the designs, and out of this melting pot the straightforward modernism of the Odeons was born.

The Warley was built by J. B. Whitehouse and Son, whose only other cinema-building work in the Black Country was later at the Clifton, Lye. Mr. Whitehouse also became a director of the company. By the time the cinema opened W. G. Elcock had joined the Board, and he later joined the companies building the Odeons in Wolverhampton and Dudley.

The Warley opened on 22nd December 1934, not long after the Odeon, Blackheath. On stage were Oscar Deutsch, R. H. Morgan M.P., Councillor Wallis, the Chairman of Oldbury U.D.C. and Mr. and Mrs. Whitehouse. However the actual opening was performed by the Earl of Dudley. The Earl had quite a lot to say. He felt that more films should portray industrial life and social problems such as housing for the working classes. He added,

"Before the War, when work was over, there was hardly anything else left to do except to get drunk. Now, instead of spending five shillings in getting

THE WARLEY,
Hagley Road West, Birmingham.

| THE WARLEY, Hagley Road West, Birmingham. | THE WARLEY, Hagley Road West, Birmingham. |
|---|---|
| Reservation Ticket for | RESERVATION TICKET for |
| OPENING PERFORMANCE on SATURDAY DEC. 22nd, 1934 | OPENING PERFORMANCE on SATURDAY, DECEMBER 22nd, 1934 |
| Doors open 7-30 p.m. Commencing promptly 8-0 | Doors open 7-30 p.m. Commencing promptly 8-0 p.m. |
| BALCONY | BALCONY |
| SEAT No. B 13 | SEAT NUMBER B 13 |

A ticket for the opening of the Warley Cinema — kept as a souvenir by Mr. Onions, who was connected with this cinema and the Clifton, Stone Cross.

141/142. The Warley Cinema: by night and by day. This cinema was a "gateway" to the Black Country and illustrates the view that cinemas often looked their best at night. It was also a key cinema in the development of the "Odeon Style". Photo taken 31st April 1935.

*(Photos: John Maltby)*

drunk, we spend sixpence on the pictures, — and a very good substitute it is too!".

Everyone admired the huge 1530 seater auditorium, decorated in terracotta and green, and, years later, some patrons can recall the strong scent of carnations in the foyer. It was equipped with BTH equipment, favoured by both Oscar Deutsch and Sidney Clift. Oscar Deutsch seems to have regarded it as an ideal showplace, conveniently close to his home in Edgbaston. He organised special shows on Sundays for his private house parties, and always came personally to thank the chief, Mr. Matheson, and the second operator, Frank Harvey, for their services. The Earl of Dudley also "borrowed" films, and the services of the operators, from the Warley to be presented in his private cinema at Himley Hall.

Very quickly the original name was dropped and it became an Odeon. With this "anonymity" I feel it slipped into the role of serving the Birmingham suburbs whatever its position in relation to local government boundaries.

The Warley Odeon lasted until 25th November 1961, closing with "Victim", starring Dirk Bogarde, supported with "Attempt to Kill". Work started immediately on turning it into a bowling alley at a cost of £200,000. As the Warley Bowl it lasted less than a decade. The last skittles fell on 29th April 1970 and this once elegant building stood boarded-up for a couple of years, while the huge areas of faience on the main elevation began to show their age. It was finally demolished in 1973.

Naunton Developments obtained planning permission to build a 120 bedroom hotel on the site but the building that eventually materialised was a massive office block. Strangely enough, since the Warley cinema's closure, the Quinton cinema seems to have made a virtue, and financial success, of showing films on the fringe of Birmingham's suburbs.

## 28. The Danilo
### (later known as The Essoldo and the Classic)
*Hagley Road West*

Fortunately, at the time of writing, one cinema still flourishes as a "Gateway to the Black Country". This is the Quinton Classic, which stands above a high brick precipice on the side of the M5 Motorway. As northbound drivers pass below it they can see the Black Country open out ahead of them.

The Classic was originally part of the Danilo circuit, in fact it served as Mortimer Dent's Head Office as it was within easy reach of his Edgbaston home. Mortimer Dent's partner in building this particular Danilo was Colonel J. Baldwin Webb. The site chosen was in an area that was fast becoming a residential suburb of Birmingham, but at that time it was in Oldbury.

Plans were drawn by Andrew Mather, in the prevailing modern style, and were approved by the Council in February 1938. The contractors were T. Elvins, who had developed considerable expertise

143. The Danilo / Essoldo / Classic, now with four screens. 1981.

*(Photo: Ned Williams)*

in building super-cinemas and had a specialised team working on such tasks. Their only other excursion into the Black Country, however, had been a decade earlier at the Beacon.

The 1600 seater cinema, with its apparently lengthy brick facade, opened on August Bank Holiday, 7th August 1939, apparently without official ceremony. The Majestic, Smethwick, re-opened on the same day. *"Charlie Chan In Honolulu"* could be heard in RCA High Fidelity Magic Sound for 6d, 1/- or 1/6d. Saturday afternoon matinees were introduced immediately, including the serial, *"Blake at Scotland Yard"*. The car park held five hundred cars: a sign of the times!

After the War the Danilo, along with the other cinemas on the circuit, passed to Mr. Southan Morris's S. M. Super Cinemas Ltd., but still retained its original name. It became part of the Essoldo group in 1961 and took the name of the new proprietors. The original Danilo name, in high stainless steel letters, was very much an integral part of the design of the front elevation and successive changes of name, and changing the canopy etc., have all spoilt its original harmony. It was given a £65,000 facelift by the Essoldo group in 1967.

After the local government reorganisation of Spring 1966 the Essoldo found itself not in Warley, as one might expect, but in Halesowen, where there was no provision for granting Sunday licences! Special steps had to be taken in mid 1967 to enable the Essoldo to open seven days a week. Two years later rumours circulated about its possible closure, probably started by the fact that the motorway looked as if it was about to be built throught it. The manager, Michael Jackson, denied the rumour and promised further improvements to the cinema after the completion of the motorway.

In April 1972 it was sold to the Classic circuit and began calling itself the Halesowen Classic. A year later work began on tripling the cinema. At first the circle was kept open with the screen hanging from the ceiling to the front wall of the circle. This could accommodate 400 patrons while two 320 seater auditoria were constructed, at night, beneath it.

The Classic opened as a triple-screen cinema on 26th July 1973 with *"Cabaret"*, *"The Ten Commandments"* and *"The Sound of Music"*. It also started calling itself the Quinton Classic as references to Halesowen had confused potential patrons! The vacant space in the former front stalls was turned into a fourth auditorium, and opened Autumn 1978. Michael Jackson now found himself managing the Black Country's only quadruple cinema — and in 1979 won the Manager of the Year award within the Classic group. Michael Hands, the chief operator, won a similar award in his field. He had successfully installed "Sound Surround" equipment for *"Earthquake"*, and four-track stereo for *"Tommy"*. Further improvements heralded the eighties when a £10,000 Dolby stereo system was installed in Classic I during April 1980, first used for the Midlands premier of *"Hair"*.

I hope the Classic will continue to survive. I have often enjoyed visiting this shrine to the Danilo circuit, particularly one Sunday afternoon when a packed cinema sat down to enjoy every single episode of *"Flash Gordon Conquers The Universe"* joined together into a marathon epic that, to me, still outshines *"Star Wars"* or the recent "remake" version of *"Flash Gordon"*. Flash will not have conquered the Universe in vain if at least a few screens survive in the Black Country.

144    "The End": The demolition of the Clifton, Wolverhampton, 5th April 1981. *(Photo: Express & Star)*

230

Usherettes line up at the Majestic about 1948 or 1949. Note the "M" motif on their caps and coats. Hewitsons Theatres were very keen on decorative monograms on buildings, stationery and uniforms!

*(Photo: Harry King)*

*That's all folks! We hope you enjoyed the show!* The author would like to hear from you if you have further information, photographs etc. on this subject.